Constitutional Law and Economics of the European Union

Edited by

Dieter Schmidtchen

Professor of Economics,
Universität des Saarlandes, Germany

Robert Cooter

Professor of Law,
University of California at Berkeley, US

Edward Elgar
Cheltenham, UK • Lyme, US

Published by
Edward Elgar Publishing Limited
8 Lansdown Place
Cheltenham
Glos GL50 2HU
UK

Edward Elgar Publishing, Inc.
1 Pinnacle Hill Road
Lyme
NH 03768
US

A catalogue record for this book
is available from the British Library

Library of Congress Cataloguing in Publication Data
Constitutional law and economics of the European Union / edited by
Dieter Schmidtchen, Robert Cooter.
Includes bibliographical references.
1. European Union—Constitutional law. 2. European Union.
I. Schmidtchen, Dieter. II. Cooter, Robert.
KJE4445.C66 1997 96–52261
341.242'2—dc21 CIP

ISBN 1 85898 598 6

Printed and bound in Great Britain by
Hartnolls Limited, Bodmin, Cornwall

Contents

PART THREE: INSTITUTIONAL CHANGE

List of Tables

List of Contributors

Bednar, Jenna, University of Southern California, US.
Berg, Sven, University of Oslo, Norway.
Bergh, Roger van den, Universities of Hamburg, Utrecht and Antwerpen, Germany and The Netherlands.
Bouckaert, Boudewijn, University of Ghent, Belgium.
Cooter, Robert, University of California at Berkeley, US.
Eichberger, Jürgen, University of Saarland, Germany.
Eichenberger, Reiner, University of Zurich, Switzerland.
Everling, Ulrich, University of Bonn, Germany.
Faure, Michael G., University of Limburg, The Netherlands.
Ferejohn, John, Stanford University and Hoover Institution, US.
Frey, Bruno S., University of Zurich, Switzerland.
Garrett, Geoffrey, University of Pennsylvania, Philadelphia, US.
Ginsburg, Tom, University of California at Berkeley, US.
Hoehn, Tom, London Economics Ltd., UK.
Holler, Manfred J., University of Hamburg, Germany.
Kirchner, Christian, Humboldt-University Berlin, Germany.
Koboldt, Christian, University of Saarland, Germany.
Lane, Jan-Erik, University of Oslo, Norway.
Maeland, Reinert, University of Oslo, Norway.
Paqué, Karl-Heinz, Institute for the World Economy Kiel, Germany.
Schlieper, Ulrich, University of Mannheim, Germany.
Schmidt-Trenz, Hans-Jörg, Chamber of Commerce Hamburg, Germany.
Schmidtchen, Dieter, University of Saarland, Germany.
Schneider, Friedrich, University of Linz, Austria.
Steunenberg, Bernard, University of Twente, The Netherlands.
Streit, Manfred E., Max Planck Institute Jena, Germany.
Tsebelis, George, Stanford University, US.
Vaubel, Roland, University of Mannheim, Germany.
Vibert, Frank, European Policy Forum London, UK.
Voigt, Stefan, Max Planck Institute Jena, Germany.
Watrin, Christian, University of Cologne, Germany.
Wickström, Bengt-Arne, Humboldt-University Berlin, Germany.

1. Introduction

Dieter Schmidtchen and Robert Cooter

As an economic area the European Community is a great success. By contrast, as a political association, the European Union is coming under enormous strain. Enlargement from a Union of 15 to a Union of 25–30 members means that the decisionmaking procedures and institutions of the Union will have to change. But there is no consensus on how the institutional and constitutional structures are to be adapted or how the present level of integration can be secured or even increased.

The power game is going on, played by the Commission, the European Parliament, the Council and the European Court of Justice, where each player has different preferences concerning the distribution of power in the European Union – but the outcome of the game is still unclear. There is a general feeling that the Council and Commission have acquired considerable power but are not sufficiently accountable to the voting public. In particular, the European Parliament laments democratic deficits, but giving it more power could result in a concentration of power at the Union level at the expense of national parliaments. Will the latter accept the diminution of power, and – most importantly – what would be the gains for the voting public?

The difficulties in the ratification of the 'Maastricht I'-treaty reveal that sensitivities have increased rather than diminished. Metaphors proliferate – Europe à la carte, multi-speed and multi-track Europe, variable geometry, concentric circles and so on – reflecting the increasing prospect of a Europe of institutional impasse where, nevertheless, nations get on the best they can. The existing institutions of the Community are criticised for their policy and management failures, in foreign affairs as well as in external and internal security matters. However, the nation states, which form the Union, are reluctant to transfer sovereignty.

All this reveals that the process of the European integration is at the crossroads. Both the Union's capability of action and its acceptance by the various peoples is at stake. What the Union needs is an effective institutional and constitutional structure which must be transparent to the citizens and must have an appropriate democratic foundation.

This volume contains revised versions of the papers and comments presented by distinguished economists, political scientists, and jurists at a conference about the constitutional law and economics of the European Union. The conference, held in Saarbrücken, Germany, in September 1995, was organised by the Center for the Study of Law and Economics, Department of Economics, Universität des Saarlandes, on behalf of the European Association of Law and Economics (EALE) and the American Law and Economics Association (ALEA).

The authors and discussants evaluate recent developments, consider the current situation, and assess prospects for the future on a wide variety of institutional and constitutional issues facing the European Union. The contributions address the big issues of the debate: decisionmaking, federal structures and institutional change. The book is of interest to observers, scholars, and students of European economic and political affairs, institutional analysis, constitutional analysis, and last, but not least, the policymakers themselves.

Part one on decisionmaking contains two papers. Geoffrey Garrett and George Tsebelis start with arguing that power indices cannot explain the decisionmaking in the European Union. According to their paper, the increasing use of qualified majority voting (QMV) in the Council of Ministers of the European Union (EU) since the mid 1980s has prompted many to analyse European decisionmaking in terms of the relative power of different national governments in the Council. While there are some differences among specific approaches, all of these power calculations are based on computations of the portion of all mathematically possible winning coalitions to which each government is pivotal (that is, without which a coalition would fall short of the QVM threshold). Scholars have used this basic 'power index' approach to make numerous assertions about the direction of policy in the contemporary European Union, such as the effects of expanding the size of the Union from 12 members to 15 and beyond, the policy consequences of different constitutional arrangements, and the likely course of outcomes in discrete issues areas.

The authors argue that conclusions about the EU based on power index analyses will invariably be wrong: first, because they fail to take into account the impact of the relative position of countries on strategic bargaining in the Council; and secondly, because all analyses based on power indices pay too little attention to the institutional rules that govern decisionmaking in the contemporary EU.

One can only understand the legislative process in Europe through detailed institutional analysis of the interactions between the Council, the Commission and the European Parliament, and in particular the sequencing of decisions. Changes in agenda-setting have had systematic policy consequences that are not appreciated by most scholars of European integration. The paper develops this point by contrasting likely policy outcomes under the four most frequently used procedures in Europe today – assent, consultation, cooperation and codecision. The paper also offers a brief critique of the power index approach to EU decisionmaking, and analyses the impact of policy preferences on likely coalitional behaviour in the Council of Ministers.

In the second paper of this part, Bernard Steunenberg, Christian Koboldt and Dieter Schmidtchen analyse game-theoretically the issue of comitology and the balance of power in the EU. The paper deals with the outcome of a power game played during the mid-1980s with three players involved: the European Commission, the Council and the European Parliament. The game started in the wake of the Single European Act when the long-standing practice of comitology received the status of primary community law, and ended with the famous comitology decision of the Council.

As is well known, the Council can delegate implementing power to the Commission. To prevent the Commission from becoming too powerful through unrestricted discretion at the implementation stage, the Council delegates powers under the condition that specific decisionmaking procedures have to be used. Although these procedures vary across different European acts, three different types can be distinguished under the comitology decision: the advisory committee procedure, the management committee procedure and the regulatory committee procedure. The committees, which are bodies of civil servants from the member states, consult, but also supervise, the Commission's execution of legal acts. They act as gatekeepers.

Using simple game theory, this paper analyses the working properties of the different procedures laid down in the comitology decision, outlines a concept of power, and asks how the balance of power is determined by the comitology decision. The main findings are that – apart from the advisory committee procedure that does not restrict the Commission in the slightest way – the management committee procedure restricts the Commission the least.

Part two on federal structures consists of three papers. Jenna Bednar, John Ferejohn and Geoffrey Garrett start with analysing the politics of European federalism. The significant increase in the pace of European integration in the past decade offers the opportunity to witness a rare kind of political process: the creation of a supranational political authority from previously independent states. Even if the European Union never becomes a true 'federation', it is now a trite truism that Europe is 'more than just another international regime'. While the creation of federations is not unprecedented, it is also clear that the process is fraught with political obstacles. Scepticism about the prospects for European federalism has strong foundations. From an internal European perspective, one can point to the difficulty of coordinating agricultural policies, and of deciding which policies should be decided at the European versus the national level. Moreover, the distance of the most powerful European actors – especially the European Court of Justice and the Commission – from the electorates sustains a concern with their democratic legitimacy that can only grow as time goes on. From a comparative perspective, we can see examples of apparently successful federal states, such as Canada, seeming to disintegrate in the face of ethnic and linguistic cleavages – divisions that are certainly no greater than those found in Europe.

Bednar, Ferejohn and Garrett argue that the most important factor that will determine the fate of Europe's would-be federation is the set of institutional choices made. The primary claim is that federal states cannot afford decisive central governments. Where such structures have evolved within federal systems, the federal structure has tended to collapse, either into fragmented states or into a centralised system. Within the European context, the authors argue that the move toward majoritarian institutions and practices (the *sine qua non* of a powerful central government) poses a genuine threat to the evolution of Europe as a federal entity.

In the second paper Robert Cooter and Tom Ginsburg present an empirical test of economic models of comparative judicial discretion. Judges have their own preferences about the political order, which they can exercise through the interpretation of statutes. Judicial lawmaking is constrained, however, by the countervailing power of other officials. A judicial interpretation of a statute can be overturned by fresh legislation that explicitly stipulates the preferred interpretation of the legislators. The discretionary power of judges increases as the probability decreases that a judicial interpretation of a statute will be repealed by fresh legislation. Fresh legislation is more difficult to enact when the constitution divides power, providing more officials with the power to veto bills. Conversely, fresh legislation is easier to enact when a single, disciplined party governs the state. Therefore, the authors predict that courts will be more adventurous in interpreting legislation as the number of independent vetoes on fresh legislation increases and as the unity and discipline of political parties decreases. They test this prediction using data from western nations and Japan. The data confirms the prediction. The implications of the model for the future of the EU are as follows: the development of the Union has brought a rise in the power of the European Parliament. This change increases legislative resistance, which should expand the judicial discretion in the European Court of Justice.

Part two closes with Roger van den Bergh examining the subsidiarity principle and the European Community competition rules. The principle of subsidiarity, which is a central concept of the European Union Treaty, has put renewed emphasis on the virtues of decentralisation. Powers should be granted to the institutions of the EC only when it has been established that they cannot be satisfactorily exercised by member states (except for matters falling within the exclusive competence of the EC institutions). An economic analysis of the subsidiarity principle allows for a better understanding of the fundamental issues in the allocation of competence between national antitrust authorities and a supranational agency.

The first section of the paper summarises the current state of the law. The next two sections elaborate further upon legal analysis, to find out whether the current allocation of competence fits with economic criteria. The second section addresses the benefits of decentralisation, whereas the third section discusses the reasons for centralisation. Because differences in lobbying power that pressure groups can exert *vis-à-vis* the national and the supranational authorities may provide an explanation for the observed allocation of competences, the fourth section of the paper analyses the current allocation of tasks in competition matters from a Public Choice perspective. The paper not only addresses antitrust issues, but the laws prohibiting unfair trade practices as well as self-regulation of competitive conduct are incorporated into the analysis.

Part three on institutional change consists of four papers. Bruno S. Frey and Reiner Eichenberger start with proposing a 'Single European Market for Governments' for securing a 'Fifth Freedom'. The EC has excelled in strengthening economic competition. In contrast, competition between governments has been neglected. This article proposes that a future European constitution should guarantee a fifth freedom allowing the evolution of functional, overlapping and competing governmental jurisdictions (FOCJ).

The federal units proposed in this paper have four major characteristics. They are:

- functional (F), that is, the new political units extend over areas defined by the tasks to be fulfilled;
- overlapping (O), that is, in line with the many different tasks (functions), there are corresponding governmental units extending over different geographical areas;
- competing (C), that is, individuals and/or communities may choose the governmental unit to which they want to belong, and have the political right to express their preferences directly via initiatives and referenda;
- jurisdictions (J), that is, the units established are governmental, they have enforcement power and can, in particular, raise taxes.

The authors propose that the future European constitution should allow, and actively promote, the evolution of functional, overlapping and competing governmental jurisdictions (FOCJ). They fulfil many of the welfare enhancing qualities suggested by theoretical concepts such as Tiebout's voting by foot, Olson's and Oates' fiscal equivalence, or Buchanan's clubs. It is shown that FOCJ are feasible, that there are successful historical examples, and that they partially exist in the form of US special districts and Swiss functional, democratic and overlapping communes.

Manfred E. Streit and Stefan Voigt continue with comparing the relative merits of enlarging versus deepening the European Union. The collapse of the centrally planned economies in 1989 has fundamentally changed Europe's political landscape. Not only do the societies of Central Europe and Eastern Europe have to rewrite their constitutions, international and supranational entities such as the OSCE, NATO, and the EU have to redefine the scope and depth of their tasks. In this paper an attempt is being made to apply the framework of constitutional economics to the question of entry into the European Union. The choice of a constitution can be thought of as a choice of rules as opposed to a choice within rules. The authors thus have to look for rules that could be chosen by rational actors to admit entry of additional states. In the first section of the paper, the current *status quo* is described and possible costs and benefits of enlarging the Union are sketched. This includes possible effects on the EU budget as well as on trade with potential member states. The following makes use of the theory of clubs in order to conceptualise the European Union for the analytical problem. The last section of this paper is an attempt to substantiate the analysis further by applying constitutional economics to the question of entry. The central hypothesis is advanced that the 'deepen or enlarge' alternative frequently discussed today is probably only half the story. If a decision to considerably enlarge the Union to the south and east is taken, people might be better off if the scope of tasks delegated to the European level were to be diminished.

In the third paper of this part Frank Vibert examines the role of the principle of non-coercion and of decision rules in the constitution. One of the most important topics for discussion in the near future will concern decision rules in the Council of Ministers. This will involve the question of what voting rules should apply to which subjects. A further part of this discussion will concern to what extent 'opt-outs' or 'opt-ins' are possible and desirable in different areas of policy and will thus be critical to the evolution of 'variable geometry' in the Union. Yet another dimension concerns the procedures for rule changing and rule keeping. In order to get some guidance on these questions about decision rules, the paper explores what constitutional economics has to offer. According to Vibert this will bring the reader fairly quickly to the non-coercion principle. In the way it has been formulated in constitutional economics, the non-coercion approach states that, in principle, the best rule for collective decisionmaking is that decisions should be taken by unanimity.

This paper explores the role played by this formulation of the non-coercion principle and discusses to what extent it offers a coherent approach to decisionmaking rules in the EU and the Council. The general conclusion is that this formulation does not capture important aspects of the nature of the choices about decision rules to be made in Europe and that other insights from constitutional economics have to be brought into play in order to achieve coherence. This does not mean that the non-coercion principle can be simply set aside. On the contrary, it is a key principle. However, as a validating principle it has to be reformulated as a normative rule for political association.

Finally, Ulrich Everling closes this part with giving a lawyer's view on the constitutional problems of the EU. The paper is based on the understanding that law is not only to be interpreted as being formed by economic and social factors and by the requirements of efficiency. Law is also the expression of traditions, of social structures and demands, of political attitudes and interests and in particular of values and sense of justice. These aspects may be less important in the field of technical rules where practical requirements are predominant. But they have a higher degree of influence on the regulations concerning the social and economic order, and, on the constitutional level, fundamental values are to be respected and are not at the disposal of the legislator. One of the crucial problems of the European integration consists in the fact that the mentioned traditions, structures and understandings of values are quite different in the member states. They must gradually be assimilated to such a degree that they may form the basis of a common consciousness of the citizens.

The paper presents some theses on European constitutional issues under four headings. First, the origin and structure of the Union and community are examined. Secondly, constitutional questions, in particular the decision-making process and the democratic deficit, are addressed. Thirdly, federal concerns such as the distribution of competences and subsidiarity are discussed. Finally, in a short outlook, perspectives of enlargement are outlined.

Such a big conference cannot be organised without the help of many others. We would like to thank the following institutions for their support: Auswärtiges Amt, Bonn; Commission of the European Union, Brussels; Fachbereich 2 der Universität des Saarlandes; Landeszentralbank in Rheinland/Pfalz und im Saarland, Mainz/Saarbrücken; Ministerium für Bildung, Kultur und Wissenschaft des Saarlandes, Saarbrücken; Sparkasse Saarbrücken; Union Stiftung e. V., Saarbrücken; Volkswagen-Stiftung, Hannover. We would also like to thank the following persons: Christian Koboldt and Patrick Steimer for their organisational support and, particularly, Eric Neumayer and Alexander Neunzig for their editorial work.

PART ONE

Decisionmaking

2. Why Power Indices Cannot Explain Decisionmaking in the European Union*

George Tsebelis and Geoffrey Garrett

1. INTRODUCTION

The increasing use since the mid-1980s of qualified majority voting (QMV) in the Council of Ministers of the European Union (EU) has prompted many to analyse European decisionmaking in terms of the relative power of different national governments in the Council. While there are some differences among specific approaches, all of these power calculations are based on computations of the portion of all mathematically possible winning coalitions to which each government is pivotal (that is, without which a coalition would fall short of the QVM threshold).[1] Scholars have used this basic 'power index' approach to make numerous assertions about the direction of policy in the contemporary EU, such as the effects of expanding the size of the Union from 12 members to 15 and beyond, the policy consequences of different constitutional arrangements, and the likely course of outcomes in discrete issues areas.

We argue that conclusions about the EU based on power index analyses will invariably be wrong because the approach is deeply flawed. First, most studies ignore the policy preferences of member governments in the Council of Ministers – leading them systematically to overestimate the power of governments that generally assume extreme positions (especially from big countries, notably the United Kingdom) and systematically to underestimate the power of more centrist governments (especially from smaller countries such as the Benelux group). Some studies seek to remedy this weakness by

* The authors would like to thank participants at the Conference on Constitutional Law and Economics of the European Union, Saarbrücken, 2–5 September 1995 for numerous helpful comments on an earlier version of this paper. Neal Jesse and Amie Kreppel provided valuable research assistance. George Tsebelis would like to recognise financial support from the Simon Guggenheim Foundation, and NSF grant #SBR 9511485.

weighting power indices by measures of policy position – most importantly Mika Widgrén's 'partial homogeneity index'.[2] These still generate misleading results, however, because they fail to take into account the impact of the relative position of countries on strategic bargaining in the Council.

Second, all analyses based on power indices pay too little attention to the institutional rules that govern decisionmaking in the contemporary EU. Most importantly, they don't fully take into account the impact of the 1986 Single European Act (SEA) and the 1992 Treaty on European Union (TEU) on interactions among the Council, the Commission and the European Parliament. In particular, we highlight the impact of changes in 'agenda-setting power' – the ability to make proposals that are difficult to amend – and 'veto power' on policymaking under the four most frequently used procedures in Europe today – assent, consultation, cooperation and codecision.[3]

The remainder of our paper is divided into four sections. Section 2 discusses the implications for the power index approach of taking into account the policy preferences of member governments in the Council of Ministers. Section 3 demonstrates the inability of the power index approach effectively to take into account the role of institutional actors other than the Council in EU decisionmaking. In Section 4, we present our own analysis of the strategic interactions among the Council, the Commission and the European Parliament under the EU's different legislative procedures. We conclude in section 5 by highlighting the implications for future research on the EU of the differences between our approach and the power index perspective.

2. POLICY PREFERENCES AND POWER INDICES

Let us begin by assuming – along with the bulk of studies based on the calculation of power indices – that the Council of Ministers is the pre-eminent decisionmaker in the EU. We will consider a seven-member Council, in which each member's vote is weighted equally and five votes constitute a qualified majority. This is the simplest way to represent decisionmaking under the qualified majority thresholds that have obtained in all actual configurations of the Council.[4] From the power indices perspective, the ability of a government to influence Council deliberations is a function of the portion of all mathematically possible 'winning' qualified majority coalitions to which it is pivotal (that is, those coalitions that would cease to attain the qualified majority threshold if the government defected). In order to determine a government's power, one simply divides the number of 'vulnerable' coalitions to which it is pivotal by the total number of vulnerable coalitions.[5] As a result, the power index of a government is a normalized score between 0 and 1, and the sum of all these indices is 1. In the case of a seven-member Council with equal voting weights, there are 21 (= 7!/5!2!) ways that five-member coalitions can be put together. Each of the seven governments would be pivotal to fifteen (= 6!/(4!2!)) of these coalitions.[6] Hence, the power of each government would be the same: 1/7.

The critical difference between our analysis and the standard power index perspective is that we include the policy preferences of member governments. In the first part of this section we demonstrate that the type of calculations performed by power indices produce completely different results if policy positions are taken into account. In the second part we compare our results with the more sophisticated partial homogeneity approach. In both cases we use a one-dimensional policy space for simplicity of presentation. However, our argument holds in any number of dimensions.[7]

We show that taking policy positions into account has two important effects on power indices. First, only connected coalitions should be considered in calculations of vulnerable coalitions. Second, oversized, rather than 'minimal winning', coalitions may often form.

Standard Power Indices

Assume that the seven members (1–7) of the Council have Euclidean preferences ('ideal points') on a one dimensional policy space from less to more European integration (see Figure 2.1). Recall that from a power index (PI) perspective, each member is equally powerful (PI(n) = 1/7). Our first argument is that a more appropriate way of calculating power would be to include from the 21 decisive coalitions only those that are connected. Consider the coalition 12346. According to the power index literature this coalition has a probability 1/21 to occur. We argue, however, that the probability of 12346 occurring is actually zero. This is because there is nothing that unites members 1, 2, 3, 4, with 6 which would not include 5.

Figure 2.1 Power indices and connected coalitions

To demonstrate this, assume that the *status quo* is to the left of government 1. All five members of the coalition 12346 prefer policy outcomes that are closer to their ideal points than is the *status quo* (for example, at the preferences of government 1). But so does government 5. When a vote is taken in the Council, the members of the winning coalition cannot stop government 5 from voting with them. A similar argument could be made if the *status quo* were somewhere between 1 and 6. There is no proposal that governments 1 and 6 would both support. In these collectively exhaustive and mutually exclusive cases, the coalition 12346 would not arise.

Coalitions such as 12346 do not occur because they are not connected; they do not include a member whose preferences are located between the preferences of members in the coalition. As a result, an agreement among the members of the coalition either is not possible or, if an agreement is possible, the excluded member will go along. This coalition is not decisive since it can reduce its size by one and still win. Consequently, non-connected coalitions do not form when voting is done on the basis of policy positions.

This outcome should be contrasted with that of coalition government formation.[8] Building a government is fundamentally different from decisionmaking in the Council of Ministers. Parties in a coalition can exclude a would-be (connected) member from participating in government (that is, holding cabinet portfolios). Moreover, they have motives to do so – for example, to increase their shares of the perquisites of office. This is impossible in the Council of Ministers. No Euro-government is formed. There are no perquisites inherent in being in the majority on a given issue. Moreover, member governments are free to vote for any policies they choose.

The possibility that oversized coalitions will form should also be considered from a power index perspective. Assume now that the *status quo* in Figure 2.1 is located far to the left of government 1, and that a decision to implement a policy at government 4's ideal point is proposed. All the members of the Council prefer 4 to the *status quo*. If one were to allow for oversized coalitions, three more could form: 123456, 234567, and 1234567. These should be included in the computation of power indices.

The consequences of the biases introduced by the unrealistic assumptions of non-connectivity and decisiveness are serious. Here we only analyse the non-connectivity assumption, although extensions to the case of oversized coalitions is straightforward. If one considers only the connected winning coalitions in Figure 2.1, it is clear that there are only three: 12345, 23456, and 34567. In these coalitions, members 1 and 7 participate once each, members 2 and 6 twice each, and 3, 4, and 5 all three times. Thus, the power index (PI) of the different members is as follows: PI(1)=1/15, PI(2)=2/15, PI(3)=3/15, PI(4)=3/15, PI(5)=3/15, PI(6)=2/15, PI(7)=1/15 ($\sum$PI(n) =1).

Thus, even though the voting weights of all members in our example are the same – and hence each member would be considered equally powerful by conventional calculations of power indices – the influence of these countries over policies is clearly related to their centrality in the policy space.

'Partial Homogeneity' Power Indices

Recent work by Mika Widgrén (1995) has attempted to deal with the problem of policy positions within the basic structure of power index calculations. Widgrén acknowledges that conventional power indices assume that the preferences of actors are 'homogenous', that is, the probability that each will vote for a given measure is the same. He suggests, however, that when this is unrealistic – as is in the case of the Council of Ministers – one can take into account the impact of 'partial homogeneity' (that is, heterogeneity in policy positions) by weighting power indices by the probabilities that members of a coalition will vote for a given measure.

To illustrate Widgrén's argument, we develop an example based on the division of government preferences into three discrete groups, though obviously the scale could be expanded.[9] In order to simplify the analysis without affecting the thrust of our argument, we consider a single value for each probability (instead of an integral over a certain domain). Let us divide governments in the Council of Ministers into likely 'supporters' of a proposal radically to increase the level of integration in the EU, likely 'opponents', and governments that are 'undecided'. The probability that 'supporters' will vote for the proposal is 0.8; that for 'undecideds' is 0.5; and 0.2 for 'opponents'. Now return to Figure 2.1. Assume that governments 1, 2 and 3 are opponents, governments 4 and 5 are undecided, and govern-ments 6 and 7 are supporters.

Widgrén suggests that under these circumstances, one can weight a conventional power index calculation by the probabilities that different members of a specific coalition will vote for a given proposal. For example, the coalition 12345 has probability $(0.2)^3(0.5)^2(=0.002)$ of occurring; 12346 has probability $(0.2)^3(0.5)(0.8)(=0.0032)$, whereas 34567 has probability $(0.2)(0.5)^2(0.8)^2(=0.032)$. A simple numerical comparison indicates that the coalition 34567 is ten times more likely to occur than coalition 12346. But this is exactly where our criticism of conventional power indices should be re-stated. In our account, the coalition 12346 is not possible, because member 5 will join any coalition that has 4 and 6 as members. In other words, the (conditional) probability of government 5 joining the coalition 12346 is 1.0 in our spatial model, whereas it is 0.5 according to the partial homogeneity approach. This is a fundamental difference between our approach and Widgrén's. In our model, we can infer the voting behaviour of member 5 from the voting behaviour of 4 and 6 (if they vote 'yes' for a given proposal, so will government 5). For Widgrén, however, no such inference can be made.

To assess the relevance of spatial positioning, let us examine one of the real world applications in Kirman and Widgrén's analysis – the EU budget.[10] Two items dominate the budget: regional development assistance and the common agricultural policy (CAP). Accordingly, Kirman and Widgrén propose very plausibly that the preferences of member governments can be arrayed on two dimensions: national per capita GDP and the share of agriculture in the labour force (poorer countries with large agricultural sectors want to increase the size of the EU budget because it redistributes wealth to them). The spatial location of national preferences over the EU budget is presented in Figure 2.2. As is well known, there is a strong correlation between the two dimensions. The wealthier, less agricultural countries of northern Europe cluster quite tightly in the upper-left corner, while the poorer and more agricultural members of the EU spread out towards the lower-right corner.

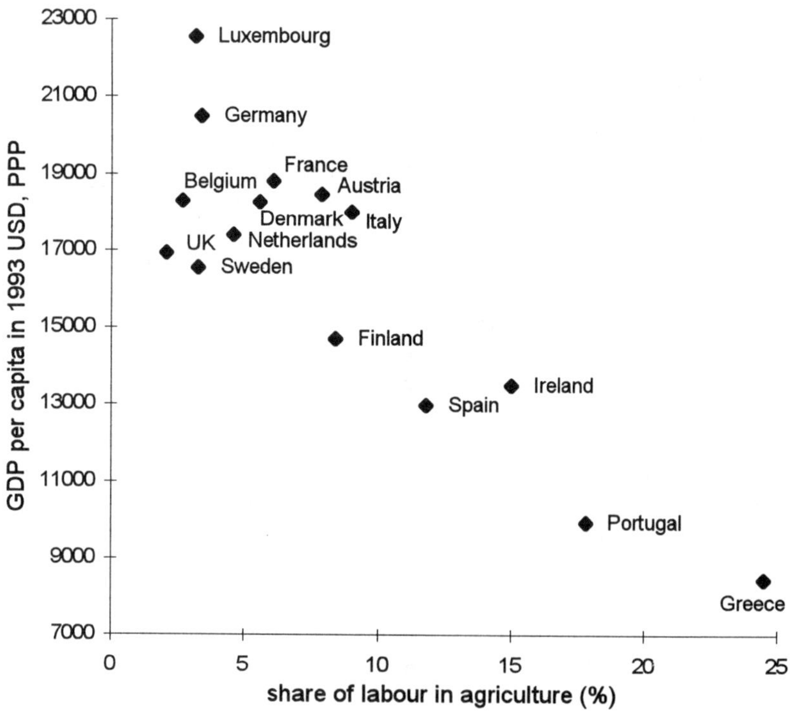

Source: Kirman and Widgrén (1995), p. 444.

Figure 2.2 Two-dimensional preferences over the EU budget

What leverage does this information give us over the likely outcome of budgetary negotiations. We can see that Luxembourg, the UK, Sweden and

Italy define the 'periphery' of a quadrangle that includes six other countries that might be considered the EU 'core' on budgetary issues: Germany, Belgium, France, Denmark, The Netherlands and Austria. We will not discuss the other countries (broadly speaking the south). Suppose that we learn from an authoritative source that the countries of the 'periphery' have decided to accept a certain budget plan. What are the implications of this piece of information?

In our model, this plan will be supported by the core with probability 1. For Kirman and Widgrén, however, this would not be the case. The likelihood that the plan would be supported by these countries would continue to be a multiplicative function of the unconditional probabilities that each country would support the plan. Unless these probabilities were one for every country (that is, national preferences were homogeneous rather than heterogeneous), Kirman and Widgrén would conclude that the chances of the core's supporting the budget plan would be considerably less than 1.

3. THE COMMISSION AND POWER INDICES

Up until now, our analysis has accepted the basic assumption of most power index analyses: that one can understand policy making dynamics in the EU by focusing exclusively on bargaining among member governments in the Council of Ministers. This assumption, however, is inappropriate. In this section, we introduce the institutional details that affect the actual course of decisionmaking in the contemporary union and analyse how the strategic interactions among the Council, the Commission and the Parliament affect legislative outcomes. We focus our critique of power indices on the work of Kirman and Widgrén since it is the most sophisticated in the genre and it is the only power index analysis that explicitly includes the impact of an actor outside the Council of Ministers – the Commission – on decisionmaking. Having demonstrated the limitations of their analysis, we describe the different legislative procedures that are used in the EU today and examine the effects of these procedures on the likely course of policy.

Kirman and Widgrén propose an ingenious way of introducing the Commission into their power index calculations.[11] According to the rules of most procedures (see section 4 for details) legislation can be adopted either by agreement of the Commission with a qualified majority of the Council (that is, five out of the seven members in our example), or by unanimity in the Council. If one includes the Commission as an actor in this process, from a power index perspective there are now 22 possible winning coalitions.[12] There are 21 combinations of the form 12345C (five members of the Council plus the Commission); there is also a single unanimity coalition in the Council (1234567). One can now re-calculate the power indices for each government in the Council and for the Commission on the basis of the number of coalitions to which each is pivotal.

There are several problems with this approach. First, as we have already shown, only the three connected qualified majority coalitions in the Council should be included. Second, the introduction of the Commission restricts the possibilities even further. Consider the preference configuration presented in Figure 2.3, where the Commission (C) is to the right of the last country (that is, the Commission is in favour of more European integration than is any member state).[13] For the reasons explained in the previous section, a coalition of 12345 and the Commission is not possible because it excludes members 6 and 7 who have intermediate preferences. Similarly, a coalition of 23456 and C is impossible, because 7 will join. Thus, only one of the three possible qualified majority coalitions in the Council can form if the agreement of the Commission is required for passage of legislation: 34567 and C. If we introduce the non-minimal coalitions, then there are actually three coalitions that could form to pass legislation: 34567 and C, 234567 and C, and 1234567.[14] Calculating power indices on the basis of the 22 mathematically possible coalitions in the Council and the Commission will thus generate extremely misleading results.

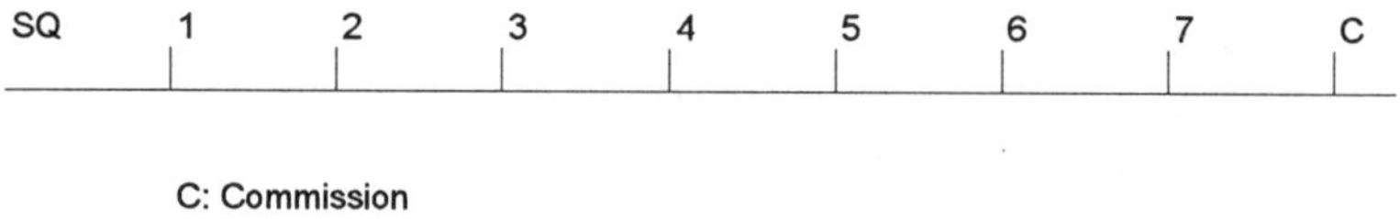

Figure 2.3 The council of ministers and the commission

The third problem with the way Kirman and Widgrén's analyse the role of the Commission is the most serious from our perspective. According to the legislative procedures of the EU, the Commission is not just one of the participants in the possible coalitions (as Kirman and Widgrén assume). Rather, the Commission has a monopoly over introducing legislative proposals around which Council coalitions form. Given the preference distribution depicted in Figure 2.3, it is clear that the Commission will try to avoid the situation where its proposal will be rejected by all Council members, and the unanimous coalition is formed in the Council.

If the *status quo* is to the right of C, the Commission can propose its own ideal point and have it adopted by the coalition 34567. If the *status quo* is between 7 and C in the figure, the best that the Commission can do is propose the ideal point of member 7 and see a unanimous Council accept its proposal. If the status quo is anywhere between 3 and 7, there is no coalition that can upset it. Finally, if the status quo is to the left of 3, the Commission can propose 3 and this will be adopted by the coalition 34567. Thus, simply acknowledging that the Commission makes proposals to the Council – the first of many institutional details concerning decisionmaking in the EU that we will discuss – introduces strategic assessments on the part of the Commission and the Council members that cannot be explored from a power index perspective. We now turn to a more complete analysis of the legislative procedures in the EU.

4. THE INSTITUTIONAL DETERMINANTS OF DECISIONMAKING IN EUROPE[15]

The balance of legislative power between the Council, the Commission and the Parliament varies systematically in the contemporary EU with the procedures under which decisions are made. As noted above, in almost all of the procedures, the right to initiate legislative proposals is vested solely in the Commission.[16] However, this does not necessarily give it effective control over the policy making process. The Commission cannot keep issues off the agenda. Since the Treaty of Rome, the Commission has been bound to make proposals when requested by the Council. This power was extended to the Parliament at Maastricht. More importantly, the fact that the Commission makes the first proposal does not mean that it can always constrain – much less determine – the ultimate proposal that is voted on in the last stage of the legislative game.

In this section, we analyse decisionmaking in Europe in terms of institutional variations in the location of 'agenda setting' power (the ability to make proposals that are difficult to amend) and 'veto' power (the ability to ensure that the status quo is maintained). In order to do this, we should begin by describing the assumptions and methods that underpin this analysis.

As in the preceding sections, we base our analysis on a one-dimensional spatial model using a seven-member Council. In order to substantiate this argument, we base our analysis on the one-dimensional spatial model presented in Figure 2.1 (in which the Council has seven members with equal voting weights). Our analysis can be generalised in multiple dimensions, but we examine the one dimensional case for ease of presentation.[17]

We assume that the *status quo ante* is a policy that reflects the preferences of the least integrationist government in the Council. This can be understood as the outcome of intergovernmental bargaining under the Luxembourg compromise that dominated decisionmaking until the ratification of the Single European Act (see below). All the other relevant actors – the other members of the Council, the Commission and the Parliament – prefer to increase the level of integration in the EU. This is the scenario that best describes the environment that has obtained since the demise of the

Luxembourg compromise. We ultimately relax this assumption to analyse the possibilities for rolling back integration under the codecision procedure.

Consistent with the qualitative literature highlighting the vested interests of Commissioners in vigorously pushing forward the integration agenda, we model the preferences of the Commission (more precisely, the median voter in the College of Commissioners) to be more extreme than those of any member of the Council (as in Figure 2.3).[18] Furthermore, we also assume that the preferences of the Parliament (the preferences of the median voter on the floor of the Parliament) are similar to those of the Commission.[19] We relax this assumption later to take into account the possibility that the degree of citizen control over Parliamentarians will increase in time.

Our analysis focuses on the last steps of different decisionmaking procedures in the EU today. For these last steps we assume complete information, that is, that all actors know each other's preferences and the location of the *status quo*.[20] We also assume that the actors engaged in EU policy making believe that it is not feasible in the short run to re-introduce a policy issue once it has gone through the relevant procedure.[21] Under this framework, the last two stages of each EU decisionmaking process are pivotal: which actor makes the final proposal? to whom? under what voting rules? We now address these questions with respect to the major decisionmaking procedures in the EU today – assent, consultation, cooperation and codecision.

The Assent Procedure

Under the Luxembourg compromise that effectively governed decisionmaking in the EU from at least 1966 until 1986, the Council of Ministers dominated the policymaking process. Though the formal right to propose lay exclusively with the Commission, proposals could only become law if they were supported unanimously in the Council. This effectively gave all the decisionmaking power to the government with the least interest in changing the *status quo* (government 1 in Figure 2.4). Some issues today are still dominated by lowest common denominator pressures in the Council.[22] First, unanimity among EU members is necessary for treaty revision, for the EU's external relationships, and for common foreign and security policy and cooperation in justice and home affairs. Second, some contentious policy issues – including indirect taxation, exchange rate parities for Economic and Monetary Union, industrial policy and some environmental matters – are decided unanimously in the Council, but on a proposal made by the Commission. Since the Council can amend Commission proposals unanimously, however, the Commission has no real agenda-setting power in these cases.

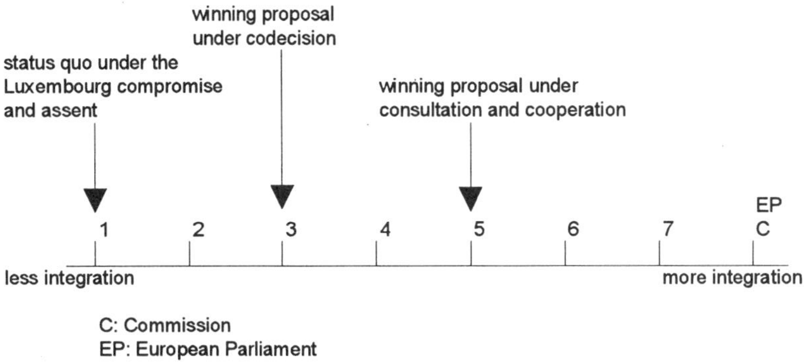

Figure 2.4 Legislative procedures and policy outcomes

The final legacy of the Luxembourg compromise is more interesting. Numerous areas are covered by the assent procedure in which the Council votes on a Commission proposal under a unanimity rule, subject to the assent of a majority in the Parliament. The policies covered by assent include establishing citizenship rights, cohesion funds, electoral rules for the European Parliament, and the accession of new members. The introduction of a parliamentary veto of Council decisions would seem to be a significant departure from the Luxembourg compromise. So long as the median voter in the Parliament is more integrationist than the least integrationist member of the Council, however, Parliament will not exercise its veto right.

In sum, in all those instances where voting in the Council is by unanimity, including the assent procedure, one can ignore the roles played by other EU institutions. For all the other areas of EU jurisdiction, however, Council votes have been by qualified majority since 1986. We now demonstrate that the consequences of qualified majority voting vary with the relationships among the Council, the Commission and the Parliament.

The Consultation Procedure

The simplest procedure using qualified majority voting in the Council is the consultation procedure elaborated in the Treaty of Rome, but blocked until 1986 by the Luxembourg compromise (see the top panel of Figure 2.5). Today, the consultation procedure applies to numerous areas, including the free movement of capital, competition policy and industrial subsidies. Under qualified majority voting, the Commission wants to make the most pro-integrationist proposal that will be supported by a qualified majority in the Council. Given the situation depicted in Figure 2.4, this coalition is clearly 34567. Moreover, government 3 replaces government 1 as the pivotal player in the Council. The Commission will make the proposal that is closest to its

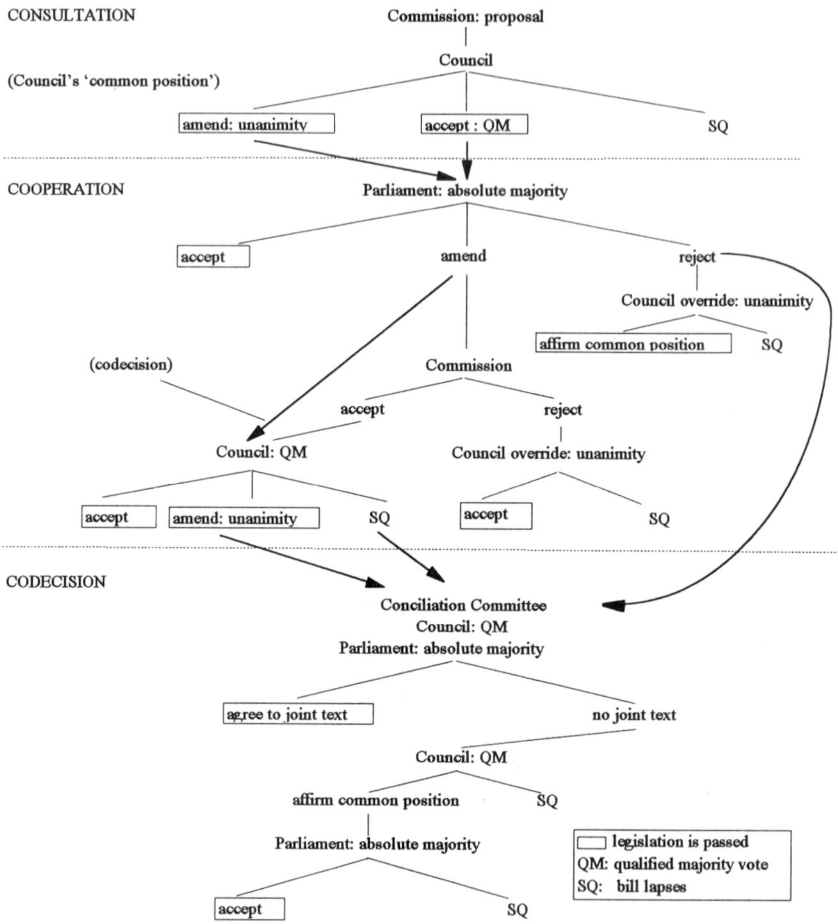

Source: Garrett (1995).

Figure 2.5 Consultation, cooperation and codecision

ideal point and that government 3 prefers to the *status quo* (and to all solutions that can defeat the *status quo* unanimously).

It is thus clear that the pace of European integration would increase under the consultation procedure. Unlike the Luxembourg compromise, recalcitrant governments can be outvoted. Moreover, since agenda-setting power lies with the Commission, the pivotal player in the Council will not be able to get policy at its ideal point. Instead, the Commission will propose a more integrationist policy, but one that the pivotal member of the Council still prefers to the *status quo*.

The Cooperation Procedure

The cooperation procedure was introduced in the Single European Act. Until Maastricht, the most important issues subject to it concerned the internal market (the '1992' agenda). Today, the cooperation procedure (Article 189c of the Maastricht treaty) applies to areas including social policy (although Britain opted out of this provision), implementation of regional funds, research and technological development, and a number of environmental issues.

The most important institutional difference between the consultation and cooperation procedures is that the European Parliament gained 'conditional agenda setting power' (see the middle panel of Figure 2.5).[23] Under cooperation, the Parliament can amend Commission proposals. If these are accepted by the Commission (which is the case for three out of four amendments), the new proposal is then presented to the Council, which votes using the same rules that pertain under consultation.[24] If the Parliament's preferences are similar to those of the Commission, the policy consequences of the cooperation procedure will be the same as those under the consultation procedure. The Commission and the Parliament will agree to make the most pro-integration proposal that will win the support of a qualified majority in the Council. In the context of Figure 2.4, this proposal would be marginally to the left of government 5's ideal point because this is the most integrationist policy that the pivotal government 3 prefers to the *status quo*.

Given the proliferation of internal market legislation since the mid-1980s, it is relatively easy to delineate the policy consequences of the cooperation procedure – and specifically the agenda setting power it grants to the Commission and the Parliament. The most important of the consequences of the introduction of the cooperation procedure is that policy outcomes may be outside the Pareto set of member governments – something that was inconceivable under the Luxembourg compromise. Consider the following example.

Most observers believe that the EU's recent legislation on health and safety at work issues is more advanced (that is, affords more protection to workers) than legislation in any of the member states.[25] Volker Eichener concluded that '[t]he European Community definitely adopted the highest health and safety at work level which is to be found among the 12 Member States'.[26] Similarly, Giandomenico Majone argued that '[i]t is difficult to find equally advanced principles (like the "working environment") in the legislation of major industrialised countries, inside and outside the EC. In order to explain such policy outputs we need new, more analytic theories of the policy process in the Community.'[27]

How was it possible for European legislation to be more stringent than that in any member state? One potential line of argument would be that while EU legislation may go further than the regulations of member countries, the existing national laws were not at the ideal points of the individual governments. Governments might have wanted more advanced regulation, but they were unable or unwilling to adopt it unilaterally. According to this account, EU members used supranational institutions to solve domestic problems. This is not plausible, however, since EU legislation clearly imposes a heavy burden on the ability of European products to compete outside the Union. Given that only around two-thirds of total EU trade is internal, it is most unlikely that governments would be unconcerned about the external competitiveness of their national economies.

The second explanation for standards for health and safety at work being higher at the EU level than in any member state concentrates on the strategic interactions inherent in the cooperation procedure. Consider the following modification of Figure 2.4. Let the first three member governments remain at the same points. But assume that the ideal points of the other four governments are tightly packed around point 4 (this is plausible with respect to health and safety at work since standards in most northern European countries are quite similar). In this case, the outcome of the cooperation procedure (still at point 5 in the figure, but now with no government holding this preference) is outside the Pareto set of the member governments.

This outcome assumes that government 1 and 2 would not be willing to support a Council amendment of regulation at point 4 (recall that the Council can always amend proposals unanimously), and hence their intransigence would leave the qualified majority (34567) with no other choice but to accept point 5. The behaviour of government 1 and 2 would thus be 'irrational', but it can be explained if one takes into account domestic political consideration in the first two countries (in this example, one could plausibly think of these countries as Greece and the United Kingdom). Governments 1 and 2 may prefer to be on the record as having voted down any significant increase in regulation, rather than to have decreased marginally the level of regulation (from point 5 to point 4) – if support of regulatory measures is very unpopular domestically.[28]

The basic point to be derived from this example is that, given the institutional innovations of the Single European Act, one should not be surprised if outcomes of the legislative process sometimes are outside the Pareto set of member governments. Under certain very plausible configurations of government preferences, this type of outcome will be the product – a very dramatic product – of the agenda-setting powers vested in the Commission and the Parliament.

The Codecision Procedure

A final decisionmaking procedure was added at Maastricht. The codecision procedure (Article 189b) replaced the cooperation procedure for internal market matters, and it also applies to new areas of EU jurisdiction such as education, culture, public health and consumer protection. There are two critical institutional differences between cooperation and codecision (see the bottom panel of Figure 2.5).

First, the agenda-setting power of the Commission is greatly reduced under codecision because Parliament's amendments of legislation do not go back to the Commission before they are re-considered by the Council. Moreover, new proposals effectively can be made if a conciliation committee is convened.

Second, the roles of the Council and the Parliament are reversed from cooperation to codecision. Under the new procedure, if parliamentary amendments to the Council's 'common position' (that is, a Commission proposal that won the support of a qualified majority in the Council) are not acceptable to a qualified majority in the Council, a conciliation committee is convened. If this committee (comprising all members of the Council and equal representation from the Parliament) cannot agree to a joint text, proposal power effectively reverts to the Council. In the final stage of the game, the Council produces the final text of the law unless an absolute majority in the Parliament vetoes it.

One can begin analysing the likely policy consequences of codecision by assuming that the structure of actors' preferences and the status quo are those in Figure 2.4. It is obvious that coalition 34567 would offer the best deal to the Parliament and hence it would generate the proposal on which the Parliament would vote. With respect to the bargaining within the Council coalition, any solution acceptable to government 3 would also be accepted by the other members of the coalition. This confines policy outcomes to the segment between 3 and 5 in Figure 2.4. Government 4 might threaten not to accept any proposal that is not at its ideal point. If this statement were credible, a policy at 4 would be the outcome of the codecision procedure. A more reasonable assumption, however, is that government 3 has the effective bargaining power, and it will be able to impose its ideal point.

Thus, there is a very important difference in expected policy outputs between consultation and cooperation, on the one hand, and codecision, on the other. If the Parliament is more integrationist than any member of the Council, and if the *status quo ante* was achieved under the Luxembourg compromise, the pace of European integration will be slower under codecision than under the older procedures. This is directly a function of the transfer of agenda-setting power from the Commission and the Parliament to the Council.

In the consultation/cooperation endgame, the Commission or the Parliament makes proposals to the Council that can only be amended unanimously. Government 3 is pivotal in the Council, but it will accept proposals to its right so long as they are preferable to the best amendment it could make that would be acceptable to all Council members (in Figure 2.4, there are no such amendments since the *status quo* is at government 1's ideal point). The agenda setters understand this and thus propose a policy to the right of government 3's ideal point. The situation is reversed under codecision because agenda-setting power rests with the Council. Government 3 effectively controls the agenda and can determine the pace of European integration.

Thus, the fact that the Parliament gained an absolute veto over Council proposals is not so important as many analysts have assumed.[29] This is because its veto power was attained at the expense of its ability to influence the Council's agenda. Under the reasonable preference configurations analysed here, the Parliament is a less effective policy maker under codecision than under cooperation. Unfortunately, however, it is not yet possible to test this argument empirically.

Before closing our discussion of codecision, we should note that our analysis has assumed that the *status quo ante* was generated under the Luxembourg compromise. This is entirely reasonable where new issue areas were brought under EU jurisdiction, but it is less appropriate for the major area under codecision – the internal market – because the volume of legislation passed in this area under the cooperation procedure was great.[30] For the internal market, it might be better to assume that the *status quo* is one in which much of the enabling legislation is already in place.

Under this scenario, the major analytic issue is whether the Council can use its agenda-setting power to roll back internal market legislation? So long as the Parliament's preferences are more integrationist than those of the Council, the answer is 'no'. This situation is depicted in Figure 2.6. We assume the extreme case in which the *status quo* is at the Parliament's ideal point. There is no proposal that a qualified majority in the Council could make that would not be vetoed by the Parliament. Here, Parliament's veto power under codecision is potentially very important – it would allow Parliament to block efforts to dismantle existing legislation.

The second assumption we have used that might be relaxed is that the Parliament is more integrationist than all the governments in the Council. This assumption is based on the freedom members of the European Parliament have to act independently of their electoral constituencies. This has been the case up until now because of the general public's disinterest in European Parliament elections.[31]

Figure 2.6 Policy stability under codecision

But this could change in the future as citizens come to understand the power of the Parliament. If the current division between political elites and the mass public continues – with the latter being more sceptical about European integration than most politicians – the preferences of the median voter in the European Parliament might come to be less integrationist than those of governments in the Council.

This scenario is depicted in Figure 2.7. We assume that the *status quo* is very integrationist, but that the Parliament prefers less integration than does government 1. In this extreme case, it is possible that some European legislation (likely concerning the internal market) could be rolled back to the preferences of the pivotal government in the Council under qualified majority voting (government 5 in this case).

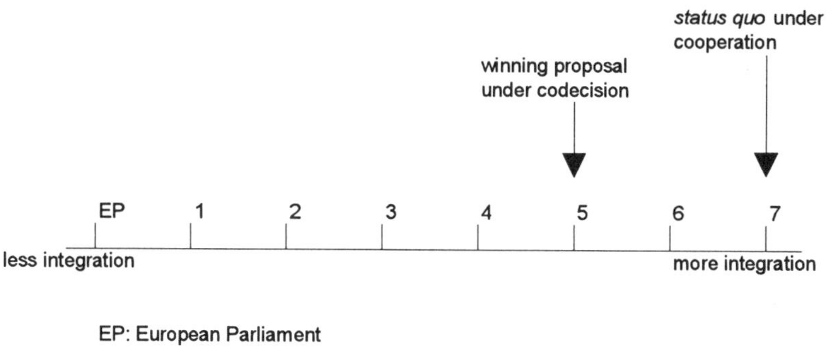

Figure 2.7 The electoral accountability of parliament and codecision

Summary

This section has demonstrated that the only way to understand decisionmaking in the contemporary EU is through detailed analysis of its legislative procedures. The Council-centric perspective of most power index studies was justified during the Luxembourg compromise period and still is useful for analysing some issues today. But here, studies should not concentrate on voting weights. Rather they should consider the ability of countries opposed to integration either to block reforms or to extract high prices for their acquiescence. In all the remaining areas of EU decision-making, one cannot analyse qualified majority voting in the Council without knowing how the agenda on which the Council deliberates is set.

5. CONCLUSION

The EU has proved fertile ground for proponents of power indices since the effective introduction of qualified majority voting to the Council of Ministers in the mid-1980s. Numerous articles using this approach have recently appeared in leading economics and political science journals. We have presented a general critique of this approach. The cooperative game-theoretic foundation on which power indices are based generates systematic biases against focusing attention on the issues that drive decisionmaking in the EU. There are two fundamental flaws in power index analysis.

First, power indices downplay the importance of the spatial location of actors' preferences to their strategic behaviour with respect to coalition formation. In our analysis we demonstrated not only that the calculations are biased, but that in addition they ignore strategic calculations of the agenda setting actor(s).

Second, power indices ignore virtually all the details of the procedures that govern interactions between Council coalitions and the supranational actors in the EU that play legislative roles – the Commission and the European Parliament. These procedures have a considerable impact on policy outcomes – as is evidenced by the fact that the different institutional actors fight over (and even take cases to the Court of Justice concerning) the institutional rules (consultation, cooperation, etc.) under which different policy decisions should be made.

We have not limited our analysis, however, to critique. We have proposed an alternative approach to the study of European decisionmaking – based on a non-cooperative game theory and taking fully into account the preferences of different actors and the institutional conditions that affect their interactions. Our approach generates considerable leverage over important policy outcomes in Europe. For example, we have shown why spatially isolated countries such as the United Kingdom have little influence over decisionmaking under qualified majority voting, why the agenda setting power of the Commission and the Parliament often results in policy outcomes that seem extremely interventionist, and why it would be wrong to conclude that the Maastricht treaty clearly increased the policy influence of the Parliament.

NOTES

1. See, for example, Brams and Affuso (1985); Hosli (1993); Johnston (1995); Lane and Mœland (1995); Widgrén (1994); Widgrén (1995) and Kirman and Widgrén (1995).
2. Kirman and Widgrén (1995) and Widgrén (1995).
3. For other studies in this vein, see Garrett (1992); Garrett (1995); Martin (1993); Schneider (1995); Steunenberg (1994; Tsebelis (1994); Tsebelis (1995).
4. The current qualified majority required is 62 out of 87 votes. Governments are allocated votes in the Council in loose approximation to their countries' populations, although the voting weights are biased in favour of smaller countries. Today, these weights are: France, Germany, Italy and the United Kingdom: 10; Spain: 8; Belgium, Greece, the Netherlands, and Portugal: 5; Sweden and Austria: 4; Denmark, Finland and Ireland: 3; Luxembourg 2.
5. This is the Banzhaf power index. Our critique applies equally to the other common method of calculation, the Shapley– Shubik index. Banzhaf (1965); Shapley and Shubik (1954).
6. The number is calculated by assuming one government is a member of a coalition and asking how many decisive coalitions can be formed with four out of the remaining six members.
7. For a multi-dimensional model criticising conventional power indices in these terms, see Garrett and Tsebelis (1996).
8. See, for example, Riker (1962) and Axelrod (1970).
9. The three category example is used by Widgrén (1995), pp. 349–352; an interval scale is used in Kirman and Widgrén (1995), pp. 434–442.
10. Kirman and Widgrén (1995), pp. 443–445.
11. Op. cit. , pp. 445–447.
12. We will exclude analysing the impact of preference heterogeneity to isolate the effects of introducing the Commission into the power index framework.
13. We discuss below why this is a representative example of actual decisionmaking in the EU.
14. The coalition 1234567 and C is theoretically possible, but the Commission is redundant to it and hence cannot be understood to have any power over it.
15. This section is drawn from Garrett and Tsebelis (1996).
16. The Commission plays no formal role in the new areas of EU jurisdictions created at Maastricht (see below).
17. For extension to multiple dimensions, see Tsebelis (1994) and Tsebelis (1995).
18. The pro-integration agenda of Commissioners may seem puzzling given that national governments select their own Commissioners and can replace them at the end of their terms. However, there are informal constraints that militate against governments' choosing their partisans as Commissioners. There is also considerable evidence that Commissioners take on increasingly pro-integration positions after they arrive in Brussels.
19. For a detailed analysis of decisionmaking within the Parliament, see Tsebelis (1995).
20. While one could readily extend the complete information assumption to the whole procedure – as opposed to the last steps – we avoid the temptation because it leads to conclusions that are difficult to support empirically. Perhaps most importantly, under complete information the decisionmaking game would never reach the final stages. The initial proposal would be accepted by all actors and the game would end. In practice, however, most deliberations reach the final stage of a given procedure. Nonetheless, the complete information assumption is reasonable at the end of the game because by this time the relevant actors have exchanged

considerable information – by their behaviour both under the decisionmaking procedure and outside it.

21. Indirect evidence supports this assumption. Most importantly, it is extremely rare for any policy initiative to end in a stalemate with no decision reached. It is thus reasonable to analyse policymaking as a one shot game in which the final player in a game will accept proposals that it prefers to the *status quo ante*. It is theoretically possible, of course, for issues on which legislative efforts fail to be raised again in the future. Introducing the possibility of indefinite iteration of these games complicates matters. One would have to analyse non-cooperative bargaining games between the agenda setter and the actor that must accept or reject the agenda setter's proposal. This latter actor must determine whether to reject a proposal it prefers to the *status quo ante* in the expectation of securing a more favourable outcome in a subsequent play of the game. While there are unique equilibria to such games in theory, it is very difficult in practice to put empirical weights on the relevant factors.
22. For detailed descriptions of the policy areas subject to the different decisionmaking procedures, see Jacobs, Corbett and Shackleton (1992), pp. 203–205.
23. Tsebelis (1994), p. 136.
24. The Parliament can also reject proposals that are accepted by a qualified majority in the Council's first reading of a bill. This rejection can only be overridden by a unanimous Council. In practice, however, this power is not very significant if the Parliament is more pro-integration than any member of the Council. A proposal that is preferred to the *status quo* by the Council will invariably also be preferred by the Parliament.
25. The relevant pieces of legislation are the 'Health and Safety at Work' directive (89/391/EEC), the 'Machinery' directive (89/392/EEC), and the 'Display Screen Equipment' directive (90/270/EEC).
26. Eichener (1993), p. 6, emphasis in the original.
27. Majone (1993).
28. For a detailed discussion of this type of 2-level strategic interaction, see Tsebelis (1990).
29. Jacobs, Corbett and Shackleton (1992), pp. 191–194; Nicoll and Salmon (1994), p. 83; Noel (1995), pp. 62–63; Nugent (1994), p. 326.
30. By the end of 1992, over 600 measures had been passed in this manner – double the number envisaged in the Commission's 1985 White Paper on the Completion of the Internal Market. See Jacobs, Corbett and Shackleton (1992), p. 193.
31. In the 1994 elections, for example, turnout was very low and the intense campaigns (most notably in Britain) were dominated by domestic considerations, rather than by EU policy issues.

REFERENCES

Axelrod, R. (1970), *Conflict of Interest*, Chicago: Markham.

Banzhaf, J. III (1965), 'Weighted Voting Doesn't Work: A Mathematical Analysis', *Rutgers Law Review*, **19**, 317–343.

Brams, S. J. and P. J. Affuso (1985), 'New Paradoxes of Voting Power in the EC Council of Ministers', *Electoral Studies*, **4**, 135–139.

Eichener, V. (1993), 'Social Dumping or Innovative regulation? Process and Outcomes of European Decision–Making in the Sector of Health and Safety at Work Harmonization', Florence, European University Institute Working Paper #92/28.

Garrett, G. (1992), 'International Cooperation and Institutional Choice', *International Organization*, **46**, 533–560.

Garrett, G. (1995), 'From the Luxembourg Compromise to Codecision: Decision Making in the European Union', *Electoral Studies*, **14** (3), 289–308.

Garrett, G. and G. Tsebelis (1996), 'An Institutional Critique of Intergovernmentalism', *International Organization*, **50**, 269–299.

Hosli, M. O. (1993), 'The Admission of the European Free Trade Association States to the European Community', *International Organization*, **47** (4), 629–643.

Jacobs, F., R. Corbett and M. Shackleton (1992), *The European Parliament*, 2nd ed., Essex: Longman.

Johnston, R.J. (1995), 'The Conflict over Qualified Majority Voting in the European Council of Ministers: an Analysis of the UK Negotiating Stance Using Power Indices', *British Journal of Political Science.*

Kirman, A. and M.Widgrén (1995),.'European Economic Decision-Making Policy: Progress or Paralysis?', *Economic Policy*, 21, 423–460.

Lane, J.-E. and R. Mœland (1995), 'Voting Power Under the EU Constitution', *Journal of Theoretical Politics*, **7** (2), 223–230.

Majone, G. (1993), 'The European Community between Social Policy and Social Regulation', *Journal of Common Market Studies*, **31**, 153–170.

Martin, L. (1993), 'International and Domestic Institutions in the EMU Process', *Economics and Politics*, **5**, 125–144.

Nicoll, W. and T.C. Salmon (1994), *Understanding the New European Community*, Hemel Hempstead: Harvester-Wheatsheaf.

Noel, E. (1995), 'Towards a New Institutional Balance of Power', in Etienne Davignon, Niels Ersbøll, Karl Lamers, David Martin, Emile Noël, and Frank Vibert, *What Future for the European Commission?*, The Phillip Morris Institute.

Nugent, N. (1994), *The Government and Politics of the European Union*, Durham: Duke University Press.

Riker, W. (1962), *The Theory of Political Coalitions*, New Haven: Yale University Press.

Schneider, G. (1995), 'The Limits of Self-Reform: Institution-Building in the European Union', *European Journal of International Relations*, **1** (1), 59–86.

Shapley, L. S. and M. Shubik (1954), 'A Method of Evaluating the Distribution of Power in a Committee System', *American Political Science Review*, **48**, 787–792.

Steunenberg, B. (1994), 'Decision-Making Under Different Institutional Arrangements – Legislation by the European Community', *Journal of Institutional and Theoretical Economics*, **150**, 642–669.

Tsebelis, G. (1990), *Nested Games: Rational Choice in Comparative Politics*, Berkeley: University of California Press.

Tsebelis, G. (1994), 'The Power of the European Parliament as a Conditional Agenda Setter', *American Political Science Review*, **88**, 128–142.

Tsebelis, G. (1995), 'Conditional Agenda Setting and Decision Making Inside the European Parliament', *Journal of Legislative Studies*, **1**, 65–93.

Widgrén, M. (1994), 'Voting Power in the EC Decision Making and the Consequences of Two Different Enlargements', *European Economic Review*, **38**, 1153–1170.

Widgrén, M. (1995), 'Probabilistic Voting Power in the EU Council: The Cases of Trade Policy and Social Regulation', *Scandinavian Journal of Economics*, **97** (2), 345–356.

Comment

Tom Hoehn

When I first received this paper I read it from the beginning to the end. I struggled with the logic of the argument. The final conclusions did not seem to follow from the discussion in the first part of the paper. When I read it again yesterday evening I started with the conclusions and found them eminently plausible and very convincing. So I am faced today with a dilemma, to praise or not to praise. I am choosing the critical path and will provide some comments on the bits that I failed to understand. I will also raise some questions about the applicability of the conclusions to some problems that I have come across in my dealings with the institutions of the EU.

My first comments are related to the critique of the use of power indices in the analysis of European policy making. If I understood the argument correctly, then there are three major problems, two can be fixed and one cannot.

1. power indices need to be recalculated to cover connected coalitions only;
2. the number of vulnerable winning coalitions should not be oversized.

These two problems are solvable. The next problem is more fundamental. Intergovernmentalism cannot take into account the agenda setting that different treaties allow. Neither does this perspective take into account the institutional rules that govern decisionmaking in Europe. Without these additional considerations decisionmaking power in Europe is wrongly identified. I am left wondering what the result of this critique is:

- what is wrong with the approach if it can be fixed?
- is it wrong in the first place?
- can you demonstrate the superiority of the proposed amendments?

The authors of this paper do not demonstrate the bias of simple power indices, they simply assert the bias. Neither do they demonstrate the superiority of their fixes. Moreover the authors do not persuade me that they know how to apply their own critique to their own solution. I am not fully convinced they have all their recalculations right:

In Figure 2.1 they recalculate power indices for a hypothetical example of a seven-member council with equal voting rights. The council decides with 5/7 majority. The seven members are positioned along a one dimensional spectrum of preferences for integration. A coalition 12346 is impossible (5 will join). There are three vulnerable connected winning coalitions:

1. members 1–5
2. members 2–6
3. members 3–7

I so far agree with Garrett and Tsebelis. They then identify 15 pivotal positions of member states and assign each member a power index that is based on their share of pivotal positions. Members 3, 4 and 5 have higher power indices and are thus more powerful in the decisionmaking in this council. I come to the contrary conclusion. In my view there are only six pivotal positions:

1. members 1 and 5 in coalition 1–5
2. members 2 and 6 in coalition 2–6
3. members 3 and 7 in coalition 3–7

Member 4 has no decisionmaking power. My view is consistent with the critique of Garrett and Tsebelis of simple power indices, their conclusion that member 4 is among the most powerful is not. This is because I acknowledge the crucial assumption of preference ordering and do not allow a member to drop out of a coalition if his preferences dictate that he would not want to leave the coalition. In other words member 4 cannot credibly threaten to leave the coalition. If member 4 was unhappy with a voting proposal then someone else with more extreme preferences would have left the coalition already. His preferences are never decisive or pivotal.

My second comment relates to the scope of the proposed approach to analysing political power in European institutions. My main concern is that the approach cannot handle the tensions between different policy objectives. From my own experience I know that integration is not the only policy objective in the EU. Competition policy is another, sometimes a conflicting policy objective. Similarly industrial policy, trade policy and so on come into conflict with the policy of integration. When these conflicts exist then the various players occupy different positions. The Commission often is very supportive of European interests and supports European companies to the detriment of integration of markets. The European Parliament is similarly not always at the most pro-integrationist end of the preference spectrum across member states. On policy issues that would threaten employment in some areas of the EU the Parliament can easily vote pro-domestic employment and industry and hence become anti-integrationist in its policy preferences.

This tension requires a multi-dimensional approach. It means that the conclusions of Garrett and Tsebelis on the lack of power of the Parliament in the case of codecision becomes reversed. If the parliament is no longer at the most extreme position *vis-à-vis* other member states then its voting power under codecision increases again. This multi-dimensionality also requires that other institutions in the EU need to be brought into play: chiefly the European Court of Justice (ECJ) and secondly the power of lobbyists with the European Parliament. If the Parliament obtains more power then the lobbyist will focus more on MEPs. MEPs are vulnerable to lobbyists. The ECJ has a very important role to play in furthering European integration. These institutional issues need to be incorporated in a more general theory of political power in the EU.

I believe we need to get back to the discussion this morning about the difference between the approach taken by Cooter and Drexl (1994) and the approach taken by Garrett and Tsebelis. I for one found the paper by the former more persuasive and convincing. This paper needs to be developed more consistently and convincingly before I am ready to accept its conclusions.

REFERENCE

Cooter, R. and J. Drexl (1994), 'The Logic of Power in the Emerging European Constitution: Game Theory and the Division of Powers', *International Review of Law and Economics*, **14**.

Comment

Ulrich Schlieper

The authors want to analyse the decisionmaking process in the EU. They claim that power indices are not sufficient to give a satisfactory explanation; one has to take into account the preferences of governments and the allocation of agenda-setting power in the EU. I think there can be hardly a question that preferences and agenda-setting power are important to understand and/or to forecast the outcome of a decision procedure, and in so far as that Tsebelis and Garrett (henceforth TG) are correct.

However, claiming that preferences and agenda-setting power are important variables is not the same as proposing that they are the most important variables. TG try to prove their point by constructing a hypothetical example and to back it up by some empirical investigations. I do not think that this can pass as sufficient proof – at most it demonstrates that their claim might be plausible.

Is TG's approach more promising in analysing decision procedures in the EU than the power index method? This question is probably difficult to answer in general since it should be possible to find instances where the power index works well and others where TG's model performs better.

TG investigate decisions of the EU concerning 'integration'. The EU does not decide on more or less integration as such but rather on more precise proposals and measures. I doubt that these can be neatly ranked on the scale of an 'integration index'. Likewise, I have my problems with presenting preferences of a government on such a simple scale. Governments are not single actors equipped with a consistent set of preferences. On at least one occasion the authors themselves refer to this when they cite 'domestic political considerations' to explain some 'irrational' behaviour. It can also be asked why the possibility of log-rolling has not been considered, as well as a large number of further items. By making this point I do not want to suggest that the authors should follow this line and increase the number of variables and complicate their model. The purpose is a different one. Any theoretical explanation relies on abstract models, where many aspects of 'reality' are left out. Whether the model is useful or adequate depends on the problem under consideration. TG say that the power index model is inadequate for analysing the decision procedure in the EU. They claim to have a better model, and they try to prove this by showing that in hypothetical situations their model performs better. If we want to compare these two models we would need a satisfactory empirical test on a sufficiently large number of decisions.

3. Comitology and the Balance of Power in the European Union: A Game Theoretic Approach*

Bernard Steunenberg, Christian Koboldt and Dieter Schmidtchen

1. INTRODUCTION

This chapter deals with the outcome of a power game played during the mid-1980s with three players involved: the European Commission, the Council and the European Parliament. The game started in the wake of the Single European Act when the long-standing practice of comitology received the status of primary community law. It ended with the famous comitology decision of the Council, in which the Council established procedures for the Commission on how to exercise its delegated policymaking powers.

In its decision of 13 July 1987 the Council laid down the procedures for the exercise of implementing powers conferred on the Commission (European Council, 1987). Articles 2 and 3 of the so-called 'comitology' decision officially established advisory committees (procedure I), management committees (procedure II, a and b) and regulatory committees (procedure III, a and b). Additionally, Article 3 introduced a procedure regarding the exercise of the Commission's power to determine safeguard measures.

The committees, which are bodies of representatives (civil servants) drawn from the member states, consult, but also supervise, the Commission's execution of legal acts. Whereas under the advisory committee procedure the committee cannot directly affect the decision adopted by the Commission, under the management committee procedure,

* The authors want to thank Sven Berg, Ronald Heiner and Manfred Holler for valuable comments, and Ige Dekker and Torsten Stein for providing them with legal material on comitology.

and under the regulatory committee procedure, the respective committees can block a measure proposed by the Commission. While not having decisionmaking power of their own, the latter committees act as *gatekeepers*. If they are in disagreement to the Commission's position, the Council will take up the matter and may overrule or just void the Commission's decision.

Although advisory committees, management committees and regulatory committees have become an integral part of the European institutional structure, there is surprisingly little research to be found in constitutional law and economics. To the best of our knowledge, our contribution can be seen as the first attempt to analyse the implementation procedure that govern policymaking in the European Union (EU) using an economic approach and, more specifically, the tools of non-cooperative game theory. We analyse the working properties of the different procedures laid down in the comitology decision, outline a concept of power, ask how the balance of power is determined by the comitology decision, and how this balance would change if the role of the European Parliament in the implementation of policy measures were strengthened.

The chapter is organised as follows: in section 2 we describe policy-making in the EU and point to ways in which the Council tries to restrict the power of the Commission in implementing European policies. In section 3 we analyse the current decisionmaking procedures, using a model in which the Commission may select a policy that is subject to review by a committee of representatives of the member states and the Council. In section 4 we add two further decision procedures in which the Parliament is given some influence on the final outcome. Section 5 examines the power of the Commission and the European Parliament under the different procedures. We present our main conclusions in section 6.

2. IMPLEMENTATION PROCEDURES

To prevent the Commission from becoming too powerful through unrestricted discretion at the implementation stage, the delegation of implementing power from the Council to the Commission is being made conditional upon the use of specific decisionmaking procedures.[1] Although these procedures vary across different European acts, three different types can be distinguished, partly based on the comitology decision.[2]

The first type is called the *advisory committee procedure* in which a committee of representatives of the member states gives its opinion on a draft measure of the Commission. The Commission has to take this advice into account and is obliged to inform the committee about the way in which it has affected its final policy choice. This procedure will not be analysed further in this paper since it does not grant any decisionmaking power to players other than the Commission.

The second type is the *management committee procedure*. In this procedure the Commission is assisted by a committee of representatives of the member states, which gives its opinion on the Commission proposal by qualified majority.[3] If the committee agrees with the Commission proposal or remains divided, the Commission proposal will be implemented. If the committee adopts a different view, the Commission reports its proposal to the Council.[4] The Council may only take a decision that deviates from the Commission proposal by qualified majority. If the Council agrees with or does not respond to the proposal, the Commission is allowed to implement its proposal.

The third procedure is the *regulatory committee procedure*. In this procedure the Commission submits its proposal again to a committee of state representatives. This committee has to give its opinion on the Commission proposal by qualified majority rule. If the committee proposes a policy that deviates from the Commission proposal, or when the committee does not reach a decision, the Commission has to submit its proposal to the Council. A divided committee in this procedure means that the Commission proposal has to be submitted to the Council. With regard to decisionmaking in the Council, two variants of this procedure can be distinguished. In both variants the Council may amend the Commission proposal by qualified majority. In variant (a), which will be called the *amendment procedure*, the Commission proposal will be adopted if the Council does not decide otherwise. A Council decision that deviates from the Commission proposal has to be based on a qualified majority. In variant (b) the Council may also veto the Commission proposal by a simple majority. This variant of the regulatory committee procedure is known as the *contrefilet* procedure. In this chapter this version will be called the *veto procedure*.

The main difference between the two variants of the regulatory committee procedure, that is, the amendment and the veto procedure, is the voting procedure. In the amendment procedure the Council can change the Commission proposal only if a qualified majority prefers a different point, including the initial *status quo*. If the Council fails to adopt a different view, the Commission proposal will be implemented. In the veto procedure the Council is able to reject the Commission proposal by a simple majority in favour of the initial *status quo*. In that case, the Council has to make a comparison between the *status quo post* and the *status quo ante*. If the Council prefers the Commission proposal to the *status quo ante*, it will not use its veto power.

3. POLICYMAKING UNDER DIFFERENT ARRANGEMENTS

3.1. Players, Preferences, and Decisionmaking Procedures

To analyse the extent to which the Commission is bound to the Council in selecting different policy measures, a model with four types of players will be used:[5]

(i) the members of the Council,
(ii) the members of the committee of state representatives,[6]
(iii) the Commission, which will be regarded as a unitary actor, and
(iv) the members of the European Parliament (in our hypothetical procedures with Parliamentary involvement).

These players are assumed to decide on some regulatory issue which can be represented by a one-dimensional outcome space $X = \mathbb{R}$. The preference of a player i over X is represented by a function $U_i = U_i(x)$ which defines single-peaked preferences.[7] The preference set of a player i, that is, the set of points a player strictly prefers to some point x, is defined as

$$P_i(x) \equiv \{y \in X \mid U_i(y) < U_i(x)\};$$

a weak version of the preference set is $R_i(x)$ which is defined as

$$R_i(x) \equiv \{y \in X \mid U_i(y) \geq U_i(x),\ y \neq x \in X\};$$

For a group of players,[8] S, these preference sets are defined as

$$P_S(x) \equiv \{y \in X \mid U_i(y) > U_i(x) \text{ for all } i \in S\},$$

and

$$R_S(x) \equiv \{y \in X \mid U_i(y) \geq U_i(x) \text{ for all } i \in S,\ y \neq x \in X\}.$$

Furthermore, player i's point of indifference to a proposal x will be denoted as $I(x)$. Decisions are assumed to be made sequentially. The sequence is based on the existing procedures that specify the order in which players are allowed to make a move. Players are assumed to have complete and perfect information. This assumption implies that the preferences of players, the structure of the game, and the fact that players behave in a rational way are assumed to be common knowledge, while only at every stage of the game one player is allowed to make a move. Second, we assume that none of the players prefers its decision to be overturned. This preference can be viewed as imposing some cost on a proposal that is not the final outcome of the decisionmaking process. These costs are assumed to reduce the final pay-off to a player. All implementation games we consider in the chapter have a unique subgame-perfect Nash equilibrium, which we take to define the outcome.

Qualified majority voting, which combines special majority voting and weighted majority voting, plays an important role in the Union's decisionmaking process. Under this rule, each voter may cast a specific number of votes, and a special majority is required to adopt a proposal. It may lead to some complications, which can be illustrated by a (hypothetical) five-member Council. In Figure 3.1, L_i denotes the ideal point of Council member i, and $L_i(x)$ stands for this member's point of indifference to the policy x. If, for instance, a two-thirds majority is needed to approve a proposal, while Council members have equivalent vote shares, member 2 or member 4 is important, since two-thirds of the ideal points in the Council are found to the right or to the left of this member, including his or her own vote. So, if the initial proposal x satisfies $x > L_4$, such as x_1 in the figure, a two-thirds majority strictly prefers an alternative proposal $y = L_4$ to the initial proposal x_1. Consequently, the Council will approve this alternative proposal y. However, if $L_2 \leq x \leq L_4$, as illustrated by x_2 in Figure 3.1, the initial proposal divides the members of the Council. Some members prefer a move to the left, others to the right. But neither fraction is able to form the required qualified majority against the initial proposal. In that case, the Council is not able to approve any new proposal, and x_2 will be implemented.

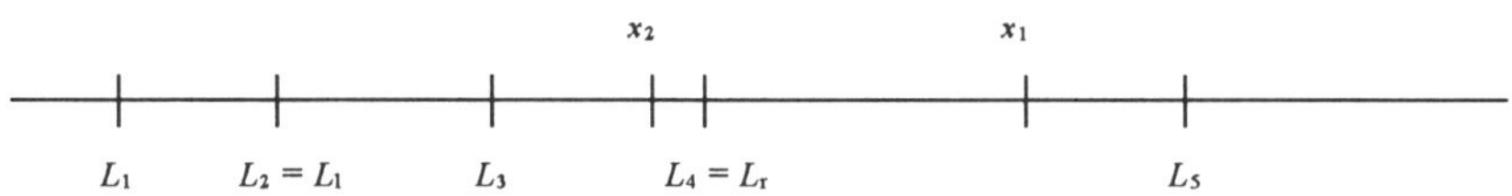

Figure 3.1 Qualified majority voting in a five-member Council

Under qualified majority rule each voter does not have just one vote, but instead may cast a number of votes which varies between voters. A decisive Council member, such as member 2 or member 4 in the example, has to be defined in terms of the number of each player's votes. Now assume, without loss of generality, that $x \geq L_m$, with L_m as the ideal point of the median Council member.[9] Given some distribution of Council members along the policy dimension X, a Council member will be called the decisive qualified majority member, L_r, if it finds to its left the ideal points of other Council members whose vote shares constitute the smallest qualified majority, including its own vote share. This group of members, of which r is the rightmost member, will be denoted as S_r^L. If all members are allowed to propose amendments,[10] qualified majority voting yields the following outcome:

$$y = \begin{cases} L_r & \text{for } x > L_r \\ x & \text{for } L_r \geq x \geq L_m \end{cases} \tag{3.1}$$

If $x > L_r$, the preference set of group S_r^L, $P_{S_r^L}(x)$ is non-empty, and the Council is able to amend the initial proposal to $y = L_r$, which is the best proposal feasible to the members of S_r^L. If $x \leq L_r$, $P_{S_r^L}(x) = \varnothing$, and the Council is not able to form a qualified majority against the initial proposal x. In general, the Council is not able to reach a decision for initial proposals that are found between its two decisive members. These proposals form the 'blocking' set for Council moves, which is defined as

$$M \equiv \left\{ x \middle| P_{S_l^L}(x) = \varnothing \text{ and } P_{S_r^L}(x) = \varnothing \right\}.$$

Initial proposals that are an element of this set are invulnerable to amendments. Now we want to analyse the decision that has to be made by the committee of representatives. This committee of representatives acts as a *gatekeeper*, but does not have the right to amend the initial proposal. Therefore, it can choose only between the initial proposal x (by keeping its gates closed) and the amended proposal y (which it can expect to result from opening its gates). Using qualified majority rule, proposals may exist that divide the committee of representatives: neither the initial proposal, x, nor the proposed amended policy, y, will be preferred by a qualified majority in the committee. If the initial proposal is selected in such a way that it makes the relevant decisive committee member indifferent between both proposals (that is, $x = C_4(y)$ or $x = C_2(y)$ in Figure 3.2), this player will not support proposal y, and the committee will not be able to reach a decision.

The proposals that will not lead to a committee decision are found in the so-called gatekeeper's 'blocking' set.

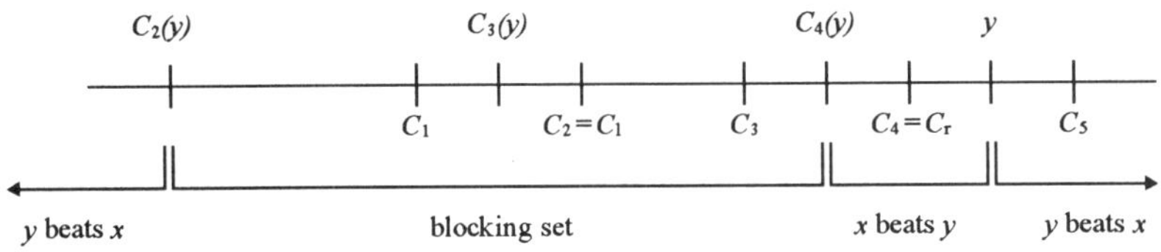

Figure 3.2 Qualified majority voting in a five-member committee of representatives

This set is defined as

$$G(y) \equiv \{x \mid C_l(y) \leq x \leq C_r(y)\},$$

with $C_l(y)$ and $C_r(y)$ as the point of indifference to y of the leftmost and the rightmost decisive qualified majority committee member, respectively. For the five-member committee in Figure 3.2, and a subsequent proposal y, this set is equivalent to the interval $[C_2(y), C_4(y)]$. If, for instance, the initial proposal is $x = C_2$, the gatekeeping committee will be divided and cannot reach a decision. Depending on the decisionmaking procedure, a divided committee may lead to either the implementation of the Commission policy or the submission of this proposal to the Council.

3.2. Management Committee Procedure

The management committee procedure can be modelled as a game that consists of three stages. In the first stage the Commission proposes a new policy x. In the second stage the committee of representatives, acting as a gatekeeper, considers the policy proposed by the Commission. Only if the committee *disagrees* on the Commission proposal by qualified majority, is the Commission proposal submitted to the Council. In the third and last stage the Council considers the Commission proposal and may propose a different measure, y, by qualified majority. Let a be the Commission; c_i, $i \in \{l,r\}$ the relevant decisive qualified majority member of the committee of representatives, and l_i, $i \in \{l,r\}$ stands for the decisive qualified majority member in the Council.[11] The game tree for this procedure is given in Figure 3.3.[12]

To solve this game, we proceed by backward induction. In the last stage, the Council will consider the Commission proposal, x, and determine whether sufficient support exists to select a different policy, y, given x. The Commission proposal, forms the *status quo post* which will be implemented if the Council does not respond. Assume, for simplicity, that the Commission has a 'progressive' preference compared to the Council, that is, $A \geq L_m$, so $x \geq L_m$. Consequently, we can restrict our attention to l_r as the relevant qualified majority member in the Council. The Council's response is now given by equation (3.1).

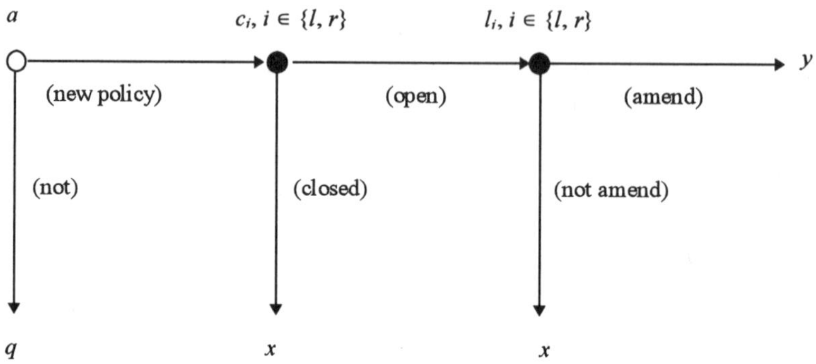

Figure 3.3 Game tree for management committee procedure

In the second stage, the committee of representatives has to determine whether or not it will accept the Commission proposal given the response of the Council. The committee keeps its gates closed when

(i) a qualified majority of the committee weakly prefers x to $y = L_r$, that is, $R_{S_i^C}(L_r) \neq \varnothing$, $i \in \{l, r\}$,[13]
(ii) the committee cannot form a qualified majority, or
(iii) the Council cannot amend the Commission proposal and therefore will accept x.

Formally, the Commission proposal will not be submitted to the Council when $x \in R_{S_i^C}(L_r) \cup G(L_r) \cup M$, $i \in \{l, r\}$. Knowing this response of the committee, the Commission selects its best proposal from this union of sets, which will be the equilibrium outcome.

Proposition 1: Under the management committee procedure, the equilibrium policy x is the Commission's most preferred point in the interval $[L_m, \max\{L_r, C_r(L_r)\}]$.[14]

3.3. Regulatory Committee Procedure: Amendment

The main difference between the management and the regulatory committee procedure is that the Commission proposal has to be submitted to the Council if the committee of representatives does not reach a decision. So the amendment version of the regulatory committee procedure can be modelled as the management committee procedure with the following modification: only if a qualified majority in the committee weakly prefers the proposal of the Commission, x, to the Council measure, y, will it keep its gates closed. This implies that the committee will accept the Commission proposal

(i) when a qualified majority of committee members weakly prefers x to y, or

(ii) when the Council cannot amend the Commission proposal and therefore will accept x.

Formally, the Commission proposal will not be submitted to the Council when $x \in R_{S_i^C}(L_r) \cup M$, $i \in \{l, r\}$. Knowing this response of the committee, the Commission selects its best proposal from this union of sets.

Proposition 2: Under the amendment version of the regulatory committee procedure, the equilibrium policy x is the Commission's most preferred point in the interval $[L_m, \max\{L_r, C_r(L_r)\}]$.

In comparison with the management committee procedure, the interval from which the Commission may select its best proposal is more restrictive. Since, by definition, $C_l < C_r$, so $C_l(L_r) < C_r(L_r)$. This is the result of the fact that the Commission has to submit its proposal to the Council if the committee does not reach a decision. This requirement increases the involvement of the Council and, at the same time, decreases the extent to which the Commission is able to formulate a new public policy that differs from the preferences of Council members.

3.4. Regulatory Committee Procedure: Veto

The veto version of the regulatory committee procedure provides the Council with an additional opportunity: besides amending the Commission proposal, the Council may also reject the new proposal by simple majority. This procedure will be modelled in the following way: after the committee's decision in the second stage, the Council first decides whether or not it will veto the Commission proposal before it considers amendments. If the Council

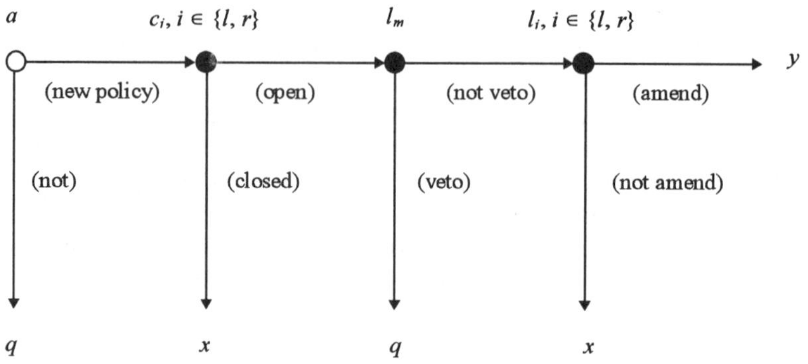

Figure 3.4 Game tree for the veto version of the regulatory committee procedure

vetoes the Commission proposal, the *status quo ante*, q, will again come into effect. The game tree[15] of this game is given in Figure 3.4.

In the last stage, the Council will consider the Commission proposal and selects $y = L_r$ if $x > L_r$ or $y = x$ if $x \leq L_r$ (see equation 3.1). The median Council member, l_m, will take this response into account and use its veto only if it prefers q to either x or L_r, that is, if x or $L_r \notin R_{l_m}(q)$. Since $L_m \leq L_r$ a veto will be issued when $q < L_r < x$, or when $q < x \leq L_r$. However, if x or $L_r \notin R_{l_m}(q)$ the median Council member will not use its veto power.[16] In the second stage, the committee has to decide whether or not to keep its gates closed, that is, give a negative opinion on the Commission proposal. It will keep its gates closed when it weakly prefers x to either q or $y = L_r$, or when the Council cannot amend the Commission proposal and therefore has to accept x, while this proposal is not being vetoed. Formally, the Commission proposal will not be submitted to the Council when $x \in R_{S_l^C}(L_r) \cup [M \cap R_{l_m}(q)]$ for $q > L_r$, or $x \in R_{S_l^C}(q) \cup [M \cap R_{l_m}(q)]$ for $q < L_r$. Knowing this response of the gatekeeping committee, the Commission selects its preferred proposal, given that this proposal will not need to be submitted to the Council.

Proposition 3: Under the veto version of the regulatory committee procedure, the equilibrium policy x is the Commission's most preferred point in the interval

(i) $[L_m, \max\{L_r, C_l(L_r)\}]$, for $q \geq L_r$, or
(ii) $[L_m, \max\{q, C_l(q)\}]$, for $L_m < q < L_r$.[17]

Note that for $q \geq L_r$, the equilibrium outcome of the veto version is equivalent to the amendment version of the regulatory committee procedure. Only when $q > L_r$, does the additional veto of the Council play a role. It may reduce the set of proposals from which the Commission may select its policy. If the Commission does not take this response by the Council into account, its proposal will be vetoed.

4. ALTERNATIVE PROCEDURES WITH PARLIAMENTARY INVOLVEMENT

In its resolution of 23 October 1986, the European Parliament stressed the 'need to limit in future the number of committee procedures', and welcomed the 'fact that the Commission is prepared to support Parliament's position, according to which the Council is urged to give precedence to the "advisory committee" procedure'. This resolution also revealed the strong preference of the Parliament not only for becoming involved in the implementation phase but also for increasing the executive power of the Commission: '[I]n accordance with its efforts over the past years to increase the executive powers of the Commission and strengthen its own supervisory power vis à vis the Commission' and 'wishing that the implementation of Community law is subject to the maximum parliamentary supervision,' the Parliament insisted 'that the reform transfers full executive power to the Commission, allowing at the same time unrestricted parliamentary supervision' (European Parliament 1986: pp. 94–95.). Furthermore, the Parliament welcomed 'the Commission's willingness to ensure comprehensive information for and consultation of Parliament about draft implementing measures' and expected 'to see a binding agreement between Parliament and the Commission on this issue in the near future'.

Obviously, there is nothing in the comitology decision which reflects the preferences of the European Parliament. Under neither procedure does the Parliament play any role in the implementation phase of legal acts in the Union. Furthermore, the decision amends the Commission proposal by adding procedures concerning safeguard measures and so-called 'variants (b)' to both the management and the regulatory committee procedure thereby changing the substance of the original Commission proposal.

Since the European Parliament revealed a strong preference for becoming involved in the implementation phase of legal acts, in this paper we analyze two alternative procedures. In the first procedure the European Parliament serves as a gatekeeper for Council review of Commission policies. The Parliament decides by simple majority whether or not a Commission proposal has to be considered by the Council before it can be implemented. This variant of the management and regulatory committee procedure will be called the *parliamentary gatekeeping procedure*. In the second procedure the European Parliament is assumed to have an absolute veto on Committee proposals: this procedure varies from the veto version of the regulatory committee procedure in the sense that Parliament may force the Commission to implement the *status quo ante*. This procedure will be called the *parliamentary contrefilet* procedure.[18]

In the first game Parliament substitutes for the committee of representatives. This game runs as follows. In the last stage the Council selects its best policy as described by equation (3.1). In the second stage Parliament has to determine whether or not it will accept the Commission proposal given the response of the Council. Parliament keeps its gates closed when:

(i) a simple majority of its members weakly prefers x to $q = L_r$, that is, $x \in R_{E_m}(L_r)$, with E_m as the median member of Parliament, or
(ii) the Council cannot amend the Commission proposal and therefore will accept x.

The Commission proposal will not be submitted to the Council when. Knowing this response, the Commission selects its best proposal from this union of sets, which will be the equilibrium outcome.

Proposition 4: Under parliamentary gatekeeping procedure, the equilibrium policy x is the point in the interval $[L_m, \max\{E_m(L_r), L_r\}]$ which the Commission prefers most.

In the *parliamentary contrefilet* procedure the European Parliament may veto the Commission proposal by simple majority. This procedure is a version of the regulatory committee procedure. After the decision of the committee of representatives, Parliament may veto the Commission proposal in view of the *status quo ante*. If the proposal is not vetoed, the Council may decide by qualified majority whether it will be amended.

In the last stage the Council selects $q = L_r$, if $x > L_r$, or $y = x$ if $q \leq L_r$, (see equation 3.1). In the third stage Parliament takes this response into account and it will not use its veto power if its median member prefers y to q, that is, if $y \in R_{E_m}(q)$. If not, the proposal will be voted in favour of q. In the second stage, the committee has to decide whether or not to keep its gates closed, that is, to give a positive opinion on the Commission proposal.

The committee will keep its gates closed when it weakly prefers x to either q or $q = L_r$, or when the Council cannot amend the Commission proposal and therefore has to accept x, in which case this proposal is not being vetoed.

Formally, the Commission proposal will not be submitted to the Council when $x \in R_{S_l^C}(L_r) \cup [M \cap R_{E_m}(q)]$ for $q > L_r$, or $x \in R_{S_l^C}(q) \cup [M \cap R_{E_m}(q)]$ for $q < L_r$. Knowing this response of the gatekeeping committee, the Commission selects its best proposal that does not lead to the submission of its proposal to the Council. For $x \geq L_m$, as we assumed, the Commission selects the following policy:

Proposition 5: Under the *parliamentary contrefilet* procedure, the equilibrium policy x is equivalent to a point, or the point in one of the following intervals which the Commission prefers most:

(i) for $E_m \leq q$:

(a) and if $q \leq L_r$,

- $[L_m, q]$ for $C_r < q$ and min $\{E_m(q), C_r(q)\} \leq L_m$,
- [min $\{E_m(q), C_r(q)\}$, q] for $C_r < q$ and min $\{E_m(q), C_r(q)\} > L_m$,
- [max$\{L_m, E_m(q)\}, q$] for $C_l \leq q \leq C_r$, or
- [max$\{L_m, E_m(q)\}$, $C_l(q)$] for $C_l > q$.

(b) and if $q > L_r \geq E_m(q)$,

- $[L_m, L_r]$ for $C_r < L_r$ and min $\{E_m(q), C_r(q)\} \leq L_m$,
- [min$\{E_m(q), C_r(q)\}$, L_r] for $C_r < L_r$ and min $\{E_m(q), C_r(q)\} > L_m$,
- [max$\{L_m, E_m(q)\}, L_r$] for $C_l \leq L_r \leq C_r$, or
- [max$\{L_m, E_m(q)\}$, $C_l(L_r)$] for $C_l > L_r$;

(ii) for $E_m > L_r$, $q > L_r$ and $E_m(q) > L_r$:

(a) [max$\{L_m, C_r(q)\}, q$] for $C_r < q$, or

(b) the *status quo ante* point q for $C_l \leq L_r \leq C_r$, or

(c) $[q, C_l(q)]$ for $C_l > q$;

(iii) for $E_m > q$:

(a) and if $q \leq L_r < E_m(q)$,

- [max $\{L_m, C_r(q)\}$, L_r] for $C_r < q$,
- $[q, L_r]$ for $C_r \geq q$ and $C_l \leq L_r$, or
- $[q, C_l(L_r)]$ for $C_l > L_r$;

(b) and if $q \leq L_r$ and $E_m(q) \leq L_r$,

- [max $\{L_m, C_r(q)\}$, $E_m(q)$] for $C_r < q$,
- $[q, E_m(q)]$ for $C_l \leq q \leq C_r$, or
- [q, max$\{E_m(q), C_l(q)\}$] for $C_l > q$.[19]

5. THE BALANCE OF POWER UNDER DIFFERENT INSTITUTIONAL ARRANGEMENTS

The power of the European Commission to set new policies that coincide with its own preferences is affected by the structural characteristics of the decisionmaking process as well as the preferences of the other players. We will define the power of the Commission with reference to the ability to set a policy according to its own preferences, given a specific procedure and a variety of possible preference constellations. Thus, the better is the outcome of the policy setting game from the perspective of the Commission, the higher can be said to be the power of the Commission.

5.1. The Measurement of Power

We can use **Propositions 1–5** to map possible preferences of the players over the policy space onto an outcome of the implementation game, where the mapping is defined by the relevant procedure. Thus, we can look at the expected outcome of policymaking, given some additional assumptions about the set of possible preference constellations that might arise.

We assume that the optimum outcome from the perspective of player i is the realisation of a random variable x_i^*. We assume that x_i^* is distributed on a subset of the policy set, that is, on an interval $[\underline{x},\overline{x}] \subset R$. For the sake of simplicity we assume that x_i^* is discrete, and that the distance between two neighbouring values is constant and denoted by δ. The number of possible realisations of x_i^* depends on the length of the interval over which the ideal points are distributed. For example, given an interval of length 3δ, there are four possible values that the ideal points may take, *viz.* some arbitrary number x, $x+\delta$, $x+2\delta$ and $x+3\delta$. In general, if the ideal points are distributed over an interval of length $n\delta$, then the number of possible values that an ideal point may take is given by $n + 1$. We will normalise δ to one, such that the length of the interval over which the ideal points are distributed is given by n.

We will define a preference profile as the vector of ideal points of the players who potentially affect the outcome of the implementation game under one of the procedures. Given the assumption that the Commission is more progressive than the median member of the Council (that is, $A \geq L_m$), these players turn out to be

- the Commission,
- the leftmost decisive member and the rightmost decisive member of the Committee,

- the median member and the rightmost decisive member of the Council, and
- the median member of Parliament.

An admissible preference profile ϕ is a realisation of the random variable

$$\phi \equiv (x_q^*, x_{cr}^*, x_{cl}^*, x_{lm}^*, x_{lr}^*, x_{em}^*)$$

that satisfies the following conditions:

$$x_q^* \geq x_{lm}^*,^{20}$$
$$x_{cl}^* \leq x_{cr}^*$$
$$x_{lm}^* \geq x_{lr}^*.$$

In some cases the *status quo ante* is also needed to determine the outcome of the decision process, so that we assume the *status quo ante* to be the realisation of a random variable x_q* that can take the same values as the optimum points of individual players. This variable is assumed to be distributed uniformly on $[\underline{x}, \overline{x}]$. Because we restricted our previous analysis to cases where $q \geq L_m$ an admissible *status quo ante* is defined by $x_q^* \geq x_{lm}^*$.

An admissible state of the world ξ can be described by the combination of an admissible preference profile and an admissible *status quo ante*. Let N denote the total number of admissible states in the world. Due to the discreteness of x_i*, the number of admissible states in the world is finite, and determined by the length of the interval $[\underline{x}, \overline{x}]$, which is denoted by n. We will assume that all admissible states in the world are equally probable.

It is important to stress that this assumption does not mean that the ideal points of the players are distributed uniformly on the interval $[\underline{x}, \overline{x}]$. Since we restrict our analysis to cases where the ideal point of the Commission as well as the *status quo ante* are not to the right of the ideal point of the median Council member, and because the ideal points of the rightmost and the leftmost decisive member of a committee must not be in descending order, the assumption of equal probability of all admissible states is different from the assumption of equal probability of every possible ideal point for each player. This difference, however, does not imply any bias, because without the restrictions $L_m \leq A$ and $L_m \leq q$, the outcomes of the policy game would be strategically equivalent to those dealt with in the paper.[21]

The assumption of equal probability of all admissible states in the world excludes correlated preferences of individual players (except for the restriction of our analysis to cases where the ideal point of the Commission as well as the *status quo ante* is not less than the ideal point of the median Council member). Particularly, we abstract from cases where the group of 'truly European players' (that is, Parliament and Commission), on the one hand, and the group of 'national players' (Council members and state representatives forming the committees), on the other hand, are more likely to have similar preferences within the group and divergent preferences between the groups.[22]

Now we can determine the outcome of a specific implementation procedure for a given profile. Let $\gamma^p(\xi)$ denote the outcome under procedure p in the state of the world ξ. These outcomes are defined for each procedure by Propositions 1–5. As the power of a player is defined with regard to the 'fit' between the policy outcome and this player's preferences, the most satisfactory way to measure the power wielded by a player would be to identify the difference between the expected utility of the different outcomes, and the ideal point of the player. Obviously, such a measure requires additional and strong assumptions about the preferences of all players beyond the assumptions of single-peakedness. For simplicity, we will leave out these assumptions and use a measure that approximates power by the distance between the actual outcome and the ideal point of a player in terms of policy rather than utility. This 'distance-measure' can be defined as

$$\pi_i^d(p) = \frac{\sum_{j=1}^{N_t} \left|\gamma^p(\xi_j) - x_i^*(j)\right|}{N_t}.$$

5.2. The Balance of Power

The resulting indices measuring the power of the Commission and the Parliament respectively, are summarised in Table 3.1.[23] Note, that with regard to Parliament the indices measure power only in those procedures where the Parliament is involved as an active player. Since Parliament is affected by the outcomes of the current procedures, the mean distance can be interpreted as a negative externality. The table gives the length of the interval over which the ideal points can be distributed (n) and the mean distances for the Commission (π_a^d) and the median member of the Parliament (π_{em}^d). An increase in n can be interpreted as a wider range over which individual preferences may diverge. In other words, the greater n is, the greater is the potential for disagreement. From these indices, several implications can be drawn:[24]

Table 3.1 Mean distance between outcome and preferred policy under different procedures

	Procedure 1: management committee		Procedure 2: regulatory committee: amendment		Procedure 3: regulatory committee: veto		Procedure 4: parliamentary gatekeeping		Procedure 5: parliamentary contrefilet	
n	π_a^d	π_{em}^d	π_a^d	π_{em}^d	π_a^d	π_{em}^d	π_a^d	π_{em}^d	π_a^d	π_{em}^d
2	0.11	0.87	0.24	0.82	0.35	0.79	0.24	0.69	0.40	0.63
3	0.15	1.22	0.34	1.14	0.48	1.09	0.34	0.97	0.56	0.91
4	0.19	1.56	0.43	1.45	0.61	1.38	0.43	1.25	0.71	1.18
5	0.22	1.90	0.52	1.76	0.74	1.66	0.52	1.53	0.87	1.44
6	0.26	2.24	0.62	2.06	0.88	1.95	0.62	1.80	1.02	1.71
7	0.29	2.58	0.71	2.36	1.01	2.23	0.71	2.07	1.18	1.97

For all n, the three 'comitology' procedures convey a different amount of power to the Commission. The mean distance between the outcomes of the implementation games and the preferred policy of the Commission is smallest in the management committee procedure and largest in the regulatory committee veto procedure. Given these results, the Commission's preference over different procedures can be written as (management committee) $\succ$ (regulatory committee: amendment) $\succ$ (regulatory committee: veto).

The difference in Commission power between the management procedure and the amendment version of the regulatory committee procedure results from the fact that both procedures differ with respect to the consequences of an undecided committee. Whereas in the management committee procedure a qualified majority is required to open the gates, in the regulatory committee procedure the committee must be able to form a qualified majority to keep the gates closed. The difference in Commission power between the veto version and the amendment version of the regulatory committee procedure results from the fact that the Commission is restricted in the veto version by the possibility that the Council may veto the Commission proposal in favour of the *status quo ante*.

Under the comitology procedures, the Parliament can be regarded as an agent who, though not involved in the decisionmaking process, is affected by its outcome. Even if Parliament is not involved in the game, it is better off under the regulatory committee procedures, among which the veto version is better for the Parliament. This can be interpreted as a result of actual outcomes being less biased in favour of the Commission's ideal point, as the figures for the Commission show. Thus, one would expect the Parliament to rank the three comitology procedures in the following way: (management procedure) $\prec$ (regulatory procedure: amendment) $\prec$ (regulatory committee: veto).

Obviously, this is not the ranking the Parliament revealed in the process preceding the comitology decision. The European Parliament clearly has an incentive to change these procedures and become more closely involved in these decisionmaking processes. One way is to propose and introduce a formal role of Parliament at the implementation stage. Another possibility is that Parliament, which may review the policy initiatives of the Commission (and dismiss the Commission with a two-thirds majority vote), uses its current powers to affect Community policies.

The position of the Parliament improves by becoming involved, where the improvement from being a gatekeeper under the parliamentary gatekeeping procedure is smaller than the improvement from having veto power (under the *parliamentary contrefilet* procedure).

The procedures in which Parliament is involved imply a change in Commission power. This is due to the fact that

- in the case of the *parliamentary gatekeeping* procedure, Parliament opens the gates with simple majority, whereas the management committee has to disagree with a qualified majority, while in the amendment version of the regulatory committee procedure a qualified majority is required to keep the gates closed;
- in the case of the *parliamentary contrefilet* procedure, an additional player can veto the Commission proposal and force the Commission to implement the *status quo ante*.

The Commission loses more power from a change to the *parliamentary contrefilet* procedure than from a move to parliamentary gatekeeping.

While Parliament gains from a change from the amendment version of the regulatory committee procedure to the parliamentary gatekeeping procedure, the position of the Commission remains the same. Therefore, the Commission should not oppose the substitution of **Procedure 2** by **Procedure 4**, which is in the interest of the Parliament.

The ranking of comitology procedures that results from the mean distances in Table 3.1, however, is valid only if there is no correlation between the preferences of the parliamentary player and the preferences of one of the players who affect the outcome of the policy setting game under any of the three comitology procedures. Thus, the European Parliament would benefit from decreasing Commission power only if the Commission is not more likely to have preferences similar to those of the members of Parliament than are the members of the Council or the respective Committee. One might infer from the fact that Parliament backed the Commission in making its final proposal concerning the implementation procedures that Parliament at least believed the Commission to prefer a policy more in line with the preferences of Parliament than the Council.

6. CONCLUSION

We have shown how the results of a policy setting game, by which the outcomes of legislative processes are put into effect, depend on the procedures used for the implementation of policy. We have analysed three prominent procedures laid down in the comitology decision, as well as two hypothetical decision procedures that involve the European Parliament. To compare these procedures we have focussed on the power of the Commission in setting the policy that best suits the Commission's own interests, as well as on the changes in the power of the European Parliament that may result from a parliamentary involvement at the implementation stage. Our main findings are that – aside from the advisory committee procedure that does not restrict the Commission in the slightest way[25] – the management committee procedure restricts the Commission the least. Under this implementation procedure, the Commission has the most power in setting public policies.

The European Parliament would rank the current implementation procedures differently, that is, it would most prefer the veto variant of the regulatory committee procedure. However, this finding is valid only as long as the preferences of the parliamentary player and of the Commission are not correlated. If both players hold comparable views on regulatory measures, the parliamentary player may prefer different procedures, even those that provide the Commission with substantial policymaking power.

We have presented a *positive* analysis of existing and conceivable procedures governing the policy implementation stage, and it seems necessary to stress that 'more' or 'less' power for the Commission does not necessarily coincide with 'better' or 'worse' decisionmaking procedures. The latter judgement has to be reserved for a *normative* analysis. For this kind of analysis, of course, one needs a normative criterion to judge the quality of different procedures in terms of their outcomes. Such a criterion would have to acknowledge that none of the institutional players should be seen as an end in itself, but rather that all of them are intended to serve the interests of the European citizens. Thus, the normative criterion would have to judge how well the preferences of the European citizens are represented in the policies that are selected at the European level.

Quite naturally, one would expect these preferences to be mirrored in the composition of the European Parliament, and, thus, best reflected in the preferences of the parliamentary players. Consequently, a decision procedure that does not allow for some influence of Parliament seems, at first sight, to be worse than procedures where the outcome is affected by parliamentary players. This conclusion, however, rests on the assumption that the preferences of these parliamentary players in fact reflect the preferences of the citizens better than the preferences of other players. These preferences are not completely exogenous, but depend on the way the members of the different bodies are appointed, and on their responsibility to the electorate of the individual member states. If the interests of the European electorate are highly valued, one may stress that the European Parliament needs to play a more substantial role in the implementation process. On the other hand, if the interests of the national electorate or the regions are regarded as important, particularly in a pursuit of European integration, the Council or an adapted voting body based on a regional representation of interests and not proportionality should be the player who is most likely to determine the outcome of an implementation process.

An answer to the question of whether and how well the individual players' preferences reflect the preferences of the citizens needs further institutional analysis. The extent to which the preferences of the electorate are represented by some of the players in the policy game, however, does not convey much information without knowing the extent to which these players do affect the outcome of this game. Our chapter has focused on the latter question and can thus be regarded as one building block in an analysis of the democratic quality of a European institutional framework, or – in a broad sense – a European Constitution.

NOTES

1. It must be noted that the Commission already plays an important role in the legislative process. In all current legislative procedures of the Union, the Commission has the exclusive power of initiative. See Cooter and Drexl (1994), Tsebelis (1994), Steunenberg (1994b), Crombez (1996) and Moser (1997) for more detailed analyses of the legislative procedures in the European Union.
2. See Kapteyn and VerLoren van Themaat (1990), pp. 240–247.
3. As provided for in Article 148(2) EC.
4. At this point two variants of the procedure can be distinguished which will not be discussed in this paper. In variant (a) the Commission may implement the measure if it is being discussed by the Council. In variant (b) this is not possible, and the implementation of the measure has to be deferred for a specific period of time.

5. See Steunenberg (1994a), for a similar model applied to policymaking in a parliamentary setting.
6. As indicated, the members of these committees of representatives are civil servants of the national administrations of the member states. Depending on the policy field involved, more than one sector specialist from the same member state can be appointed to these committees. Furthermore, changes in appointments to these committees occur relatively infrequently. So, in our view, it is *a priori* not clear that committee members have preferences identical to those of the ministers in the Council.
7. Since players have single-peaked preferences along a single dimension, the well-known median voter theorem (Black 1987: 18) applies if a decision has to be made on the basis of simple majority voting.
8. A group of players constitutes a voting body or, as it is called in the literature, a committee (Black, 1987). In this respect, the Council and the committees of representatives are committees in the technical sense.
9. The interested reader should be able to derive the results for $x \leq L_m$, which contains strategically equivalent cases to the ones discussed in this paper.
10. We assume that the Council, or in general any committee (in the technical sense), uses a well-ordered agenda in the following sense: first, all proposed amendments are collected and ordered according to their deviation from the initial proposal; second, each amendment is compared with the initial proposal in a binary vote, starting with the amendment that deviates most from the initial proposal.
11. In this paper we use the following convention: players are indicated with lower case letters, while players' ideal points will be given in capitals.
12. Note that the endnodes are labelled with the outcomes in terms of the policy that is selected rather than with the individual payoffs. These payoffs, however, can be obtained by substituting the policy outcome into each player's utility function. For example, the policy x results in individual payoffs to the players equal to $(U_a(x), U_{c_i}(x), U_{l_i}(x))$.
13. Recall that S_i^C is a qualified majority coalition of gatekeeping committee members with i as its leftmost or rightmost member. Note that the committee might be able to form a qualified majority in favour of y in two cases:
    (a) if $C_r < L_r$, so $y > C_r$, or
    (b) if $C_l > L_r$, so $y < C_l$.
14. See the Appendix for a proof of all results.
15. See note 13 for the labelling of the endnodes.
16. Note that, in those cases, the response of the Council is as follows: it will propose $y = L_r$ if $x > L_r$ and $q \geq L_r$, or $y = x$ if $x \leq L_r$ and $q \geq x$.
17. For $q \leq L_m$ the following solution can be derived: the equilibrium policy x is the Commission's preferred point in the interval
    (i) $[L_m, \max\{C_l(q), L_m(q)\}]$ for $L_m(q) < L_r$ or
    (ii) $[L_m, \max\{C_l(L_r), L_r\}]$ for $L_m(q) \geq L_r$.
18. Game trees for these procedures can be constructed from those presented above. The parliamentary gatekeeping procedure is built upon the management committee procedure, whereas the *parliamentary contrefilet* procedure can be regarded as a modification of the regulatory committee veto procedure.
19. For $q \leq L_m$, comparable results can be derived, which are based on cases that are strategically equivalent to the ones discussed in the Appendix.
20. This restriction allows the use of only **Propositions 1–5** to determine the outcome of a specific procedure given a specific preference constellation. It is important to note that this restriction does not imply any bias, because with $A < L_m$ the policy games would be strategically equivalent to the games with $A \geq L_m$. This is to say that without this restriction, the number of admissible preference profiles would increase, but the power indices would remain the same, as the outcomes just mirror the outcomes given by **Propositions 1–5**.
21. In regard to the ideal points of the rightmost, median, and leftmost decisive members of the committee, the Parliament, or the Council, one could imagine the following modelling approach: if we assume that the preferences of the a individual members are distributed

identically over the interval $[\underline{x}, \overline{x}]$, then the probability of the ideal point of the decisive member being at some point x is given by the probability that the ideal points of $f < e$ members are smaller then x and the ideal points of $e-f$ members are greater or equal to x, where f or $e-f$ is the number of members who are required to vote for or against a proposal. This probability can easily be calculated, using a binomial distribution. In this case, the distribution of the ideal points of the ***decisive members*** may depend on the size of the body.

22. Nevertheless, such a constellation of preferences seems to be quite plausible, and we will point to the implications that can be derived from an intra-group similarity of preferences.
23. Note that we can interpret the values defined with respect to the ideal point of the median member of the Parliament as a useful measure for the power of the Parliament even if the identity of the median member is not the same for all possible preference constellations. Suppose that rather than the Commission following the delegation of implementation power from the Council and using one of the procedures, Parliament would decide itself with simple majority on the policy to be implemented. In this case, the ideal point of the median member of the Parliament determines the outcome. Thus, regardless of the identity of the median member, the mean distance captures the difference between the best outcome that a Parliament could guarantee, and the outcome that results from the use of a specific procedure.
24. We want to stress that neither the absolute nor the relative change in the respective power indices should be generalised, because the figures are highly sensitive with respect to the assumption about the probability of different states of the world. Thus, we want to consider only implications drawn from the direction of change.
25. This result has not been proved in the chapter, but given the description of the advisory committee procedure from section 3, it should be straightforward.

REFERENCES

Black, D. (1987 [1958]), *The Theory of Committees and Elections*, Boston: Kluwer.

Cooter, R. and J. Drexl (1994), 'The Logic of Power in the Emerging European Constitution: Game Theory and the Division of Powers', *International Review of Law and Economics*, **14**, 307–326.

Crombez, C. (1996), 'Legislative Procedures in the European Community', *British Journal of Political Science*, **76**, 199–228.

European Council (1987), 'Council Decision of 13 July 1987 Laying Down the Procedures for the Exercise of Implementing Powers Conferred on the Commission (87/373/EEC)', *Official Journal of the European Union*, **L 197/33**.

European Parliament (1986), 'Resolution of the European Parliament of 24 November 1986', *Official Journal of the European Union*, **C 297**.

Kapteyn, P.J.G. and P. VerLoren van Themaat (1990), *Introduction to the Law of the European Communities: After the Coming into Force of the Single European Act*, Deventer: Kluwer.

Moser, P. (1997), 'A Theory of the Conditional Influence of the European Parliament in the Cooperation Procedure, *Public Choice*, forthcoming.

Steunenberg, B. (1994a), 'Regulatory Policymaking in a Parliamentary Setting', in P. Herder-Dorneich, K.-E. Schenk and D. Schmidtchen (eds), *Jahrbuch für Neue Politische Ökonomie, Band 13*, Tübingen: Mohr, pp. 36–57.

Steunenberg, B. (1994b), 'Decision Making Under Different Institutional Arrangements: Legislation by the European Community', *Journal of Institutional and Theoretical Economics*, **150**, 642–669.

Tsebelis, G. (1994), 'The Power of the European Parliament as a Conditional Agenda Setter', *American Political Science Review*, **88**, 128–142.

APPENDIX

A. Notation

The following notation is used in this paper:

i: player (a: Commission, c: member of a committee of representatives, l: member of the Council, e: member of the European Parliament).
i_l: leftmost member of a committee (in the technical sense, that is, the Council or a committee of representatives), who finds to its right the ideal points of other members whose vote shares constitute a qualified majority, including its own vote share ($i \in \{c, l\}$).
i_m: median member of a committee in the above sense ($i \in \{c, l\}$), or the European Parliament.
i_r: rightmost member of a committee in the above sense who finds to its left the ideal points of other members whose vote shares constitute a qualified majority, including its own vote share ($i \in \{c, l\}$).
q: *status quo ante*.
I: player i's ideal point ($I \in \{A, L_m, L_r, C_l, C_r, E_m\}$).
$I(q)$: player i's point of indifference to q.
P_i: strict preference set of player i.
R_i: weak preference set of player i.
S_i^j: qualified majority coalition of members of a committee j of which i is the leftmost or rightmost member.
N_t: total number of possible preference constellations (including ideal points and *status quo ante*).
$x_i{}^*$: random variable indicating the ideal point of player i.
$x_q{}^*$: random variable indicating the *status quo ante*.
$x_i{}^*(j)$: ideal point of player i in the state of the world j.
$\gamma^p(\xi)$: outcome of procedure p given preference constellation ξ.
$\xi\,(j)$: admissible state of the world.
$\pi_i{}^d(p)$: mean distance between the outcomes of a policy implementation game defined by procedure p and the ideal point of player i.

B. Proof of the Propositions

Proposition 1:
Note that for $x \geq L_m$, the set M is equivalent to $[L_m, L_r]$. For $x \leq L_r$ the Council selects $y=x$ and the gatekeeper will not open its gates, since any other action will lead to a lower payoff. The Commission with an ideal point $A \leq L_r$, selects $x=A$. More interesting cases occur when the Council will propose $y=L_r$, that is, if $x > L_r$. Now, three cases need to be distinguished:

(a) If $C_r < L_r$, C_r is the relevant decisive committee member, and $C_r(L_r) < C_r < L_r$. $R_{S_r^C}(L_r)$ is non-empty and equivalent to $[C_r(L_r), L_r]$. However, for $x \geq L_m$, $R_{S_r^C}(L_r) \subseteq M$, and the gatekeeper will always keep its gates closed given the response of the Council.

(b) If $C_l \leq L_r \leq C_r$, the committee opens its gates when $x > C_r(L_r)$. Then, its decisive member r strictly prefers y to x. Only if $x \leq C_r(L_r)$, and thus $x \in G(L_r)$ the gatekeeper cannot reach a decision and keeps its gates closed. Note that $G(L_r)$ is equivalent to $[C_l(L_r), C_r(L_r)]$ with $C_l(L_r) \leq L_r$, so M and $G(L_r)$ have a non-empty intersection.

(c) If $C_l > L_r$, C_l is decisive. The committee keeps its gates closed either if $x \in R_{S_l^C}(L_r)$ or $x \in G(L_r)$. Since $R_{S_l^C}(L_r)$ is equivalent to $[L_r, C_l(L_r)]$, and $G(L_r)$ is equivalent to $[C_l(L_r), C_r(L_r)]$, its union is $[L_r, C_r(L_r)]$.

The Commission selects its best x such that the gatekeeper does not open its gates. The set of points that satisfy this condition is equivalent to $[L_m, L_r]$ for $C_r < L_r$, or $[L_m, C_r(L_r)]$ for $C_r \geq L_r$. The equilibrium policy will be: $x = A$ for $L_m \leq A \leq \max\{L_r, C_r(L_r)\}$, or $x = \max\{L_r, C_r(L_r)\}$ for $A > \max\{L_r, C_r(L_r)\}$.

Proposition 2:
See Proposition 1. For $x \geq L_m$, three cases need to be distinguished:

(a) If $C_r < L_r$, as before, the gatekeeper will keep its gates closed.

(b) If $C_l \leq L_r \leq C_r$, the committee cannot form a qualified majority in favor of x given y, since $P_{S_r^C}(y) = \varnothing$ and $P_{S_l^C}(y) = \varnothing$. Consequently, the committee will only keep its gates closed when $x \in M$.

(c) If $C_l > L_r$, C_l is the decisive committee member. Now, the committee will not open its gates when $x \in R_{C_l}(L_r)$.

The Commission selects its best x such that the gatekeeper does not open its gates. The set of points that satisfy this condition is equivalent to $[L_m, L_r]$ for $C_l < L_r$, or $[L_m, C_l(L_r)]$ for $C_l \geq L_r$. The equilibrium policy will be: $x = A$ for $L_m \leq A \leq \max\{L_r, C_l(L_r)\}$, or $x = \max\{L_r, C_l(L_r)\}$ for $A > \max\{L_r, C_l(L_r)\}$.

Proposition 3:
For $q \geq L_r$, see Proposition 2. The Council will not veto the Commission proposal x, since its median member prefers $y = x$ for $x \leq L_r$ or $y = L_r$ for $x > L_r$. For $q < L_r$ and $q \geq L_m$, the set of proposals that will not be vetoed is $[L_m, q]$. Now, three cases need to be distinguished:

(a) If $C_r<q$, the gatekeeper weakly prefers proposals in $R_{S_r^C}(q)= [C_r(q),q)$. However, these proposals are also veto-proof proposals, that is, will be accepted by the Council, so the gatekeeper will keep its gates closed.

(b) If $C_l \leq q \leq C_r$, $R_{S_r^C}(q)=\varnothing$ and $R_{S_l^C}(q)=\varnothing$, so the committee cannot form a qualified majority in favour of x given q. The committee will only keep its gates closed when x is veto-proof, that is, $x \leq q$.

(c) If $C_l>q, R_{S_l^C}(q)\neq\varnothing$, C_l is the decisive committee member. Now, the committee will not open its gates when $x \in R_{C_l}(q)$ which is equivalent to $(q, C_l(q)]$.

The Commission selects its best x such that the gatekeeper does not open its gates. The set of points that satisfy this condition is equivalent to $[L_m, q]$ for $C_l \leq q$, or $[L_m, C_l(q)]$ for $C_l>q$. The equilibrium policy will be: $x=A$ for $L_m \leq A \leq \max\{C_l(q), q\}$ or $x=\max\{C_l(q), q\}$ for $A>\max\{C_l(q), q\}$. Similarly, the solutions for $q \leq L_m$, and therefore $L_m(q)>L_m$, can be derived.

Proposition 4:
Knowing the policies the Council will select, Parliament has to decide whether or not to give a positive opinion on the Commission proposal. The following two cases have to be distinguished:

(a) If $E_m \leq L_r$, the preference set of the median representative in Parliament is either $R_{E_m}(x)=\varnothing$ for $x \leq L_r$, or $R_{E_m}(L_r)$ for $x>L_r$. Note that $E_m(L_r)<L_r$, since $E_m \leq L_r$, so $R_{E_m}(y) \subseteq M$. In either case, will Parliament keep its gates closed.

(b) If $E_m>L_r$, $E_m(L_r)>L_r$. Then, Parliament will keep its gates closed when $x \in R_{E_m}(L_r)$, since it prefers this policy to $y=L_r$.

Knowing this, the Commission selects its best x such that the gatekeeper does not open its gates. The set of points that satisfy this condition is equivalent to $[L_m, L_r]$ for $E_m \leq L_r$, or $[L_m, E_m(L_r)]$ for $E_m>L_r$. The equilibrium policy will be: $x=A$ for $L_m \leq A \leq \max\{E_m(L_r), L_r\}$, or $x=\max\{E_m(L_r), L_r\}$ for $A>\max\{E_m(L_r), L_r\}$.

Proposition 5:
Knowing the Council's response, Parliament will not use its veto when it prefers y to q, that is, if $x>L_r$, $L_r \in R_{E_m}(q)$, or, if $x \leq L_r$, $x \in R_{E_m}(q)$. Given

the preference of the median member of Parliament, and for $x \geq L_m$ and $q \geq L_m$, the following cases can be distinguished:

(a) $M \cap R_{E_m}(q) \neq \varnothing$ and $R_{E_m}(q) \subseteq M$: there exist veto-proof proposals that will not lead to a response of the Council, since it will not be able to amend the Commission proposal. This occurs when $q \leq L_r$ and $E_m \leq L_r$, while also $E_m(q) \leq L_r$.

(b) $M \cap R_{E_m}(q) \neq \varnothing$ and $R_{E_m}(q) \not\subset M$: for some veto-proof proposals, the Council will amend the proposal to $y = L_r$. This occurs when $q > L_r$ and $E_m \leq L_r$, or when $q \leq L_r$ and $E_m(q) > L_r$.

(c) $M \cap R_{E_m}(q) = \varnothing$: then the Commission proposal will always be vetoed by the Parliament. This occurs when $q > L_r$ and $E_m > q$, while also $E_m(q) > L_r$.

Given these responses the committee decides in the second stage whether or not it gives a positive opinion on the proposal, that is, to keep its gates closed. For $q \geq L_m$, the following cases need to be distinguished:

(a) (i) $M \cap R_{E_m}(q) \neq \varnothing$ and $R_{E_m}(q) \subseteq M$: Furthermore, assume $E_m \leq q$, so $E_m(q) \leq E_m$. Proposals not in the subset will be vetoed, which results into the outcome q. For $C_r < q$, the committee prefers proposals in $R_{S_r^C}(q) = [C_r(q), q)$. Similarly, for $C_l > q$, a qualified majority prefers proposals in $R_{S_r^C}(q) = (q, C_l(q)]$, $C_l \leq q \leq C_r$, $R_{S_r^C}(q) = \varnothing$ and $R_{S_l^C}(q) = \varnothing$, so the committee cannot form a qualified majority. The committee keeps its gates closed when a proposal is either preferred, that is, $x \in R_{S_r^C}(q)$ or $x \in R_{S_l^C}(q)$, or veto-proof, that is, $x \in R_{E_m}(q)$.

(ii) $M \cap R_{E_m}(q) \neq \varnothing$ and $R_{E_m}(q) \not\subset M$. Furthermore, assume $E_m < q$, so $E_m(q) < E_m$. Veto-proof proposals not in M will be amended by the Council resulting into the outcome $y = L_r$. In addition, Parliament will veto proposals to the left of $E_m(q)$. For $C_r < L_r$ and thus $C_r < q$, the committee prefers proposals in $R_{S_r^C}(q) = [C_r(q), q)$. Similarly, for $C_l > L_r$, a qualified majority prefers proposals in $R_{S_l^C}(L_r) = (L_r, C_l(L_r)]$. For $C_l \leq L_r \leq C_r$, $R_{S_r^C}(L_r) = \varnothing$ and $R_{S_l^C}(L_r) = \varnothing$, so the committee cannot form a qualified majority. The committee keeps its gates closed when a proposal is either preferred, that is, $x \in R_{S_r^C}(q)$ or $x \in R_{S_l^C}(L_r)$, or veto and amendment proof, that is, $x \in R_{E_m}(q) \cap M$.

(b) $M \cap R_{B_m}(q) = \varnothing$, so a proposal will always be vetoed. The committee will keep its gates closed when it prefers a proposal to q, that is, $x \in R_{S_r^C}(q) = [C_r(q), q)$ for $C_r < q$, or $x \in R_{S_l^C}(q) = (q, C_l(q)]$ for $C_l > q$. For $C_l \le q \le C_r$, $R_{S_r^C}(q) = \varnothing$ and $R_{S_l^C}(q) = \varnothing$, so the committee cannot form a qualified majority in favor of a Commission proposal. It will open its gates, with the exception of a proposal $x = q$.

(c) (i) $M \cap R_{B_m}(q) \ne \varnothing$ and $R_{B_m}(q) \not\subset M$. Furthermore, assume $E_m > q$, so $E_m(q) > E_m$. See (a-ii). The committee keeps its gates closed when a proposal is either preferred, that is, $x \in R_{S_r^C}(L_r)$ or $x \in R_{S_l^C}(L_r)$ or veto and amendment proof, that is, $x \in R_{B_m}(q) \cap M$.
(ii) $M \cap R_{B_m}(q) \ne \varnothing$ and $R_{B_m}(q) \subseteq M$. Furthermore, assume $E_m \ge q$. See (a-i). The committee keeps its gates closed when a proposal is either preferred, that is, $x \in R_{S_r^C}(q)$ or $x \in R_{S_l^C}(q)$, or veto-proof, that is, $x \in R_{B_m}(q)$.

The commission selects its best x such that the gatekeeper does not open its gates. The set of points that satisfy this condition is equivalent to

(a) (i) if $q \le L_r$ and $E_m \le q$: $[L_m, q]$ for $C_r < q$ and $\min\{E_m(q), C_r(q)\} \le L_m$, $[\min\{E_m(q), C_r(q)\}, q]$ for $C_r < q$ and $\min\{E_m(q), C_r(q)\} > L_m$, $[\max\{L_m, E_m(q)\}, q]$ for $C_l \le q \le C_r$, or $[\max\{L_m, E_m(q)\}, C_l(q)]$ for $C_l > q$.
(ii) if $q > L_r$ and $E_m(q) \le L_r$: $[L_m, L_r]$ for $C_r < L_r$ and $\min\{E_m(q), C_r(q)\} \le L_m$, $[\min\{E_m(q), C_r(q)\}, L_r]$ for $C_r < L_r$ and $\min\{E_m(q), C_r(q)\} > L_m$, $[\max\{L_m, E_m(q)\}, L_r]$ for $C_l \le L_r \le C_r$, or $[\max\{L_m, E_m(q)\}, C_l(L_r)]$ for $C_l > L_r$.

(b) if $q > L_r$, $E_m > L_r$ and $E_m(q) > L_r$: $[\max\{L_m, C_r(q)\}, q]$ for $C_r < q$, the point q for $C_l \le q \le C_r$, or $[q, C_l(q)]$ for $C_l > q$.

(c) (i) if $q \le L_r$ and $E_m(q) > L_r$: $[\max\{L_m, C_r(q)\}, L_r]$ for $C_r < q$, $[q, L_r]$ for $C_r \ge q$ and $C_l \le L_r$, or $[q, C_l(L_r)]$ for $C_l > L_r$;
(ii) if $q \le L_r$ and $E_m(q) \le L_r$: $[\max\{L_m, C_r(q)\}, E_m(q)]$ for $C_r < q$, $[q, E_m(q)]$ for $C_l \le q \le C_r$, or $[q, \max\{E_m(q), C_l(q)\}]$ for $C_l > q$.

So the Commission will select the following policy, which will be the equilibrium policy:

(a) (i) if $q \le L_r$ and $E_m \le q$:
- and if $C_r < q$ and $\min\{E_m(q), C_r(q)\} \le L_m$: $x = A$ for $L_m \le A \le q$, or $x = q$ for $A > q$;

- and if $C_r<q$ and $\min\{E_m(q), C_r(q)\}>L_m$: $x=A$ for $\min\{E_m(q), C_r(q)\}\leq A\leq q$, or $x=\min\{E_m(q), C_r(q)\}$ for $A<\min\{E_m(q), C_r(q)\}$, or $x=q$ for $A>q$;
- and if $C_l\leq q\leq C_r$: $x=A$ for $\max\{L_m, E_m(q)\}\leq A\leq q$, or $x=E_m(q)$ for $A<E_m(q)$ if $E_m(q)>L_m$, or $x=q$ for $A>q$;
- and if $C_l>q$: $x=A$ for $\max\{L_m, E_m(q)\}\leq A\leq C_l(q)$, or $x=E_m(q)$ for $A<E_m(q)$ if $E_m(q)>L_m$, or $x=C_l(q)$ for $A>C_l(q)$;

(ii) if $q>L_r$ and $E_m(q)\leq L_r$:

- and if $C_r<L_r$ and $\min\{E_m(q), C_r(q)\}\leq L_m$: $x=A$ if $L_m\leq A\leq L_r$, or $x=L_r$ if $A>L_r$;
- and if $C_r<L_r$ and $\min\{E_m(q), C_r(q)\}>L_m$: $x=A$ if $\min\{E_m(q), C_r(q)\}\leq A\leq L_r$, or $x=\min\{E_m(q), C_r(q)\}$ if $A<\min\{E_m(q), C_r(q)\}$, or $x=L_r$ if $A>L_r$;
- and if $C_l\leq L_r\leq C_r$: $x=A$ if $\max\{L_m, E_m(q)\}\leq A\leq L_r$, or $x=E_m(q)$ if $A<E_m(q)$ and if $E_m(q)>L_m$, or $x=L_r$ if $A>L_r$;
- and if $C_l>L_r$: $x=A$ if $\max\{L_m, E_m(q)\}\leq A\leq C_l(L_r)$, or $x=E_m(q)$ if $A<E_m(q)$ and if $E_m(q)>L_m$, or $x=C_l(L_r)$ if $A>C_l(L_r)$;

(b) if $q>L_r$, $E_m>L_r$ and $E_m(q)>L_r$:

- and if $C_r<q$: $x=A$ for $\max\{L_m, C_r(q)\}\leq A\leq q$, or $x=C_r(q)$ for $A<C_r(q)$ if $C_r(q)>L_m$, or $x=q$ for $A>q$;
- and if $C_l\leq q\leq C_r$: $x=q$ for all $A\in X$;
- and if $C_l>q$: $x=A$ for $q\leq A\leq C_l(q)$, or $x=q$ for $A<q$, or $x=C_l(q)$ for $A>C_l(q)$;

(c) for $E_m>q$:

(i) if $q\leq L_r$ and $E_m(q)>L_r$:

- and if $C_r<q$: $x=A$ for $\max\{L_m, C_r(q)\}\leq A\leq L_r$, or $x=C_r(q)$ for $A<C_r(q)$ for $C_r(q)>L_m$, or $x=L_r$ for $A>L_r$;
- and if $C_r\geq q$ and $C_l\leq L_r$: $x=A$ for $q\leq A\leq L_r$, or $x=q$ for $A<q$, or $x=L_r$ for $A>L_r$;
- and if $C_l>L_r$: $x=A$ for $q\leq A\leq L_r$, or $x=q$ for $A<q$, or $x=C_l(L_r)$ for $A>C_l(L_r)$;

(ii) if $q\leq L_r$ and $E_m(q)\leq L_r$:

- and if $C_r<q$: $x=A$ for $\max\{L_m, C_r(q)\}\leq A\leq E_m(q)$, or $x=C_r(q)$ for $A<C_r(q)$ if $C_r(q)>L_m$, or $x=E_m(q)$ for $A>E_m(q)$;
- and if $C_l\leq q\leq C_r$: $x=A$ for $q\leq A\leq E_m(q)$, or $x=q$ for $A<q$, or $x=E_m(q)$ for $A>E_m(q)$;

- and if $C_l > q$: $x=A$ for $q \leq A \leq \max\{E_m(q), C_l(q)\}$ or $x=q$ for $A<q$, or $x=\max\{E_m(q), C_l(q)\}$ for $A>\max\{E_m(q), C_l(q)\}$.

The solutions for $q \leq L_m$ can be derived similarly.

Comment

Sven Berg, Reinert Maeland and Jan-Erik Lane

There is certainly a need for a science of committee decisionmaking, predicting which alternatives will be the social choice given the preferences of different actors and the employment of various aggregation procedures. Comitology would, for example, be highly relevant in relation to the analysis of the European Union, whose complicated decisionmaking rules have attracted substantial interest among social scientists lately.

Looking at the Union from an institutional point of view, one key question concerns the power differences between the three main institutions: the Commission, the Council and the Parliament. Assuming that the Commission is one player and the Council and the Parliament consist of many players, which player prevails under alternative arrangements for the making and implementation of EU legislation?

One may approach this question from two angles. Either one looks at the initiation process, focusing critically upon agenda-setting power. Or one deals with the implementation stage, examining how EU norms are taken from legislative outcomes into administrative practice. This article is a very interesting attempt to model the implementation game in the EU, analysing the opportunities for the Commission to favour its preferences over or against those of the special implementation committees and, in the final resort, those of the Council.

To us, the nice results of this analysis, showing that the Commission indeed can influence how EU norms are to be implemented, amount to a *caveat* against the often repeated position that the Commission is the only decisive player among the three key institutions. The complicated implementation mechanism in the EU entails that the work of the Commission is checked and that it may be rejected by the true legislative body of the Union, the Council.

In order to identify how much space for manoeuvring the Commission has, the article uses non-cooperative game theory. We believe that co-operative game theory should be employed in the analysis of the power interaction between the Commission, the Council and the Parliament. Let us give a fresh example.

Generally, in any decisionmaking process in the EU, either at the initiation stage or at the implementation stage, the Commission has agenda power but the power of resolution rests with the Council. Adding the role of the Parliament or that of the implementation committees changes the players but not the basic game which is one of agenda power in combination with resolution power. This may be modelled by means of cooperative game theory with each player looking for the coalition which will maximise his/her capacity to carry through his/her preferences. Even if all the coalitions are only one-shot temporary formations, there is no way that a player can do better by not searching for his/her best coalitions, since the rules of the EU require the making of either simple majority coalitions or qualified majority coalitions. What is the best the Commission can do under, for instance, the cooperation procedure? Table 3.2 has the answer.

Table 3.2 Voting power under the cooperation procedure

Players	Votes	Banzhaf normalised
Commission	aye/nay	0.133
Germany	10	0.097
Italy	10	0.097
United Kingdom	10	0.097
France	10	0.097
Spain	8	0.080
The Netherlands	5	0.051
Belgium	5	0.051
Greece	5	0.051
Portugal	5	0.051
Austria	4	0.042
Sweden	4	0.042
Finland	3	0.031
Denmark	3	0.031
Ireland	3	0.031
Luxembourg	2	0.020

The result here is unambiguously clear: the Commission is in no way stronger than the Council. The Commission may use its agenda setting power in such a manner that it becomes the strongest player – that is true. But it is only marginally stronger than each of the largest players in the Council and can exercise only 13 per cent of the entire voting power in a game including both the Commission and the Council, the rest being divided upon the member states as a function of their different votes cast.

More research is necessary on the EU institutions in order to arrive at more certain estimates of the power of the various players. This article is a most valuable contribution in this line of research. However, non-cooperative game theory should not be considered the only approach. This is because the power indices present a useful approximation of the average capacity of each player to maximise his influence through being decisive in collective choice, that is, by forming temporary coalitions.

Comment

Manfred J. Holler

1. AN OVERVIEW

The chapter by Steunenberg *et al.* gives an example of how to analyse the power of various bodies that are jointly involved in collective decision-making – when the preferences of the individual members of these bodies matter since decisions are made by voting. They study EU decisionmaking which involves the Council, the Commission, advisory committees, management and regulatory committees and, although merely potentially, the European Parliament. The Commission is considered a unitary actor while the Council, the various committees and the European Parliament are characterised by their members' preferences. These preferences are assumed to be single-peaked with respect to a one-dimensional left–right policy space. Further, it is assumed that the distribution of these preferences differs from one decision body to another so that the median members of the various bodies are characterised by different preferred positions.

Given the decision rules of the various bodies, the prescribed sequence of the decisionmaking steps and the aggregation rules which transform the decisions made by the individual bodies into a collective decision, an EU decisionmaking problem can be interpreted as a sequential game. This game is of perfect information with respect to the decision bodies as all previous decisions are known to a decision body when a decision has to be made, and decision bodies do not decide simultaneously. The members of a body decide simultaneously. Since each member votes sincerely and thus opts for the preferred alternative, sequential voting would lead to the same results. Of course, each set of preference distributions, which specifies the preferred policy positions for the members of the various decision bodies (that is, a preference profile of the joint collective decision body), defines another game. Each modification of the decision rules also does. This becomes obvious if the Council is given the power to veto a proposal of the Commission by a simple majority of votes instead of limiting the Council to the amendment procedure which only allows a qualified majority of the Council to approve a proposal which deviates from the proposal of the commission.

Steunenberg *et al.* derive subgame perfect equilibria for these games. These equilibria give unequivocal answers to questions of which positions on the one-dimensional left–right policy space can be achieved (or blocked) by, for example, a regulatory committee or the Council. From this result a measure of power is straightforward. For example, the power of a regulatory committee refers to the difference between the outcome of the decisionmaking and the committee's preferred position, that is, its ideal point.[1] This distance could be zero, and thus indicate a power maximum, if the committee's ideal point were identical with the result derived from the decisionmaking of the other bodies involved – even if the committee has no decisive influence on the outcome of joint decisionmaking. In this case the committee is lucky, but has no power. Steunenberg *et al.* take care of the distinction of 'luck and power'[2] by taking all admissible preference profiles and all admissible *status quo* policy points into consideration. The set of admissible preference profiles differs from the set of all possible preference profiles inasmuch as it takes care of the spatial order of the ideal points and the assumption that the ideal point of the Commission and the *status quo* are not to the right of the ideal point of the median member of the Council. The latter assumption facilitates the analysis.

Since ideal points are discrete, the set of admissible preference profiles and admissible *status quo* policy points depends on how many potential ideal points (that is, slots) are admitted, or, equivalently, on the length of the interval over which the ideal points are distributed if the distance between two ideal points is fixed. Steunenberg *et al.* show that their power measure depends on the number of slots. We come back to this issue in the discussion which follows.

2. DISCUSSION

The analysis of Steunenberg *et al.* is very lucid and this lucidity makes their arguments very convincing. I was even willing to accept that 'it is *a priori* not clear that the committee members have preferences identical to those of the ministers in the Council' (see endnote 4) although the committee members are civil servants from the national administration of the member states. I was prepared to praise the model developed in this paper as a general approach to the analysis of multi-body decisionmaking which includes voting. To be fair, the authors do not pretend that this generalisation was possible. However, once we try to take this step some constraints of the present model become obvious. The results hinge upon the presumption that well-defined decisions derive from the preferences by means of voting. This is assured by the assumption of a one-dimensional left–right policy space. However, is this assumption justifiable?

It is well known from the literature that if the policy space has more than one dimension, the median voter theorem no longer applies. Majority circles can be observed, which lead to results depending on the voting agenda, that is, the sequence of voting, and encouragement of sophisticated (strategic) voting and therefore a misrepresentation of preferences. In general, well-defined equilibria cannot be derived.[3] Only if the preferred position of a voter is the median on dimension-by-dimension, this voter qualifies as median voter and his/her preferred position qualifies as equilibrium for simple majority voting (see Kadane 1972). The corresponding problem also applies to the other 'distinguished points' in the analysis of Steunenberg *et al.* such as the preferred policy points of the decisive qualified majority members of the Council: L_r and L_l.

Since the policy space is assumed to be discrete, the chaos problems present in the continuous spatial setting do not prevail. However, is a discrete policy space an adequate assumption for a theory which should be applied to reality and the political institutions we find there? The answer is Yes and No. It depends on the issue which defines the dimension. Nevertheless, a high degree of indetermination remains if there is more than one dimension, even if we assume discreteness for the policy space. It is, of course, an empirical question whether we map the policy space to one dimension or not, but given the various national interests which enter EU decisionmaking and the increasing weakness of the left–right dimension if defined ideologically, it does not seem very likely that this could be successful. Moreover there is even the danger that dimensionality could fully break down if questions of distribution become dominant. It is well known that the core of a simple-majority voting game is empty if the decision is on the distribution of a constant sum or cake (see, for example, Friedman, 1986, p.191). As a result there is always a feasible allocation y which beats any feasible allocation x by a majority of votes. I have been told that with the economic crisis in Western Europe the importance of the distribution problem in the EU is expected to increase.

If the simple one-dimensional left–right policy space is no longer valid, then we run into various bargaining problems related to multiparty systems.[4] However, there is a set of rather plausible assumptions about the formation and operation of coalition governments from which equilibria are derived for a multi-dimensional discrete policy space. It seems straightforward that, at least to some extent, the portfolio model which builds on these assumptions could be applied to EU decisionmaking.[5] Laver and Shepsle (1990a, 1990b) treat government as a coalition which decides on the allocation of portfolios as its policies. The portfolios (defined by policy jurisdictions) are assigned to ministers who form the cabinet which corresponds to the coalition in government. Coalition bargaining is over credible policies. A policy suggested by a minister is credible if it coincides with the ideal point of his or her party. As a consequence, there is only a finite number of portfolio allocations among the parties forming a government. The dimension of the policy space is defined by the salient policy jurisdiction, that is, ministries, and the credible portfolio allocations form a lattice of points L.

We assume that the parties try to move government policy outputs as closely as possible to their ideal points. In this type of model the policy space is represented by a two-dimensional Euclidean space and closeness is expressed by the Euclidean distance from the ideal point.

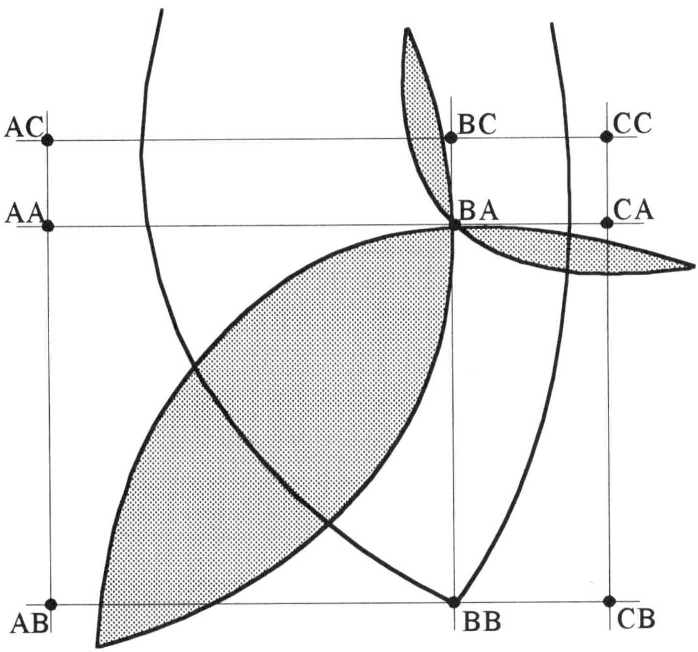

Figure 3.5

The consequences of the objectives of the politicians and the above credibility assumption are illustrated by Figure 3.5 (which derives from the third diagram of Figure 1 in Laver and Shepsle (1990a, 1990b)). The point AB means that A and B form a coalition. This coalition establishes the preferred position of A in the jurisdiction which is controlled by A and illustrated by the vertical dimension and ideal point of B in the jurisdiction which is controlled by B and represented in the horizontal dimension. We see that BA is the dimension-by-dimension median. In other words, the winset[6] of BA is empty: the shaded area in Figure 3.5 does not intersect with the (discrete) lattice *L*. However, party B might veto on the coalition BA (which is feasible since B is a member of BA) in order to establish BB. By the same reasoning B can veto BC. Note that B can veto any point in the winset of its ideal point BB. This makes BB a likely candidate for an equilibrium outcome. A and C can instead propose CC which is not vulnerable to a veto by party B. But CC is not an equilibrium as BA is in the winset of CC and C is unable to block BA. Again B might wish to veto BA in order to achieve BB, but B might be hesitant to do so if it risks a potential path through CC.

From the model of Laver and Shepsle (1990a, 1990b) it seems straightforward that the analysis by Steunenberg *et al.* can be extended to the multi-dimensional case. Inasmuch as the portfolio approach is applicable to EU decisionmaking, it delivers a strong argument in favour of a discrete policy space which supports the model presented by Steunenberg *et al.* Moreover, the portfolio arguments give a conceptual framework from which the number of slots can be derived (see above) which is exogenous to the model by Steunenberg *et al.* Given this possible extension, the analysis of Steunenberg *et al.* has the potential to lead to more general results than I conjectured at the beginning of this section.

NOTES

1. Of course, the authors are aware that the strict cardinality of the implied distance concept is hard to defend.
2. See Barry (1980) for the relationship of these two concepts and Holler and Packel (1983) for a discussion and application with respect to measuring power.
3. See McKelvey (1976, 1979) and Schofield (1983) for chaos results for a multi-dimensional continuous policy space.
4. See Schofield (1987) for an application to portfolio distribution.
5. The portfolio model has been developed by Laver and Shepsle (1990a, 1990b) and Austen-Smith and Banks (1990).
6. A point y is in the winset of x, if the combined weight of parties for which y is preferred to x exceeds the majority rule. If the voting weight of each party is less than 0.5 and the decision is made by simple majority voting, then the winset of point x is the set of points preferred by a pair of parties.

REFERENCES

Austen-Smith, D. and J. Banks (1990), 'Stable Governments and the Allocation of Policy Portfolios,' *American Political Science Review*, **84**, 891–906.

Barry, B. (1980), 'Is it Better to be Powerful or Lucky: Part I and Part II', *Political Studies*, **28**, 183–194 and 338–352.

Friedman, J.W. (1986), *Game Theory with an Application to Economics*, New York and Oxford: Oxford University Press.

Holler, M.J. and E.W. Packel (1983), 'Power, Luck and the Right Index', *Journal of Economics (Zeitschrift für Nationalökonomie)*, **43**, 21–29.

Kadane, J.B. (1972), 'On the Division of the Question', *Public Choice*, **13**, 47–54.

Laver, M. and K.A. Shepsle (1990a), 'Coalitions and Cabinet Government', *American Political Science Review*, **84**, 489–507.

Laver, M. and K.A. Shepsle (1990b), 'Government Coalitions and Intraparty Politics', *British Journal of Political Science*, **20**, 489–507.

McKelvey, R.D. (1976), 'Intransitivities in Multidimensional Voting Models and Some Implications for Agenda Control', *Journal of Economic Theory*, **12**, 472–482.

McKelvey, R.D. (1979), 'General Conditions for Global Intransitivities in Formal Voting Models', *Econometrica*, **47**, 1085–1111.

Schofield, N. (1983), 'Generic Instability of Majority Rule', *Review of Economic Studies*, **50**, 695–705.

Schofield, N. (1987), 'Bargaining in Weighted Majority Voting Games – with an Application to Portfolio Distributions', in M.J. Holler (ed.), *The Logic of Multiparty Systems*, Dordrecht, Boston and Lancaster: Kluwer.

PART TWO

Federal Structures

4. The Politics of European Federalism*

Jenna Bednar, John Ferejohn and Geoffrey Garrett

1. INTRODUCTION

The European Union (EU) is manifestly different from other international 'regimes'.[1] Even if it never becomes a genuine federation, the EU is a much more powerful economic, juridical and political entity than the myriad intergovernmental institutions that dot the international landscape. Indeed over the course of its short history, the governing institutions of the EU have successfully claimed wider and wider jurisdictions despite the resistance of numerous actors in member states.

This chapter considers the development of EU within an explicit model of federalism. We take a different perspective on the familiar terrain of institutional research on the EU – the interactions among the Commission, the Council of Ministers, the European Court of Justice and the European Parliament.[2] We ask how these 'horizontal' facets of European integration have affected what we call 'vertical' federalism – that is, relations between the member states and 'Brussels'. More specifically, we consider the impact of the changes in these institutionalised interactions at the Brussels level signalled by the 1986 Single European Act (SEA) and the Treaty on European Union signed at Maastricht in December 1991 (the Maastricht treaty) on the support for further integration among European governments and citizens.

William Riker argued long ago that politics – most importantly, the need to provide for common defence against a powerful enemy – rather than economics – in terms of the optimal level of public goods production – is the glue that holds federations together.[3] In the post cold war world, there is no major external military threat to contemporary Europe, but there may be an internal analogue. The French–German alliance continues to be at the centre

* We would like to thank the participants at the conference on Constitutional Law and Economics of the European Union, and especially Robert Cooter and Jürgen Eichberger for helpful comments on an earlier draft of this paper.

of the European integration dynamic, and the shared goal of both governments is to eliminate the possibility of another military conflict on the continent – using ever-more federal arrangements in the EU as the means to this end.[4]

There is little to be gained from speculating as to whether the security motive will prove strong enough to forge a stable federation of European states in the future because of substantial opposition to the current level of integration. Most notably, political support for the European Union has declined in the past decade (and especially since Maastricht) among citizens in the founding members of the EU – the countries that have traditionally been the strongest supporters of European integration – relative to the newer members. What explains this decline in support in the EU's 'core'? Deep recession in the early 1990s clearly played an important role. Popular perceptions of a burgeoning 'democratic deficit' may also have adversely affected support for the Union.

In this chapter, we offer an alternative explanation for the recent decline in support for the European Union among citizens from the core member states. Our analysis is based on the relationship between the horizontal and vertical dimensions of European integration. We contend that decisive central government (in the extreme, a unicameral legislature that can make or change law by a simple majority of its members) is incompatible with federal (that is, vertically separated) political arrangements. Central governments cannot easily commit *ex ante* to respect the decisionmaking jurisdictions of their regional constituents; there will be a constant temptation to pull decisionmaking authority away from other levels of government, either directly or by regulating the actions of the member states. In turn, state governments can be expected to try to resist such efforts by the central authority. This is a damaging dynamic that threatens to unravel all federal bargains.

To prevent the centre from encroaching on the domain of the member states, and to prevent member states from rationally anticipating this encroachment, federal power must be restrained. There are two ways of accomplishing this objective. Either the autonomy of the central government could be checked by another actor – such as a court – or the ability of the central government to act decisively could be constrained – by the imposition of super-majority rules, multiple veto points, and the like. The adjudication of federal disputes by a politically independent court would, in theory, increase the confidence of member states that the centre will respect their autonomy. But the experiences of federal structures in Canada and the United States suggest that even politically independent judiciaries cannot necessarily be relied upon to protect provincial governments against the centre. National courts in these two countries seem, for whatever reasons, to see things from a national point of view and are often systematically more deferential to national than state interests.[5]

Alternatively, the powers of the central government may be restrained politically, as James Madison argued, by the suitable arrangement of institutions. If national powers are divided and fragmented, and if state governments are given checking powers within the national government, centralising tendencies may be effectively held in check.

Moreover, it is important to note that the burdens of centralisation are not equal across all members of a federation. Using a simple model of political capture in which the behaviour of the administrative actors policing federal bargains favours certain states over others, we hypothesise that the burdens of centralisation would fall asymmetrically on the states that haven't managed to institutionalise their interests. As a federation adds members, it is reasonable to presume that bureaucracies set up early on in a federation's history will tend to act in ways that favour older members over newer ones.

We expect that the development of federalism, European style, has been and will continue to be affected by considerations of this sort. The European Court of Justice (ECJ) has played an active role in defining the jurisdiction of European institutions, but it has done this largely by limiting the jurisdiction of the national states in favour of an expanded role for European institutions.[6] For this reason, the existence of a powerful and independent ECJ is not likely to provide much assurance to member states that their legitimate interests will be respected within the EU. Such assurances are likely to arise, if at all, from political rather than legal sources.

From the mid-1960s until the mid-1980s, the 'Luxembourg compromise' curtailed the volume of legislation in Europe – by giving all members the right of unconditional veto. At the same time, however, the Treaty of Rome signed in 1957 significantly increased the discretion of the EU's executive branch – the Commission – and its judicial branch – the ECJ – to administer and interpret Community laws. In turn, the Commission and the Court acted in ways that favoured the interests of the founding members of the EU, by pursuing a trade liberalisation agenda in which the more competitive economies of northern Europe could flourish.[7] Not surprisingly, in this climate, there was considerable political resistance to EU policies in the more peripheral states – led by Britain after its accession in 1973.

The unanimity requirements embedded in the Luxembourg compromise were overturned by the passage of the Single European Act. The Maastricht treaty increased still further the scope of majoritarianism, while limiting the agenda-setting powers of the Commission. As is well known, these moves to majoritarianism have increased the pace of European legislation dramatically. However, it is less well understood that the treaty reforms also significantly reduced the administrative discretion available to the Commission and the Court. This outcome has been most harmful to the founding members of the EU. Thus, it is not surprising from our perspective that there has been the cooling of popular ardour for European institutions in recent years in these countries.

The chapter proceeds as follows. In section 2, we briefly outline the general argument about the relationship between horizontal and vertical federalism. Section 3 articulates postulates regarding administration and legislation in federal polities. We generate hypotheses that apply specifically to the European case in section 4. These hypotheses are tested in section 5. We make a number of concluding remarks in section 6.

2. HORIZONTAL AND VERTICAL ASPECTS OF FEDERALISM

Federations are political systems in which decisionmaking authority is divided among layers of government. Such polities are characteristically vulnerable to opportunistic behaviour on the part both of the central government and those from member states.[8] Membership in federations is costly; members hope to increase their security or rates of economic growth, but they pay for these benefits by ceding some authority to the central government. Thus, they have incentives to renege on federal bargains to regain autonomy. For example, it is common for state governments to use non-tariff barriers to trade or otherwise to subsidise local firms in violation of federal trade agreements. At the same time, central decisionmakers often are tempted to make incursions on state jurisdictions. Federal encroachment is often justified as a political or economic necessity (as with New Deal legislation in the US and Canada), but it always represents an intrusion on the jurisdictions of member states.

These mutual incentives to renege on centre–state bargains threaten the stability of federal arrangements. Even though both the central and state governments would benefit from the mutual respect of established jurisdictional lines, they face temptations to cheat that are often irresistible. In this sense, federal bargains – even those embodied in formal constitutions – lack credibility. Even if the federation survives as a formal entity, the lack of trust fostered by these unresolved incentives to renege may generate both economic inefficiency and political instability.[9] In unstable federations, both state and central laws can be unpredictable, creating disincentives for investment that politicians can only counteract by offering other enticements to economic agents.

The credibility problem inherent in federalism can be mitigated, however, by the careful design of political institutions. Decentralisation and fragmentation of federal authority constrain the ability of the central government to encroach upon the jurisdiction of member states. Furthermore, independent national courts can adjudicate federal disputes, to correct or dissuade actions taken by a state that create negative externalities for the rest of the federation. Thus, institutions that fragment and constrain the central governments are instruments of horizontal federalism. Our central claim is that the balance of power among federal institutions also affects the viability of vertical federalism, the relationship between the centre and the regional units. We develop this argument in the next section.

3. AGENDA-SETTING AND ADMINISTRATIVE POLICY MAKING IN FEDERAL POLITIES

Let us begin by distinguishing between two models of policy making: legislative and administrative.[10] In legislative policy making, the *status quo* policy is set exogenously; we assume it to be the product of previous legislation. The *status quo* can only be changed if a new law is passed by the legislature. In administrative policy making, the policy *status quo* is set by prior administrative action. A bureaucracy, court, or some other actor determines the *de facto* policy outcome unless that action provokes the legislature to override it with a new statute.

Consider first the legislative model. Suppose an odd-numbered unicameral chamber can pass legislation by a simple majority of its members. The set of possible policies is arrayed unidimensionally. Each member of the legislature has an 'ideal point', and has preferences over all policies that depend only on the Euclidean distance of the policy outcome from her ideal point. Employing the median voter theorem, a policy set at the preference of the median member of the legislature, M, is the only stable outcome under majority rule, that is, it is the only policy that cannot be defeated by any other in pair-wise voting (see Figure 4.1).

$c \quad Q \quad c' \quad M \quad c'' \quad M(Q)$

Figure 4.1

Now suppose that some agent, C, has the monopoly power to make proposals, and that Q, the *status quo*, continues in effect unless the legislature agrees by majority rule to some other policy. Let the ideal point of the agenda-setting agent be c. In this case, the agenda-setter will not make a proposal, since any policy she could suggest to move the policy closer to her ideal point than Q would be defeated by a majority. If $C=c'$, however, she could propose c' and a majority would prefer that to Q. Similarly, if $C=c''$, she could successfully propose c'', since c'' is closer to M than is Q. Finally, if $C>M(Q)$, where M is indifferent between $M(Q)$ and Q, she can do no better than to propose $M(Q)$ itself.

Policy can only be changed in this model to the benefit of the median voter, relative to Q. The agenda-setter can obtain any policy between Q and $M(Q)$, but if her ideal point lies outside of this segment of the policy space, she will not make a proposal that would be approved by M. As long as Q is not equal to M, the agenda-setter will be able to manipulate policy. Whether or not she chooses to make a proposal will depend upon the location of her ideal point.

Now consider other legislative voting rules. Instead of simple majority rule, assume that legislation requires a super-majority to pass, with a fraction $s>1/2$ votes required for enactment of a proposal (thus, unanimity is the case where $s=1$). Let S be the policy position with s votes to its right and S' be the position with s votes to its left, and continue to assume that C has a monopoly proposal power (see Figure 4.2). Therefore, unlike Figure 4.1 in which the only stable point was at M, no point between S and S' can be defeated. As above, for any Q, there exists a policy $S(Q)$ such that the pivotal voter is indifferent between Q and $S(Q)$. In this case, since $Q<S$, C can employ her the proposal power obtain any outcome between Q and $S(Q)$. If Q is between S and S', C cannot make any proposal that will defeat Q as long as the supermajority is required.

Q S $S(Q)$ M S'

Figure 4.2

We can measure the proposal power of the agenda-setter by the size of the set of policies that she can alter. For a fixed Q and the same distribution of ideal points in the legislature, the power of the agenda-setter is a function of the voting rule. The agenda-setter has the most power when $s=1/2$, that is, under simple majority rule. In that case, Q is distinct from M, and the only unalterable policy is M. As the size of the required majority increases, the impact of agenda-setting diminishes monotonically, reaching its low point at unanimity, where $s=1$. The set of *status quo* points that the agenda-setter cannot alter (those between S and S') expands; fewer *status quo* points will lie outside of this band. Note also that this diminished set lies fully within the set when $s = 1/2$ (that is, the voting games are nested).

Proposition 1: As the size of the majority required by a legislative voting rule increases, the power of the legislative agenda-setter decreases.

The preference distribution of Figure 4.2 also illuminates the effects of changing the voting rule on administrative policy making. Recall that in the administrative policy model, the *status quo* is set by a court or agency. As the size of the majority required for the passage of bills is reduced, the legislature becomes more decisive. Put differently, the more majoritarian is the legislature, the more easily it can overturn agency or court policy through new legislation. Therefore, we can think of the power of the court or agency also as a function of s, the size of the majority. Instead of decreasing in s (the case for the agenda-setter), the administrative power for courts and the bureaucracy increases monotonically with s.

Proposition 2: As the size of the majority required by a voting rule increase, courts and bureaucratic actors will have more discretion to choose policy.

In sum, while moves away from unanimity increase the power of legislative agenda-setters, they decrease the range of administrative authority that can be exercised by bureaucratic agents.

Thus far we have only discussed the horizontal institutions of federalism. Let us now add the vertical dimension (see Figure 4.3). Consider a state government, G, with preferences different from M, the median state in the federation. Let U and U' represent the preferred policies of the most extreme state governments in the federation, and S and S' stand for the position of the pivotal voters under the qualified majority rule in the central legislature. Assume that the agenda-setter's ideal point is c.

$U \quad G \quad S \quad S(G) \quad c \quad S' \quad U'$

Figure 4.3

Assume also that policy is set at the state level unless the central government of the federation overrides it.[11] The voting rule employed by the central government will affect the freedom of individual member state governments to pursue their ideal policies. Following the legislative model, under unanimity rule ($S = U,\ S' = U'$), government G would be free to pursue its own policies without interference from the centre – because the centre would not be able to agree upon a legislative correction. If voting were by qualified majority, S, the agenda-setter could propose $S(G)$ and it would be enacted. The member state, knowing that the result of pursuing G would be $S(G)$, would have a powerful incentive to adjust its own policies accordingly and pick $G = S$. Obviously, under simple majority rule, there would be only one politically viable policy at $G = M$.

Now suppose that an administrative actor can overturn the action of a member state and substitute another outcome, Q, in its place, subject to the possibility of a legislative override. In this case, the administrative actor could pick any point between S and S' without fear of legislative correction.

Proposition 3: Within the legislative model, as the size of required majority (s) increases the autonomy of member state governments increases. Within the bureaucratic model, increases in s lead to a decrease in member state autonomy.

Proposition 3 relates the horizontal dimensions of administration and legislation to the context of a federation. The analysis suggests that decreases in the majority requirement in the central government can affect member states in two different ways. One route is direct: there is an increase in the likelihood that central legislation would set policies far from the preferences of some state governments. The second route is indirect: the increased probability of central legislation constraining administrative actors from implementing certain policies. Which of these effects is most significant for a particular member state is an empirical question that depends on the policy preferences of the central bureaucratic actor and of the legislative agenda-setter.

The impact of changes in decision rules evidently depends on which model – the legislative or the administrative – is a more accurate depiction of how policy is made in a given federation. But, if we recognise that member states have heterogeneous preferences, we can exploit the results of these propositions to say something about state preferences for decision rules themselves. Assume in the European case, for example, that member states and EU institutions can be ranked in terms of how 'integrationist' their preferences are. If a member state has similar preferences to a key administrative actor at the EU level, it would prefer unanimous decision rules, since under such a rule the policy outcomes would be integrationist. Conversely, states whose preferences are far from those of EU administrative agents would prefer more majoritarianism in the legislative process – to slow the pace of integration.

Proposition 4: Member states prefer unanimity rule when the preferences of courts and bureaucratic agents are close to their own ideal points.

Proposition 4 assumes that the preferences of the central bureaucratic actors and agenda-setters are close to those of one or more of the member states (which we call the 'core' states). Obviously, a core state weakly prefers to make policy bureaucratically. While such a state may do as well with legislative policymaking, it cannot do better. If, however, policy must be made legislatively, a core state would prefer that the required majority be as small as possible. To see this, refer to Figure 4.4.

Q S $S(Q)$ M C $M(Q)$ S'

Figure 4.4

Assume the core state preference is C and the *status quo* is Q. Then if S is a supermajority rule, the best policy the core state can obtain legislatively is $S(Q)$, whereas it could get its preferred position C under majority rule. As long as Q is on the opposite side of M from C, C strictly prefers majority rule to any supermajority rule. If, Q is on the same side of M as C, C is indifferent among the set of voting rules.

Proposition 5: Core states prefer, *ceteris paribus*, bureaucratic policy making; if policy must be made legislatively, core states prefer majority rule to supermajority rule.

Finally, within the legislative policymaking model we may relax the assumption that C has monopoly agenda-setting power. Suppose, instead, that while C can place items on the agenda, it cannot keep proposals off the agenda that have the support of a sufficient majority (this is the case for the European Commission). In other words, we assume that both C and S or S' can make proposals. In this case, the outcome will depend on the amendment procedures. In the case illustrated in Figure 4.4, if anyone is free to offer amendments to C's proposals, the outcome of the legislative policy model would be either S. If Q is between S and S', it will remain fixed under any agenda rule, and if Q is to the right of S' the outcome would be S'. If simple majority rule is used, M is the unique sustainable policy. Thus, with competitive agenda-setting, C's preferences over voting rules depends on the actual distribution of preferences and the location of the *status quo*.

4. AGENDA-SETTING, ADMINISTRATIVE POWER AND THE STABILITY OF FEDERAL ARRANGEMENTS IN THE EUROPEAN UNION

The preceding section generated propositions about the impact of legislative decision rules on administrative discretion in a generic federation. In this section, we apply our theoretical perspective to the case of the European Union and pose a question that is critical to the stability of this variant of federalism: how should we expect public support for the Union in member states to have been affected by the moves to majoritarian decisionmaking embodied in the Single European Act and the Treaty on European Union? A principal finding of our theoretical analysis is that impact of such institutional change is likely to be uneven across members depending both on the spatial location of their policy preferences and the extent to which these are aligned with those of legislative agenda-setters and administrative agencies.

Let us consider first the location of agenda-setting and administrative power. The European Union has two major administrative actors – the Commission and the European Court of Justice. The 'constitutional' obligation of both actors is to uphold and to further the treaties on which the Union is founded. The Commission is the EU's executive branch; it implements the treaties and secondary legislation made pursuant to them. The Court of Justice is bound to ensure that the behaviour of all actors in Europe is in accordance with the treaties and secondary legislation. The Commission monitors compliance with EU law and brings potential breaches to the attention of the Court.

The history of legislative agenda-setting in the EU is more complex. The Treaty of Rome dictates that proposals for new legislation can only be made by the Commission. However, two qualifications must be made to the notion that agenda-setting power in the European Union lies exclusively with the Commission. First, the Commission is not a 'gatekeeper'; it cannot keep issues off the legislative agenda. Since the Rome treaty, the Council has had the right to demand that the Commission submit proposals on a given issue and this right was extended to the European Parliament at Maastricht.

Second, the effective location of agenda-setting power has varied over time with the different institutional rules that govern the passage of laws in the European Union.[12] Under the Luxembourg compromise that governed the European legislative process until the passage of the SEA, the Commission effectively ceded agenda-setting power to the national government with the least interest in changing the *status quo* – because legislation could only be passed unanimously.

The passage of the Single European Act changed this dramatically. While some issues are still subject to unanimity in the Council, most day-to-day legislative decisions are now made under a qualified majority (QMV) rule: approximately 5/7ths of the weighted votes in the Council are required for passage. However, the location of effective agenda-setting power varies with the different legislative procedures that use QMV.[13] Under the consultation procedure, covering areas such as the free movement of capital, competition policy and industrial subsidies, the Commission makes proposals to the Council that are passed by QMV but may only be amended unanimously. Therefore, under the consultation procedure the Commission possesses agenda-setting power because it can make proposals to the Council that are difficult to amend.

The SEA introduced another procedure, the cooperation procedure, that applied (up until Maastricht) to all matters pertaining to the completion of the internal market. Under this procedure, the Commission's agenda-setting power is shared with the Parliament. Council decisions are made by QMV, but the European Parliament may amend Commission proposals, and the Commission has strong incentives to accept parliamentary amendments.

The Treaty of European Union extended still further the scope of majoritarian decisionmaking. It applied the cooperation procedure to new areas such as social policy (although Britain opted out of this provision), implementation of regional funds, research and technological development, and a number of environmental issues. Maastricht also created a new procedure, the codecision procedure, to replace cooperation with respect to internal market issues.

For our purposes, the most important element of the Maastricht treaty is its impact on agenda-setting.[14] Most analysts focus on the fact that the Parliament gained an unconditional veto over internal market policy. However, there is a less well-appreciated facet of codecision: it effectively returned agenda-setting power to the Council, at the expense of the Commission. The reason for this is that the Commission is excluded from deliberation in the conciliation committee that is formed if the Council and Parliament still cannot agree on legislation. If the Council and Parliament cannot agree in this committee, the Council makes the ultimate proposal that the Parliament must accept or reject.

Taking all of these institutional details as a whole, one can make the following conclusions about the location of agenda-setting power and administrative discretion in the European Union. First, while *de jure* administrative authority continues to be vested in the Commission and the Court of Justice, the legislative constraints that affect *de facto* administrative discretion have tightened substantially. Second, there are three distinct periods in the history of agenda-setting in the EU. Up until 1986, this power lay with the member government in the Council of Ministers whose preferences were closest to the policy *status quo*. In the period between 1986 and 1991, the legislative agenda was set by the Commission, which shared its power with the Parliament under the cooperation procedure. Since the passage of the Maastricht treaty, agenda-setting power has reverted to the Council of Ministers, and more specifically to the pivotal voter under QMV.

In order to assess the impact of these developments on the stability of federal arrangements in Europe, it is necessary first to make judgements about the preferences of the administrative actors and the agenda-setters. This is clearly not an easy matter. None the less, we believe that certain generalisations can be made.

We use a simple understanding of political capture to hypothesise that the Commission and the Court of Justice act in ways that favour the founding (or core) members of the EU: France, Germany, Italy and the Benelux countries. Since these countries were present when the Commission and Court were established, it is reasonable to assume that their institutional rules were set up so as to ensure that their behaviour was consistent with the preferences of the median member of this European core. This presumption is strengthened by taking into account some well-known facets of European integration, especially concerning trade liberalisation (which remains the centrepiece of the EU's economic agenda).

Both the Commission and the Court have aggressively pursued a pro-free trade agenda. The Commission has always proposed legislation to achieve this end (such as the 1985 White Paper on Completing the Internal Market). The Court has made decisions that have furthered trade liberalisation (including such landmark decisions as Cassis de Dijon, which established the mutual recognition principle). In turn, recent studies have argued that Germany, France and the Benelux countries (and to a lesser extent, Italy) stand to gain the most from the progressive removal of non-tariff barriers in the EU, because these are the economies with the most competitive firms in the sectors most affected by the completion of the internal market.[15]

Assuming some institutional inertia (whether generated by rules or norms), this suggests, in turn, that with each expansion of the EU – from the original six to the current fifteen – the behaviour of the Commission and the Court of Justice will have not shifted fully towards the new median member of the Union. This will thus often have been damaging to the interests of the newer members.

Combining these assumptions as to the SEA and the Maastricht Treaty with the theory in the previous section allows us to formulate simple hypotheses and corollaries about the effects of the Single European Act and the Maastricht treaty.

H1: By increasing majoritarianism in the Council of Ministers, the SEA and Maastricht reduced the administrative discretion of the Commission and the Court of Justice.

C1: Declining administrative discretion adversely affected the interests of the core of the EU relative to the periphery, which in turn reduced support for the Union in the core.

H2: The SEA increased the agenda-setting powers of the Commission.

C2: The increased agenda-setting power of the Commission between 1986 and 1991 adversely affected the interests of the periphery of the EU relative to the core, which in turn reduced support for the Union in the periphery.

H3: The Maastricht treaty decreased the agenda-setting powers of the Commission.

C3: The decreased agenda-setting power of the Commission since 1991 has adversely affected the interests of the core of the EU relative to the periphery, which in turn has reduced support for the Union in the core.

Summing these conjectures, we would thus expect:

C4: The SEA and Maastricht should have increased support for the EU among peripheral members but decreased it among the core.

C5: Declining support for the EU in the core should have been greater after Maastricht than after the SEA.

5. PUBLIC SUPPORT FOR THE EUROPEAN UNION

In this section we test our theoretical argument. While our hypotheses about changes in agenda-setting and administrative power are difficult empirically to evaluate, this is not true for our corollaries about support for the EU among member states. Thus, we examine the empirical veracity of C4 and C5 using aggregated Eurobarometer data for eight countries for the period 1975–92 – France, Germany, Belgium, The Netherlands, Italy (the EU's founding 'core'); and Denmark, Ireland, the UK (the 'periphery').[16]

Table 4.1 presents descriptive data on support for the EU using two survey items that have been asked in almost every Eurobarometer since 1975 – the proportion of respondents saying that EU membership is a 'good thing' (in the regressions that follow, this variable is labelled 'eugood'), and the fraction saying they approve of efforts to unify Western Europe ('unifgood').[17] Two elements of these data are consistent with C4 and C5. First, the difference in support for the EU among the founding members and those that joined in 1973 decreased after the signing of the Single European

Act. Second, support for Europe declined in absolute terms in the core in 1992 – after the Maastricht treaty was signed – whereas this did not happen in the periphery. Although we do not have access to all the data, the patterns of support in 1992 seem not to have changed significantly in the ensuing years.

Table 4.1 Citizen support for the EU

	core*	periphery**
Membership in the EU is a good thing***	%	%
1975–85	65	40
1986–91	72	54
1992	69	61
Favour efforts to unify Western Europe***		
1975–85	90	69
1986–91	90	75
1992	83	75

Notes: * Belgium, France, Germany, Italy, Netherlands. ** Denmark, Ireland and the United Kingdom. *** Percentage of respondents agreeing with statement.

Of course, one cannot rely on these descriptive data to support for our argument because attitudes to the EU are undoubtedly affected by numerous other variables. Accordingly, we sought to isolate the effects of the SEA and Maastricht on citizen evaluations of Europe using multivariate regressions employing a pooled time series cross section design and estimating fixed effects models that are robust to arbitrary covariance structures within each national time series. This model corrects for both heteroskedastic errors and also autocorrelation of any order.[18]

We began by constructing a baseline model of support for European integration, excluding the effects of treaty revisions (see Table 4.2). Following existing studies, we included both national economic conditions (inflation and unemployment) and exposure to trade (both within the EU and in general) in the regressions.[19] We would expect that support would be decreasing in both economic variables and increasing with total trade (as a portion of GDP) and the portion of that trade done within the EU. We also thought it plausible that the (un)popularity of a nation's government could 'rub off' on European institutions, disposing citizens with relatively popular governments to support (not support) European institutions as well.[20]

Table 4.2 contains the results of fixed effects regressions of EU evaluations, for our two dependent variables. In general, the results are considerably stronger for eugood than for unifgood – arguably a product of the fact that there is less variance both over time and among countries in the latter measure of support for the EU. While the results are somewhat mixed, both models suggest that the business cycle has a consistent effect – lower inflation and unemployment are associated with greater support for the EU. Both total trade and the portion of intra-European trade had the expected effects with respect to the eugood variable, but and this was not true for unifgood. Finally, the popularity of the national governments seems to have had no effect on either variable. Whether these results are due in part to the substantial difference in the marginal distributions on the dependent variables we cannot say. None the less, we continued to deploy the trade and economic variables in our subsequent analyses.

Table 4.2 The baseline regression model of support for the EU

	Eugood	Unifgood
Eutrade	0.544	–0.05
	(0.154)*	(0.215)
Trade	0.136	–0.106
	(0.069)	(0.083)
Inflation	–0.009	–0.004
	(0.002)	(0.002)
Unemployment	–0.009	–0.003
	(0.003)	(0.003)
Government support	0.006	0.047
	(0.064)	(0.039)
N	144	128
R square net of fixed effects	0.41	0.16

Note: * standard errors.

Table 4.3 presents results that seek to capture the effects of the enactment of the SEA on support for the EU in both the core and periphery. In this model, SEA is a dummy variable scored as one for the years 1986–91; SEA*Core is a multiplicative interaction term scored one for the same years but only for observations concerning the core founding members of the EU.

The pattern of results for the trade and economic controls variables in Table 4.3 is very similar to that in Table 4.2. Again, while the anticipated effects are clearly evident with respect to evaluations of whether membership in the EU is a ‘good thing’, the battery of four control variables had a much weaker impact on support for the unification of Western Europe. However, what is more important for our purposes is that the results for the SEA and SEA*Core terms are exactly as we predicted.

Table 4.3 The effects of the SEA on support in core and periphery states

	Eugood	Unifgood
Eutrade	0.298	0.112
	(0.230)	(0.201)
Trade	0.101	–0.074
	(0.039)	(0.078)
Inflation	–0.003	–0.004
	(0.002)	(0.002)
Unemployment	–0.006	–0.003
	(0.003)	(0.004)
SEA	0.131	0.026
	(0.015)	(0.011)
SEA*Core	–0.097	–0.061
	(0.019)	(0.012)
R square net of fixed effects	0.56	0.24
N	144	128

The enactment of the SEA made the EU and the ideal of European unification more popular in the peripheral states, although this effect was much larger with respect to eugood than unifgood. In terms of our theoretical argument, this suggests that these moves to majoritarianism after 1985 were unambiguously positive for the peripheral states because they lessened the administrative discretion of the Commission and the ECJ. In contrast, however, citizen evaluations in the core countries suggest that the impact of treaty reforms on the interests of the EU's founding members was very different. Here, the positive effect on Eugood was much smaller than in the periphery (0.131–0.097=0.034, implying an increase in popular support for the EU of 3.4 percentage points), whereas the coefficient was negative with respect to unifgood (0.026–0.061=–0.035, a decline in support of 3.5 per cent). This suggests that the SEA was more effective in restraining central bureaucratic actors than in enhancing their legislative agenda-setting powers (since the former was harmful to the core whereas the latter was beneficial).

Finally, Table 4.4 distinguishes between the effects of the SEA and the Maastricht treaty on popular support for the EU. We do so by introducing two dummy variables, Maas and Maas*Core constructed in the same way as the terms measuring the impact of the SEA. In this case, however, we only had one year to estimate popular opinion after the Maastricht treaty was signed – 1992 – so caution is warranted in interpreting the coefficients for these two terms.

Table 4.4 The effects of the SEA and Maastricht on support in core and periphery states

	Eugood	Unifgood
Eutrade	0.269	0.151
	(0.212)	(0.184)
Trade	0.110	–0.047
	(0.033)	(0.076)
Inflation	–0.003	–0.004
	(0.002)	(0.003)
Unemployment	–0.007	–0.003
	(0.003)	(0.003)
SEA	0.123	0.028
	(0.019)	(0.011)
SEA*Core	–0.082	–0.057
	(0.019)	(0.014)
Maas	0.070	–0.012
	(0.030)	(0.023)
Maas*Core	–0.106	–0.055
	(0.035)	(0.027)
R square net of fixed effects	0.58	0.31
N	144	128

Once account is taken of both SEA and Maastricht, the impact of the economic and trade variables is smaller than in the previous tables. The unemployment and total trade variables are still significant in the Eugood model, but none of the other variables had any discernible impact. This suggests the plausibility of a political rather than an economic account of European integration. Moreover, as our theoretical analysis predicts, the effects of the SEA and Maastricht are heterogeneous in both equations.

The effects of the SEA variables were very similar to those reported in Table 4.3. Recall, however, that what is distinctive about Table 4.4 is that it explicitly estimates the impact of the signing of the Maastricht treaty in December 1991 on citizens' attitudes towards Europe in 1992. The results here reinforce those for the SEA. The Maas coefficient was significantly positive in the Eugood equation, whereas that for the Maas*Core term was negative – and larger in absolute magnitude. That is, the signing of the Maastricht treaty not only depressed support for the EU in the core relative to the periphery, but in absolute terms as well (by 3.6 per cent of citizens in the core countries). This was also true for the Unifgood equation, although here Maastricht had a negative but insignificant impact on support in the periphery as well.

From our theoretical perspective, the effects of the signing of the Maastricht treaty on support in the core for the EU – above and beyond those captured by the SEA terms – are consistent with the view that Maastricht disadvantaged the founding members of the EU even more. The further extension of majority rule reduced again the administrative discretion of the Commission and the ECJ – to the detriment of the core. In this case, however, this was not offset by an increase in agenda-setting power for the Commission – because the codecision procedure effectively removes the Commission from the legislative loop. Thus, Maastricht was an unmitigated negative for the founding members of the core, with respect to the mix of administrative and legislative power at least.[21]

6. CONCLUSION

This chapter has developed a political model of federalism in which institutional choices aimed at increasing the level of integration can determine the viability of the federation. The basic idea is that the impact of institutional change is often quite heterogeneous. Such changes create winners and losers and – for this reason – are often sharply contested. We also found some support for the model in data drawn from the rich series of Eurobarometer studies. While it was necessary to make some assumptions in order to create operational tests and to interpret the statistical results in ways that might be debated, we none the less think the statistical estimates are generally plausible and worth further investigation.

Our empirical results suggest that, historically, policymaking in the EU was largely formulated bureaucratically, and that its effects were generally favourable to citizens in the core countries. The effects of the SEA and Maastricht were to erode this administrative discretion. The direct legislative effects of the SEA – the move away from unanimity rule and the concomitant vulnerability of peripheral states to the agenda-setting powers of the Commission – seem to have been less significant from the standpoint of the core states. In turn, the effects of Maastricht can be interpreted as an amalgam of direct and indirect effects. The treaty continued to limit administrative and judicial discretion while also diminishing the agenda powers of the commission. Whether these changes were favourably received in the periphery or not, citizens of core countries seemed to lose some of their attachment to European federalism.

The analysis also implies that there is a growing rift between governments and their citizens within the core countries of the EU. After all, these governments were instrumental in the passage of the SEA and the Maastricht treaty. However, our interpretation of this rift is different from – or at least more nuanced than – the conventional wisdom. Instead of presuming that the primary concern of citizens is that the EU is eroding national sovereignty, our analysis implies that citizens in the EU's founding members understand that the EU worked well for them when it was governed by a unanimity rule that gave considerable discretion to supranational actors (the Commission and the ECJ). The move to majoritarianism embodied in the SEA and Maastricht eroded citizen support in the core because this lessened the probability that developments would be in their interests.

Elsewhere two of us have examined empirical predictions derived from a model similar to the one in this chapter with respect both to the historical record in Britain, Canada and the US.[22] Using a much different set of materials and methods, we found results that are broadly similar to those reported here. The institutional choices made in those countries significantly shaped the possibility of developing and maintaining a stable system of decentralised or federal policymaking. The European case is too new and its path of federalisation too untried to make strong conclusions now. None the less, we suspect that the political consequences of hurrying the process of establishing a powerful supranational authority are probably larger than many of the political actors would care to admit.

NOTES

1. This is the term used by international relations scholars to describe international institutions 'above' the nation state. See for example Krasner (ed.) (1983).
2. See for example, Cooter and Drexel (1994); Garrett (1995); Steunenberg, Koboldt and Schmidtchen, 'Comitology, and the Balance of Power in the European Union: a Game Theoretic Approach', chapter 3 of this volume; Tsebelis (1994).
3. Riker (1964). For an economic analysis of federalism in Europe, see Inman and Rubinfeld (1992).
4. See, for example, Garrett (1996).

5. Bednar, Eskridge and Ferejohn (1996).
6. Weiler (1991).
7. Garrett (1992); Garrett and Weingast (1993).
8. The material in this section is drawn from Bednar (1995); Bednar, Eskridge and Ferejohn (1996); Bednar and Eskridge; Eskridge and Ferejohn (1994).
9. Weingast (1995); North and Weingast (1989).
10. Ferejohn and Shipan (1990).
11. In Europe, this assumption is embodied in the subsidiarity principle.
12. Garrett (1995).
13. The current qualified majority required is 62 out of 87 votes. Governments are allocated votes in the Council in loose approximation to their countries' populations, although the voting weights are biased in favour of smaller countries. Today, these weights are: France, Germany, Italy and the United Kingdom: 10; Spain: 8; Belgium, Greece, The Netherlands, and Portugal: 5; Sweden and Austria: 4; Denmark, Finland and Ireland: 3; Luxembourg 2.
14. Thus, we do not analyse the path to the creation a monetary union in Europe that was laid out at Maastricht.
15. Smith and Wanke (1993).
16. We did not include data for the countries that joined the EU after 1973 in order to balance the sample years between those before and after the signing of the Single European Act. It was not possible to include data for the years since 1992.
17. The item asking attitudes towards European unification was not asked in 1976 or 1977. Not surprisingly, the two items are highly correlated. However, their marginal distributions are quite different. For example, 84 per cent of all respondents with opinions on the matter favoured efforts to unify Western Europe, while only 68 per cent approved of their nation's membership in the EC.
18. See Dubin and Rivers (1996).
19. Eichenberg and Dalton (1993).
20. We measured governmental support by aggregating responses to the Eurobarometer question asking which party they would support if there was an election, according to which parties were in government at the time.
21. At this point, it is worth remembering that our analysis does not speak to the effects of the EMU agreement on the core and the periphery. For an analysis of this issue, see Garrett (1996).
22. See Bednar, Eskridge and Ferejohn (1996).

REFERENCES

Bednar, J. (1995), 'The Federal Problem', manuscript.

Bednar, J. and W. Eskridge, 'Steadying the Court's "Unsteady Path": A Theory of Judicial Enforcement of Federalism', *Southern California Law Review*, **68** (6), 1447–1491.

Bednar, J., W. Eskridge and J. Ferejohn (1996), 'A Political Theory of Federalism', in John Ferejohn, Jack Rakove and Jonathan Riley (eds), *Constitutions and Constitutionalism.*

Cooter, R. and J. Drexl (1994), 'The Logic of Power in the Emerging European Constitution: Game Theory and the Division of Powers', *International Review of Law and Economics*, **14**, 307–326.

Dubin, J. and D. Rivers (1996), 'Truly Robust Standard Errors for Pooled Time Series Cross Section Models', manuscript.

Eichenberg, R. and R. Dalton (1993), 'Europeans and the European Community', *International Organization*, **47**, 507–534.

Eskridge, W. and J. Ferejohn (1994), 'The Elastic Commerce Clause: A Political Theory of American Federalism', *Vanderbilt Law Review*, **47**, 1355–1400.

Ferejohn, J. and C. Shipan (1990), 'Congressional Influence on the Bureaucracy', *Journal of Law, Economics and Organization*, **6**, 1–20.

Garrett, G. (1992), 'International Cooperation and Institutional Choice', *International Organization*, **46**, 533–560.

Garrett, G. (1995), 'From the Luxembourg Compromise to Codecision: Decision Making in the European Union', *Electoral Studies*, **14** (3), 289–308.

Garrett, G. (1996), 'The Transition to Economic and Monetary Union', in Barry Eichengreen and Jeffry Frieden (eds), *The Political Economy of European Integration: The Challenges Ahead*, Ann Arbor: University of Michigan Press, forthcoming.

Garrett, G. and B. Weingast (1993), 'Ideas, Interests and Institutions', in Judith Goldstein and Robert Keohane (eds), *Ideas and Foreign Policy*, Ithaca: Cornell University Press.

Inman, R. and D. Rubinfeld (1992), 'Fiscal Federalism in Europe', *European Economic Review*, **26**, 654–660.

Krasner, S. (ed.) (1983), *International Regimes*, Ithaca: Cornell University Press.

North, D. and B. Weingast (1989), 'Constitutions and Commitment: The Evolution of Institutions Governing Public Choice in 17th Century England', *Journal of Economic History*, **49**, 803–832.

Riker, W. (1964), *Federalism: Origin, Operation and Significance*, Little Brown: Boston.

Smith, D. and J. Wanke (1993), 'Completing the European Single Market', *American Journal of Political Science*, **37**, 529–554.

Steunenberg, B., C. Koboldt and D. Schmidtchen, 'Comitology, and the Balance of Power in the European Union: a Game Theoretic Approach', chapter 3 of this volume.

Tsebelis, G. (1994), 'The Power of the European Parliament as a Conditional Agenda Setter', *American Political Science Review*, **88**, 128–142.

Weiler, J. (1991), 'The Transformation of Europe', *Yale Law Journal*, **100**, 2403–2483.

Weingast, B. (1995), 'The Economic Role of Political Institutions: Federalism, Markets, and Economics Development', *Journal of Law, Economics and Organization*, **11** (1).

Comment

Jürgen Eichberger

In 1861, John Stuart Mill noted in his Considerations on Representative Government three conditions for the stability of a federation:

> To render a federation advisable, several conditions are necessary. The first is, that there should be a sufficient amount of mutual sympathy among the populations. [...] A second condition of the stability of a federal government, is that the separate states be not so powerful, as to be able to rely, for protection against foreign encroachment, on their individual strength. [...] A third condition, not less important than the two others, is that there be not a marked inequality of strength among the several contracting states. (pp. 435–436)

When the founding states of the European Community embarked on the creation of a common market, they intended to set in motion a process which eventually would lead to some form of European state. Given the threat from the strong block of the communist countries and facing the collapse of their colonial empires, European states satisfied at least the last two of the conditions advanced by John Stuart Mill a century earlier. Though mutual trust and sympathy may have been weak, the mutual need for protection and the declining self-sufficiency of European states provided the necessary background for a willingness to abandon sovereignty in favour of common institutions.

Following two decades of slow and gradual progress, over the past ten years the European Community suddenly leaped towards greater political union as new members joined the union, the institutional structure of the union became more refined with a directly elected European Parliament, and the powers of the European Council were enlarged when the unanimity principle, adopted in the late sixties, was finally abandoned. The more surprising is the apparent disenchantment with the idea of a political union which has grown among the citizens of the member states of the European Community just when power and influence of the European institutions appear to have reached a new peak.

Moves towards greater European unification which might eventually lead to a federation have traditionally been observed with reservations by some member states. More surprisingly however, founding members of the community, who were the promoters and strongest supporters of the idea of a politically unified Europe, began to show waning enthusiasm for the idea of central European authorities taking on more of the responsibilities of nation states.

In their stimulating paper, Jenna Bednar, John Ferejohn and Geoffrey Garret (henceforth BFG) trace these changes in the mood for a unified Europe to a shift in power arising from new voting procedures established by the Single European Act (SEA) in 1986 and the Maastricht Treaty (MT) in 1991. Their argument consists essentially of three propositions:

- Qualified majority voting restrains the discretion of administrative decisionmakers.
- The European administrative agencies were captured by the core members.
- If a country loses influence in the European decisionmaking process this will lead to declining support for the European idea among its citizens.

My comments will deal with these three propositions in turn.

1. QUALIFIED MAJORITY VOTING AND ADMINISTRATIVE DISCRETION

The claim that a move away from the unanimity principle towards less comprehensive voting rules reduces the influence of the administrative agencies, that is, the European Commission (EC) and the European Court of Justice (ECJ), is supported by a formal model. Preferences of the member states regarding policies are measured along the real line by the members' *ideal points*. Policies that do not coincide with an ideal point of a member state are ranked according to their distance from the ideal point.

BFG assume that the administrative agencies determine policies which the European Council can overturn only by moving a counter-proposal that is accepted by the qualified majority. Given the proportion of delegates necessary for the acceptance of a proposal, only policies outside the interval formed by the pivotal voters' ideal points can be overturned by a counter-proposal of the council. A counter-proposal between the pivotal voters' ideal points will not attract sufficient votes to defeat the administrators' policy. Policies, however, that rank outside the interval of the pivotal voters' ideal points can be defeated by proposals that are preferred by one of the pivotal voters.

An immediate corollary of this proposition is that administrative policies are the better immunised against counter-proposals the higher the qualified majority is. Assuming that the policies of the administrative agencies lie within the range of ideal points of the member states, the following extreme cases can be distinguished. If a counter-proposal requires unanimity, no administrative policy can be defeated by a vote of the Council. On the other hand, for the simple majority rule, there are counter-proposals that will attract the required majority for every policy that does not coincide with the median voter's ideal point. In particular, the further away from the median voter's ideal point a policy lies, the more viable counter-proposals exist. In general, a qualified majority rule will define a range of policies that cannot be defeated and a range for which there are counter-proposals that will win a contest with the administrative policy.

Within this model two parameters are of crucial importance: who determines the policies of the administrative agencies and who can initiate a counter-proposal. In order to apply this model to the analysis of the recent developments in the European community one has to locate the preferences of the administrative agencies relative to the preferences of the member states on the policy issue line. Such assumptions are indeed made and will be discussed in the next section. Some other assumptions which are important for some of the formal propositions advanced in the chapter are however left implicit and will therefore be discussed here briefly.

First, it appears as if the authors assume that the ideal points of the member states lie equally spaced along the issue line. Without such an assumption some statements about the increase or decrease in the likelihood of proposals being defeated appear difficult to justify. Though it is never explicitly stated, this likelihood seems to be measured by the length of the intervals of policies that can be defeated by counter-proposals compared to the length of the interval of policies that cannot be defeated. For instance, the claim that 'an increase in the required majority increases the autonomy of member state governments' (Proposition 3) is based on the observation that, with an increase in the required majority, the interval of policies (of the member states) that can be defeated by a counter-proposal in the council decreases relative to the interval of policies that can never be defeated. The proposition would fail, if, for instance, several state governments had identical ideal points. In the latter case, the required majority could be increased without changing the proportion of policies that can never be defeated by a counter-proposal.

2. THE EUROPEAN ADMINISTRATIVE AGENCIES CAPTURED BY THE CORE MEMBERS

BFG assume that policies determining the *status quo* are chosen by the Commission and the ECJ. A central tenet of their proposition that changes in voting procedures introduced in the SEA and the MT would disenfranchise the founding members of the European community rests on the presumption that these agencies were captured by the core members. According to this argument, the administrative bodies of the community were heavily, if not exclusively, influenced by the core members and would exercise their discretion to introduce policies which reflected the interest of the core members of the community. Moreover, these policies were sheltered from modification by the council as long as the unanimity rule was maintained. This way of ruling the community was threatened by the new and less comprehensive voting procedures which were instituted by the SEA.

There are some problems with this argument. Firstly, it remains unclear how the core members could capture the administrative agencies and maintain their influence for so long. Secondly, why were the core members in favour of abolishing the unanimity rule? Thirdly, one would expect conflicting issues between core members and other members, which were settled in favour of the core members before 1986, to be reversed afterwards. Yet, there seems to be little evidence for such policy reversals.

A further implicit assumption behind BFG's proposition concerns the location of preferences of agenda-setting agents in the European Council. The paper never really identifies who these agenda-setters actually are and where their preferred policies lie. The proposition that a less comprehensive voting rule will reduce the influence of the core members requires the preferences of these agenda-setters to be different from the preferences of the core members. This point deserves more elaboration, since these assumptions link the theoretical model with the empirical analysis.

3. INFLUENCE IN THE EUROPEAN DECISIONMAKING PROCESS AND DECLINE OF POPULAR SUPPORT

According to BFG's argument, the power of the core countries was diminished substantially by the move towards qualified majority voting in the European Council. As a consequence of this loss of influence BFG predict declining support for the European idea among the citizens of the core member countries. In a simple econometric model they find that, after controlling for trade, inflation and unemployment, there remains a statistically significant decrease of enthusiasm for Europe among the population of the core countries following 1986, the year of the SEA, and 1991, when the MT was agreed upon.

These observations require an explanation, but one need not be convinced by the authors' argument that the disenchantment with Europe is caused by a loss of influence. After all, there is little evidence in the public debate of the founding member countries that indicates a concern about the lack of influence by the European administrative agencies. The willingness to accept the argument of BFG as an explanation for the observed shifts in popular support for Europe rests therefore on the belief that European citizens in the core states were concerned about their loss of influence in shaping European policy.

Many other events took place during the period from 1986 to the present. The collapse of the communist regimes in Eastern Europe, for example, coincides with the implementation of the SEA. Many new European states with a great diversity in economic and military power have been established since. Borders became more open and new economic opportunities arose in the east. Thus, one could also appeal to the reasons advanced by John Stuart Mill more than a century ago that states are nowadays in a better position for relying on their own strength against potential enemies, thus reducing the need to team up for mutual protection.

REFERENCE

Mill, J.S. (1991 [1861]), 'Considerations on Representative Government', reprinted in J.S. Mill: *On Liberty and Other Essays* (ed. J. Gray), Oxford: Oxford University Press.

Comment

Bengt-Arne Wickström

1. INTRODUCTION

In their chapter, Bednar *et al.* explain the support for the EU among its citizens as a function of the voting rules in the EU organs. For this purpose the authors develop a model of federalism based on the public-choice literature on agenda-setting. The model, in my opinion, catches some essential points and contributes to our understanding of the development of federal structures and their acceptance in the EU. My task here, however, is to attempt to find weak or incomplete points in the analysis. For this purpose, I will first concentrate on the specifics of the theoretical model and then briefly comment on the general approach.

2. THE THEORETICAL MODEL

The authors use a very simple median-voter model to model the importance of the voting rules in a legislative and an administrative setting. An implicit assumption, that is necessary to define the point $M(Q)$ with reference only to the median voter, is that all voters have cardinal preferences over the one-dimensional policy space, only differing in an absolute intensity term and a fixed translation term in the policy variable. That is, the corresponding utility function of voter i belongs to the family

$$u^i = u(p-\alpha^i) + k^i,$$

where u is some given, symmetric, and single-peaked function, p the policy variable, and α^i and k^i some constants. This rather strict assumption is however not necessary for any of the results. All that is needed for Propositions 1–4 is that preferences are single-peaked and that the policy space is one dimensional. As a matter of fact, it is very simple to demonstrate that Proposition 1 holds in a much more general setting with, among other things, multidimensional policy spaces:

Simply define A_i as the set of policy variables, p, in some space, P, that are equivalent or superior to Q for individual i:

$$A_i(Q)=\{p\in P|p\ R_i\ Q\},$$

where R_i represents the preference ordering over P of individual i. Then for any c, we can define the support for c, $\mu(c)$, as the cardinality of the set of individuals supporting c in comparison with the *status quo*, having normalised the cardinality of the set of all individuals to one:

$$\mu(c;Q)=\#\{i|c\in A_i(Q)\}.$$

For any voting rule, s, the set of alternatives open to the agenda-setter, $C(s;Q)$, is now

$$C(s;Q)=\{c|\mu(c;Q)\geq s\}.$$

It is obvious that $C(s;Q)$ for a large class of policy spaces, P, has all the properties of the corresponding set in the much more restrictive model of the paper.

For Proposition 2, on the other hand, the assumptions are much more crucial. Here one has to find a *status quo*, Q, such that $C(s;Q)$ is empty or equal to $\{Q\}$. This is in general not possible, unless $s=1$, in which case all Pareto-efficient alternatives are possible, or unless the policy space is one dimensional and the preferences single-peaked. In all other cases, the problem of non-existence of equilibria and cyclical majorities can occur. In other words, the results for the legislative model are much more robust than the corresponding results of the administrative model.

One could therefore expect that the agenda-setting, legislative aspects of the problem are to be more relevant than the administrative ones. This should also be reflected in the further analysis.

3. THE GENERAL APPROACH

A constitutional-economics approach to European federalism should also explain the evolution of the European institutions. The authors, however, only attempt to explain the reaction of the European citizens to the institutions. The theoretical analysis shows, in the legislative setting, that a move from unanimity towards majority rule leads to less autonomy for the federal states, that is, to centralisation at the federal level. The question that now poses itself is in whose interest is such a change.

Could it be that such a change towards majority rule is in the interest of the core and that the core therefore pushes for a weakening of the unanimity rule? Isn't this an aspect that has to be balanced with the result that majority rule undermines the power of the core on the central level? In short, the analysis in the chapter is in some aspects very partial and their model needs to be closed. One should not only analyse the effects of changes but also the cause of these changes.

Presumably, many other variables like the increasing number of members in the Union will also alter the constitutional equilibrium. The analytical framework of the paper, hence, far more opens up roads of inquiry than it answers questions.

5. Comparative Judicial Discretion: An Empirical Test of Economic Models

Robert Cooter and Tom Ginsburg

INTRODUCTION

The European Union (EU) is one of the great economic and political success stories of modern times. It now faces a period of uncertainty as to whether and how it will widen and deepen. Some commentators have begun to speak of a 'democratic deficit' in the Union, and have proposed a number of changes in the Union's governance structures.[1]

Our belief is that much of the future legitimacy of the European Union rests on its judicial development rather than its democratic development *per se*. The American experience of federalism shows that courts can play a central role in facilitating economic and political integration. By safeguarding minority interests against abuse, courts encourage parties to trust in the process of integration. Without such protection, parties will be reluctant to deepen integration within the Union because of fears of subordination to the will of the majority.

To protect minority interests, courts must have power *vis-à-vis* other actors in the political system. To date, there has been little comparative research on what circumstances give rise to powerful and independent courts. This chapter presents a theory about the power of courts in different countries to interpret legislation. It then tests the theory against the behaviour of national-level courts in Europe and elsewhere.

1. FRAMING THE PROBLEM OF DISCRETION

One indicator of judicial power is the amount of discretion judges have in interpreting statutes. Comparative law scholars describe several factors which contribute to the relative amount of judicial discretion in a particular legal system.[2] These factors include traditional conceptions of the proper role of judges,[3] the structure of the judicial profession,[4] and its degree of independence from political branches of government.

Taken on their own, these factors cannot explain why judicial activism and creativity vary across countries. The examples of the United Kingdom and the US should serve to illustrate the point. Both countries share a common law tradition, prize judicial independence, and have a 'status' (as opposed to civil service) judiciary. Both judiciaries are staunchly independent of their respective political systems. Yet American judges are usually considered far more adventurous than their British cousins.[5]

We approach this problem from the perspective of game theory. We think of judges as participating in a game of power against other officials. Judges have their own preferences about the political order. The court has a range of possible interpretations of any statutory language. The judges can satisfy their political preferences by exercising their power to interpret statutes. Judges are constrained, however, by the countervailing power of other officials. A judicial interpretation of a statute can be overturned by fresh legislation that explicitly stipulates the preferred interpretation of the legislators. The judges are constrained by the possibility of legislative repeal of their decisions, so the space of judicial discretion expands as overriding the court becomes more difficult. Game theory thus suggests the following prediction: *Courts will be more adventurous in interpreting statutes when the probability decreases of legislative repeal of their decisions.*

An obvious way to test this theory may come to mind: when the preferences of court and legislators diverge, legislatures should frequently enact fresh legislation to repeal the judicial interpretation of statutes. Research has discovered some illuminating examples that confirm this prediction.[6] The relative frequency of legislative overrides of judicial decisions would appear to be a useful variable for the comparative analysis of judicial discretion. This obvious empirical test, however, is incomplete. To understand why, consider the analogy to bargaining games. The players in a bargaining game seldom carry out their threats, yet their relative power determines the terms of their cooperation. Similarly, judges seldom go so far as to provoke legislative repeal of interpretations, even though the possibility of repeal may determine how far the judges go in pursuing their own political preferences. When the political vision of judges conflicts with legislators, prudent judges pursue their own preferences to a point that stops short of provoking legislative repeal. Thus the relative power of officials controls their behaviour, even though they seldom exercise their power against each other.

This chapter approaches the relationship of judicial discretion to other branches in a different way. First we quantify two variables affecting the probability of legislative repeal of the judicial interpretation of statutes. One of these variables concerns the constitution and the other variable concerns political parties. Next we develop a series of indicators for how adventurous courts are in different countries. Finally, we regress the latter variables on the former variables. Section 2 explains the theory and sections 3–5 test the model.

2. A MODIFIED SPATIAL MODEL: LEGISLATIVE RESISTANCE

Constitutional law and economics has analysed how the division of powers among the branches of government affects the discretionary power of courts.[7] The theory predicts that a court's ability to diverge from legislative preference is a function of the number of independent vetoes on passing overriding legislation. Thus, a constitutional system like the American, which requires two independent houses of the legislature and the president to agree before a bill can become law, provides more room for judicial creativity than the British parliamentary system, wherein one house of parliament can pass most bills on its own. By imposing three independent vetoes on new legislation, the American system allows the court to diverge further before provoking a legislative correction.

The division of powers in the constitution provides one determinant of the probability that fresh legislation will repeal the judicial interpretation of a statute. This determinant is central to models in the existing literature.[8] As conventionally stated, however, the model does not adequately reflect politics. The difficulty of the legislative process, which we call 'legislative resistance', is also affected by politics. We believe that the underlying point of the model, namely that judicial discretion expands with the difficulty of passing legislation, to be a valid one, but politics is as important as the constitution.

One way politics determines legislative resistance is through political parties. The greater the degree of party discipline, the more party leadership can influence outcomes in a predictable way. Legislative systems with undisciplined parties may require more negotiation to form coalitions to enact legislation. The need for legislative bargaining to enact legislation may give courts more space to interpret statutes.[9] Besides party discipline, the number of member parties in the governing coalition and its stability affect resistance to legislation. If there are many political parties in the governing coalition, new legislation requires more extensive inter-party negotiation than in a system where there is a single disciplined party.[10] Again this increases room for judicial action. By contrast, a single dominant party with discipline can easily impose its preferences upon the legislature.

The number of independent vetoes on fresh legislation provided in the constitution of a nation can be counted. Similarly, the stability of the governing coalition can be quantified. We will explain how we quantify these variables for purposes of our statistical analysis.

Legislative Vetoes

Narrowly interpreted, 'legislative veto' refers to the formal power to veto legislation. Broadly interpreted, any body whose assent is required to create new law has a veto, because such a body may choose not to allow the legislation to proceed. We will describe the number of vetoes in various political systems, broadly interpreted. This description is stylised because certain kinds of exceptional legislation, like the budget, may require special procedures involving otherwise dormant upper houses. In some countries, such as Germany and Israel, legislation requires a presidential signature, but this is a ceremonial and not a real veto. Furthermore, in some countries the drafting of legislation is performed by the civil service, which may itself have an independent policy preference. For simplicity, these factors are not fully taken into account. Our model concerns only ordinary legislation, and only counts vetoes that are regularly exercised.

The Constitution determines the number of legislative vetoes in a political system. In unicameral parliamentary systems, where the government is formed by the majority coalition in the legislature, there is essentially one veto on legislation.[11] This describes the situation in the United Kingdom, Sweden, Israel, and Japan.[12]

Other systems have two vetoes on new legislation. Such would be the case in either a bicameral parliamentary system (as in Germany), or an essentially unicameral parliamentary system with a strong president (as in France.)[13] Finally, as described above, the United States is exceptional in that it has three legislative vetoes: the two independent houses of the legislature and the president. The column labelled 'Vetoes' records these facts in Table 5.1.

Dominant Disciplined Party and Coalition Duration

The exercise of legislative vetoes depends on the party system. For example, if a single coalition holds both houses of parliament in a bicameral parliamentary system, the key determinants for whether a particular bill will be passed lie within that coalition. Bargaining will first take place within the governing coalition, and only later between the two houses of the legislature. The most important bargaining involves developing the proposal.[14]

Several factors can minimise the salience of institutional vetoes. If parties are disciplined so that individual members seldom defect from bargains, party leadership can control the votes of backbenchers. This means that party leaders in a coalition can bargain on a given proposal with relative certainty that they will be able to deliver their votes. Once such a bargain is struck, it does not much matter how many legislative vetoes exist, as long as they are all controlled by the coalition.

If the governing coalition consists of a single disciplined party, bargaining over the proposed bill takes place entirely within that party. This is the case, for example, in the United Kingdom, which has well-disciplined parties and a unicameral legislature that is controlled for long periods by a single party. We characterise this situation as the Dominant Disciplined Party (DDP), because the position of the party and its internal discipline mean that any proposal it wishes to impose on the country can be passed with relatively little resistance from the legislature.

There are several possible variables which might indicate the presence or absence of a DDP. Ideally we would like to have a measure of the ability of a party to impose its substantive preferences through the political process. One measure would be the success rate of party proposals. However, counting every instance where a party proposes legislation requires extensive information not easily available for comparative research. Furthermore, such a measure would miss those instances where a relatively weak ruling party wants to propose legislation but does not do so because it anticipates failure.

In a parliamentary system, where the government serves at the pleasure of the legislature, the average duration of the cabinet is one possible indicator of party dominance. As long as the governing coalition commands the support of the parliament, the cabinet continues in office. When the parliament withdraws its support (for example, by rejecting an important government bill) the government falls. A DDP should be able to maintain cabinets for longer than weaker parties.

Cabinet duration, however, is affected by constitutional rules about elections as well as by the party system. This is because elections mandate a formal change in government even if the ruling party stays in power, and all democratic constitutions provide for a maximum duration between parliamentary elections. Thus a dominant party in a system which requires elections at least every five years will have longer cabinets than an equally dominant party in a system with triennial elections.

A simpler indicator of party dominance is coalition duration. A dominant party will be able to hold power through multiple elections. An extreme example is the Liberal Democratic Party of Japan, which formed 14 consecutive governments and ruled from its formation in 1955 until 1993. Similarly, the United Kingdom has been ruled by disciplined Conservatives for a decade and a half. Systems where party discipline is low or where no dominant party holds sway will tend to have shorter coalitions.

We counted the number of changes in the party composition of the governing coalition for each of twenty countries and then divided by the number of years to determine the average coalition duration.[15] For most countries the period of study was 1945–93, but in certain cases we adjusted the period to reflect constitutional change. Thus in France, we began with the founding of the Fifth Republic in 1958. In Germany, we began with the founding of the Federal Republic in 1949. The details are given in Appendix A.

One theoretical problem comes in applying this indicator to countries such as the US with a presidential system or countries like France with a mixed system. In both cases, there is the possibility of divided government wherein one party controls the legislature and another the presidency. For example, from 1981 until the most recent elections in 1995, France has enjoyed mainly socialist rule under a socialist president with brief periods of Gaullist government. In the US, divided government is the norm.[16] We used the party composition of the cabinet as the indicator for both kinds of systems. Thus in the US, the composition of the cabinet changes whenever there is a change in the party controlling the presidency. In France, the prime minister is typically drawn from the majority coalition in the legislature, so control over the legislature becomes the basic indicator of coalition duration.

Some countries have political systems wherein one party is at the centre of coalitions but must rely on smaller parties to govern. We believe our coalition duration variable captures the relative stability of these systems. For example, the Christian Democrats have been at the centre of almost every post-war Italian government, much as the Social Democrats have been in Sweden. The Christian Democrats have been unable to form stable coalitions however, and have had to adjust the composition of the cabinet almost annually since World War II.

According to our hypothesis, longer coalitions would tend to correlate negatively with legislative resistance. This is because longer coalitions indicate governments ability to maintain discipline and enact its legislative programme. The average cabinet duration for each country for this variable is presented in Table 5.1.

Table 5.1 predicts that judicial discretion is lowest in those countries with a low number of vetoes and a high average coalition duration, such as Japan and the United Kingdom. Judicial discretion will be highest in countries with either a large number of vetoes, such as the US, or low average cabinet duration, such as Italy and Israel. Other countries in the middle include Germany and France. The following sections of the chapter test this prediction. The first test consists of a simple questionnaire of experts. The second consists of a study of one area of law which has been especially suited to judicial daring, namely the move to strict liability for tort claims dealing with defective products. The final test concerns the pattern of environmental regulation in various legal systems.

Table 5.1 Legislative resistance

Country	Vetoes	Avg.Coalition Duration (in years)
Australia	2	9
Austria	2	8
Belgium	2	4.8
Canada	2	8
Denmark	1	8
Finland	2	4.8
France	2	6.8
Germany	2	6.3
Ireland	1	6.4
Israel	1	2.4
Italy	2	1.3
Japan	1	9.4
Luxembourg	2	4.4
The Netherlands	2	2.5
New Zealand	1	6
Norway	1	4
Sweden	1	4.2
Switzerland	2	12
United Kingdom	1	8
United States	3	6.9

Sources: E. Browne and J. Dreijmanis (1982), A. Lijphart (1984), Keesing's Contemporary Archives; A. Blaustein (1984).

3. TEST ONE: EXPERTS' VIEWS

As a first test, we asked a small number of comparative law scholars for their views on the degree of judicial daring in the various countries. The questionnaire, which is attached as Appendix B, asked experts to rate the adventurousness of courts in different countries on a five-point scale. For example, one expert assigned the US courts a 5 to indicate they were the most daring, courts in the UK a 1, and German and French courts a 3. The various experts' ratings were then averaged so that each country had a single number.

Table 5.2 shows the results of regressing the expert ratings on the two variables in Table 5.1. The explanatory variables have the predicted signs. The coalition duration variable is highly significant and the Vetoes variable is less significant. The two variables explained over 60 per cent of the variance, which is very high for such a simple model.

Table 5.2 Expert ratings of judicial daring regressed on two determinants of legislative resistance

Variable	Coefficient	Std. error	T-stat.	2-tail sig.
Constant	2.94	0.96	3.06	0.03
Vetoes	0.89	0.41	2.16	0.08
Coalition duration	−0.18	0.10	−1.71	0.14
R-squared = 0.61				
Prob (F-statistic) = 0.097569				

Note: Only countries for which three or more experts responded are included in the regression.

4. TEST TWO: THE MOVE TO STRICT LIABILITY

To test further our prediction of judicial daring, we examined one area of law as a case study, the adoption of strict liability for consumer product injuries. We found that courts with high predicted daring were willing to innovate in this area of private law more than other courts. Courts with low predicted daring, by contrast, were content to wait for legislative adoption of the new standard.

Before the move to strict liability for product defects, liability had usually been based on traditional standards of negligence in tort doctrine. Traditional doctrine required the plaintiff to prove the defendant's negligence caused the sale of a defective product. Alternatively, many jurisdictions had a contract law doctrine which allowed buyers to sue sellers for breach of contract (sometimes using an 'implied term' or warrant of merchantability). Contract liability was strict, but when narrowly construed the doctrine had limited utility in product liability cases. For example, contract liability is usually restricted to the actual seller of the product, so it does not extend easily back to the manufacturer.

As the number and type of consumer products have expanded with the modern economy, most wealthy countries have moved to strict liability for injuries caused by defective products. (A large debate concerns whether this change increased or decreased economic efficiency.[17])

The key question for our model is whether the jurisdiction adopted strict liability through judicial or legislative mechanisms. We hypothesise that more daring courts would sooner overturn a traditional tort law standard than would more conservative courts. Conservative courts may be more likely to defer to strict terms of legislative doctrine.

The first jurisdiction to move to a strict liability standard was California, and some form of its rule was adopted by all US jurisdictions. The first European jurisdiction to move to a strict liability standard for product liability claims was France. Product liability claims were traditionally based on either contract or tort provisions in the French code. The Cour de Cassation gradually unified the remedies available to consumers.[18] While the French system of consumer protection is extremely complicated, the main point is that in the US and France courts led the way in changing liability law.

There are three possible ways in which strict liability could be adopted. In some jurisdictions, as described above, courts moved to a strict liability standard before the legislature mandated it, overturning traditional doctrine (and sometimes the explicit text of the codes). This was the case in France and the US.[19] In other countries, such as in Germany, Italy and Israel, courts went part of the way by reversing the burden of proof. Under traditional law in product liability cases, the plaintiff must prove that the defendant was negligent, whereas under revised law the defendant must prove that he was not negligent. Reversing the burden of proof helps plaintiffs overcome evidentiary problems and thereby significantly expands liability for manufacturers. Finally, certain courts neither moved to strict liability nor reversed the burden of proof, and the move to strict liability was initiated by the legislature (as in the United Kingdom, Sweden and Japan).

These facts provide a basis for quantifying judicial daring in the area of consumer products liability (see Table 5.3). Countries where courts moved to strict liability without legislative construction are assigned a 3. Countries where courts went part-way, a lesser but still significant judicial innovation, are assigned a 2. Finally, courts which refused to innovate are assigned a 1.

Table 5.3 Judicial role in developing strict liability

Country	Judicial role in SL*	Vetoes	DDP
Australia	1	2	9
Austria	2	2	4.8
Belgium	3	2	4.8
Canada	2	2	8
Denmark	1	1	8
Finland	1	2	4.8
France	3	2	6.8
Germany	2	2	6.3
Ireland	1	1	6.4
Israel	2	1	2.4
Italy	2	2	1.3
Japan	1	1	9.4
Luxembourg	3	2	4.4
The Netherlands	2	2	2.5
New Zealand	1	1	6
Norway	1	1	4
Sweden	1	1	4.2
Switzerland	1	2	12
United Kingdom	1	1	8
United States	3	3	6.9

Note: * 3 indicates judicial move to strict liability; 2 indicates Courts reverse burden; 1 indicates leg. adopts strict liability

Sources: W. Freedman (1995), P. Kelly and R. Attree (1992), G. Howells (1993) and A. Mottur (1994)

Table 5.4 shows what happens when we regress these results against our two variables indicating legislative resistance. The results of the regression in Table 5.4 are similar to the results in Table 5.2. Specifically, the two explanatory variables have the predicted sign, Vetoes is highly significant, and Cabinet Duration relatively high as well. The regression explains over half the variance.

The data in Table 5.3 is simplified, so we provide more detail on some of the larger countries. The European jurisdictions are complicated by EU intervention into accident law. On 25 July 1985, the European Council issued a Directive on Product Liability.[20] Directives are essentially orders to member country legislatures to upgrade their domestic laws in a particular area.

Table 5.4 Judicial innovation concerning consumer products' liability regressed on two determinants of legislative resistance

Variable	Coefficient	Std. error	T-stat.	2-tail sig.
Constant	0.72	0.38	1.87	0.07
Vetoes	0.81	0.17	4.60	0.0002
Coalition Duration	–0.08	0.04	–1.89	0.08
R-squared = 0.57				
Prob (F-statistic) = 0.0004				

Following a directive, each country's legislature must act to bring the legal system into compliance. Directives use the method of 'approximation' wherein they specify a range of outcomes, within which national regulation may fall.

The objective of the Products Liability Directive was to unify law within the Common Market related to defective products, which had historically been quite different across legal systems. The Community felt that the varying levels of consumer protection would act as a barrier to free trade within the community.

What were the effects of the Community Directive on member countries' legal systems? Although the Directive was 'a welcome opportunity to harmonise and simplify existing law' for France[21], the parliament has not yet passed legislation to implement the directive. The European Commission issued a warning to France in this regard in 1990, and apparently there is a pending lawsuit to force the French to comply with the Directive. Given that the Directive is not as strict in some areas as existing French law,[22] the legislative reluctance is puzzling.

Prior to the issuance of the directive Germany did not have strict liability, but rather based product liability damages on traditional contract and tort doctrines.[23] Whether found in contract or tort doctrine, remedies have been comparable, although subject to technical differences.[24] German courts reversed the burden of proof from the plaintiff so as to substantially protect the consumer from defective products.[25] The result is much like strict liability for practical purposes, but still the courts were reluctant to directly challenge the legislature.

After the Directive, Germany passed a Product Liability Act,[26] which introduced the strict liability standard and provides relief for certain classes of cases not previously covered by judicially created doctrine. With its emphasis on consumer protection, the European Directive called for less liability for products used for business/professional use, so old tort-based doctrine will continue to be important in this area.[27] The Directive did not much change German law for practical purposes, as evidenced in part by the fact that product liability insurers did not raise their rates after the new legislation entered into force in 1990.[28]

In Italy the Directive was implemented by Governmental Decree[29]. Like the German implementing legislation, it does not exclude other causes of action, so previously valid tort rules still apply. Again, similar to Germany, the traditional tort doctrine burden of proof had already been reversed by courts with regard to negligence in product liability cases.[30] Contract claims are also allowed for financial damages. The Directive did introduce some changes into Italian law, including 'the concept of willing assumption of risk which is different from the contributory negligence hitherto known in Italy'.[31] As in Germany, contributory negligence of the plaintiff still provides a defence.

Traditionally, product liability in Sweden had been covered by tort and contract doctrines as well as a Consumer Safety Act. Where contract and tort doctrines are applicable, the burden of proof rests with the plaintiff, but court practice has somewhat diminished the standards of evidence.[32] Nevertheless, there was in no sense a judicially mandated move to strict liability, nor the general reversal of the burden of proof as found in Germany.[33] Of special importance in Sweden are legislatively created social insurance programmes, which protect consumers as would a regime of strict liability in many cases.[34] Courts had little incentive to impose strict liability in such a context. After many years of discussion, a Products Liability Act was passed in 1992, substantially conforming with the Community Directive. (Even before becoming an EU member, the Swedish legal authorities sought to harmonise national rules with Community law.)

Prior to the Directive, the United Kingdom system was characterised by a multiplicity of laws under which product liability claims may be lodged. These include standard tort and contract doctrine, and a number of pieces of legislation. The statutory scheme is complicated, but the important point is that prior to 1987, liability was not strict. Judicial tests of remoteness and the doctrine of contractual privity limited damages in many cases. Much changed with the Consumer Protection Act of 1987, which consolidated existing legislation as well as implemented the Community Directive, moving to a strict liability standard for most cases. The UK act diverged from the Directive in the area of development risks, and has proved controversial.[35] But the UK was the first country to pass implementing legislation after the directive, illustrating our contention that legislative resistance is low in the UK.

The above descriptions cover selected European countries, but the other countries in our study show similar patterns. Israel's law had been derived from the United Kingdom's traditional reliance on fault as the source of tort liability. But as in Germany, the courts had shifted the burden of proof from plaintiff to defendant because of the evidentiary difficulties plaintiffs would face. In 1980, the Knesset passed a Defective Products Liability Law, imposing strict liability.[36]

In Japan, the move to strict liability was long-delayed, the first statute not emerging until June 1994.[37] Although product liability reform received extensive discussion by both scholars and judges for many years, the legislature resisted a change and the courts were not powerful enough to mandate the switch on their own. The resistance of the legislature has been said to reflect industry strength, but the judicial reluctance to move reflects a conservatism that is extraordinary among industrial democracies.[38]

Of the countries in our study, only France, Belgium, Luxembourg and the US had judicially created strict product liability. The other countries moved legislatively to strict liability, although courts in Germany, Italy, Israel and other countries had gone part way by reversing the burden of proof. Japanese, UK and Swedish courts had not reversed the burden. The ten countries from our sample which fell into the latter group had, on average, fewer vetoes and longer cabinet duration than the ten in the other two groups.[39]

5. TEST THREE: POLLUTION REGULATION

Judicial innovation in private law is one indicator of discretion. We believe that the logic of judicial discretion operates in public law as well, and in this section we extend our argument to another area of legal change, specifically pollution regulation. The argument here is a bit more complex. We argue that countries with greater legislative resistance are more likely to judicialise public policy tasks, and are also likely to write detailed statutes to try to constrain courts with otherwise broad discretion.

Public law complicates the model because of the continental tradition of separate administrative courts.[40] Administrative courts are different because the judges tend to be tangled in administration and not independent of it. For simplicity, our discussion concentrates on countries with unified court systems, where courts of general jurisdiction hear disputes on administrative matters. This group includes Japan, the US and the UK.

Let us consider why politicians in some countries might prefer independent courts. Politicians need the power to commit themselves to policies. The power to commit enables politicians to bargain with others and strike mutually beneficial deals. In general, commitment can occur in two ways. One way is for a disciplined party with enduring control over government to develop a reputation for keeping promises. Having invested in reputation, the party can guarantee its promises by backing them with its valuable reputation. Under such conditions, independent courts only hinder political action.[41] This method of commitment, however, is unavailable to governments without an enduring, disciplined and dominant party. Short-lived coalition governments need another way to make commitments.

The other way is to create independent courts with the authority to interpret bargains embodied in laws. Courts serve as agents of enacting coalitions by insulating policies from reversal after electoral losses.[42] Governments run by Dominant Disciplined Parties can make commitments without independent courts, whereas other governments may need independent courts to make credible commitments. Thus, J. Mark Ramseyer argues that ruling politicians will prefer independent courts where they believe (a) there is a high likelihood of continuing elections, and (b) they are not likely to continue winning the elections.[43] Ramseyer only illustrates the argument with evidence from America and Japan. Generalising, we conclude that Dominant Disciplined Parties are unlikely to prefer independent courts to protect their policies. Furthermore, they are likely to *avoid* judicialising new policy areas because courts could deny the politicians the flexibility needed for political bargaining with various actors. We predict less 'judicialisation' of public policy in countries with a strong DDP.

One indicator of judicialisation is statute length. When governments are confident in their ability to informally control courts and agencies, there is little need to write detailed and precise statutes. Where they are not so confident, they will want to write detailed statutes so they can use courts to monitor agencies.

The case of pollution regulation in the US, Japan, and the UK illustrates this point. Table 5.5 presents data on the length of air and water pollution control statutes in these countries.

Table 5.5 Length of pollution control statutes (est. # words)[44]

	Japan	UK	US
Air Pollution Statute	12,675	62,475	544,980
Air Pollution Regulations	16,025	46,980	729,120
Water Pollution Statute	42,900	29,400	240,560
Water Pollution Regulations	189,150	29,970	854,980
TOTAL	360,750	168,825	2,379,640

It is clear that even from our crude estimates, US statutes are of an order of magnitude more lengthy (and by extension more specific) than similar laws in the other jurisdictions. While this may not establish a causal relationship between legislative resistance and judicial discretion, it does provide one more piece of evidence consistent with our prediction.

We now provide more detail on the pattern of pollution regulation in our three countries. In Japan, high-growth policies created significant pollution problems by the end of the 1960s.[45] After severely damaged children were born at Minamata, plaintiffs sued polluting companies in tort and won in the so-called 'big four' cases. Faced with a new public policy problem, the bureaucracy intervened and drafted a statute with a mediation and compensation scheme for future cases. The bureaucracy thus usurped the process of pollution compensation from the courts. American style environmental legislation was adopted with environmental impact assessments and public hearing process, but with important modifications that minimised the impact of either innovation. The Japanese version of the Environmental Impact Assessment, for example, was unenforceable in court, and participation in public hearings was structured by the bureaucracy which tended to only give voice to local interests. In general, Japanese administrative law severely limits access to the courts, as one might expect in a system with little legislative resistance. In sum, although courts attempted to innovate by holding industry liable, pollution compensation was quickly removed from courts. Pollution control schemes were developed through bureaucratic consultation and discussion with industry, rather than through legal challenge.

Environmental regulation in the United Kingdom follows a similar pattern of utilising informal discussions between regulators and businesses, not courts.[46] Environmental statutes are broadly written and provide administrative flexibility in implementation so that the particular circumstances of each polluter and community can be met. This flexibility is captured in the statutory requirement that clean-up efforts must use the 'best practicable means' with sensitivity to cost, capacity of the environment to absorb pollution and pace of modification. Standards are met through voluntary compliance far more than government prosecutions. Political control is ensured through the Secretary of State for the Environment, who can hear appeals arising from the pollution control agency decisions.

In the US, by contrast, statutes are written with strict detail. The Clean Air Act of 1970 is a good example. Pollution-clean-up efforts are required to use the 'best available technology' regardless of costs or environmental necessity, and sometimes regulations are 'technology forcing'.[47] Citizens have the right to sue the administering agency, the Environmental Protection Agency, and the EPA itself may sue polluters. Access to courts allows citizens to sue, but judicial solutions often allow polluters to delay compliance efforts.[48]

Extending the analysis to other countries shows a similar pattern to the tort area discussed above. In France, environmental liabilities arise out of general civil and criminal codes, which are judicially interpreted. The law of industrial nuisance, for example, was judicially rather than legislatively created. Legislation has come only later. A new environmental code is in draft from, but has not yet been passed. So judges have had more of a say in this area than their counterparts in other countries. By contrast, the Swedish legislature has been very active, with more than 260 relevant acts and ordinances as of 1987.[49] As in the British case, Swedish agencies are required to balance several competing interests in a flexible manner.

The example of environmental regulation shows that judicial discretion may be minimised simply by the legislature not judicialising a policy area. Courts cannot exercise discretion in cases that are not brought before them. Where a DDP holds sway, as in the UK, Japan and Sweden, judges will not be as involved in implementing pollution regulation. In contrast, where power is divided and split, independent courts may be created so that policy decisions can be legalised and maintained after the enacting coalition has faded away. Detailed statutes are needed both to control courts and to empower courts to monitor bureaucratic agencies.

6. OMITTED VARIABLES

We should mention two variables not taken into account in our model. The first is the material independence of the courts from the political process. Where judges are dependent on politicians for their budget, promotions, and other assignments, they are likely to decide cases in accordance with the wishes of the politicians who control their purse strings. We do not include this variable because we believe it may be congruent with our measure of DDP. Dominant parties can easily impose their preferences on judges because judges know that the party is likely to continue to be in power and there is little to be gained from defying it. Where parties alternate in power, any attempt to coerce the judiciary through manipulation of material incentives will likely provoke the other political parties to do the same. It is therefore in neither party's interest to begin to politicise the judiciary. Furthermore, without a DDP, individual judges may resist such attempts, since they know that eventually the other party will 'rescue' them from the imposition of a particular political viewpoint. Where a DDP holds power for a long period, judges are likely to be shaped during formative periods of their careers in directions consistent with DDP views. Finally, a DDP will gain a sophisticated understanding of mechanisms to control judges through long experience. For these reasons, material dependence on politicians is more salient when there is a DDP than where there is not.

The second omitted variable concerns the bureaucracy. In many systems it is the bureaucracy and not the legislature which actually drafts laws. The administration might be argued to constitute another legislative veto. But the bureaucracy also can veto judicial decisions in other ways, for example by failing to enforce judgements or judicial orders. For simplicity, we leave the bureaucracy out of the model, and assume that it acts as an agent of the legislature.

Clearly, judicial discretion is difficult to measure. In some areas of the law where the legislature has been inactive, the courts have moved away from old, out-of-date rules without specific instruction from the legislature. Nevertheless, this does not mean that the sitting legislature has a different policy preference from that of the courts. Rather it might mean that the legislature does not have a strong preference, or prefers to leave innovation to judicial authorities.

Another problem is the difficulty of comparing legal systems. In most every country, whether a recipient of the common law or continental tradition, judges do make law. While this is explicitly acknowledged and even celebrated in the common law, civil law tradition is more suspicious of judicial creativity. In the civil law system, law making is allegedly the function of the legislature, and law-applying is the function of courts.

This difference in conception mirrors deeper difficulties around what constitutes discretion. Is a court that invents a standard where none previously existed exercising greater discretion than another court which expressly contradicts an outmoded legislative provision? Might a court acting to create law in a civil law system where such functions are formally denied be more daring than a common law court adopting the same standard? In countries where courts' primary job is to interpret generalised codes, judges often must invent new standards to keep up with changing socio-economic conditions. Is such judicial innovation greater when the code is older (under a theory that courts are tinkering with more-established tradition), or where the legislature has spoken more recently (in which case the court might be said to show greater defiance)? What about cases where judges have discretion but do not use it to create new law because their policy preferences are congruent with the legislature? These and other issues illustrate the comparative difficulties involved in discussing discretion in cross-national terms.

7. CONCLUSION

We now return to the implications of our model for the future of the EU. We expect that as legislative resistance increases, the power of the ECJ expands. The development of the Union has brought an increase in the power of the European Parliament. While primary legislative powers still belong to the Council, the strengthening of the parliament is a move towards bicameralism. This change increases legislative resistance, which should expand the judicial discretion in the European Court of Justice.[50]

The legitimacy of the EU rests in large part on the legitimacy of its courts. While this chapter does not address legitimacy directly, we believe the positive political theory we have provided and tested is relevant. Judicial legitimacy can only come from the appropriate exercise of judicial power. We have shown that the power of courts is to a great extent a function of constitutional rules and political factors. In its efforts to design institutions for deeper and wider integration, European leaders ought to ensure that power is divided sufficiently so that the ECJ can continue to play an active role in the process.

NOTES

1. These proposals include expanding the role of the European Parliament, restructuring the Council and strengthening the powers of the Commission President. See Hesse and Johnson (1995), pp. 17-19.
2. See for example Capelletti (1989). For a theoretical account by the Chief Justice of Israel, see Barak (1989).
3. In the common law tradition, judges may have a legitimate role in the creation of norms. This is less true in the continental or civil law tradition, where judges are urged to apply legislatively-created norms.
4. A key variable here is whether the judiciary is organised along the lines of a hierarchical civil service model, in which judges enter the profession at a relatively young age and advance through adherence to internally maintained professional norms. In the common law tradition, entry to the judiciary is a prestigious appointment which comes at the end of a distinguished legal career. Advancement is less of a concern, and the upper echelons of the profession have fewer collateral means of controlling the incentives of lower-court judges (though they do maintain control over legal norms through the appeals process).
5. See for example Holland (1991).
6. The model is developed in Gely and Spiller (1990). For a discussion of the US Congress correcting judicial interpretation of civil rights legislation, see Mikva and Bleich (1991).
7. Our research draws upon similar models developed for the United States in Ferejohn and Weingast (1992a), Ferejohn and Weingast (1992b), and Eskridge (1991). For the same model with an administrative agency, see Weingast and Moran (1979), Ferejohn and Shipan (1990), Spitzer (1990), and Rose-Ackerman (1990).
8. For an empirical study of American court decisions based on the model, see Spiller and Gely (1992). The framework is developed in Gely and Spiller (1990).

9. Note it could also mean that courts have less information about stable legislative preferences, which may lead the court to be cautious for fear of over-reaching. Alternatively, courts may underestimate legislative concern, in which case their innovation could provoke legislative correction because of the uncertainty of legislative preferences. Current demands for tort reform in the United States may reflect such dissatisfaction with judicial innovation.
10. The structure of the party system itself is heavily influenced by electoral laws. For an empirical study, see Taagepera and Shugart (1989). Also see Grofman and Lijphardt (1986).
11. This is the case whether proposals for new legislation originate in the government or the legislature.
12. Note that in Japan and the UK, there is an upper house of parliament, but their assent is only required for the budget and not for most ordinary legislation. Israel recently modified its Basic Law so that after 1996, the prime minister will be directly elected. This will increase the number of legislative vetoes to two.
13. The French system is formally bicameral, but in fact the Senate is indirectly elected and can only delay lower house legislation and not block it. While this has the effect of imposing additional transaction costs and thereby increasing legislative resistance, for simplicity such partial vetoes are not counted in our model.
14. Nelson Polsby characterises these kind of legislatures as arenas, in contrast with transformative legislatures which regularly modify the legislation in substantial ways. Polsby (1975).
15. For purposes of this chapter, changes in composition occur only when a party is added or dropped from the coalition, and not when the cabinet seats are merely reshuffled among existing coalition members. Nor is there a change when the same coalition continues in power after new elections.
16. Jacobson (1990).
17. See discussion in Cooter and Ulen (1988). George Priest argues that the use of tort rather than contract doctrine in products liability cases is inefficient, Priest (1985). Landes and Posner take a slightly different view in Landes and Posner (1985).
18. See Art 1641 of the Civil Code, which provides that the seller is liable in respect of hidden defects which render the product unsuitable for its intended use.
19. The strict liability standard is a feature of state, not federal, law in the US. This is a minor but not insurmountable problem for our model, since our assessments of DDP and Vetoes in the various countries were made at the national level. We believe that the constitutional framework of most states is consistent with the federal scheme, since all states but Nebraska have bicameral legislatures. Furthermore, fragmented national parties may be replicated at the state level.
20. Council Directive 85/374/EC.
21. Kelly and Attree (1992), p. 103.
22. For example, in that the seller of a defective product can be held jointly liable with the producer *vis-à-vis* hidden defects in the product. This principle derives from the French contract law origins of product liability.
23. The Civil Code (BGB) of 1896 dealt in only a general way with contract law. There was a separation of warranty doctrine, which dealt with a consumer interest in a properly functioning product, and the problem of damages to health or property resulting from a defective product.
24. For example in tort, product requirements are standardised, whereas in contract breach cases they must be determined with regards to the specific contract. The seller duties to inform the buyer are stricter in contract cases. Damages from pure financial loss is not recoverable under tort, but only under breach of contract actions (Kelly and Attree (1992), pp. 132, 138). In contract, the defendant must prove that he was not at fault. Tort claims are more often used.
25. According to a 1988 decision (BGH in NJW 1988, 2611 ff. 'Mehrwegflasche II') the burden of proof depends on several factors: whether there has been a defect that affects the claimant's right, whether the defect results from the production process, whether there has been a

negligent or intentional disregard of due care related to the defect. The defendant must exonerate himself from liability from fault for matters related to internal production, and 'in practice, this exoneration almost never succeeds.' (Kelly and Attree (1992), p. 147).

26. Passed on 15 December 1989, it came into force on 1 January 1990. For the text of the Act, see Bundesgesetzblatt I 1989 p. 2198.
27. Kelly and Attree (1992), p. 152.
28. Schwartz (1991), p. 46 at 49.
29. Decree 224 of 24 May 1988. Note that decrees are frequently used when the Italian legislature is paralysed, but that there is rarely conflict between the versions of a law promulgated by decree and those subsequently promulgated by the legislature.
30. This occurred with the 1964 decision of the highest court of appeals, the Corte di Cassazione, of 25 May 1964, no. 1270 in Foro Italiano, 1965, 1, 2098. Kelly and Attree (1992), p. 226.
31. Ibid. p. 234.
32. See discussion of a 1989 case of foodstuffs poisoning in Howells (1993), p. 151.
33. Magrell, Nillson and Sandeun (1988), p. 16.
34. Kelly and Attree (1992), p. 334.
35. See Howells (1993).
36. In the words of one commentator, the 1980 law 'cannot be explained in terms of a political decision to rectify any social or economic wrong or resolve any particular legal problem stemming from products liability ... the law can rather be explained in terms of the legislator's awareness of the new developments in the advanced legal systems, and its realisation that the law should adapt to the changes in the Israelis' socio-economic organisation.' Moe (1988), p. 3.
37. A translation appears in Lloyds' Prod. Liab. Int'l, 31 July 1994, p. 101.
38. J. Mark Ramseyer has shown the variety of collateral incentives that the long-ruling Liberal Democratic Party imposed on the Japanese Supreme Court. See Ramseyer and Rosenbluth (1993), and also Ramseyer and Rasmusen.
39. The mean number of vetoes for the latter group was 1.3, compared with 2.0 for the first two groups combined. The mean coalition duration was 7.18, compared with 4.62 for the first two groups.
40. These separate courts began in France and have been adopted in most continental jurisdictions. Jacobini (1991).
41. Ramseyer (1994).
42. Landes and Posner (1975).
43. Ramseyer (1994).
44. We began by counting the total number of pages in the country's general air and water pollution statutes at the national level. We then took a ten-page sample and counted the number of words on each page. Next we multiplied the total number of pages by the average number of words in the ten-page sample to produce our estimates. To compensate for the different structure of the Japanese language, we used a crude measure by which two characters are equivalent to one English word. Note that even with this adjustment, our estimate probably overstates the number of English-language equivalent words in the statute.
45. An excellent discussion of environmental regulation in Japan is found in Upham (1987).
46. Vogel (1986).
47. See Badaracco (1985).
48. Vogel (1986), at 173.
49. Nillson (1993), p. 433.
50. This argument is developed at greater length in Cooter and Drexl (1994).

REFERENCES

Badaracco, J. (1985), *Loading the Dice: A Five Country Study of Vinyl Chloride Regulation*, Cambridge: Harvard University Press.

Barak, A. (1989), *Judicial Discretion*, Cambridge: Harvard University Press.

Blaustein, A. (ed.) (1984), *Constitutions of the World.*

Brealey, M. (ed.) (1993), *Environmental Liabilities and Regulation in Europe*, The Hague: International Business Publishing Ltd.

Brown, E. and J. Dreijmannis (eds) (1982), *Government Coalitions in Western Democracies.*

Capelletti, M. (1989), *The Judicial Process in Comparative Perspective*, Oxford: Clarendon.

Cooter, R. and J. Drexl (1994), 'The Logic of Power in the Emerging European Constitution: Game Theory and the Division of Powers', *International Review of Law and Economics*, **14**.

Cooter, R. and T. Ulen (1988), *Law and Economics*, Glenview, Il.: Scott Foresman.

Eskridge, W. (1991), 'Overriding Supreme Court Statutory Interpretation Decisions', *Yale Law Journal*, **101**.

Ferejohn, J. and B. Weingast (1992a), 'A Positive Theory of Statutory Interpretation', *International Review of Law and Economics*, **12**, 263–279.

Ferejohn, J. and B. Weingast (1992b), 'Limitation of Statutes: Strategic Statutory Interpretation', *Georgetown Law Journal*, **80**, 565–582.

Ferejohn, J. and C. Shipan (1990), 'Congressional Influence on Bureaucracy', *Journal of Law, Economics and Organization*, **6**, 1–20.

Freedman, W. (ed.) (1988), *Product Liability: an International Manual of Practice*, Dobbs Ferry: Oceana.

Gely and Spiller (1990), 'A Rational Choice Theory of Supreme Court Statutory Decisions with Applications to the State Farm and Grove City Cases', *Journal of Law, Economics and Organization*, **6**.

Grofman, B. and A. Lijphardt (1986), *Electoral Laws and their Political Consequences.*

Hesse, J. and N. Johnson (eds) (1995), *Constitutional Policy and Change in Europe*, London: Oxford University Press.

Holland, K. (ed.) (1991), *Judicial Activism in Comparative Perspective*, New York: St. Martin's Press.

Howells, G. (1993), *Comparative Product Liability*, Brookfield, Ma: Dartmouth.

Jacobini, H.B. (1991), *An Introduction to Comparative Administrative Law*, New York: Oceana.

Jacobson, G. (1990), *The Electoral Origins of Divided Government.*

Kelly, P. and R. Attree (1992), *European Products Liability*, London: Butterworths.

Lijphardt, A. (1984), *Democracies.*

Landes, W. and R. Posner (1985), 'A Positive Economic Analysis of Products Liability', *Journal of Legal Studies*, **14**.

Landes, W. and R. Posner (1975), 'The Independent Judiciary in an Interest Group Perspective', *Journal of Law and Economics*, **18**.

Magrell, R., O. Nillson and S. Sandeun (1988), 'Sweden', in Warren Freedman (ed.), *Product Liability: an International Manual of Practice*, Dobbs Ferry: Oceana.

Mikva, A. and J. Bleich (1991), 'When Congress Overrules the Court', *California Law Review*, **79**.
Moe, D. (1988), 'Israel', in W. Freedman (ed.), *Product Liability: an International Manual of Practice*, Dobbs Ferry: Oceana.
Mottur (1994), 'European Product Liability', *Law and Policy in International Bussiness*.
Nillson, T. (1993), 'Sweden', in M. Brealey (ed.), *Environmental Liabilities and Regulation in Europe*, The Hague: International Business Publishing Ltd.
Polsby, N. (1975), 'Legislatures', in F. Greenstein and N. Polsby (eds), *Encyclopedia of Political Science*, Redding, MA: Addison Wesley, volume 1.
Priest (1985), 'The Invention of Enterprise Liability: A Critical History of the Intellectual Foundations of Modern Tort Law', *Journal of Legal Studies*, **14**.
Ramseyer, J.M. and E. Rasmusen, 'Judicial Independence in Civil Law Regimes: Econometrics from Japan', manuscript.
Ramseyer, J. M. and F. Rosenbluth (1993), *Japan's Political Marketplace*, Cambridge: Harvard University Press.
Ramseyer, J. M. (1994), 'The Puzzling Independence of Courts: A Comparative Approach', *Journal of Legal Studies*, **23** (2).
Rose-Ackerman, S. (1990), 'Comment on Ferejohn and Shipan's "Congressional Influence on Bureaucracy"', *Journal of Law, Economics and Organization*, **6**, 21–27.
Schwartz, G. (1991), 'Product Liability and Medical Malpractice in Comparative Context', in P. Huber and R. Litan (eds), *The Liability Maze*, Washington: Brookings.
Spiller and Gely (1992), 'Congressional Control or Judicial Independence: The Determinants of U.S. Supreme Court Labor-Relations Decisions, 1949–1988', *Rand Journal of Economics*, **23**.
Spitzer, M. (1990), 'Extensions of Ferejohn and Shipan's Model of Administrative Agency Behavior', *Journal of Law, Economics, and Organization*, **6**, 29–43.
Taagepera, R. and M. Shugart (1989), *Seats and Votes: The Effects and Determinants of Electoral Systems*, New Haven: Yale University Press.
Upham, F. (1987), *Law and Social Change in Postwar Japan*, Cambridge: Harvard University Press.
Vogel, D. (1986), *National Styles of Regulation*, Ithaca: Cornell.
Weingast, B. and M. Moran (1979), 'Bureaucrats vs. Voters: On the Political Economy of Resource Allocation', *Quarterly Journal of Economics*, **93**.

APPENDIX A

Coalition Duration

Table 5.6 Coalition duration

Country	Start year[1]	End year	Total years	Number of coalitions[2]	Avg. duration (years)
Australia	1958	1994	36	4	9
Austria	1945	1993	48	10	4.8
Belgium	1945	1993	48	10	4.8
Canada	1945	1993	48	6	8
Denmark	1945	1993	48	6	8
Finland	1945	1993	48	10	4.8
France	1958	1992	34	5	6.8
Germany	1949	1993	44	7	6.3
Ireland	1948	1993	45	7	6.4
Israel	1948	1993	45	19	2.4
Italy[3]	1948	1993	45	34	1.3
Japan	1946	1993	47	5	9.4
Luxembourg	1958	1993	35	8	4.4
The Netherlands	1945	1993	48	19	2.5
New Zealand	1945	1993	48	8	6
Norway	1957	1993	36	9	4
Sweden	1951	1993	42	10	4.2
Switzerland[4]	1945	1993	48	4	12
United Kingdom	1945	1993	48	8	8
United States[5]	1945	1993	48	6.9	6.9

APPENDIX B

Questionnaire Text

A model based on game theory predicts that judicial discretion depends on the number of independent vetoes on passing overriding legislation. For example, in a bicameral, presidential system, the two chambers of the legislature and the executive each have a veto on new legislation. We are trying to establish an empirical relationship between the difficulty of passing legislation (= legislative resistance) and judicial discretion (which we call judicial daring) in a number of different countries.

For each of the following countries, how much discretion do courts exercise in interpreting legislative statutes? (1 = low; 5 = high)

Country	Judicial daring

NOTES

1. The start year usually begins with 1945 or with the subsequent establishment of a new constitutional order. Occasionally, problems in gathering the data forced us to modify the original start date.
2. A coalition change only occurs when the party composition of the cabinet changes. A simple reshuffling of seats among existing coalition partners is not counted as a change (with the exception of the Swiss system described below).
3. Although Italy has had over 50 governments in the post-war period, some of these cabinets replaced earlier cabinets of exactly the same party composition. For purposes of our calculations we did not count such instances as a break in the coalition.
4. Seats in the collective Federal Council are traditionally accorded to the parties by a 'Magic Formula' which has changed three times in the post-war period.
5. For the US, the only changes in coalition occur when the presidency changes hands. Hence the average duration is higher than the constitutionally-mandated four-year presidential term.

Comment

Christian Kirchner

I.

Judicial discretion of the European Court of Justice (ECJ) is an essential factor of the institutional framework of the European Union (EU). It has a direct impact on

1. centralisation or decentralisation of the EU.
2. democratic legitimisation of political decisions within the EU (agency problems).

The emerging constitution of the EU can only be evaluated correctly if we are in a position to understand the present discretionary power of the ECJ, its history over the various stages of the formation of the EU and its political development in the future. Any discussion on the future role of the ECJ, or any other European court, and its role in the constitutional framework of the EU presupposes an understanding of this issue which goes beyond common sense assumptions on the role of courts in different systems of separation of powers. The chapter by Cooter and Ginsburg is helpful in creating a fundament for this deeper understanding.

II.

The chapter deals with an important issue concerning the separation of powers in any political system in which law courts are engaged in the law-making process. Their power to make law is confined by legal constraints; for instance, the German Federal Labour Court cannot extensively engage in so-called free law-making if the German Federal Constitutional Court can declare decisions of the labour court unconstitutional if it violates the principle of separation of powers, guaranteed by the German constitution, the 'Grundgesetz'.[1] But such a test of whether or not a court decision is unconstitutional or not is normally not existent for decisions of a country's supreme court or the constitutional court. No German court has the power to declare such a court decision void. In the court hierarchy the ECJ may declare decisions by any court of a member state of the EU to be in violation of community law. But there is no other European court which could declare a decision to the ECJ unconstitutional in respect of the 'European Constitution'.[2] Thus we are confronted with the problem of how to control the law-making power of such courts which are at the top of the court hierarchy.

The chapter points to the fact that control may be exercised by such other legislative institutions which have the power to overturn decisions of the court by introducing fresh legislation. One should clarify exactly what the other institution is doing here: it does not change the court decision, it does not override the interpretation of the old law; it rather changes the law which then has to be applied and interpreted by the law court again. It may formulate the new law in a manner which makes it difficult for the law court to reach the same results as on the basis of the old law. Let us take the following example: the member states of the EU – before the Single European Act – were unsatisfied with the interpretation of Art. 30 and 37 EEC by the ECJ. This interpretation had left in place the originally intended balance between the goal of free flow of goods and the sovereignty of member states. The series of decisions by the ECJ had interpreted Art. 30 EEC extensively and Art. 36 EEC very strictly, thus effectively restricting the sovereignty of member states. The member states then realised the threat and have tried to solve the problem in the following way: if an issue – for example, quality standards for pharmaceuticals – is being regulated by secondary Community law,[3] the court is no longer in a position to declare provisions of the law of member states to be in violation of primary community law which would thus restrict the sovereignty of member states. The process of bargaining between the goal of free flow of goods and the sovereignty of member states becomes, rather, a political one in the phase of promulgating new secondary community Law. Art. 100 a EEC – as created by the Single European Act – provides a legal framework for a negotiation process between Community institutions and a member state which feels its sovereignty has been violated by this new secondary community law. But Art. 100 a EEC gives the last word to the ECJ. The Court thus has the chance to use this power to come to results very similar to its traditional decisions concerning Art. 30 EEC. The endeavours of the fathers of the Single European Act has largely been futile.

The example presented should demonstrate that other institutions engaging in law-making have to act themselves within the legally defined boundaries of the system of separation of powers. The game is a very intricate one. It is not just a system of countervailing powers but a system in which certain legal norms define the power of the various institutions. In the case of the ECJ one therefore has to analyse the legally defined powers of such European institutions which may try to exert control over the ECJ. The shortcomings of such an analysis are derived from the fact that the legal definition of powers of the various players of the game does not contain any information on how these players may actually make use of this power. Legal norms are important institutional variables, but there are other variables which should be taken into account. The progress of this chapter over traditional institutional analysis of the problem of separation of powers is the identification of new variables which are relevant for the system of separation of powers.

III.

The idea to bring new variables into play is fascinating, because it may open the typical economic institutional analysis to ingredients of political science with variables such as party discipline, stability of the governing coalition, and the existence of dominant disciplined party. These variables are not institutional variables. On the other hand, variables like majoritarianism or bicameralism, which have been introduced in earlier papers by Robert Cooter[4] are institutional variables. Such variables are part of the constitutional design whereas the political science variables as such are not part of this framework. If one is interested in normative aspects of constitutional design, one has to construct a connection between both types of variables. Or one has to take the given political science variables into account and try to propose such constitutional reforms which are supposed to best reach the given goal under such circumstances. One may choose one way or the other but one has to clearly understand the foundation on which one is working. If we look into the potential connections between the political science variables, which have been introduced by Cooter and Ginsburg, and institutional variables one has to analyse the institutional preconditions of the political science variables. Let us take two examples:

1. Party discipline has to do with the position of individual members of parliament and the (legally defined) power of the party to discipline dissenting party members. The crucial factor will be under which circumstances a member of parliament has to give up his seat and give it back to the party. One may also be interested in the rules which are applicable for selecting the candidates for the following elections. Such legal provisions define the institutional framework. Institutional analysis is interested in the effects of changes of such legal provisions.

2. Whether or not dominant disciplined parties exist within a national political system has much to do with election law. If small parties are confronted with certain obstacles like the German 5 per cent clause, there will be a tendency to form larger parties which in themselves are coalitions between various party factions. Institutional analysis is interested in the effects of legal changes of election laws on the existence of a dominant disciplined party.

As has been mentioned, the distinction between political science variables and institutional variables is relevant if one is interested in normative issues. If one has come to the conclusion that the existence of dominant disciplined parties constitutes a controlling factor on the law-making power of law courts, one is confronted with the problem that the creation of such dominant disciplined parties is not just a matter of political will but depends on changes of the institutional framework. The potential shortcomings of using just political science variables are not visible as long as one is mainly interested in a positive analysis. But in the moment one has to come to normative proposals it may be helpful to clarify the institutional background of such political science variables.

IV.

The chapter is extremely helpful in adding to our understanding of the position of law courts in the system of separation of powers. It makes us aware of the fact that various political science variables are decisive factors in defining the legislative power of law courts. On the other hand it is not easy to formulate normative proposals on the foundation of such a positive analysis. Is the message that – if we are interested in controlling the law-making power of the ECJ – we should create dominant disciplined political parties in a European Parliament? Even if we were in a position to do this, we could not be sure of the real impact of such a development.

The positive analysis of this chapter is a necessary ingredient for the discussion on constitutional design in Europe. But up to now the information provided by those insights are quite weak to form the fundament for normative proposals. In order to overcome these shortcomings one proceeds in the following directions:

1. Analysis of the institutional preconditions of political science variables brought into play.
2. Analysis of the side-effects of proposed institutional changes.

3. Analysis of alternative instruments to constrain the law-making power of the ECJ like the creation of a European Court of Review as has been proposed by the European Constitutional Group[5].

NOTES

1. Decision of the Federal Constitutional Court, BVerfGE, 65,182.
2. Today one may well argue that the three treaties establishing the three European Communities, the Single European Act and the EU Treaty (Maastricht Treaty) together are forming a core-constitution of the EU.
3. Secondary community law is law created by the legislative institutions of the Community whereas the three treaties establishing the three European Communities, the Single European Act and the EU Treaty (Maastricht Treaty) together are forming the so-called primary community law.
4. See Cooter (1994).
5. See European Constitutional Group (1993).

REFERENCES

European Constitutional Group (1993), *A Proposal for a European Constitution, part 2b, 4. Justiciability*, London: European Policy Forum.

Cooter, R. and J. Drexl (1994), 'The Logic of Power in the Emerging European Constitution: Game Theory and the Division of Powers', *International Review of Law and Economics*, **14**, 307–326.

Comment

Karl-Heinz Paqué

This is a most interesting chapter with a very simple structure. There is first a brief summary of the underlying theory, and then come the empirical tests of that theory. My comments will essentially replicate this simple structure.

Hence let us first turn to theory. In the first section of this chapter, the authors mention three alternative hypotheses about the degree of judicial discretion or judicial daring, namely tradition, the structure of the judicial profession and the degree of independence. None of these theories is further considered, let alone tested in the chapter.

This is a pity. Any econometrics that does not give a fair chance to the alternative hypothesis is seriously incomplete: whatever the estimated coefficients and t-statistics may be, we simply do not know whether they would robustly survive if the model were respecified along the lines of the major alternatives. Unfortunately, these alternatives are very plausible and important on *a priori* grounds. Let me briefly explain why.

It is perfectly reasonable to assume that every adult human being has political preferences. From this innocent assumption, however, it is a huge further step to assume that these political preferences influence professional behaviour. In fact, an economist who likes to assume that any individual maximises her personal utility over some lifetime horizon will predict that an individual will act so as to conform to the professional quality standards of her job, and these standards may be political or not.

For a politician, these standards are obviously political or ideological; her quality and thus her pecuniary and/or non-pecuniary rewards are directly linked to her ability to accomplish whatever political objectives. At the other extreme, there is, say, the soccer player who may have very strong political preferences and maybe also considerable leverage to influence public opinion, but who usually refrains from political statements because he assumes – and on average, I guess, correctly – that political action does no good to his professional career.

Somewhere in-between, there is the judge. She will engage in political law-making only when she can expect that political action through judicial discretion raises her credentials. More technically speaking: if, and only if, judicial discretion is part of the professional quality standards, and thus a long-term guarantee of high income or reputation, will a judge engage in it.

Hence it all depends on these professional standards, which may vastly differ between countries and call for a specification in any empirical model. They may of course be a function of the package of variables mentioned in the chapter, notably tradition and the structure and degree of independence of the judicial profession; and if they are, then these variables should be included. To me, the major theoretical weakness appears to be that they are in fact not included. It is simply assumed that judges have an inner drive towards seeing the world shaped according to their political or ideological preferences, independent of the personal opportunity cost that this political action through the judicial backdoor involves. And this appears to me highly implausible.

Let us now come to the econometric testing. Taken at face value the results presented for the first test run (Table 5.2) of the authors' theory – using the expert ratings as an endogenous variable – seem to provide good evidence in favour of their theory. Apart from my general theoretical critique, however, serious doubts arise for a number of more technical reasons.

1. The authors leave us in the dark about sample size: while there are 20 countries in the sample of Table 5.1, which contains the data for the right-hand-side variables in Table 5.2, the actual number of observations underlying the estimates in Table 5.2 is probably much smaller because only those countries are included for which three or more experts responded. In an earlier version of the chapter, which contained a slightly different specification but, I assume, the same expert ratings as the left-hand side variable, the number of countries included was eight, which means five degrees of freedom – hardly enough to speak of a serious test of whatever theory[1].
2. The authors leave us completely in the dark as to the robustness of their results. Partly, this may be the mere consequence of the low number of observations: how can you run sensible tests on, say, structural stability between subsamples when the sample contains just eight countries? None the less, there are some straightforward questions that may be addressed. In particular, one would love to know how the most conspicuous observation, the United States, influences the results. After all, the United States is the country with the highest ranking of the persistently most significant right-hand-side variable ('Vetoes'), and the highest ranking of, I guess, expert opinions on judicial discretion in test one, and of autonomous court movements towards strict liability in test two. Hence the simple question would be:

if the United States is left out of the regressions, what happens to the coefficients and the R^2? If they all drop down significantly in such a simple Chow-test, then the estimates in the chapter may not be much more than a quantification of a general US/rest-of-the world gap in judicial daring, which would be a result that is intuitively appealing but not very impressive in terms of theory testing.

3. In both econometric test runs, there is a certain inconsistency between the authors' theoretical argument and its translation into the model for testing purposes. In their theoretical reasoning, the authors argue – I think convincingly – that once a bargain is struck among a governing coalition, it does not much matter how many legislative vetoes exist, as long as they are all controlled by that coalition. If this is so, however, one should not enter a separate right-hand-side variable for legislative vetoes because it is not assumed to have an independent additive influence on judicial discretion.

   For example, adding further lower houses to the British parliament – all firmly controlled by the conservative party – should not be expected to raise the level of judicial discretion. On the other hand, adding more political instability should raise the level of judicial discretion, other things being equal; and the extent of this rise may depend on the number of houses, if the indecisiveness of the political process works through, say, different parties controlling different houses.

   Hence a theory-consistent specification may be to regress judicial discretion on an appropriate variable for political stability – expecting a positive sign, and the product of this variable and legislative vetoes – again expecting a positive sign, but not on legislative vetoes *per se*. Alas, any such specification may exacerbate the multicollinearity problem; but, clearly, the poor information content of the data should not lead to theoretical inconsistencies.

4. There are awesome measurement problems involved in the definition of some important variables. In my view, they go somewhat beyond what the authors mention in the chapter. Take average cabinet duration as an indicator for party dominance. Countries with a long post-war history of factual one-party dominance – Social Democrats in Sweden, Norway and Finland, Christian Democrats in Italy, Belgium, and Luxembourg, the Labour Party in Israel – have lived through many formal adjustments of ruling coalitions and thus show rather low average durations of coalition governments. However, a more rigorous analysis of the internal political equilibrium in these countries would probably show that there was more one-dominant-party-continuity in

> these countries than, say, in the UK and the US with their sharp, though infrequent changes of political establishments.

As to judicial discretion, the problems are obvious enough. It really goes beyond the limits of my imagination of how legal experts could consistently rank countries so diverse as Israel, Japan and Sweden in terms of judicial discretion – and this problem will be further exacerbated when the authors add further countries to the sample. For more prominent and historically similar legal systems like those of the US and the UK, this may still be possible. For most others, however, the experts' scepticism that the authors report looks to me well-taken.

The second test run is based on 20 countries and thus has a somewhat broader statistical basis. However, it suffers from a serious problem of identification and interpretation. This lies in the definition of the endogenous variable as, roughly speaking, the degree to which the judiciary preceded or even replaced the legislature in moving towards stricter liability.

Given the fact that virtually all countries moved in the direction of stricter liability, it is highly plausible that there is a common trend in all industrialised countries whose cause lies outside the model. One may speculate whether it was a change of preferences or fairness conceptions in the population at large or – the hypothesis I would prefer – a change of manufacturing technology that called for a new risk allocation. In any case, the legal system adjusted everywhere; the difference was only in who was first in initiating the change, the judiciary or the legislature.

If this is the case, however, the endogenous variable for the judicial role that the authors choose may be interpreted more as a proxy of the judicial alertness to changing trends in society (relative to the alertness of the political system) rather than a proxy for judicial discretion in the pursuit of autonomous political preferences of the judges. After all, why should the judges have a genuine preference for strict liability?

Hence the significant coefficients that the authors estimate may be no more than statistical support for the hypothesis that, for example, in those countries where there is no dominant disciplined party, it will be the judiciary rather than the political establishment which senses new trends. And there will of course be a nice private reward for this alertness because, given the trend, the judiciary will in the end be praised as the pioneer – as will be the political establishment in the country with the dominant disciplined party!

Let me conclude by repeating that this is a most interesting and courageous empirical chapter. To a large extent, its shortcomings are inevitable in a field where quantification is extremely difficult.

NOTE

1. Note that the number of experts asked is irrelevant for the number of observations in the regression. This is so for two reasons. (i) The experts' ratings were averaged for each country. (ii) even if they were not averaged, the informational content of the data for the regression would be constrained by the variation of the right-hand-side variables.

6. The Subsidiarity Principle and the EC Competition Rules: The Costs and Benefits of Decentralisation*

Roger van den Bergh

INTRODUCTION

The principle of subsidiarity, which is a central concept of the European Union Treaty, has put renewed emphasis on the virtues of decentralisation. The most detailed statement of the principle can be found in Article 3 B (2) of the EC-Treaty: 'In areas which do not fall within its exclusive competence, the Community shall take action, in accordance with the principle of subsidiarity, only if and in so far as the objectives of the proposed action cannot be sufficiently achieved by the member states and can therefore, by reason of the scale or effects of the proposed action, be better achieved by the Community.' Powers should thus be granted to the institutions of the European Community (EC), only when it has been established that they cannot be satisfactorily exercised by member states (except for matters falling within the exclusive competence[1] of the European Community institutions).

The principle of subsidiarity has been criticised because of its vagueness. It remains also unclear, to what extent judicial review by the European Court with respect to Community regulations that have been issued in violation of the principle is possible.[2] In this article the subsidiarity principle is taken seriously. It is considered necessary to ask fundamental questions about the role European institutions are playing and about their capacity to exercise the powers they enjoy in a way that enhances economic welfare. The opinion will be advanced that an economic analysis of the subsidiarity principle is

* This chapter was written during a stay at the Centre for Advanced Study of the Norwegian Academy of Sciences and Letters in Oslo. The author wishes to thank the Centre for excellent research opportunities.

particularly well suited to answer these questions. The wording of article 3 B (2) itself invites such an economic analysis: to justify the exercise of powers by European Community institutions 'the scale or effects of the proposed action' must be taken into account. This formulation allows for the consideration of scale economies and externalities; both factors are powerful efficiency arguments in favour of centralisation. Moreover, by stressing the need to take the effects of the proposed action into account, the EC Treaty itself rejects a pure legal formalistic approach. Because law on its own does not provide sufficiently accurate and reliable standards for evaluating the effects of legal rules, economic theory must be incorporated into the legal analysis. In contrast to the abundant legal literature on the subsidiarity principle,[3] which is only concerned about the internal consistency of the EC-Treaty, the economic analysis of the subsidiarity principle focuses on the consequences of the diffusion of powers between different levels of government for economic welfare in the European Community.

This chapter attempts to answer the question whether competition between legislators in the field of competition law is desirable from an efficiency viewpoint, and if so under what conditions. For the purposes of this discussion, competition law will be understood to mean the formulation and policing by the state of rules governing the competitive conduct of private actors. Rephrased in legal terms, the scope of the study comprises competition law *sensu stricto* (also denominated antitrust law), the laws banning 'unfair' competition and self-regulation of competitive behaviour by trade associations, supervised by the state. The term competition law is thus used in a broader sense than in much of the legal literature.[4] An economic analysis of the subsidiarity principle necessitates a scope of analysis, which is not limited by technical legal distinctions, such as the one between competition law *sensu stricto* (arguably efficiency oriented) and the law prohibiting unfair trade practices (allegedly fairness oriented). Also, self-regulation of competitive conduct must be incorporated into the analysis. Governments often grant executive powers to trade associations, which issue professional rules of conduct restricting competition.

For all three areas of law, the presumption of the subsidiarity principle is that member states are better able to issue and implement rules governing competitive conduct. As put by article 3 B (2) EC Treaty, *only if and in so far as* centralisation leads to superior (welfare) effects should the Community intervene. Decentralisation is to be preferred to centralisation as long as the benefits of competition between legal orders outweigh its costs. This chapter seeks to provide some useful insights into these costs and benefits as far as regulation of competitive behaviour is concerned. Its purpose is not to add to the economic literature, but to make the available economic know-how useful to law-makers. The first section of the chapter summarises the current state of the law. It will be investigated how decisionmaking powers in competition matters are diffused between the EC and the member states. The following sections of the chapter elaborate further upon the legal analysis, to find out whether the current allocation of competence fits with economic criteria. The second section addresses the benefits of decentralisation; the third section discusses the reasons for centralisation. In both sections the current diffusion of powers is confronted with the normative economic theory on (de)centralisation. Political realities may not be ignored when it comes to policy prescriptions. Differences in lobbying power that pressure groups can exert *vis-à-vis* the national and the supranational authorities may provide an explanation for the observed allocation of competence. Therefore, the fourth section of the chapter analyses the current allocation of tasks in competition matters from a Public Choice perspective. Finally, some conclusions are presented.

1. THE CURRENT DIFFUSION OF POWERS BETWEEN THE EC AND THE MEMBER STATES

1.1. Competition Law *sensu stricto*

Competition policy is not an exclusive competence of the EC. Member states have retained the power to enact own competition laws. There are, however, a number of qualifications to this rule. First, in the field of merger control, supervision by antitrust agencies of member states is excluded for mergers having a 'community dimension'. Secondly, the EC rules governing cartel agreements and abuses of dominant position apply to activities which 'affect trade between member states'. These terms are widely interpreted, so that EC competition rules will often take precedence over national competition laws because of the supremacy of Community law. Thirdly, there are great similarities between the EC competition rules and the competition laws of many member states. Besides from the substantive law, attention must also be paid to the allocation of tasks in the field of enforcement. As will be shown below, there is a remarkable combination of centralised rule-making and decentralised enforcement.

When mergers have to be supervised several times, legal uncertainty will increase, especially when the appraisal criteria differ across countries. To avoid double control, the EC Merger Regulation functions as a *one-stop-shop* for merger supervision. A choice of the applicable merger law is in principle excluded when the merger has a 'community dimension'. Mergers having a community dimension will be supervised only by the European Commission. In contrast, mergers that lack sufficient community impact will be controlled by national authorities only. A merger has a community dimension if two positively formulated conditions and one negatively worded requirement are met. First, the combined aggregate world-wide turnover of all the undertakings concerned must exceed 5,000 million ECU and the aggregate Community-wide turnover of each of at least two of the undertakings concerned must be more than ECU 250 million. Secondly, even if these thresholds are reached, the merger will not be supervised by the European Commission if each of the undertakings concerned achieves more than two-thirds of its aggregate Community-wide turnover within one and the same member state (Article 1 (2) Regulation 4064/89). Exceptions to these two principles are embodied in the so-called German and Dutch clauses. The German clause (Article 9) creates the possibility for a member state itself to control a merger falling under the EC Regulation, if it fears that a dominant position is created or strengthened in a distinct market within that state. The Dutch clause (Article 22(3)) allows member states without merger control regulations of their own to ask the Commission to supervise mergers that would otherwise fall below the thresholds.

The scope of this chapter does not allow for an in-depth discussion of the requirement that agreements only have significance under Articles 85–86 EC Treaty if they may affect trade between member states. For the purposes of the economic analysis of the subsidiarity principle, it may, however, suffice to indicate that the door for supervision by the European Commission remains open, even in cases in which there are no significant cross-border effects. Also purely national agreements may have effects on inter-state trade in the sense of Article 85 (1). The Commission, following the *Völk v. Vervaecke* judgement[5] issued a 'Notice concerning decisions and concerted practices of minor importance which do not fall under Article 85 (1) of the Treaty.[6] This document, however, does not have a major effect upon the interpretation of the phrase 'may affect trade between member states', for several reasons. The Notice does not bind the European Court or the national courts, which may also apply the EC competition rules. In addition, the Commission itself reserves an escape route by stating that the quantitative criteria given in the Notice do not constitute an absolute yardstick. Moreover, agreements may not be treated individually when there is a network of similar agreements. The European Court has decided that, in assessing whether an individual agreement is in breach of Article 85 (1), not simply the individual agreement but the entire context, both economic and legal, must be investigated.[7] The Court has pointed out also that the proper interpretation of the requirement of effect upon trade between member states is not simply one of preventing the partitioning of the market into separate national markets, but principally one of maintaining competition in a healthy state throughout the Common Market.[8]

For several years many member states did not have competition laws or, if such laws had been enacted, applied them with great discretion. In recent years several member states have introduced new competition laws, which are almost exact copies of the EC competition rules. Nowadays the national competition laws of Belgium, Greece, Italy, Portugal, Spain and Sweden look very much like European competition law. The Italian legislation is the most faithful copy of the EC competition rules. According to Article 2 of the Italian law vague concepts must be interpreted in conformity with the case-law of the European Commission and the European Court of Justice.[9] The number of member states where EC-like competition rules apply may increase in the near future. In the United Kingdom recent suggestions for reform of the present complex legislation advocate the adoption of EC-type rules.[10] Even in The Netherlands, which has long been considered 'a cartel paradise' because of the almost non-existent control on restrictions of competition, the Ministry of Economic Affairs is now seriously considering proposing to Parliament a new competition law based on the European approach. It is significant to add that many East European countries, anticipating future EC-membership, have already adopted competition laws based on the Articles 85–86 EC-Treaty.[11]

The European Commission increasingly solicits the help of national courts to enforce the EC competition rules.[12] This decentralised implementation of EC competition rules would follow from reasons of 'administrative efficiency'. The inadequate resources of the Commission in general, and of DG IV in particular,[13] necessitate that responsibility for the enforcement of competition policy within the Common Market is shared by Community competition authorities and national competition authorities. In practice national judges,[14] jointly with the European Commission, implement the EC competition rules. By using the additional resources of the national courts the general level of enforcement of these rules tends to increase.

The Commission's desire to see greater decentralised application of the EC competition rules is clearly expressed in its own policy document on decentralisation. In the 'Notice on co-operation between national courts and the Commission in applying Articles 85 and 86 of the EEC Treaty' it is stated that the Commission itself intends to concentrate on those matters which have 'particular political, economic or legal significance for the Community'.[15] According to the Commission, national judges should apply European competition rules when clear infringements can be established or solving the case requires the answer to technical legal questions only. Straightforward cases are those where there is a clear prohibition or where the rules are not applicable because of a block exemption.[16] In cases of doubt the judge may ask the Commission for advice. Doubts may arise as to whether concerted practices affect inter-state trade or may qualify for an exemption. The Commission is not only open to requests for information of a procedural nature. It may also be consulted on points of law and it will provide factual data to the national courts.[17] Although the Commission's advice is not binding, it is clear that in practice judges will attach much weight to it. It should be stressed that national judges are not empowered to grant exemptions on the basis of Article 85 (3) EC Treaty and are bound by exemptions granted by the Commission.[18] Since the Commission has the sole authority and enjoys a broad discretion to grant exemptions, it keeps the ultimate say concerning the most difficult issues of European competition policy.

1.2. The Laws Prohibiting 'Unfair' Competition and Self-regulation of Competitive Conduct

Traditionally there have been remarkable differences in the laws banning unfair trade practices, ranging from the sophisticated to the non-existent. In some member states, such as Germany and Belgium, very detailed rules with respect to the legality of marketing practices (for example, advertising and promotion) apply. In addition there is a general clause, allowing judges to prohibit certain types of business behaviour as 'unfair'. It is remarkable that German and Belgian judges consider themselves competent to decide upon the fairness of certain business practices without any hindrances. In the United Kingdom the tradition is remarkably different. The legal discipline of unfair competition law still does not exist. General clauses are viewed with disapproval. The words of a senior judge in 1889 still apply: 'To draw a line between fair and unfair competition, between what is reasonable and unreasonable passes the power of the courts.'[19] Up until now differences in the laws restricting unfair competition across member states of the EC are greater than the remaining differences in competition laws *sensu stricto*. In the law of unfair trade practices there has not been a similar trend of 'spontaneous harmonisation'. Moreover, direct harmonisation by means of Directives has remained limited.[20]

Trade associations may also regulate competitive conduct. In all member states the privilege of self-regulation is enjoyed by the liberal arts, although the scope for professional rules differs. Medical doctors, attorneys and other 'professions' have succeeded in convincing governments that the quality of their services can only be guaranteed through the granting of monopoly rights and the imposition of professional ethics. Potential professionals must seek a licence from a regulatory body (for example, the 'Order' of attorneys) to undertake a regulated activity.[21] Ethical rules governing all aspects of professional conduct (including prices) have been issued by public professional bodies. After approval by a government minister or some independent authority, the rules are binding and apply to all suppliers in the regulated market. Self-regulatory agencies may exploit their regulatory powers to establish anti-competitive conditions and thus generate rents for existing practitioners. There is ample evidence that this has happened in the markets for medical and legal services.[22] In some European countries (United Kingdom, The Netherlands) governments have responded to the abuse of the self-regulatory powers by introducing liberalisation measures. For example, there have been efforts to transform prior approval regimes into certification systems, which allow for greater consumer choice. However, the degree of liberalisation varies across countries and some national markets (Germany, Belgium) remain heavily regulated.

The scope for national rules imposing 'fairness' in competitive behaviour was limited for a long time because of the requirement of proportionality put forward by the European Court of Justice in cases concerning free movement of goods within the EC. Recently more scope for rules prohibiting 'unfair competition' (and thus necessarily restricting competition) has been created. The French prohibition of sales to consumers at loss prices was challenged before the European Court of Justice, on the ground that it was likely to hinder free movement of goods between member states. The European Court took the opportunity to undertake a remarkable change in direction. Until the *Keck and Mithouard* decision Article 30 EC Treaty which applies not only to outright quantitative import restrictions but to all 'measures having equivalent effect' was broadly interpreted. Since the 1979 *Cassis de Dijon* judgement,[23] the prohibition in Article 30 has also been held to be applicable to non-discriminatory measures. Measures applying to both national and imported products without distinction could be struck down when an additional difficulty for imports was demonstrable. The prohibition was to be applied in a reasonable way, however. Under the *rule of reason* non-discriminatory measures only violate Article 30 if they do not serve a purpose which is in the general interest and as such take precedence over the requirement of the free movement of goods. Bans on 'unfair competition' and legal rules aimed at consumer protection could be justified as necessary to attain a goal of public interest. Additionally, if such rules did not cause a disproportionate effect on imports, they could withstand the prohibition of Article 30. The impact of the non-discriminatory measures on inter-state trade was assessed on a case-by-case basis. The resulting case law of the European Court of Justice was not always consistent.[24] Consequently it became difficult to predict what national regulations would fall under the prohibition of Article 30. The result was a growing legal uncertainty: in the first place it became almost unpredictable whether an impact on inter-state trade would be established. If the European Court did find such effect, a further uncertainty arose with respect to the justification under the *rule of reason*. In the *Keck and Mithouard* decision the Court distinguishes between measures regulating production and national rules which restrict or prohibit certain 'selling arrangements'. Whereas rules of the first category remain within the reach of the prohibition of Article 30 (and the *rule of reason*), national rules of the latter category are no longer considered as measures having equivalent effect.[25] In a later case the European Court of Justice has confirmed that the new learning also applies to rules of conduct issued by professional bodies. A prohibition to advertise non-medical products imposed by a Professional Chamber of Pharmacists was held compatible with the principle of free movement of goods within the EC.[26]

2. BENEFITS OF DECENTRALISATION

Economic arguments in favour of decentralisation follow from the economics of federalism, which deals with the allocation of functions between different levels of government. Put simply, the message of economic federalism is that competition between sellers of laws may be analogised to competition between sellers of 'ordinary' products. Legislators compete just as sellers of cars or toothpaste do. People may 'vote with their feet' (Tiebout)[27] by moving to the jurisdiction where the laws are best adapted to their preferences. Theory tells us that, if competition between sellers of products may lead to allocative efficiency, the same beneficial results may be reached when legislators compete. A competitive equilibrium will ensue, but only if imperfections on the market for competition laws do not impede efficient outcomes. It will be shown below that in reality the conditions for Tiebout-competition are not met. Market imperfections which may necessitate centralisation to improve upon efficiency will be discussed in the next section. A preference for decentralisation also follows from the need to cope with informational asymmetries. In legal commentaries a greater involvement of national antitrust authorities, especially judges, in the enforcement of the competition rules is defended for reasons of administrative efficiency. This argument may be criticised because it neglects transition costs, which may be substantial. The need to cope with asymmetric information seems to be a more powerful argument in favour of decentralised enforcement. Finally, arguments in favour of competition between legal rules follow from a dynamic approach. Competition is a learning process; differences in rules allow for different experiences and may improve an understanding of the effects of alternative legal solutions to similar problems. This advantage relates both to the formulation of the substantive rules and enforcement.

2.1. From Tiebout's World to Reality

A case could be made for divergent competition laws, because preferences may differ with respect to the goals to be achieved (allocative efficiency or rather distributive goals). Moreover, in Europe state territories were, and still are, distinct economic entities bearing their particular market characteristics. Both firms and consumers may wish competition laws reflecting these differences. However, as it is the case on markets for ordinary goods and services, to ensure efficiency competition requires a large number of competitors. In theory, in the European Community a choice among 15 different competition laws is possible. In practice, the choice is more limited. Three reasons for this reduction of the number of alternative legal rules to choose between have been indicated above. There is no scope for competition between antitrust agencies for controlling the mergers achieving the largest turnovers. A further limitation on the choice between competing rules of competition law is the broad interpretation of the requirement in Articles 85 and 86 EC-Treaty that inter-state trade must be negatively affected. Finally, it should be obvious that the transplantation of EC rules into the national legal orders restricts the choice between competition laws. A choice among 15 rules already seems to be rather small to guarantee that any competitor will find the competition rules that best suit his needs. When member states copy each other's legislation this choice is further limited. To generate efficient outcomes, competition in the market for competition laws requires a sufficient number of sellers of competition rules. Instead of creating the conditions for Tiebout-competition, the current trend of 'spontaneous harmonisation' is rather moving away from the conditions to reach a competitive equilibrium.

In addition, efficient competition between legislators according to Tiebout's theory supposes that the 'buyers' of legislation select among the competing sellers by moving to the place where the legal rules are better. The question thus arises whether firms are able to move to states that have adopted competition laws that better suit their preferences. Mobility of firms requires mobility of capital, goods and workers. Obviously capital is more mobile than labour. For citizens the decision to migrate is dependent upon family ties and friendships. Moreover, in Europe many movements are still retarded by linguistic and cultural differences. Barriers to mobility within Europe in terms of language and culture are more significant for goods than for capital and for labour they will be the most significant of all. Because mobility of firms requires mobility of capital, goods and labour, one should be cautious of advocating competition between legal orders as long as actual mobility remains modest. In the United States and Canada competition on markets for legislation may be more potent, because mobility barriers are less important. So far the figures available about movements within EC countries show that mobility is moderate at best.[28] It remains to be seen how these figures will evolve in the future. On the one hand a number of factors may increase mobility: the removal of physical barriers,[29] and the mutual recognition of diplomas and educational degrees.[30] On the other hand different factors, such as the convergence of real wages in an economic and monetary union and the possible harmonisation of income taxation and social security may have the opposite effect.[31] In the field of competition policy a generous treatment of mergers across borders by the European Commission may also increase mobility. Managers working at the headquarters are generally more mobile (linguistic barriers are less severe for them) than other workers, who do not necessarily have to move or may be newly hired.

2.2. Informational Asymmetries

Tiebout's theory supposes that the buyers of legal rules understand the differences between alternative legal rules and are thus able to make an informed choice. For firms this requirement may be met, because they will be able to rely on specialists' advice in case of uncertainty. Consumers will face greater difficulties in assessing differences in legal rules.

Information asymmetries may also exist between regulatory authorities and the regulated firms. The latter asymmetry of information may be analysed as a principal–agent problem.[32] Competition authorities (both national and supranational) have an information disadvantage *vis-à-vis* the firms they have to control; the former may be seen as the principals and the latter as the agents. Out of self-interest the agents may be unwilling to reveal all the information needed by the principals. A related danger is the communication of false information. It may be argued that it is more difficult for firms to hide or misrepresent information to decentralised agencies than to a more remote agency. Information provided by firms may be cross-checked against information from competitors, consumer organisations and official sources. If such cross-checking is difficult, local agencies will still have a better view of the market than a supranational antitrust agency. Decentralisation may thus be advocated, because it reduces the agency problem.

There is, naturally, also an intermediate solution between full decentralisation and full centralisation. Decentralised information gathering can help to remove much of the information asymmetry faced by centralised antitrust agencies. Under current EC-law member states have an obligation to cooperate with the investigation procedures of the Commission. The Commission is empowered to obtain all necessary information from both governments and competent authorities of member states as well as from undertakings and associations within those member states.[33] Moreover, the competent authorities of member states may be asked to carry out on-the-spot investigations on the Commission's behalf.[34] This power has never been used,[35] but may become important in the future. When the Commission carries out its own investigations, it may require the assistance of national authorities.[36] There are similar provisions in the Merger Regulation.[37]

An obvious alternative for the choice between centralisation and decentralisation is the co-existence of national and supranational procedures. In a recent paper Smets and Van Cayseele (1995) explain why it could be profitable to have such a combination. Different national competition authorities may cooperate and exchange information, so that the mark-ups due to information asymmetries on production costs are reduced and that it becomes more difficult for the firms not to reveal the amount of profits repatriated to the headquarters of the post-merger firm. There is, however, a danger of cheating and keeping information secret when national authorities try to promote national industries. In addition, the danger of regulatory capture[38] may increase if industrial lobby groups are more powerful on the national level. Hence there is a need for an additional supranational authority that controls the national authorities to limit lobbying. When the supranational authority acts as a controller, the problem becomes a multiple agent problem. One principal (the supranational authority) delegates the policy decision to different agents (the national authorities that have an informational advantage). The national authorities will become players in a game that only the best can win. According to Smets and Van Cayseele the best regulatory structure for antitrust policy is, therefore, to have different national authorities trying to cooperate and exchange information. In addition, a second tier, supranational authority is necessary for cases with a certain magnitude and as a control on national authorities.[39]

The current allocation of competence between the national antitrust authorities and the European Commission only partially conforms to the optimal regulatory structure suggested above. In Article 85-86 cases (including cooperative mergers) the Commission keeps the ultimate say in cases having particular legal or economic significance. The *one-stop-shop* principle in current European merger law, however, does not allow the European Commission to act as a controller of the national authorities. Therefore, for those concentrative mergers that fall below the Community thresholds, regulatory capture must be combated at the national level.

The need to cope with asymmetric information is a more powerful argument in favour of decentralised enforcement than the argument concerning 'administrative efficiency' advanced in the legal literature. In assessing changes of the rules relating to enforcement, the transition costs may not be neglected. In many member states national judges have minimal knowledge of or experience in applying EC competition law. One cannot expect national judges to have developed the same skills and expertise as members of the Commission who have been working in the field for many years. A highly evolved decentralisation requires thorough additional training, to make judges better aware of all relevant legal and economic issues. The transplant of EC-like competition rules in the legal orders of the member states and the establishment of new national antitrust authorities has already caused substantial transition costs: for instance, in Belgium national administrative judges and bureaucrats were trained by EC bureaucrats. From an efficiency viewpoint, decentralisation should not be pursued if the costs of transition outweigh its benefits. Quantifying costs and benefits is a difficult thing to do. As far as decentralised implementation is concerned, the costs may be more easily quantified than the benefits. It is clear that the Commission did not undertake such a cost–benefit analysis to justify its reliance upon national judges in the enforcement of Articles 85–86 of the EC Treaty.

The argument relating to 'administrative efficiency' also starts from the assumption that enforcement by national judges will be effective. There are reasons to doubt the effectiveness of decentralised enforcement. First, there will be significant differences across member states. It is well-known that UK judges are rather reluctant to adopt an active role in EC competition law enforcement. Secondly, the costs involved in proceeding with an action before national courts tend to be higher than the cost incurred in taking the matter to the Commission. The Commission hopes that the prospect of damages, which are unavailable at the Community level, will attract potential complainants to their own national courts. In reality, however, damages are not readily available. Procedures to obtain damages are more cumbersome (relative to injunctive relief) and the amount awarded will be rather low due to problems of proof. Thirdly, remedies awarded by a national court only take effect in the member state in which the court is based. In sum, the Commission's proposition that 'greater effectiveness on the part of the national courts has a general advantage in that it reflects the spirit of the subsidiarity principle'[40] is arguably flawed.

A final remark with respect to a decentralised implementation of competition law should be made. In the legal literature the suggestion has been made to increase the role of national antitrust authorities in the implementation of EC competition rules.[41] This proposal must be criticised. There are good reasons to limit the devolution of powers to national judges. National antitrust authorities do not have the same task as the European Commission. They apply national rules which are sometimes remarkably different from the EC rules. Not all member states copied Articles 85–86 and the Merger Regulation. Germany, France, the United Kingdom, Denmark and The Netherlands have different solutions to some controversial antitrust problems, although the scope of these national rules is limited because of the broad interpretation of the requirement of impact on interstate trade. National antitrust authorities may also be captured by national interest groups (see 4.1).

2.3. Competition as a Learning Process

As stated by von Hayek, competition is the most effective discovery procedure which leads to the finding of better ways for the pursuit of human aims.[42] Competition between legal orders promotes the search for new legal arrangements that might be adopted by other states or by the central rule-maker itself. If states do not amend their codes in response to another state's innovation, they run the risk that firms will move to the state which is most responsive to firms' and consumers' demands for legislation. Such a competition between legal orders does not imply that rules will greatly differ, so that transaction costs and especially uncertainty as to the law will increase. The result of the process of innovation and subsequent amendment may be a substantial uniformity across the states. Competition between legal orders and uniformity are not mutually exclusive. Whereas harmonisation by means of centralised rules (EC Regulations and Directives) implies forced coordination of national legislative provisions, dynamic competitive processes may produce voluntary harmonisation. The scope of such a voluntary harmonisation may be larger than the degree of uniformity brought about by centralisation. Directives, for example, often contain escape clauses or grant the member states a number of options to choose between, that impede full harmonisation. If states voluntarily choose to adapt their legislation to superior rules of competing states, a greater degree of uniformity may be reached.

It was mentioned above that many member states have adapted their national competition laws to the EC competition rules, contained in Articles 85–86 and Regulation 4064/89. This raises the interesting question whether this 'spontaneous harmonisation' may be seen as the result of a dynamic competitive process between different legal orders. There are reasons to doubt that the member states copied the EC rules because of their superior quality as allocative efficiency enhancing mechanisms. The main argument in favour of the adoption of the EC rules was the strongly perceived need for legal certainty. This argument will be criticised below; in section 4.1 it will be argued that this argument is used by pressure groups profiting from uniform rules across the EC.

The current 'spontaneous harmonisation' inhibits trial-and-error processes in the area of competition law *sensu stricto*, where learning-by-doing is very important. The EC competition rules and procedures may be criticised in many respects: they are not very accurate and often rely on qualitative hunches where quantitative evidence is available; they do not pay sufficient attention to the achievement of production efficiencies and may lead to effects which are exactly opposite to the goals for which they were enacted. The limited format of this chapter does not allow for an extensive discussion of the inefficiencies, inconsistencies and adverse effects of current EC competition law. Readers who are sufficiently interested (or provoked) are advised to read another paper by this author.[43]

For the purposes of this chapter, it suffices to briefly demonstrate that in several fields national competition laws do a better job. Again, the scope of this chapter does not allow for an extensive discussion. Two examples, taken from German competition law (*Gesetz gegen Wettbewerbsbeschränkungen,* (*GWB*)) must suffice. In contrast with Article 85 EC Treaty, the German *GWB* clearly distinguishes between horizontal and vertical agreements. At the outset it seems rather odd to qualify vertical restrictions, contained in contracts between manufacturers and distributors, as agreements restricting competition, because manufacturers and dealers are not competitors. Only in rare circumstances, when markets are concentrated and significant entry barriers exist, may vertical restraints endanger competition. Therefore, a control of vertical restraints *ex post* by means of an abuse principle, as it exists under German law, seems preferable to submitting vertical restraints to a prohibition principle, as is the case under current EC competition law.[44] The anti-competitive effects of horizontal agreements are much more worrisome than the limited foreclosure effects of vertical restrictions. The treatment of vertical restrictions under EC law is also at the same time inconsistent and ineffective: fully integrated firms are allowed to implement almost any contract internally, whereas the legality of vertical agreements between independent firms depends upon the legal form.[45] A second example relates to merger control. Under EC merger control, the danger of oligopoly does not get sufficient attention. The Merger Regulation does not explicitly allow for the possibility of oligopolistic behaviour. In German competition law there is a presumption that three or fewer enterprises having the highest market shares are presumed each to be market-dominating if together they have a market share of at least 50 per cent. In EC law there is no such presumption and the Commission faces great difficulties in proving that mergers would create a situation of oligopolistic dominance. It took until the recent decision in the *Nestlé/Perrier* case to establish as a precedent the ability of the Commission to control collective as well as single firm dominance. The Commission's decision was appealed before the Court of Justice, but the case was decided upon procedural grounds, so that no further clarification on the problem of controlling collective dominance was provided.[46] These two examples illustrate how a comparison with national competition laws may reveal that the EC competition rules are either over-inclusive or under-inclusive. Such learning processes are excluded if competition rules are made uniform throughout the entire Common Market.

3. REASONS FOR CENTRALISATION

In this section a number of arguments in favour of centralisation will be addressed. When state territories are smaller than economic territories, central rules will be required to internalise external effects. Also scale economies or transaction cost savings may require large jurisdictions. If such economies are important, harmonisation of legal rules may be necessary to create legal orders of an optimal geographical size. To justify central European rules, the argument is often advanced that disparities in legislation may create unequal conditions of competition and hamper the functioning of the Common Market. In this view differences in competition law and policy are to be avoided for the sake of competition itself. The reasoning goes that states may engage in a 'race for the bottom' to attract firms. If legislators compete under *prisoners' dilemma* conditions, too lax competition rules may ensue. Centralisation is seen as a remedy to overcome the inefficiencies of prisoners' dilemmas. These arguments will be critically assessed now.

3.1. Externalities

In the field of environmental policy, the externalities problem is a major argument in favour of centralisation.[47] Externalities also occur in competition law and policy. The approval of a merger by member state A may have negative effects in member states B and C. The question then arises whether the merger should be controlled by the antitrust authorities of the three member states or by a central European authority. Cartel agreements may be concluded by firms residing in different member states. A firm may enjoy a dominant position in member state A and try to extend this position by means of exclusionary practices in member state B. Also in the last two cases the question arises whether the practices should be subjected to antitrust scrutiny in one or both of the member states or, alternatively, may be better controlled by a supranational antitrust authority. Finally, some types of competitive conduct (for example, comparative advertising or aggressive sales promotion) also occur outside the territory where the firm has its head office. Also in the latter case, the question arises whether several prohibitions of unfair competition and self-regulatory rules of conduct should apply at the same time or the business conduct should be governed by the same central rule of law.

At the outset it should be made clear that, contrary to competing national environmental regulations, decentralised competition laws are able to cope with negative external effects. A downstream member state cannot use a veto right to ban emissions from an upstream member state. In contrast, mergers that would allow firms to extract consumer surplus abroad will not pass without the consent of the antitrust authority of the harmed country. Under competing national antitrust laws mergers having extra-territorial effects will be controlled by the competition authorities of all member states involved. The externality problem in competition law is thus not comparable to the spillover effects in the field of environmental policy. The same reasoning applies with respect to cartel agreements and abusive practices by dominant firms. For the different national competition laws to apply, it suffices that anti-competitive effects occur on the territory of the supervising member state. Of course, such a supervision is only possible if the member states have an own competition law. Whereas when the Treaty of Rome was first signed, there was no member state which had a competition law of a comprehensive nature and proven effectiveness, today rare is the member state without its own competition law and in many cases, though not all, an increasing determination in its enforcement.[48] Finally, unfair trade practices may also be banned by all member states in which they occur. The principle of *lex locus delicti* implies that in cases of multi-state commerce each domestic market will apply its own law.[49]

In most of the legal literature the necessity to cope with externalities is not explicitly mentioned as a reason to introduce a centralised competition policy. To lawyers legal certainty is a much more powerful motive. As will be indicated below, legal certainty cannot on its own justify centralisation. Lawyers should therefore realise that international spillover effects between jurisdictions provide a solid case for central rule-making. Transactions with substantial externalities must be supervised by antitrust authorities to prevent a bias in favour of national interests. Significant cross-border effects will not be adequately internalised by national agencies: 'typically the costs of market power to foreign customers will be given less weight than the rents of market power to domestic interests.'[50] An excessively national focus in the control of such mergers may thus lead to distorted judgements. Starting from the insight that externalities are a powerful argument in favour of centralisation, the case for EC merger control will be stronger as the externalities' problem becomes more significant. As mentioned above, the scale of the parties to the transaction is crucial for determining whether the merger will be supervised by the European Commission. The combined world-wide turnover of the parties must exceed ECU 5 billion and at least two of them must have an EC-wide turnover exceeding ECU 250 million. Moreover, mergers between firms conducting two-thirds or more of their business in one and the same member state fall outside the scope of the Regulation. Consequently the relevant consideration is the scale of the transaction and not the magnitude of the spillovers, measured by a certain absolute sum. Neven, Nuttall and Seabright argue that it would be more natural to let the absolute size of the spillovers determine whether the EC Merger Regulation should apply. Small transactions may have substantial spillovers, which will not always appropriately be considered by national antitrust authorities. To avoid this kind of distortion, they suggest a threshold requiring that of the world-wide annual turnover, half of the turnover within the EC must take place outside the member state with the largest share of the combined turnover.[51] Such a rule would better enable the EC to investigate transactions that give rise to significant international spillovers.

As it is the case for mergers with substantial spillovers, cartel agreements and abuses of dominant position may also be better controlled by a centralised antitrust agency if significant cross-border effects occur. A centralised supervision will mitigate both judgements biased in favour of national interests and difficulties of monitoring co-operation between competing antitrust authorities. The thresholds of the EC Merger Regulation may be seen as an attempt to limit intervention by the centralised authority to cases which may not be appropriately dealt with by national agencies. It was mentioned above that the regulation does not adequately reach this goal, because the scale of the transactions is not the best way of determining the magnitude of the spillovers. Though not perfect, the thresholds may nevertheless avoid a too broad scope of community intervention. This is unfortunately not the case for the control of cartel agreements and abusive practices by dominant firms. In these fields the boundary between community competition law and that of the member states is the requirement that the agreements or practices 'may affect trade between member states' (Article 85 (1) EC-Treaty). This expression has been widely interpreted by the European Court of Justice (see 1.1). The very broad interpretation brings many agreements of an apparently domestic nature within the reach of the prohibition. It has enabled the Commission to exercise jurisdiction in a number of areas, where the degree of effect on trade between member states appears to be minor. A few examples may illustrate this point. According to the case-law of the European Court of Justice, the Commission has jurisdiction over nation-wide distribution systems reducing the attractiveness of market entry for importers,[52] aggregate rebate systems discouraging the imports of foreign products[53] and refusals to supply local retailers without objective justification.[54] The latter case is the most dramatic example of the use of EC competition rules to combat restrictive practices without any international spillovers. The market affected was clearly national (even local) with at most minor effects on imports or exports. Also with respect to the other cases the argument may be advanced that the costs of market power were borne by the consumers of the country to which exports were discouraged. Therefore, it seems more natural to have the foreclosure effects controlled by the antitrust agencies of the import country. In this respect, it is interesting to mention that on some occasions EC competition rules provide scope for a more stringent control by national authorities if the anti-competitive effects of the agreements consist mainly in the foreclosure of national markets. Thus the group exemption on exclusive purchasing permits national legislatures or competition authorities to impose stricter limits upon the period for which service station exclusive purchasing agreements may be permitted.[55] It is remarkable that the same freedom is not explicitly provided for with respect to similar arrangements in beer supply agreements and for exclusive purchasing agreements in general.[56]

Spillovers due to 'unfair' trade practices may be combated by the member states in which they occur, thanks to the principle of *lex loci delicti.* In the fields where harmonisation was brought about by Directives, the need for uniformity was motivated by other reasons. The Commission feared that divergence would lead to a distortion of competitive conditions in the member states. Such distortion may occur if competition between legal rules causes a 'race for the bottom'. In the latter case member states behave as prisoners in the famous *prisoners' dilemma.* This problem will be discussed below (see 3.3). Other arguments for EC intervention may be the informational advantages of the Community legislator (see 3.2) or simply the wish of the EC bureaucracies to maximise their budget and gain additional prestige.

3.2. Scale Economies and Transaction Cost Savings

The new national competition laws, which are almost identical with the EC competition rules, were welcomed by the great majority of lawyers and business people. The argument in favour of uniformity rests on the strongly perceived need for legal certainty. In spite of the efforts of legal realism to show that discretion is always present, the myth of legal certainty is still very much kept alive by European lawyers. The reasoning goes that if competition laws varied across member states, more uncertainty as to the precise contents of competition rules would result. Different rules or interpretations make the outcome of antitrust proceedings less predictable. If European competition law was the only yardstick, legal certainty would follow from the Community antitrust practice. Although legal certainty may be rephrased in economic terms as a factor that reduces information costs, there are serious problems with the argument. A wholesale adoption of the EC competition rules necessarily entails the importation of the inefficiencies that are inherent in them. To put it simply: lawyers might feel happy with certainty about the contents of inefficient rules. The reduction of information costs is only one part of the economic analysis; another part is the assessment of incentive costs due to legal rules that may induce inefficient behaviour or simply ban efficient conduct. These inefficiencies may outweigh any savings on information costs. An analysis that only considers information costs and neglects incentive costs is necessarily incomplete. Moreover, economic analysis has shown that inefficient rules will be challenged in the courts.[57] Inefficiencies may also induce lobbying with the regulator to change the rules to the benefit of interest groups only. The history of the European group exemptions illustrates that powerful interest groups, such as the car manufacturers, were able to get approval of their distribution agreements by the Commission.[58] These agreements contain restrictions on competition, which are generally not accepted by the Commission, even though they may be justifiable because of free-riding concerns.[59] The possibility of obtaining block exemptions restricted to specific sectors of the industry invites additional rent-seeking. Given the degree of discretion enjoyed by decisionmakers and the risks of regulatory capture (see 4.2), the adoption of inefficient rules will therefore increase legal uncertainty, instead of reducing it.

From an efficiency viewpoint centralisation to solve information problems may be defended because of scale economies or transaction cost savings. If scale economies are important, central rule-making may be required. National defence is an obvious example; this public good could not be efficiently provided by local communities. Scale economies may also be important in the production of the information needed to formulate legal rules. Some information relevant to the entire European Community can be most efficiently provided by Community institutions. Uniform rules also maintain economies of scale in production and distribution arrangements. If diversity in rules prohibits firms from using the same production and marketing techniques in larger areas, scale economies may be lost. The well-known 1992 Programme aimed at the removal of technical barriers caused by divergence in national regulations. The savings resulting from this removal were estimated to be substantial, although different in magnitude across industries.

In the legal literature no arguments of legal certainty are advanced that reveal significant scale economies in the field of competition policy. The arguments rather point in the direction of transaction cost savings. The relevant question is then whether transaction costs of diversity in rules outweigh the benefits. Under uniform Community regulation, firms and consumers must not expend resources on search costs. They do not have to inform themselves about differences in the substantive law of the member states and the way in which these rules are enforced. These transaction cost savings may be very important for firms that are active in inter-state commerce. Uniformity tends also to produce a more stable and predictable jurisprudence.[60] However, before concluding in favour of centralisation, the costs of uniformity must be taken into account. Currently these costs are quite substantial because of the inefficiencies inherent in EC competition law (see 2.3).

3.3. Prisoners' Dilemmas

Competition between legislators is often criticised because it would cause a 'race for the bottom'. When the European Commission proposes harmonisation of laws, it usually refers to the need to prevent inequality of competitive conditions across the member states. This fear may be rephrased in economic terms as the danger of *prisoners' dilemmas*.

States may operate, not in a market-like setting, but in a prisoners' dilemma game. When legislators can be analogised to firms selling in a competitive market, decentralised rules may be preferable. In contrast, when states compete under prisoners' dilemma conditions national rules will produce a result that is worse than a federal rule.[61] The relevant question is whether states may try to attract business through a lax competition policy. Laxness may occur when substantive rules have to be enacted and may also occur at the implementation stage. A state will only gain in the struggle to attract business by choosing in favour of laxness, when other states do not act in the same way. However, if all other states follow, only the businesses will gain. The result of this prisoners' dilemma game is a race for the bottom and centralisation may be required to generate efficient outcomes. In the USA the question of whether competition between legislators may cause a race for the bottom has been heavily discussed with respect to corporate law. For a long time it was thought that Delaware led the 'race for the bottom' to attract corporations. More recent research questions this belief and argues that the race has been for the top, rather than for the bottom.[62] In Europe, competition on the market for corporate charters is excluded by the 'real seat rule'. There is not a similar rule with respect to competition law. Hence, the danger of prisoners' dilemmas must be investigated further.

For this chapter the relevant question is whether competition on the market for competition law may lead to a result which benefits firms, but harms society at large. What would a race for the bottom on the market for competition law look like? Easterbrook suggests the following wish list for firms in search of monopoly profits. First on the list would be a monopoly protected by the state but not regulated in any other way. Second on the list would be a cartel enforced by the state. Third on the list would be a law lifting the antitrust laws.[63] Current EC law limits the scope for member states to grant firms any of these wishes. Existing state protected monopolies have been deregulated, including markets which were long considered natural monopolies.[64] Cartels protected and enforced by state regulation may be combated on the basis of a combined use of the Articles 3(g), 5 and 85 EC-Treaty.[65] Member states may not adopt or maintain in force any measure which could deprive the competition rules of their effectiveness. Following this principle, the European Court of Justice struck down several national regulations restricting competition, such as the Belgian rule requiring travel agents to observe the prices laid down by tour operators and prohibiting the granting of rebates to consumers.[66] Price restrictions may also be considered as measures having an equivalent effect contrary to the Articles 30 and 34 EC Treaty.[67] A complete lifting of national antitrust laws seems unrealistic. However, there are different statutory traditions in Europe. Countries adopting the *abuse principle* rather than the *prohibition principle* are often qualified as 'cartel paradises'.[68] Today Denmark and The Netherlands are the only countries which still have an abuse principle, rather than a prohibition principle. Under the former, restrictive agreements are valid until the competition authority is able to prove that any particular agreement constitutes an abuse, and then with prospective effect only. Under the latter, agreements are prohibited and exemptions only possible after notification. In addition, private parties may also sue in court. These divergent systems reflect differences in the support for the competition principle.

In addition to the rules mentioned above, which substantially reduce the risk of destructive competition on the markets for competition laws, attention must be drawn to other rules which may have the opposite effect. Some rules increase the scope for prisoners' dilemmas rather than reducing it. Although the diffusion of powers between antitrust authorities has been fixed by the Merger Regulation and the free choice of the controlling agency has consequently been limited, in practice firms may seek to change the contents or the form of the contemplated transactions in order to have them controlled by a preferred antitrust agency.[69] Although the prospect of alternative jurisdictions will presumably be a relatively minor consideration in the majority of deals where the commercial rationale dominates, these considerations may matter at the margin. If control of a merger by the

European Commission is preferred to control by national antitrust authorities, a (presumably large) minority partner may be added to increase the turnover of the undertakings concerned and make the merger a matter for the Community authorities. The European Commission may be the preferred agency when national antitrust authorities treat potentially anti-competitive mergers more strictly. It is for instance remarkable that German firms prefer the EC system to that of the Bundeskartellamt.[70] Also, changing the form of the contemplated transaction may create scope for 'forum shopping'. With respect to joint ventures there is some evidence that firms have changed the form of the joint venture, because they wanted it to count as concentrative.[71] The Commission issued a Notice to inform parties about the characteristics which qualify the contemplated transactions either as concentrative or as co-operative.[72] The latter qualification brings the transactions within the scope of Article 85 EC Treaty. Procedures under Article 85 are more cumbersome: they are open ended and tend to be lengthy; their implementation is perceived to be rather more inflexible and decisions have limited duration, whereas there is no time limit under the Merger Regulation.[73] It must be stressed that changes to the form of the transactions add to the indirect costs of the merger control. The trend to change the form of the joint venture to make it concentrative is worrisome. The Commission's current policy induces firms to engage in concentrations which tend to be durable, rather than in cartel agreements which are unstable by their very nature. Since the *one-stop-shop principle* excludes control of mergers by member states above the Community thresholds, the current lax European merger control[74] may favour substantial increases of the concentration ratios in many European industries. In sum, in the field of merger control there remains some scope for tailoring deals which preserves competition between legal rules, even where the choice of jurisdiction is supposed to be excluded. This competition may concern both the choice of the supervising agency as well as the control procedure.

Is there a risk of destructive competition in the treatment of cartel agreements and dominant firms? Because of the very wide interpretation of the phrase 'trade between member states', there are not many agreements of commercial significance which remain outside the range of Community law. In general agreements must satisfy both Article 85 and national law. If the agreement is forbidden by Article 85(1), the rule of supremacy of EC law makes national exemptions impossible. In such a case member states can not 'undersell' each other (race for the bottom) in allowing anti-competitive practices. In the converse case, where the cartel is outside the scope of the European prohibition[75], national authorities are still free to intervene, so that competition between competition laws remains possible. This competition may be for the 'top', instead of being a race for the bottom. If the agreement has been exempted under Article 85(3), either because the Commission has given an individual exemption or when a Regulation containing a group exemption applies, the national courts and competition authorities may not disregard the terms of the exemption. Hence, there is no scope for the application of a different and stricter national solution and competition on the market for competition laws is again excluded.

Also, outside the field of merger control, deals may be tailored differently to bring them within the reach of preferred alternative competition rules. For example, firms may choose in favour of a franchising formula instead of a selective distribution network, not because of reasons of efficient organisation of production and distribution but only because a group exemption applies for the former[76] and not for the latter formula. Distorted business decisions may not be excluded when firms choose the form of the transaction because of the more lenient treatment of a less efficient alternative.

After having focused on competition law *sensu stricto,* the danger of a 'race for the bottom' in the field of unfair competition and self-regulation must now be assessed. The applicability of the EC rules regarding free movement of goods creates an important escape route for national legislation restricting competition. In the *Keck and Mithouard* decision the French legislation prohibiting sales at loss prices was held compatible with Article 30 EC-Treaty, which provides for free movement of goods. Rules prohibiting sales at loss prices are part of the law against unfair competition. This judgement of the Court of Justice shows that inefficiencies may occur, when technical legal categories determine the outcome of cases. The prohibition of sales at loss prices is a surrogate for a hardly feasible cartel of retailers. There is no sound economic reason to differentiate between national legislation prohibiting price reductions and the qualification of such reductions as unfair competition. When rules against unfair competition are judged on the basis of Article 30 EC Treaty, leaving articles 3(g), 5 and 85 EC Treaty aside, different forms of cartel-like regulation will continue to be in existence. A list includes the following dramatic examples: price-undercutting, prohibition of comparative advertising, in particular price comparisons, and rules limiting the opening hours of shops. Thus, in the field of competition law *sensu stricto* some scope for a 'race for the bottom' remains.

It may be concluded that destructive competition on the market for competition law is not totally excluded. The argument is mainly theoretical, however, and lacks sufficient empirical proof. A decision to move to 'cartel paradises' will primarily be made for commercial reasons and not because of the prospect of a lax antitrust jurisdiction. Nevertheless, it may not totally be excluded that the latter considerations matter at the margin. However, as explained above, most of the cartel agreements covering territories of small member states (such as Denmark and The Netherlands) will come within EC jurisdiction because of the wide interpretation of the phrase 'affect trade between member states'. Obviously, the Community antitrust authorities also take part in the competition. In the field of merger control, where some scope for tailoring deals in such a way that they fall under a preferred jurisdiction exists (see above), the Commission has responded by the introduction of a flexible procedure, allowing for decisions to be taken within short time limits. The 'race for the bottom' may thus be won by central rules.

4. A PUBLIC CHOICE PERSPECTIVE

The efficiency analysis of the previous sections has made clear that arguments may be advanced both in favour of decentralisation and centralisation. The current division of powers reveals a somewhat greater degree of centralisation than would be warranted for efficiency reasons. It is well-known that private interests may have an important impact on decisions about whether to regulate at Community or national levels. Interest groups will have a preference for rules being formulated at the level where their strength is greatest relative to that of other groups with divergent interests in the same area.[77] In this section of the chapter it will be investigated which interest groups may succeed in *rent-seeking* at the expense of the public at large (4.1).

In the field of enforcement, the above analysis has shown that there is a clear tendency towards decentralisation. Also in the latter case the private interest explanation may be more powerful than the public interest (efficiency) explanation. Interest groups may be strong enough to pervert regulatory agencies. When not all interests are equally well represented, regulatory capture becomes possible. The possibilities of regulatory capture have their limitations in the design of regulatory institutions. Although appropriate institutional design will not prevent regulatory capture altogether, it may nevertheless limit its scope. In section 4.2, it will be investigated whether and to what extent institutional design, both at the level of the member states and at the community level, hinders or enhances rent-seeking by interest groups.

4.1. Pressure Groups, Bureaucracies and Utility Maximising Judges

Public Choice teaches us that industrial groups will be more successful than consumer groups in influencing the contents of competition laws. The costs of a too lax competition policy are borne by the consumers, who lack information about the activities of the regulatory agencies. The abilities of pressure groups to influence decisionmaking, either at the supranational or national levels, differ across industries (or occupations) and may further vary depending on the subject matter. Some private interests are represented by well-organised interest groups that are able to cope with the free-riding problem easily through compulsory membership. This explains why the 'professions' have been successful in generating rents for existing practitioners (see 4.1.1). Large firms will also be powerful lobbyists: they may gather information about the substantive and procedural issues concerned at low cost (as a by-product of their other activities); they may also have more at stake and may therefore be better able to spread the fixed costs of information acquisition.[78] It will be demonstrated below that large firms had an important impact on the decisions whether to regulate at the Community level or to adopt EC-like rules at the national level (see 4.1.2). Finally the problem of rent-seeking through legal rules banning unfair competition will be addressed (see 4.1.3). In each of these subsections, attention will also be drawn to the bureaucrats' self-interest in power and prestige and to the behaviour of utility maximising judges.

4.1.1. Self-regulation

The problem of rent-seeking tends to be rather serious in the case of self-regulation which is approved and supervised by the state. At the member state level, rules governing competitive conduct may be issued within different regulatory frameworks: governmental regulation, supervised self-regulation (neo-corporatism) and regulation by means of cartel agreements, subject to antitrust scrutiny. Direct regulation by the government may take different forms. Economic regulation may concern marketing practices (advertising, promotion efforts) and prices. Self-regulation may be preferred to government regulation because of the information advantages of private firms and its greater flexibility. There is, however, a major danger that self-regulation is used by professional groups to erect entry barriers to new competition. This danger increases with supervised self-regulation.[79] In the latter case the government grants a monopoly position to professional associations, subject to some conditions. Thanks to this monopoly, the organised firms are able to force the unorganised business to respect cartel agreements in which they originally took no part. Specific forms of supervised self-regulation exist within neo-corporatist institutions. The government not only consults with these institutions, but also grants them executive powers in many fields. In most member states public self-regulatory bodies exist for the liberal arts. Medical doctors, attorneys, architects and other lobby groups that have been able to appropriate the status of a 'liberal profession' have not only succeeded in having their professional title protected, but also enjoy monopoly rights in the provision of certain professional services. Public professional bodies issue ethical rules governing conduct. Economic analyses of these rules have shown that they cause societal costs well in excess of the benefits gained by the professional groups in terms of restricting competition.[80] The 'public interest' arguments advanced in defence of the rules of conduct are not convincing: it is remarkable that the rules go much farther than would be necessary to cure market failures. The rules restricting advertising are a clear example. Although the problem of asymmetric information is especially serious with credence goods and might cause a breakdown of the market,[81] not all services offered by professionals are credence goods. There is thus no justification for a flat prohibition of advertising and such a remedy is not an appropriate market-oriented response. Ethical rules imposing such a prohibition impede the functioning of the market mechanism.[82]

Can the problem of regulatory capture be mitigated by allocating decisionmaking power to the appropriate level of authority? On the one hand, one could argue in favour of centralisation. Indeed, the neo-corporatist frameworks have been created by member states. In order to limit the welfare losses due to self-regulation by professional groups, centralisation may be considered. There are, however, reasons to be pessimistic as far as the ability of Community institutions to prevent rent-seeking by professional groups is concerned. In a recent judgement the European Court of Justice refused to invalidate restrictions on advertising in the pharmacists' profession.[83] On the other hand, decentralisation does not necessarily enlarge the scope for successful rent-seeking. In recent years some member states have started deregulation programmes in the sector of the liberal professions. A few examples may be mentioned. In the United Kingdom steps have been taken to liberalise the market for legal services. In The Netherlands proposed reforms concern *inter alia* the notaries' profession. In sum, the scope for rent-seeking will depend upon the relative strength of the professions in the various EC member states, compared to their impact on centralised rule-making in the Community.

4.1.2. Competition law *sensu stricto*

Legal certainty is a very important issue for lobby groups representing large industries. Large business firms want to be informed as soon as possible about the legal validity of cartel agreements or the compatibility of a proposed merger with the applicable supervisory regulation. The legislative records of recent national competition laws make clear that imitation of the EC rules was defended by large firms. In Sweden it was argued that uniformity between EC law and national law will be an advantage for export businesses since the same rules will be operable in the Common Market and at home.[84] Large Dutch firms consider certainty as to the law of utmost importance in the competitive struggle in the European markets, because American firms may be tempted to use the possibility of initiating legal proceedings with the European Commission or national judges as a competitive weapon.[85] The transplant of EC competition rules into national legal systems increases the predictability of the decisions by national antitrust authorities. It also excludes the danger that economic analysis is going to play a greater role than it currently does, which would benefit American firms and antitrust practitioners, who are familiar with the most recent economic reasoning in competition matters.[86] In small countries (such as Belgium and The Netherlands) where EC competition rules have been used for many years because the requirement that agreements must affect inter-state trade is easily met, established antitrust lawyers also prefer imitation of EC rules to the adoption of American-like solutions. The governments of these countries tend to consult specialists in the field, who obviously want to protect their human capital and prefer a quiet life to a hard time of study. A preference for EC rules is also to be found in the advice of the Economic and Social Committee on merger control. European industry favours a lowering of the thresholds, because controls by different national authorities would increase uncertainty. The EC Merger Task Force is applauded for its flexibility and ability to reach decisions with only short delays. More scope for national merger controls is rejected, because an extension of national competence would only result from wrong ideas concerning subsidiarity.[87]

It is important to realise that the universal application of EC-like rules, advocated by large firms, may harm smaller firms. The savings in search costs (thanks to legal certainty) accrue to export industry but are achieved at the expense of industries competing only in the home markets.[88] The adoption of the EC competition rules also entails the acceptance of the inefficiencies inherent in them. The European Commission is unwilling to take account of the free-riding argument with respect to the legality of vertical restrictions in distribution agreements between manufacturers and small retailers.[89] Again, only well-organised larger industries (car dealers, franchised networks) succeed in getting their distribution agreements exempted from the scope of the EC rules. In sum, pleas for legal certainty seem to be the flag under which powerful interest groups (large firms, antitrust lawyers) achieve benefits at the expense of interests that are not well-organised (small firms, consumers).

Obviously, the growth of centralisation increases the workload of the central authorities. Bureaucrats motivated by self-interest may want to maximise the budget of the bureau[90] or try to achieve higher status, while at the same time making work more agreeable.[91] The latter option, reducing the workload while at the same time gaining more prestige, was on the top of the Commission's wish list. A reduction of the workload is achieved by leaving the treatment of the 'simple' cases and the purely technical legal questions to national judges. As soon as matters become more complicated and especially when economic and political arguments may influence the ultimate decision, the Commission will have the last word. With the exception of the granting of exemptions,[92] the Commission's advice on legal issues is not binding. However, given their unfamiliarity with competition law, national judges will probably follow the Commission's advice in most cases.[93] Consequently, the Commission's ability and willingness to help poorly qualified national judges will certainly add to its prestige.

4.1.3. The law prohibiting unfair competition

As far as the substantive rules are concerned, increased centralisation in competition law *sensu stricto* goes hand in hand with increased decentralisation in the field of the law banning unfair competition. This remarkable opposite tendency may again be explained from a Public Choice perspective. Industries and occupations without self-regulatory power may achieve similar rents through regulation. For example, the prohibition in French and Belgian fair trade laws of sales to consumers at loss prices or with an exceptionally low profit margin can be seen as a surrogate for hardly feasible cartel agreements between retailers. Cartels with a too large number of members may easily unravel when outsiders, offering lower prices, enter the retailing business. Legal rules that qualify sales at loss prices as dishonest trade practices force outsiders, especially newcomers, to ask cartel-like prices. The welfare reducing effects of bans on 'unfair trade practices' (such as the prohibition of true comparison advertising or sales at 'unreasonably low prices' by retailers without market power) remain hidden to the public at large. It is obvious that the *Keck and Mithouard* judgement of the European Court of Justice enlarges the scope for rent-seeking by interest groups of the small and medium sized retailing trade. The validity of national rules concerning sales methods, such as the prohibition of sales at loss prices or with low profit margins and comparative advertising, can no longer be challenged upon the basis of the provisions of the EC-Treaty guaranteeing free movement of goods. Lobby groups from the small and medium sized retailing trade have easier access to national governments than to the European decisionmakers. In Belgium, for instance, lobby groups have succeeded for many years in blocking a legislative amendment allowing new entrants to sell at loss prices during a specified period of time.[94]

Looking for an explanation for the remarkable change of direction by the European Court of Justice, it may immediately be noted that the judges' behaviour is not understandable as implicit attempts to achieve efficiency in the Posnerian sense. On the contrary, significant inefficiencies may ensue as a consequence of the new interpretation of Article 30 EC-Treaty. It should also be mentioned that it is highly unlikely that the European Court of Justice has been 'captured' by interest groups from the retailing trade. Following the assumption that judges behave rationally, explanations will have to be found by looking at the desire of judges to improve their own position. It may be expected that they will try to maximise their utility by gaining prestige with their audience (attorneys and process parties)[95] or by lowering the pressure of work.[96] The latter explanation is the most powerful one. In the *Keck and Mithouard* judgement the Court itself took notice 'of the increasing tendency of traders to invoke Article 30 of the Treaty as a means of challenging any rules whose effect is to limit their commercial freedom' and therefore considered it 'necessary to re-examine and clarify its case law on this matter' (paragraph 14). The new ruling will not bring greater legal certainty because the wording 'selling arrangements' is unclear and vague. A lot of new cases may be brought, but the Court will be able to reach a decision without additionally having to investigate justification upon the basis of the rule of reason.

4.2. The Problem of Regulatory Capture

It was mentioned above that information asymmetries between competition authorities and firms may argue in favour of a decentralised competition policy. These benefits in terms of reduction of information costs may, however, be outweighed by the increased danger of capture. If information asymmetries exist between regulatory agencies and the public at large, there will be scope for regulatory capture. In the absence of such asymmetries, there would be much less difficulty in ensuring that public agencies took welfare enhancing decisions. For these reasons it is important to look for devices that may alleviate problems of excessive capture. An answer to the question whether enforcement decisions should be taken at the level of the European Community institutions or those of member states requires a comparison of the possibilities of decentralisation and centralisation to cope with the problem of regulatory capture.

A lax enforcement of the competition rules widens the scope for self-regulation by means of cartel agreements. With respect to competition policy in general and merger control in particular Neven, Nuttall and Seabright indicate three different responses to the problem of regulatory capture: accountability, independence and transparency. Mobility is one of the best guarantors of accountability. When mobility is limited, other devices are necessary to guarantee that regulatory agencies are held accountable to the general public through the political process. The argument for political independence rests on the fact that compared to the voting public at large special interest groups can more easily influence politicians. Finally, transparency may reduce the informational asymmetries, aid regulatory agencies to commit themselves to a given regulatory policy, and cope with unequal costs of gathering information.[97]

Some national competition laws contain rules which try to improve political accountability. For example, the Belgian antitrust authority must submit a report to parliament which informs all interested parties about the enforcement of the competition rules. The German Monopolies Commission (Monopolkommission) publishes every two years a report concerning the evolution of concentration in Germany. These reports are submitted to the government, which must then clarify its position *vis-à-vis* the legislator.[98] This broadens and deepens public debate of competition policy issues. So far, there is no European Monopolies Commission with similar tasks.[99]

The procedures for the control of cartels, dominant firms and mergers have a noticeable influence on the degree of independence of the antitrust authorities and the transparency of the decisionmaking process. For example, a competition agency can only be truly independent if it is not forced to take account of political arguments in the assessment of anti-competitive practices. Real independence requires that political modifications of decisions are taken by a separate agency. A division between the decision stage and the stage of political review will thus contribute to the independence of the antitrust agency. Such a division may also contribute to transparency. It would be naive to think that political arguments will not be considered if they are not explicitly mentioned in the relevant antitrust provisions. The advantage of a division of functions is that political modifications can only be made after the decision by the antitrust agency. If this decision is previously published, the political arguments for changing the decision will have to be spelled out clearly. A comparison between the antitrust procedures of the European Community and those of the member states may reveal how far independence and transparency is currently achieved under both centralised and decentralised antitrust laws. If such a comparison is able to show that decentralised antitrust agencies enjoy a greater degree of independence and that the decisionmaking at national levels is more transparent than at the level of the Community, the argument in favour of decentralisation will be strengthened.

From an examination of the antitrust procedures, at least three differences immediately appear. First, in the EC a single body (the European Commission) is responsible for antitrust enforcement. The European

Commission is both prosecutor and judge.[100] Conversely, in some member states a functional division of powers between different bodies has been preferred. Secondly, the head of the Community antitrust agency is a politician, whereas the antitrust agencies of the member states are usually headed by civil servants or administrative law judges.[101] Thirdly, in some member states scope for considerations other than competition aspects is explicitly provided for: for example, an efficiency defence is available both in the United Kingdom and in Germany. In the EC, decisions should be taken solely on competition grounds, at least in theory.

In the EC all stages of the procedures (notification, investigation, negotiation, decision and political review) are assigned to a single body, the European Commission. In some member states the body responsible for notification and investigation is not the party taking the decision. For instance, in Belgium the *Dienst voor de Mededinging* (Competition Agency) has to be notified in regard to restrictive practices and mergers, and will carry out the investigation, but decisions will be taken by the *Raad voor de Mededinging* (Competition Council). The Agency is composed of civil servants, whereas the Council has 12 members, half of whom are administrative law judges, the other half being experts in competition matters. The Council is presided over by a judge.[102] The separation of powers is even clearer in the UK. The body responsible for investigation of a proposed merger (the Monopolies and Mergers Commission) is neither the party to whom mergers must be notified (being the Director General of Fair Trading), nor the party taking the decision, who is the Secretary of State for Trade and Industry. As far as EC antitrust procedures are concerned, the picture is different. It is true that notification and investigation of mergers are carried out by a notionally separate body, the Merger Task Force, but this acts more as a support unit to the Commission than as a genuinely and visibly separate agency. The Merger Task Force is not comparable to the notification and investigation bodies in member states which have legal personality. The unification of roles in the EC may improve the efficiency of the procedure and its clarity and predictability to the parties concerned, but it reduces transparency from the point of view of the general public.[103]

A second difference relates to the degree of political independence of the antitrust agencies. At the EC-level, the competition agency is more directly under political control than in most of the member states. The heads of the competition agencies in the member states are either civil servants or administrative law judges. Political independence is further guaranteed by rules imposing incompatibilities between membership of the antitrust authorities and leading functions in firms or professional associations.[104] On the contrary, European Commissioners are politicians. Although they are required to forswear national allegiances on joining the Commission, it would be naive to think that there is no risk of national capture. This risk has even been institutionalised in the antitrust procedures. Before taking formal decisions, whether favourable (negative clearances) or adverse to the addressee (refusal of exemption), the Commission is required to consult the Advisory Committee on Restrictive Practices and Monopolies. This Committee is composed of representatives of the member states' competition authorities. The meetings of the Committee are not open to the public. The Committee's opinion is attached to the draft decision when it is sent up to the Commissioners for approval, but it is not published or made available to the defendants.[105] Although the Committee's opinion is not binding, it is clear that the decision procedure with respect to Articles 85–86 EC-Treaty has many features which allow for capturing by national interests. The same is true for the procedure of merger control. The Advisory Commission on Concentrations, which consists of representatives of the member states, meets with the Commission's staff during the investigation and before the results of the investigation are published.[106] It is significant to add that there are also Advisory Committees for specific sectors of the economy.

Transparency is improved if the influence of considerations, other than competition aspects, is made visible. In contrast with the competition laws of some member states, the EC rules do not explicitly allow for the consideration of other arguments than competition aspects. It would, however, be naive to think that considerations of productive efficiency or political considerations do not play a role in practice. Efficiency considerations can make an otherwise anti-competitive merger worthwhile. Neven, Nuttall and Seabright report that efficiency gains are insisted upon by firms during the negotiations and that favourable assessments of dominance or lax remedies may hide some concern for efficiency.[107] In contrast with efficiency considerations, political considerations have a greater potential of generating decisions which are detrimental to society at large and only benefit small interest groups. The main weakness of the EC procedures is that political considerations will be considered even though they are not supposed to be mentioned. The current procedures obscure which kinds of political pressures were actually most influential in determining the outcome of cases. To reduce the risk that political pressures cause decisions which are biased in favour of rent-seeking groups, these pressures must be made visible. The same is true for efficiency considerations. If there is no explicit scope for an efficiency defence in merger cases, this may give rise to distorted efficiency claims by firms which are not seriously examined but nevertheless influence the ultimate decision.

The risks that political negotiations will distort the character of the investigations and influence the final decision without clearly being visible appears also to be less serious in the member states. Many provisions of the

German law aim at protecting the Bundeskartellamt from political influence. A first rule which deserves attention in this respect is § 8 *GWB* concerning 'Sonderkartelle'. According to this paragraph cartel agreements may be allowed if the restrictions of competition are exceptionally necessary because of predominant grounds of economic welfare and public interest ('aus überwiegenden Gründen der Gesamtwirtschaft und des Gemeinwohls'). It is, however, not the Bundeskartellamt but the Minister of Economic Affairs who will take a decision to this effect.[108] The paragraph on 'Sonderkartelle' served as an example for the similar provision with respect to merger control, which was introduced later. According to § 24 III *GWB* mergers may get the approval of the Minister of Economic Affairs if the restrictions of competition are made good by general economic advantages or predominant motives of public interest. Experience with this rule made clear that the political pressure exerted upon the Minister of Economic Affairs was greater than expected. To cope with this problem the law was changed. An approval now requires a report by the Monopolkommission prior to the decision by the Minister. The new procedure does not succeed in entirely banishing the influence of political pressures, but makes those pressures visible without disguise. The German system clearly contrasts with EC law, where economic and political influences may distort the actual analysis of the competition aspects of cases.

The previous analysis has shown that centralisation is not the perfect institutional design that will exclude the scope for regulatory capture. In general, the antitrust authorities in the member states are independent of the Government, whereas the European Commission is a collegiate, political body.[109] Decentralisation does a better job in mitigating the risk of regulatory capture than is often assumed. Of course, the relative strength of the interest groups will differ across countries and industries. If agencies are captured by national interests, supranational bodies will be able to reach more objective decisions. If lobbies represent sector rather than national interests, centralisation by itself will not cure the problem. Centralisation may weaken the power of some interest groups (for instance, middle class retailers), but other groups may gain when competition policy is centralised (e.g. farmers). Some interest groups (e.g. insurance companies) appear to be equally powerful both at the supranational and the national levels, although there may exist some differences across member states. The group exemption for cartels on insurance markets illustrates how centralisation may even cause market power costs in member states, where competitive markets existed before.[110]

CONCLUSION

European competition rules have existed for many years as instruments to promote the integration of national markets. If the subsidiarity principle is to be taken seriously, the Community institutions must prove why a centralised competition policy remains necessary even in a mostly realised internal market. The major arguments advanced by legal commentators in favour of central rule-making relate to 'legal certainty' and 'administrative efficiency'. Taken together, these arguments favour a remarkable combination of centrally made uniform substantive rules and decentralised enforcement. Uniform rules would make the outcome of anti-trust cases more predictable; and enforcement by national authorities, in particular judges, would enhance the effectiveness of the prohibitions. In this chapter both arguments were criticised. The emphasis put on legal certainty neglects the current inefficiencies, inconsistencies and adverse effects of EC competition law. The argument in favour of decentralised enforcement omits the transition costs which are quite substantial in many member states. It is also remarkable that a preference for centrally made competition laws *sensu stricto* goes hand in hand with a tendency to decentralisation in the field of unfair competition law. Bans on 'unfair' competitive behaviour, together with rules of conduct issued by self-regulatory professional bodies, may limit competition contrary to the goals of competition law *sensu stricto*. To avoid inconsistencies, the allocation of competence should be the same for both branches of competition law.

An economic analysis of the subsidiarity principle allows for a better understanding of the fundamental issues involved in the allocation of competence between national antitrust authorities and a supranational agency. Decentralisation creates scope for competition between legislators which, at least theoretically, allows firms and consumers to 'vote with their feet' by moving to their preferred jurisdiction. In reality, an efficient outcome on the market of competition laws will not ensue because of insufficient choices, information problems and restricted mobility. A more powerful argument in favour of decentralisation is the information advantage of national competition authorities. The danger of regulatory capture, which is often advanced as an argument against decentralisation, does not appear to be more serious than with a supranational authority. Industry generally prefers the current decisionmaking process under EC competition law to national procedures, which provides support to the belief that regulatory capture may be even more worrisome at the central level. A further powerful argument in favour of decentralisation follows from a dynamic approach. Trial-and-error is most relevant in the field of competition policy. If antitrust rules vary across countries, policy errors will be recognised more rapidly and better devices may be developed sooner.

Some arguments in favour of centralisation are not particularly strong. The externality problem can be dealt with by the cumulative applicability of the national competition laws of all countries where spillover effects emerge. The danger that divergent competition laws may cause a 'race for the bottom' is not empirically substantiated. The scope for prisoners' dilemmas is, moreover, limited by legal devices. Centralisation may not be the appropriate remedy anyway, since the European Commission seems to take an active part in the 'race for the bottom'. A major argument in favour of centralisation is the achievement of scale economies and transaction cost savings. Firms active in inter-state trade will profit when they do not have to adapt their business practices to divergent competition laws. In addition, transaction costs will decrease (and 'legal certainty' will increase) if business practices and mergers will not have to be controlled by several antitrust authorities. These benefits must, however, be balanced against the costs of centralisation. As mentioned above, decentralisation allows national antitrust authorities to take profit from information advantages and has a potential to improve existing competition laws through learning-by-doing.

The current allocation of competence between national competition authorities and the European Commission shows a greater degree of centralisation than would be warranted for efficiency reasons. It is clear that the broad interpretation of the requirement in Article 85 that inter-state trade must be affected also makes EC competition rules applicable in the absence of externalities between member states. It also hampers innovations in the field of competition policy. Given the magnitude of the spillovers and the important savings on transaction costs, the rule in the Merger Regulation limiting supervision by the European Commission to mergers having a 'community dimension' better fits into the economic analysis. However, the current criteria are a poor indicator of the magnitude of the externalities involved.

The high degree of centralisation in the field of competition law, combined with a tendency towards decentralised enforcement, can best be explained from a Public Choice perspective. Both interest groups and bureaucrats influence the decision how to allocate tasks. 'Legal certainty' brought about by an extensive use of EC or EC-like rules benefits large firms, which are powerful lobby groups. The increasing involvement of national judges in the enforcement of EC competition law is, in the Commission's eyes, an appropriate reflection of the spirit of the subsidiarity principle. This can be easily understood if the self-interest of the EC bureaucrats is taken into account. Decentralised enforcement reduces the workload of the European Commission, while at the same time adding to its prestige. Public Choice also provides an explanation for the opposite tendency towards decentralisation in the field of unfair competition law. Bans on unfair trade practices benefit interest groups from the small and medium sized retailing trade, which cannot achieve similar rents through cartel agreements. These interest groups are more powerful at the national level than at the EC level. Due to information deficiencies the costs of the rent-seeking remain hidden to the public at large. The change in direction in the case-law of the European Court of Justice may also be understood. Not only bureaucrats, but also judges want to reduce the workload and focus on solving problems which add to their prestige.

NOTES

1. The notion 'exclusive competence' is narrowly defined. See Lenaerts and van Yperseele (1994).
2. See Toth (1994).
3. A list of more than 350 references could be given but is omitted here taking into account that the marginal cost of such a list considerably exceeds its marginal benefit.
4. This distinction may be explained on historical grounds and has been upheld mainly because of successful lobbying by small and medium-sized retailers and the insertion into the laws banning unfair competition of rules that allegedly aim at consumer protection. In many European countries (for example in Germany and Belgium) rules prohibiting unfair conduct preceeded the introduction of a competition law. The former rules were enacted at the beginning of the century, in order to protect small and medium-sized retailers from so-called 'unfair competition' by the upcoming large retail stores and travelling salesmen. From the 1970s on, the laws against unfair competition (for example, the German *Gesetz gegen den unlauteren Wettbewerb (UWG)* and the Belgian *Wet betreffende de handelspraktijken en de voorlichting en de bescherming van de verbruiker*) have been amended to also incorporate consumer protection issues. The inevitable result of trying to reconcile business and consumer interests is a great degree of inconsistency. Moreover, by prohibiting certain modes of conduct as unfair competition, the scope for competitive conduct is limited. This raises the question whether conduct which is lawful according to the competition law (and must be encouraged from a viewpoint of allocative efficiency) may nevertheless be prohibited as being unfair (because of distributive issues, such as the protection of small businesses). The uneasy coexistence of the German competition laws (*Gesetz gegen Wettbewerbsbeschränkungen (GWB)* and *UWG*) is extensively commented upon in the legal literature. See, for instance, Ulmer (1977) and Lehmann (1977).
5. Case 5/69 [1969] ECR 295 ; CMLR 273.
6. According to this Notice the following quantitative criteria apply: (a) the product and its immediate substitutes should not constitute more than 5 per cent in a substantial part of the Common Market, and (b) the aggregate annual turnover of the undertakings participating in the agreement should not exceed ECU 200 million units of account.
7. Case 23/67, *Brasserie de Haecht v. Wilkin-Janssens* [1967] ECR 407 ; [1968] CMLR 26.
8. Case 73/74, *Groupement des Fabricants de Papiers Peints de Belgique v. Commission* [1975] ECR 1491; [1976] 1 CMLR 589.
9. See Frignani (1993).
10. See the White Paper *Opening Markets: New Policy on Restrictive Trade Practices*, Cm 727 (1989).
11. This is the case in Hungary, Poland and Romania.

12. Two important judgements of the European Court of Justice (Case C-234/89, *Stergios Delimitis v. Henninger Bräu AG* [1992] 5 CMLR 210; Case T-24/90 *Automec v. Commission* [1992] 5 CMLR 431) paved the way for the Commission's own policy document on decentralisation: the Notice on co-operation between national courts and the Commission in applying Articles 85 and 86 of the EEC-Treaty [1993] OJ C 39.
13. The Directorate-General for Competition, known as DG IV, has a total staff of approximately 350 persons, around half of these being professional lawyers and economists. See Ritter, Braun and Rawlinson (1991) at p. 601.
14. National competition authorities may enforce Articles 85 and 86 EC-Treaty unless and until the European Commission itself commences proceedings in the instant case (Article 9(3) of Regulation 17). National authorities have rarely exercised their jurisdiction, possibly because they lack adequate powers of investigation. See: Ritter, Braun and Rawlinson (1991) at p. 604–605.
15. Paragraph 14 of the Notice, *supra,* footnote 12.
16. Block exemptions, which have been used since 1967, are an early example of decentralisation at work. They free the Commission from having to deal with exempted agreements and pass on the responsibility to national judges to ensure compliance with the block exemptions.
17. Paragraphs 37, 38 and 40 of the Notice, *supra,* footnote 12.
18. An exemption requires an express decision by the Commission, which grants exemptions either by an individual decision (granted upon an application made in the form of a notification) or by a block exemption regulation.
19. L.J. Fry in the *Mogul* case, (1889) 23 Ch. D 598, 625–626.
20. Council Directive 84/450 EEC relates to the approximation of the laws, regulations and administrative provisions of the member states concerning misleading advertising [1984] OJ L 250/17. This Directive has been implemented in all EC member states, including the United Kingdom (Control of Misleading Advertisements Regulation 1988).
21. See in general on prior approval regimes: Ogus (1994), at p. 214–244.
22. See Faure, Finsinger, Siegers and van den Bergh (1993).
23. Case 120/78, *Rewe-Zentral AG v. Bundesmonopolverwaltung für Branntwein* [1979] ECR 649.
24. See Steiner (1992).
25. Cases C-267 and C-268/91, *Bernard Keck and Daniel Mithouard* [1993] ECR I-6097. There are exceptions to the new rule if the provisions do not apply to all affected traders operating within the national territory and if they, in law or in fact, do not affect the marketing of imported and of domestic products in the same manner (paragraph 16 of the Court's judgement).
26. Case C-292/92, *Ruth Hünermund et al. v. Landesapothekerkammer Baden-Württemberg* [1993] ECR I-6787.
27. This idea builds upon a now classic article by Tiebout (1956) on the optimal provision of local public goods. Tiebout's theory is specially relevant for the provision of public services for which tastes may differ considerably from locality to locality. The underlying assumptions appear to be highly severe when the original scenario is left and conditions for efficient outcomes of competition between legal rules have to be formulated. See van den Bergh (1994).
28. In 1986 almost 2 million EC citizens worked in other EC countries, which is only 1.5 per cent of the total working force (138 million people). See Hansen *et al.* (1992) at p. 92–93.
29. The Schengen Treaty has removed physical barriers to the free movement of persons within Belgium, the Netherlands, Luxembourg, France, Spain and Portugal. Other EC Member States will join the Schengen area at a later stage.
30. Directive 89/48 [1989] OJ L 19.
31. Hansen *et al.* (1992) at p. 92–93.
32. See Smets and van Cayseele (1995).
33. Article 11(1) Regulation 17.
34. Article 13(1) Regulation 17.
35. Ritter, Rawlinson and Braun (1991) at p. 605.

36. Article 14 Regulation 17.
37. Articles 11-13 Regulation 4064/89.
38. The problem of regulatory capture is discussed more extensively in section 4.2.
39. For the formal analysis, see Smets and van Cayseele (1995).
40. 22nd Report on Competition Policy, paragraph 299.
41. See Riley (1993).
42. von Hayek (1978).
43. See van den Bergh (1996).
44. The prohibition principle flatly outlaws particular business practices in a statute, unless a statutory exemption or individual dispensation again makes them lawful. The abuse principle does not ban particular business practices, unless and until the competition authorities use their review powers to intervene against such practices.
45. For example, the limitation of the number of dealers is not allowed in exclusive distribution agreements and in systems of selective distribution (except for car dealerships), but is considered a lawful business practice in franchised networks.
46. Case T-12/93 *Comité central d'entreprise de la société anonyme Vittel et al. v. Commission* [1995] ECR II-1247.
47. See van den Bergh, Faure and Lefevere (1996).
48. The most comprehensive competition law is the German *Gesetz gegen Wettbewerbs-beschränkungen* (an excellent textbook is Immenga/Mestmäcker (1992)). The most lax competition law is to be found in The Netherlands, which have been considered a 'cartel paradise' for several decades (see Mok (1993). Recently the supervision of cartel agreements has increased, but the country still has no merger supervision. However, the introduction of EC-like competition rules in The Netherlands is scheduled for 1997 (see Bos (1995). The Netherlands will thus follow the example of many other member states, such as Belgium, Italy and Greece, which have already transplanted EC competition rules in their own legal order.
49. See Dyer (1988) and Schricker (1982), who also discusses some ways of softening the harsh consequences of the territorial point of view in cases of unintentional overspill of advertising abroad.
50. Neven, Nuttall and Seabright (1993) at p. 196.
51. Neven, Nuttall and Seabright (1993) at p. 198.
52. *Centraal Bureau voor de Rijwielhandel (Dutch bicycles)* [1978] OJ L 20/18.
53. As in the case of the Belgian wallpaper manufacturers, see note 8.
54. Case 126/80, *Salonia v. Poidomani and Baglieri* [1981] ECR 1563; [1982] 1 CMLR 64. This case concerned a complaint by a retailer in Ragusa, who was not supplied with newspapers and periodicals by a wholesaler who also had his warehouse in Ragusa.
55. Recital 19 Regulation 1984/83 on Block Exemption of Exclusive Purchasing Agreements [1983] OJ L 173/5.
56. According to Goyder, this does not necessarily imply that the benefit remains restricted to service station exclusive purchasing agreements. (Goyder (1988) at p. 351–352). This author also draws attention to a similar degree of flexibility for member states in the group exemption concerning agreements for the resale of automobiles (Recital 29 of Regulation 123/85).
57. See Rubin (1983).
58. Regulations 123/85 [1985] OJ L 15/16 and 1475/95 [1995] OJ L 145/25 on Block Exemption of Motor Vehicle Distribution and Servicing Agreements.
59. See van den Bergh (1996).
60. Rose-Ackerman (1992) at p. 172.
61. Rose-Ackerman (1992) at p. 167.
62. Compare Cary (1974) and Romano (1985).
63. Easterbook (1983).
64. The deregulation of the telecommunications sector may serve as an example.
65. Case 13/77, *Inno v. ATAB* [1977] ECR 2115; [1978] 1 CMLR 283.

66. Case 311/85, *Vereniging van Vlaamse Reisbureaus v. Sociale Dienst (Flemish Travel Agents)* [1987] ECR 3801; [1989] 4 CMLR 213.
67. Case 229/83, *Association des Centres Distributeurs Edouard Leclerc et al. v. Sarl 'Au Blé Vert' et al. (French Books I)* [1985] ECR 1; [1985] 2 CMLR 286. In this case resale price maintenance for imported books was held to violate the free movement of goods; the only exception to that would be if it was established that the original exports of the books had been for the sole purpose of circumventing the French legislation by subsequent reimportation.
68. In the real world, no system operates in a pure form. For instance, in the German system, which is based on the prohibition principle, various modifications are interjected by distinguishing between different types of cartel agreements. Some cartel agreements become valid after simple notification ('Anmeldekartelle'); others become valid unless the competition authority opposes such validity within three months ('Widerspruchskartelle') and a third category comprises agreements which need explicit permission ('Erlaubniskartelle'). Systems that at the outset ascribe to the abuse system have one or more flat bans against particular business practices: for example, the ban against resale price maintenance in Denmark and The Netherlands.
69. The arguments are derived from Neven, Nuttall and Seabright (1993) at p. 79–80.
70. The German antitrust authorities have expressed concern from the outset that the Merger Regulation may be too lax. Officials from the Bundeskartellamt indicated that their assessment would probably have been different in some cases, such as *Varta/Bosch* (see Neven, Nuttall and Seabright (1993) at p. 81).
71. Neven, Nuttall and Seabright (1993) at p. 145.
72. Notice the distinction between merger-type and cooperative operations [1990] OJ C 203/10. A joint venture may be characterised as concentrative if it performs on a lasting basis all the functions of an autonomous economic entity (positive condition) and if it does not have as its object or effect the co-ordination of the competitive behaviour of undertakings that remain independent of each other (negative condition).
73. Neven, Nuttall and Seabright (1993) at p. 79, with further references.
74. For prohibitions of mergers, see *Aérospatiale-Alenia/De Havilland* [1991] OJ L 334/42 and *MSG Media Service* [1994] OJ L 364/1.
75. There may of course exist uncertainty as to whether the agreement affects interstate trade or, if it does, will remain free from challenge by the European Commission on competition policy grounds. The notion of 'competition' in Article 85 is vague and allows for a great degree of discretion. In some cases restrictions of competition were not prohibited because they were held not to interfere with the goal of 'workable competition'. In cases of doubt judges may ask the Commission for advice if the practices are challenged before national courts. National judges may also enquire about the chances that an individual exemption will be granted (see Notice on cooperation, *supra*, footnote 12).
76. Regulation 4087/88 on Block Exemption of Franchising Agreements [1988] OJ L 359/46.
77. Noam (1982).
78. Neven, Nuttall and Seabright (1993) at p. 175.
79. Bos (1995).
80. See Faure, Finsinger, Siegers and van den Bergh (1993).
81. Akerlof (1970).
82. According to recent theoretical research, the market mechanism may solve the problem of fraudulent sales of credence goods. See Emons (1995).
83. Case *Hünermund*, cited, note 26.
84. See the Swedish Promemoria (Ny konkurrenslag - en promemoria från Näringsdepartementet 1992), at p. 32–33 and the Swedish proposition (Regeringens proposition 1992/93: 56 Ny konkurrenslagstiftning), at p. 18–20.
85. See the arguments advanced by Philips in *Staatscourant*, 10 maart 1995, 5.
86. At present the quality of economic reasoning in EC antitrust cases is poor, if not totally absent. See van den Bergh (1996).
87. Advice 94/C 388/09 [1994] OJ C 388/41.
88. See with respect to the Swedish law Stray Ryssdal (1996).

89. van den Bergh (1996).
90. Niskanen (1971).
91. Dunleavy (1991).
92. In recent legal literature the (minority) opinion is advanced that national judges are also bound by negative clearances (decisions of the Commission that an agreement does not fall within the scope of the prohibition of Article 85 (1) EC-Treaty) if the factual circumstances of the case have been entirely known to the Commission and have remained unchanged until the decision by the national judge (see Gyselen (1993)). According to this view, only comfort letters would still leave scope for independent decisionmaking by national judges.
93. 'What would be the point of such opinion if the Commission does not expect that they will be followed by national courts?' (Bourgeois (1994) at p. 493).
94. See van den Bergh (1985).
95. Cooter (1983) at p.129.
96. Rubin (1983) at p.134.
97. Neven, Nuttall and Seabright (1993).
98. § 24 b V GWB. The Monopolkommission may also draft reports concerning competition issues on its own initiative.
99. The establishment of a European Monopolies Commission is defended by Ehlermann (1995).
100. In reaction to complaints about this improper combination of functions, a Hearing Officer has been appointed within the Directorate General for Competition.
101. The only countries in which decisions are taken in ministries are the United Kingdom and The Netherlands. In the latter country the creation of an independent competition authority is envisaged. See Ehlermann (1995).
102. See for more information Steenlant (1992).
103. Neven, Nuttall and Seabright (1993), p.215.
104. See § 48 *GWB* (Bundeskartellamt) and § 24 b *GWB* (Monopolkommission).
105. Ritter, Rawlinson and Braun (1991) at p. 662.
106. Neven, Nuttall and Seabright (1993) at p. 218.
107. Neven, Nuttall and Seabright (1993) at p. 240.
108. § 8 I *GWB* is used *inter alia* to accept cartel agreements which contribute to the protection of the environment (Immenga/Mestmäcker, § 8, nr 41).
109. There are proposals to establish an independent European Cartel Office. See, for a critical analysis of these proposals, Ehlermann (1995).
110. See Faure and van den Bergh (1995).

REFERENCES

Akerlof, G. (1970), 'The Market for "Lemons": Qualitative Uncertainty and the Market Mechanism', *Quarterly Journal of Economics*, **84**, 488–500.

Bergh, R. van den (1985), 'Belgian Public Policy Towards the Retailing Trade', in J.-M. von der Schulenburg and G. Skogh (eds), *Law and Economics and the Economics of Legal Regulation*, Nijhoff, pp. 185–205.

Bergh, R. van den (1994), 'The Subsidiarity Principle in European Community Law: Some Insights from Law and Economics', *Maastricht Journal of European and Comparative Law*, **1**, 337–366.

Bergh, R. van den (1996), 'Modern Industrial Organisation *versus* Old-Fashioned European Competition Law', *European Competition Law Review*, **17**, 75–87.

Bergh, R. van den, M. Faure and J. Lefevere (1996), 'The Subsidiarity Principle in European Environmental Law: an Economic Analysis', in E. Eide and R. van den Bergh (eds), *Law and Economics of the Environment*, Oslo: Juridisk Forlag, pp. 121-166.

Bos, D.I. (1995), *Eindrapportage literatuurstudie Onderzoeksproject Marktwerking in Nederland*, OCfEB.

Bourgeois, J.H.J. (1994), 'EC Competition Law and Member State Courts', in B.E. Hawk (ed.), *1993 Fordham Corporate Law Institute. Antitrust in a Global Economy,* New York: Transnational Juris Publications.

Cary, J. (1974), 'Federalism and Corporate Law: Reflections upon Delaware', *Yale Law Journal*, **83**, 663 *et seq.*

Cooter, R.D. (1983), 'The Objectives of Private and Public Judges', *Public Choice,* **41**, 107–132.

Dunleavy, P. (1991), *Bureaucracy and Public Choice: Economic Explanations in Political Science,* New York: Harvester Wheatsheaf.

Dyer, A. (1988), 'Unfair Competition in Private International Law', *Receuil des Cours*, **211**, 373–446.

Easterbrook, F. (1983), 'Antitrust and the Economics of Federalism', *Journal of Law and Economics,* **26**, 23–50.

Ehlermann, C.-D. (1995), 'Reflections on an European Cartel Office', *Common Market Law Review*, **32**, 471–486.

Emons, W. (1995), 'Credence Goods Monopolists', Working paper Universität Bern.

Faure, M., J. Finsinger, J. Siegers and R. van den Bergh (eds) (1993), *Regulation of Professions*.

Faure, M. and R. van den Bergh (1995), 'Restrictions of Competition on Insurance Markets and the Applicability of EC Antitrust Law', *Kyklos*, **48**, 65–85.

Frignani, A. (1993), 'Art. 1. Ambito di applicazione e rapporti con l'ordinamento comunitario', in A. Frignani, R. Pardolesi, A. Patroni Griffi and L. Ubertazzi, *Diritto antitrust italiano*, Bologna: Zanichelli, pp. 93–143.

Goyder, D. (1988), *EEC Competition Law*, Oxford: Clarendon Press.

Gyselen, L. (1993), 'Le juge national face aux règles de concurrence communautaire applicables aux entreprises', *Journal des Tribunaux. Droit Européen*, 25–33.

Hansen, J.D. *et al.* (eds) (1992), *An Economic Analysis of the EC*, McGraw-Hill.

Hayek, F.A. von (1978), 'Competition as a Discovery Process', in *New Studies in Philosophy, Politics, Economics and the History of Ideas*, Chicago: University of Chicago Press.

Immenga and Mestmäcker (eds) (1992), *GWB. Gesetz gegen Wettbewerbs-beschränkungen,* München: Beck.

Lehmann, M. (1977), 'Wettbewerbspolitik, Strukturpolitik und Mittelstandsschutz', *Gewerblicher Rechtsschutz und Urheberrecht*, 580–588 and 633–642.

Lenaerts, K. and P. van Yperseele (1994), 'Le principe de subsidiarité et son contexte. Etude de l'article 3B du Traité CE', *Cahiers de Droit Européen*, 3–85.

Mok, M.R. (1993), 'Nederland kartelland? Plaats en toekomst van het nationaal kartelrecht naast het Europese recht', *Rechtsgeleerd Magazijn Themis,* **3**, 116–127.

Neven, D., R. Nuttall and P. Seabright (1993), *Merger in Daylight. The Economics and Politics of European Merger Control*, CEPR, London.

Niskanen, W. (1971), *Bureaucracy and Representative Government,* Chicago: Aldine.

Noam, E. (1982), 'The Choice of Governmental Level in Regulation', *Kyklos*, **35**, 278–291.

Ogus, A.I. (1994), *Regulation. Legal Form and Economic Theory*, Oxford: Clarendon Press.

Riley, A.J. (1993), 'More radicalism, please: the Notice on Co-operation between National Courts and the Commission in Applying Articles 85 and 86 of the EEC Treaty', *European Competition Law Review*, **14**, 91–96.

Ritter, L., F. Rawlinson and W.D. Braun (1991), *EEC Competition Law: a practitioner's guide*, Deventer: Kluwer.

Romano, R. (1985), 'Law as a Product: Some Pieces of the Incorporation Puzzle', *Journal of Law, Economics and Organization*, **1**, 225 *et seq*.

Rose-Ackerman, S. (1992), *Rethinking the Progressive Agenda*, Free Press.

Rubin, P.H. (1983), 'The Objectives of Private and Public Judges. A Comment', *Public Choice*, **41**, 133–137.

Schricker, G. (1982), 'Die Durchsetzbarkeit deutscher Werberegelungen bei grenzüberschreitender Rundfunkwerbung', *Gewerblicher Rechtsschutz und Urheberrecht. Internationaler Teil*, 720–726.

Smets, H. and P. Van Cayseele (1995), 'Competing Merger Policies in a Common Agency Framework', *International Review of Law and Economics*, 425–441.

Steenlant, J. (1992), 'De nieuwe wet tot bescherming van de economische mededinging', *Tijdschrift voor Privaatrecht*, **29**, 337–392.

Steiner, J., 'Drawing the Line: Uses and Abuses of Article 30 EEC', *Common Market Law Review*, **29**, 749–774.

Stray Ryssdal, A.C. (1996), 'Towards a Nordic Competition Law', *Tidsskrift for Rettsvitenskap*, 332–357.

Tiebout, C. (1956), 'A Pure Theory of Local Expenditures', *Journal of Political Economy*, **64**, 416–424.

Toth, A.G. (1994), 'Is Subsidiarity Justiciable?', *European Law Review*, 268–285.

Ulmer, P. (1977), 'Der Begriff "Leistungswettbewerb" und seine Bedeutung für die Anwendung von GWB und UWG-Tatbestanden', *Gewerblicher Rechtsschutz und Urheberrecht*, 565–580.

Comment

Manfred E. Streit

The author has presented an interesting and empirically knowledgeable study of (1) the current diffusion of competences in competition policy in a wider sense within the EU, (2) arguments related to subsidiarity as an economic demarcation principle regarding the distribution of competences, and (3) reasons for the present handling of competition law in a narrow sense and for laws banning unfair competition by employing public choice theory and the theory of regulation.

In my comment, I shall focus on two issues: (1) the frame of reference used when discussing subsidiarity as an economic demarcation principle and (2) the answer to the question raised in the title of the chapter, namely does competition on the market for competition laws work?

The problem of the frame of reference has to be somewhat differently phrased than is done by the author. Considering his reasoning, the problem is not one of moving 'from Tiebout's world to reality'. If I take his reference to Hayek seriously, the question must be how to get from Tiebout to Hayek to reality. This is much more difficult than the author suggests. The basic problem is that throughout he uses neoclassical welfare economics as the relevant approach. He claims to answer the question 'whether and if so, under what conditions, competition between legislators in the field of competition law is desirable from an efficiency viewpoint'. He also tries to solve the demarcation problem by making centralisation dependent upon 'superior (welfare) effects'.

Regarding 'efficiency', the verdict of inefficiency is passed by the author quite frequently, but without clarifying how his judgement came about. Only the general theoretical approach, not its empirical application, is revealed. The author's point of reference is 'competitive equilibrium'. It includes the reference to rather naïve models of competition among systems of law (see below). To quote: 'Theory tells us that, if competition between sellers of products may lead to allocative efficiency, the same beneficial results may be reached when legislators compete'. Thereafter the author takes up the conventional 'market imperfections', that is, market structure ('number of competitors'), barriers to mobility, informational asymmetries, externalities and scale economies. However, I was unable to find out where he parts with the conventional approach to public policy which has been criticised by Demsetz (1969/1971, 160) as a 'nirvana approach'.

Given the basic line of reasoning, it is very difficult to see how the author can view the move from a modified Tiebout world to Hayek's competition as a discovery procedure. He tries to make this move under the subtitle 'competition as a learning process'. He further stresses that 'competition between legal orders promotes the search of new legal arrangements'. Hence, he definitely does not conceive this kind of competition as a purely adaptive process in which the 'best' institutional solution ultimately survives as an institutional equilibrium. However, this deviation from one aspect of the naïve model of competition among systems already has important consequences. It requires one to treat competition as an evolutionary process. This, in turn, implies true uncertainty in a Knightian sense. To share Hayek's view of competition also requires one to accept his disquieting but inescapable conclusion: 'If we do not know the facts we hope to discover by means of competition, we can never ascertain how effective it has been in discovering those facts that might be discovered' (Hayek 1968/1978, 181). This means that, once again, conventional efficiency evaporates as an empirically meaningful point of reference. Hayek's competition is an open process. Whether it may lead to a substantial uniformity of rules across the states must be left to the process itself. This is a conclusion which the author seems to support, at least in principle.

Related to this result is the author's reference to transaction costs. When discussing uniformity versus diversity in rules, he redefines the implied problem of legal certainty as follows: 'The relevant question is then whether transaction costs of diversity in rules outweigh the benefits'. I can agree with the emphasis being placed upon transaction costs. However, the suggested cost–benefit analysis has problems of its own. The author's assertion that the current costs of uniformity 'are quite substantial because of the inefficiency inherent in EC competition law' remains unfounded if efficiency is an inappropriate frame of reference. Competition among systems depends – like economic competition – on the propensity of the actors to incur transaction costs.[1] However, neither on the individual nor on the aggregate level is there any possibility of making a cost–benefit analysis which deserves that name. If Arrow's 'fundamental paradox in the demand for information' (Arrow 1962/1971, 140) holds, the benefits are not known until one has the information. Furthermore, the benefits themselves are the uncertain outcome of the process of competition which is driven by the costly acquisition of information. Given these properties of competition, competition laws cannot be an instrument to produce results of competition which could be identified as allocatively efficient. Distributional goals may be pursued by employing rules which tend to restrain competition. However the results are uncertain and include unpredictable side-effects. Hence I cannot see that a case can be made for instrumentalising competition laws to pursue concrete objectives. This is an issue which is touched upon by the author without pursuing it any further.

Considering the second issue – 'does competition on the market for competition laws work?' – it appears useful to deal at least briefly with what I call the naïve view of competition among systems. As already pointed out, the author employs this view as a frame of reference, adding the conventional 'imperfections' as qualifications. However in my view, it is even more important to reflect on the basic abstractions which allow to derive results like a 'race to the bottom', a 'competition in laxity' or 'zero regulation'. A few remarks must suffice here.[2] Thereby I do not discuss the problem, that some of the so-called imperfections are methodologically much more questionable than usually suggested. Even then, the aforementioned results can only be safely obtained (1) if economic competition is merely modelled as an adaptation to objectively given 'data' and not as a discovery procedure based on subjective knowledge, and (2) if political competition is modelled like adaptive economic competition, following the logic of equilibrium analysis.[3] Under these conditions, the interaction between the two partial processes hardly poses any serious analytical problems. However, the basic abstractions mentioned appear to be totally inadequate in view of the real processes.

From a Hayekian or Austrian perspective it is easier to agree with the author when – after having referred to the 'imperfections' – he points out that 'A more powerful argument in favour of decentralisation is the information advantage of national competition authorities'.[4] I can also agree with his finding, that 'decentralisation creates scope for competition between legislators', and that – within the EU – Public Choice can be employed to provide plausible reasons why such a decentralisation only exists in the field of unfair competition law .

With regard to the question whether at present competition on the market for competition laws works within the EU, the author appears to suggest a negative answer. His main argument is the present degree of centralisation, given the quasi-constitutional framework, under which the EU operates. Two questions remain open: From a constitutional point of view it has to be asked how the constitutional design in the area of competition policy could look like in order to allow a competition of legislators. Competition among competition policies itself requires rules of conduct for the competing legislators. At present, this problem of a superior level of rules is discussed with regard to international competition rules within the GATT/WTO system. Applying some of the results obtained so far to the EU would be quite interesting. In order to see what may be involved, I can only point at two avenues worth exploring: (1) A full application of the so-called effects doctrine of national antitrust law. In this case, each member country of the EU would apply its own competition laws on all activities if they have effects on domestic markets, notwithstanding whether these effects originate from actors inside or outside the domestic territory. The problem of jurisdictional conflicts due to diverging national competition laws and their extraterritorial enforcement would have to be solved by developing a collision norm in the sense of Savigny's principle of comitas or comity (for example, Hauser, Schoene 1994; Mestmäcker 1985/1993). It would be an extreme case in the sense that the competition rules of the EC-Treaty would be replaced by an agreement of comity in order to remove frictions resulting from a competition of competition policies between the member states. (2) As a second avenue an analogy to the Draft International Antitrust Code (see Fikentscher, Drexl 1995) could serve. In this case harmonisation would be combined with institutional competition. The element of harmonisation would be a minimum standard of competition rules which have to be applied by all member states of the EU. The element of competition would consist of rules of member states stricter than those of the minimum standard. The standard and deviations from it would have to be enforced by the member states only. However, there would be an EU antitrust authority entitled to take cases of alleged violation of the common minimum standard to the courts of the member states. As a consequence, the European Court of Justice would no longer be involved in matters of antitrust.

The two avenues demonstrate how competition among systems or – for that matter – among competition laws is related to sovereignty of the member states. Compared to these and similar arrangements, the EC-Treaty entails a solution to antitrust problems with inherent tendencies to centralisation, as set out by the author with regard to competition law sensu stricto.

This leads me to the second issue and to my final point. Even if rules for competition between competition policies were found, it could be asked how effective such a competition could be in view of the fact, that competition policy is but one of a multitude of factors affecting border-crossing factor movements and trade which provide the linkage between economic competition and competition among legislators. However, the answer to the question raised in the title of the chapter is not one of straightforward expediency. Given the properties of competition, it is difficult to establish its particular effects in advance. In addition there is a normative constitutional aspect. It is related to competition between legislators as a potential controlling device. To give competition at least a chance would require that the legislators themselves agree to a hands-tying by competition rules for competition policy.

NOTES

1. For analysis of the role of transaction costs in the process of economic competition see Streit and Wegner (1992).
2. For an assessment with special reference to the European integration process see Streit (1995).
3. A thorough analysis of the deficiencies of modelling political competition as an analogy to economic competition in general and the particular problems related with neoclassical and evolutionary models see Wohlgemuth (1995).
4. In fact, I would go much further than that. Taking Hayek and the non-constructivist approach seriously, identifying restrictive business practices (RBP) in itself becomes a problem. Elsewhere (Streit 1996), I have tried to show that this approach and the related concept of freedom to compete requires one to take a fresh look at what could be considered a RBP and whether requirements as to general properties of competition laws can be identified.

REFERENCES

Arrow, K.J. (1962/1971), 'Economic Welfare and the Allocation of Resources for Invention', in D.M. Lamberton (ed.), *Economics of Information and Knowledge*, Harmondsworth: Penguin, pp. 141–159.

Demsetz, H. (1969/1971), 'Information and Efficiency: Another Viewpoint', in D.M. Lamberton (ed.), *Economics of Information and Knowledge*, Harmondsworth: Penguin, pp. 160–186.

Fikentscher, W. and J. Drexl (1995), 'Der Draft International Antitrust Code – Zur institutionellen Struktur eines künftigen Weltkartellrechts', in W. Fikentscher and U. Immenga (eds), *Draft International Antitrust Code*, Baden-Baden: Nomos, pp. 35–52.

Hauser, H. and R.E. Schoene (1994), 'Is there a Need for International Competition Rules?', *Außenwirtschaft*, **49**, 205–222.

Hayek, F.A. (1968/1978), 'Competition as a Discovery Procedure', in F.A. Hayek, *New Studies in Philosophy, Politics and the History of Ideas*, London and Henley: Routledge, pp. 179–190.

Mestmäcker, E.-J. (1985/1993), 'Rechtsfragen einer Ordnung der Weltwirtschaft', in E.-J. Mestmäcker, *Recht in der offenen Gesellschaft*, Baden-Baden: Nomos, pp. 122–182.

Streit, M.E. (1995), 'Systemwettbewerb und Harmonisierung im europäischen Integrationsprozeß', in D. Cassel (ed.), *Entstehung und Wettbewerb von Systemen, Schriften des Vereins für Socialpolitik, 246,* Berlin: Duncker und Humblot, pp. 223–244.

Streit, M.E. (1996), 'Constitutional Ignorance, Spontaneous Order and Rule-Orientation – Hayekian Paradigms from a Policy Perspective', in S. Frowen (ed.), *Hayek: Economist and Social Philosopher: A Critical Retrospect*, London: Macmillan.

Streit, M.E. and G. Wegner (1992), 'Information, Transactions, and Catallaxy: Reflections on Some Key Concepts of Evolutionary Market Theory', in U. Witt (ed.), *Explaining Process and Change – Approaches to Evolutionary Economics*, Ann Arbor: University of Michigan Press, pp. 125–149.

Wohlgemuth, M. (1995), 'Economic and Political Competition in Neoclassical and Evolutionary Perspective', *Constitutional Political Economy*, **6**, 71–96.

Comment

Christian Watrin

Professor van den Bergh presented a truly valuable and stimulating contribution to our conference. Especially his comments on the working and inefficiency of the European Union's (EU) legal system are highly interesting. The reader can learn much about the confusing criteria the Commission uses in its role as prosecutor and judge. Also note 86 should not be overlooked, where the author states that 'at present the quality of economic reasoning in EC antitrust cases is poor, if not totally absent'.

One particular point should definitely be addressed: Professor van den Bergh's defence of the subsidiarity principle. Contrary to the vagueness attributed to it by many critics, he claims that he would take it seriously as a workable device for the assignment of powers to the different layers of government in the member states and in the EU. In the final section of his chapter, he comes to the conclusion that 'if the subsidiarity principle is to be taken seriously, the Community institutions must prove why a centralised competition policy remains necessary even in a mostly realised internal market'. He demonstrates that neither 'legal certainty' nor 'administrative efficiency' are convincing arguments for the present allocation of powers in the Community, in which lawmaking is centralised and law enforcement decentralised. This outcome is further explained in other parts of the chapter.

But is the subsidiarity principle truly a workable device for the assignment of powers in a polity like the European Union? First of all, it should be taken into account, that there are competing definitions of this principle. Professor van den Bergh, for instance, uses the term as a sort of synonym for decentralisation. James M. Buchanan and Dwight R. Lee describe it as 'the ideal of not letting a higher level of government perform a task that can be performed as well or better by a lower level of government'. And it can be expected that a review of the literature will lead to the conclusion that the ideal of subsidiarity is interpreted in many ways. This can be confirmed by the definition which has been chosen in the Maastricht Treaty. Article 3a first states that the principle applies only to those areas not falling into the Community's exclusive competence. In other words, subsidiarity is not an idea for reviewing the whole political and administrative structure of the Treaty. If a power has already been assigned to the supranational level, it should remain there forever. This can be interpreted as a defence of the legal *status quo*.

Further, the legal text states that action can be taken by the Community in areas outside its exclusive competence only if, and in so far as, the objectives of the proposed action cannot be sufficiently achieved by the member states. In this case, by reason of the scale or effects of the proposed action, the aims must be 'better achieved' by the Community. Seen economically, the question arises whether objective standards exist that assist in deciding which institutional arrangement – centralisation or decentralisation – can be judged as 'better achieving' the purposes of the subsidiarity principle. Professor van den Bergh tries to answer it by reverting to static and dynamic efficiency. But in economic policy affairs efficiency criteria perform poorly. Also, questions of the assignment of state powers, which define the rules of the game, are too complicated to be easily subsumed under the heading of static or even dynamic efficiency. It is difficult to determine in advance how, for instance, a specific set of competition rules might work and what their outcome might be. Further, if the outcome of stiffening competition rules is an emergence of winners and losers, the respective losses and gains have to be weighed. What weight should be placed on the costs and on the benefits? The social value of a specific competition policy is – in practice – always controversial. And in the end a collective decision has to be reached, whether a policy is compatible with the subsidiarity principle or not.

All in all, the subsidiarity principle is open to value-loaded or political interpretations. This is the reason why one should join the ranks of those criticising it as being vague. Or to put it differently, the normative content of the subsidiarity principle is rather low. Here the notion of 'normative content' should be used in analogy to Karl Popper's idea of the 'empirical content' of positive theories. An empirical testable theory must have a class of events, which are incompatible with it. Otherwise, it would not be refutable. In the same way we can talk about a normative criterion. It must define a class of outcomes incompatible with the respective norm. A centralised unitary state might be incompatible with the subsidiarity principle, but how about a highly centralised federal state, where some provinces have rights of autonomy and others do not? And how does the structure of the European Union fit into the subsidiarity principle? According to some, it is a 'federation or supranational state in process' as the centralists claim, whereas the decentralists stress its character as an international treaty or alliance resting on the principle of unanimity – a 'Europe of Nations' according to de Gaulle's famous phrase. If both structures would fit into the subsidiarity principle, then it is not very helpful for deciding practical problems.

Professor van den Bergh does not discuss the subsidiarity principle in detail, but tries to apply it to a very special case, European competition law. There are, at least, three different ways to assign the power to make competition rules. Decentralised lawmaking, centralised law-making and competition among national and EU-law-makers. It seems Professor van den Bergh favours decentralised law-making. He argues that more efficient rules would be initiated by competition among states and that costs are higher in centralised law-making. This evaluation is fully in line with my own prejudices. But are they logical implications of the subsidiarity principle? Should Professor van den Bergh's argument that harmonisation of competition law is not necessary and that we all can live together under differing competition laws be so easily accepted? In international trade, for instance, competition law in a foreign country is of less interest, when trade is established and performed. But in a more closely integrated organisation like the EU, the minimum provision must be that a segmentation of markets through cartel-like agreements must be prevented. There has to be an authority monitoring this simple rule. Then it turns out that the meaning of subsidiarity principle applied to competition policy is just another way to express the liberal idea that all markets – not only the ones in the EU – should be open to competition. Enforcing this simple rule inside the Single Market and also with respect to all third countries would be sufficient to reap substantial economic benefits from the division of labour.

From this perspective competition policy takes on a wider meaning. Competition cannot only be strengthened by antitrust laws and laws prohibiting 'unfair' competition, but also by trade liberalisation. According to experiences in the Common Market, neither national nor European competition policies (in the narrow sense) have had a decisive effect on improving competition. On the contrary, as Professor van den Bergh rightly emphasises, there are countless examples, where interest groups undermine the aims of competition policy successfully. Even the European Commission, which should be the guardian and protector of competition in the Single Market, 'seems to take an active part in the race for the bottom', that is, prefers lax competition instead of strengthening the rules. This is underlined by Article 130 TEU in which industrial policy is introduced as a new competence of the community. This could lead to a serious set-back for all endeavours towards building the Common Market on the rules of an internationally open market economy.

PART THREE

Institutional Change

7. FOCJ: Creating a Single European Market for Governments*

Bruno S. Frey and Reiner Eichenberger

1. LIBERALISED ECONOMIC AND RESTRICTED POLITICAL MARKETS IN EUROPE

European integration was outstandingly successful at granting the four freedoms related to the movement of goods, services, labour and capital. As a result of establishing a single, competitive European *economic* market, the citizens of the countries forming the European Union (EU) have certainly experienced a significant increase in welfare. However, no such open and competitive *market for politics* has been established. On the contrary: the competition between governments was successfully restricted by the various European treaties and institutions. While the European Union's power in politics, including economic policy, are still quite limited, no steps have been undertaken to actively institutionalise competition between governmental units at all levels. Such competition has only been considered for national governments. However, from a constitutional perspective other forms of political competition should be envisaged, too. We argue that welfare can be improved substantially by promoting competition between newly emerging jurisdictions that are organised along functions instead of territories. The *fifth freedom* we suggest allows for such *functional, overlapping and competing jurisdictions*. They will be called by their acronym FOCJ (one such jurisdiction will be called FOCUS). FOCJ form a federal system of governments that is not dictated from above, but emerges from below as a response to citizens' preferences. This fifth freedom requires a *constitutional decision* (see, for example, Frey 1983, Mueller 1996) which ensures that the emergence of FOCJ is not blocked by existing

* We thank Iris Bohnet, Isabelle Busenhart, Felix Oberholzer-Gee, Daniel Rubinfeld, Hans-Jörg Schmidt-Trenz, Dieter Schmidtchen and Jürg de Spindler for useful suggestions. Financial support from the Swiss National Fund, Project No. 12-42480.94, is acknowledged.

jurisdictions such as direct competitors or higher level governments. Every citizen and community must have the right to appeal directly to the European Court if barriers to the competition between governments are established. The European Constitution must give the lowest political units (communities) a measure of independence so that they can engage in forming FOCJ. The citizens must be given the right to establish FOCJ by popular referenda, and political entrepreneurs must be supported and controlled by the institution of popular initiatives. The FOCJ themselves must have the right to levy taxes to finance the public services they provide.

These FOCJ strongly contrast with the concepts of federalism currently existing or being proposed in the European Union. We intend to show that FOCJ are well-grounded in economic theory. Successful precursors of these institutions existed in European history. Indeed, Europe owes its rise to a economic and intellectual centre to the competition among governmental units. Moreover, such functional competing units already partially exist in present-day Europe and elsewhere, where they perform well within the space accorded to them. The idea of continuing European integration at different speeds, and thus having various subgroups of countries within the European Union, is also related though it is far more restrictive than our concept of FOCJ.

The chapter is organised as follows: section two specifies the concept of FOCJ and puts it into theoretical perspective. The third section compares FOCJ to existing federal institutions in the European Union. The next section analyses the working of FOCJ and discusses how the problems related with this type of jurisdiction may be overcome. For this purpose, our concept of competitive federalism is contrasted to all-purpose jurisdictions confined to one particular geographical area. The fifth section asks why FOCJ do not yet exist in reality on a large scale. However, section six shows that FOCJ partially exist in both European history and today. The relationship to US special districts and in particular to functional communities in Switzerland is emphasised. Concluding remarks are offered in the last section.

2. CONSTITUTING ELEMENTS

The federal units here proposed have four essential characteristics: they are

- *Functional* (F), that is, the new political units extend over areas defined by the tasks to be fulfilled;

- *Overlapping* (O), that is, in line with the many different tasks (functions) there are corresponding governmental units extending over different geographical areas;
- *Competing* (C), that is, individuals and/or communities may choose to what governmental unit they want to belong, and they have political rights to express their preferences directly via initiatives and referenda;
- *Jurisdictions* (J), that is, the units established are governmental, they have enforcement power and can, in particular, levy taxes.

FOCJ are based on theoretical propositions advanced in the economic theory of federalism. They nevertheless form a governmental system completely different to the one suggested in that literature. While the economic theory of federalism (see Bird 1993 and Breton 1996 for surveys on its present state) analyses the behaviour of *given* political units at the different levels of government (Weingast 1993: 292), FOCJ *emerge* in response to the '*geography of problems*'.[1]

The four elements of FOCJ are now related to economic theory as well as to existing federal institutions, pointing out both similarities and differences to existing concepts.

2.1. Functions

A particular public service which benefits a certain geographical area should be financed by the people living in that area, that is, there should be no spillovers. The different governmental units can cater to differences in the populations' preferences or, more precisely, to its demands. To minimise cost, these units have to exploit economies of scale in production. As the latter may strongly differ between functions (for example, between schools, police, hospitals, power plants and defence) there is an additional reason for uni-functional (or few-functional) governmental units of different sizes. This is the central idea of 'fiscal equivalence' as proposed by Olson (1969) and Oates (1972). This endogeneity of the size of governmental units constitutes an essential part of FOCJ.

However, fiscal equivalence theory has been little concerned with decisionmaking within functional units. The supply process is either left unspecified or it is assumed that the mobility of persons (and of firms, a fact rarely mentioned) automatically induces these units to cater to individual preferences. This criticism also applies to a closely related concept of fiscal federalism, namely 'voting by foot' (Tiebout 1956). This preference-revealing mechanism makes comparatively efficient suppliers grow in size, and the others shrink. According to this model of federalism, the political jurisdictions are exogenously given, are multi-purpose, and do not overlap, while the political supply process is left unspecified. In contrast, we emphasise the need to study explicitly the political supply process. In line with Epple and Zelenitz (1981), exit and entry is considered insufficient to eliminate rent extraction by governments. Therefore, individuals must have the possibility of raising voice in the form of voting. There is a certain similarity between Buchanan's (1965) 'clubs' and FOCJ because the size of both is determined endogenously by the benefits and costs of the club members (see Sandler and Tschirhart 1980). Another concept related to FOCJ are functional parliaments serving both allocative and distributional functions. Such institutions have been suggested for the European Union by Teutemann (1992), yet they differ in an important respect from FOCJ. They are determined and imposed from outside and above whereas FOCJ emerge in response to the demand by individuals or, in a more aggregate way, by communities as the smallest existing political unit.

2.2. Overlaps

FOCJ may overlap in two respects: (i) FOCJ catering to different functions may overlap; (ii) two or more FOCJ catering even for the same function may geographically intersect (for example, a multitude of school FOCJ may exist in the same geographical area). The two types of overlap may coexist; however, a constitutional decision can be taken to restrict FOCJ of some specific functions to the first type because this alleviates free-riding problems (see below). An individual or a political community normally belongs to various FOCJ at the same time. FOCJ need not be physically contiguous, and they need not have a monopoly over a certain area of land. Thus, this concept completely differs from archaic nationalism with its fighting over pieces of land. It also breaks with the notion of federalist theory that units at the same level may not overlap. On the other hand, in this respect it is similar to Buchanan-type clubs which may intersect.

2.3. Competition

The heads of FOCJ are induced to conform closely to their members' preferences by two mechanisms: while the individuals' and communities' possibilities to *exit* mimics market competition (Hirschman 1970), their right to *vote* establishes political competition (see Mueller 1989). It should be noted that migration is only one means of exit; often, membership in a particular FOCUS can be discontinued without changing one's location. Exit is not restricted to individuals or firms; as said before, political communities as a whole, or parts of them, may also exercise this option. Moreover, exit may be total or only partial. In the latter case, an individual or community only participates in a restricted set of FOCUS activities. This enlarged set of exit options makes 'voting by foot' function properly.

The importance of 'secession' (that is, exit of jurisdictions such as communities) for restricting the power of central states has been recognised in the literature (for example, Zarkovic Bookman 1992, Drèze 1993). Secession has been suggested as an important ingredient for a future European constitution (Buchanan 1991, European Constitutional Group 1993). The right to secede stands in stark contrast to the prevailing concepts of nation states and federations where this is strictly forbidden and often prevented by force, as is illustrated, for example, by the American Civil War 1861–65, by the Swiss 'Sonderbundskrieg' 1847, or more recently by the wars in Katanga (1960–63), Biafra (1967–70), Bangladesh (1970–71), and presently in former Yugoslavia. Current European treaties do not provide for the secession of a nation from the European Union, and *a fortiori* for part of a nation. The possibility of lower-level jurisdictions to exit at low cost from the European Union as a whole as well as from particular subunits (nations, states, Länder, autonomous regions, and so on) thus depends strongly on the future European constitution.

For FOCJ to establish competition between governments, exit should be as unrestrained as possible. In contrast, entry need not necessarily be free. As for individuals in Buchanan-type clubs, jurisdictions and individuals may be asked a price if they want to join a particular FOCUS and benefit from its public goods. The existing members of the particular FOCUS have to decide democratically whether a new member pays an adequate entry price and is thus welcome. 'Free' mobility in the sense of a disregard for the cost imposed on others is overcome by internalising the external cost of movement. In addition, FOCJ do not have to restrict entry by administrative and legal means such as zoning laws. Explicit, openly declared entry fees substitute implicit restrictions resulting in high land prices and housing rents. The commonly raised concern that pricing could be exploitative and mobility strongly curtailed is unwarranted as FOCJ are subject to competitive pressure. Moreover, the possibility to impose an explicit entry fee gives incentives to FOCJ-governments to care not only for the preferences of actual, but also of prospective members.

Competition also needs to be furthered by political institutions as the exit option does not suffice to induce governments to act efficiently. The citizens should directly elect the persons managing the FOCJ, and should be given the right to initiate popular referenda on specific issues. These democratic institutions are known to raise efficiency in the sense of caring well for individual preferences (for elections, see Downs 1957, Mueller 1989; for referenda Frey 1994).

2.4. Jurisdictions

A FOCUS is a democratic governmental unit with authority over its citizens, including the power to tax. According to the two types of overlap, two forms of membership can be distinguished: (i) The lowest political unit (normally the community is a member), and all corresponding citizens automatically become citizens of the FOCJ to which their community belongs. In that case, an individual can only exit via mobility. (ii) Individuals may freely choose whether they want to belong to a particular FOCUS, but while they are its citizen, they are subject to its authority. Such FOCJ may be non-voluntary in the sense that one must belong to a FOCUS providing for a certain function, for example, to a school-FOCUS, and must pay the corresponding taxes (an analogy here is health insurance which in many countries is obligatory but where individuals are allowed to choose an insurance company). The citizens of such a school-FOCUS may then decide that everyone must pay taxes in order to finance a particular school, irrespective of whether one has children. With respect to FOCJ providing functions with significant redistributive effects, a minimal regulation by the central government may be in order so that, for example, citizens without children do not join 'school-FOCJ' which in effect do not offer any schooling but have correspondingly low (or zero) taxes.

FOCJ as jurisdictions provide particular services but do not necessarily produce them themselves if contracting-out to a public or private enterprise is advantageous. But present-day outsourcing by communities does not lead to FOCJ as the former is restricted to production while FOCJ care for provision (and are directly democratically controlled). In this respect, Buchanan-type clubs differ from FOCJ, too, because they are always voluntary while membership in a FOCUS can be obligatory.

3. FOCJ AND EUROPE

3.1. Comparison to Actual and Proposed Federalistic Institutions

FOCJ differ in many crucial respects from scholarly *proposals* for a future European constitution. One of the most prominent was Buchanan's (1991) who stresses an individual nation's right to secede but, somewhat surprisingly, does not build on Buchanan-type clubs. The European Constitutional Group (1993) focuses on the example of the American constitution, and presents constructivist proposals with respect to the houses of parliament and the respective voting weights of the various countries. Overlapping jurisdictions and referenda are not allowed for, and the exit option is strongly restricted. Other economics scholars (for example, Blöchliger and R.L. Frey 1992, Schneider 1992) suggest a strengthening of federalism in the traditional sense (that is, with multi-purpose federal units) but do not envisage overlapping jurisdictions. The report by the Centre for Economic Policy Research (1993) criticises 'subsidiarity' (as used in the Maastricht Treaty) as an empty concept arguing that good theoretical reasons must be provided for central government intervention. But the report does not deal with the institutions necessary to guarantee that policy follows such theoretical advice. The idea of overlapping, not geographically based jurisdictions is shortly raised but is not institutionally or practically worked out, nor is the need for a democratic organisation and the power to tax acknowledged.

The recent proposal from politicians (Herman report of the European Parliament, 1994) mainly deals with the organisation of the parliamentary system (the houses of parliament and the national vote weights) and to a substantial extent accepts the existing treatises as the founding blocks of the European constitution. The idea of competition between governments (which is basic for FOCJ) is neglected or even rejected in favour of 'cooperation' between governments.

FOCJ are also quite different from the regions envisaged in existing *European treaties* and *institutions* (see, for example, Adonis and Jones 1991). A major difference is that FOCJ emerge from below while the 'European regions' tend to be established from above. Moreover, their existence strongly depends on the subsidies flowing from the European Union and the nation states (Sharpe 1993). In contrast, the concept of FOCJ corresponds to Hayek's (1960) (and Buchanan's) non-constructivist process view. It cannot *a priori* be determined from outside and from above which FOCJ will be efficient in the future. This must be left entirely to the competitive democratic process taking place at the level of individuals and communities. The central European constitution must only make sure that no other government units, in particular the nations, may obstruct the emergence of FOCJ. In contrast to Hayek, however, our scheme allows for a (closely restricted) set of central regulations, as mentioned above. Moreover, Hayek measures efficiency by survival in the evolutionary process while we define efficiency more directly in terms of the fulfilment of citizens' demands.

'Subsidiarity' as proclaimed in the Maastricht Treaty is generally recognised to be more a vague goal than a concept with content (see, for example, Centre for Economic Policy Research 1993: pp. 19–23). Even if subsidiarity were taken seriously, it would not lead to a real federal structure because many (actual or prospective) members of the European Union are essentially unitary states without federal subunits of significant competence (examples are The Netherlands, France or Sweden). The 'regions' existing in the European Union (examples are Galicia and Cataluña in Spain, or South Tyrol and Sicily in Italy) are far from being units with significant autonomous functional and fiscal competencies.

The Council of Ministers is a European decisionmaking institution based on federal principles (but nations only are represented) and organised according to functional principles (or at least according to the corresponding administrative units). However, this Council is only indirectly democratic (the ministers are members of governments which are democratically legitimised by the representative system) and the deliberations are not public. Exit from the European Union is not formally regulated, and exceptions to specific aspects of agreements reached (as in the Maastricht Treaty concerning the European Monetary Union and the Protocol on Social Policy, or in the Schengen Treaty concerning the free movement of persons) are granted reluctantly. Indeed, they are seen as damaging the 'spirit of Europe'. Whether differential degrees of European integration are framed as models of variable geometry, multi-track, multi-speed, two-tier, hard core, concentric circles, or as Europe *à la carte* (*The Economist*, 1994, 22 October, 'Survey of the European Union', p. 15; Pitschas 1994), it always evokes fierce opposition. In a system of FOCJ, in contrast, functional units not covering everyone are taken as a welcome expression of heterogeneous demands among Europeans.

3.2. Applications

It might be argued that the idea of FOCJ is exotic and has no chance of ever being put into practice in Europe. A careful consideration reveals, however, that there is a wide range of functional issues to which FOCJ could profitably be applied. A practical example is the policing of the Lake of Constance (which borders on two German Länder, two Swiss Cantons, and one Austrian Land) which involves the regulation of traffic, environmental protection, the suppression of criminal activities and the prevention of accidents. Formally, the various local police departments are not allowed to collaborate directly with each other, not even to exchange information. Rather, they must advise the police ministries of the Länder and cantons, which then have to notify the respective central governments which then interact with each other. Obviously, such a formal procedure is in most cases vastly inefficient and unnecessarily time consuming. In actual fact, the problems are dealt with by direct contact among the local police commissioners and officers. However, this is outside the law and depends to a substantial extent on purely personal relationships (which may be good or bad). A FOCUS committed to policing the lake would allow a pragmatic, problem oriented approach within the law – and would, moreover, be in the best 'spirit' of Europe.

FOCJ are not restricted to such small-scale functional issues but are relevant for all levels of government and major issues. An example would be Alsace which, while remaining a part of France in other respects, might partially exit by joining, say, the German social security or school system (with German as the main language), or might join a university-FOCUS involving the Swiss university of Basle and the German universities of Freiburg and Karlsruhe. Actually, the first steps for establishing such a university-FOCUS are under way. But these efforts contrast with the idea of regions as set out in the Maastricht Treaty (and elsewhere), not least because one of the participants (the university of Basle) is not part of the European Union. Another example refers to Corsica which according to Drèze's (1993) suggestion should form an independent region of Europe because of its dissatisfaction with France. However, the Corsicans are most likely only *partially* dissatisfied with France. This suggests that one or several FOCJ provide a better solution in this case; they may, for instance, especially focus on ethnic or language boundaries, or on Corsica's economic problems as an island. This allows the Corsicans to exit France only partially instead of totally. Quite generally, tourism and transport issues, in particular railroads, are important areas for FOCJ. It should be noted that, despite the membership of various countries in the (then) European Community, railroad policy was not coordinated to exploit possible economies of scale; a FOCUS may constitute a well-suited organisation to overcome such shortcomings.

4. HOW FOCJ WORK

4.1. Beneficial Effects

FOCJ compare favourably to traditional forms of federalism. One aspect concerns the governments' incentives and possibilities of satisfying heterogeneous preferences of individuals. Due to the concentration on one functional area, the citizens of a particular FOCUS have better information on its activity, and are in a better position to compare its performance to other governments. As many benefits and costs extend over a quite limited geographic area, we envisage FOCJ to be often small which is also helpful for voters' evaluations. The exit option opened by the existence of overlapping jurisdictions is also an important means to make one's preferences known to governmental suppliers.

On the other hand, FOCJ are able to provide public services at low cost because they are formed in order to minimise interjurisdictional spillovers and to exploit economies of scale. When the benefits of a specific activity indivisibly extend over large areas, and there are decreasing costs, the corresponding optimal FOCUS may cover many communities, several nations, or even Europe as a whole. An example may be defence against outward aggression where the appropriate FOCUS may extend over the whole of Europe (even beyond the European Union). That such adjustment to efficient size is indeed undertaken in reality is shown by the Swiss experience. Communities decided by referendum whether they wanted to join the new canton Jura established in 1978, and in 1993 communities in the Laufental opted to belong to the canton Basel-Land instead of Berne. Communities also frequently change districts (the federal level below cantons) by referendum vote, which suggest that voters perceive the new size of jurisdictions and the new bundle of services to be more efficient. The same holds for American special districts (see below).

The specialisation in one or a few functions further contributes to cost efficiency due to the advantages of specialisation. As FOCJ levy their own taxes to finance their activity, it pays to be economical. In contrast, in APJ (All-Purpose Jurisdictions) financed from outside lacking such fiscal equivalence, politicians have an incentive to lobby for ever increasing funds, thereby pushing up government expenditures. The incentive to economise in a FOCUS induces its managers to contract-out whenever production cost can thereby be reduced. While FOCJ are more market oriented than APJ, they reduce the size of the public sector. However, they differ from today's one-shot privatisation, which usually does not impact on the governments' basic incentives and thus is subsequently often reversed by deregulation and deprivatization. In contrast, in a system of FOCJ privatisation emerges endogenously and is sustainable, as the politicians' incentives are changed fundamentally.

The threat of dissatisfied citizens or communities to exit the FOCUS, and the benefit of new citizens and communities joining, gives an incentive to take individual preferences into account and to provide the public services efficiently. Quite another advantage of FOCJ is that they open up the politicians' cartel ('classe politique') to functionally competent outsiders. While all-purpose jurisdictions attract persons with broad and non-specialised knowledge to become politicians, in FOCJ rather persons with a well-grounded knowledge in a particular functional area (say education or refuse collection) are successful.

The possibility to form FOCJ helps to deal with issues raised by fundamentalist sentiments. Political movements focused on a single issue (for example, ethnicity, religion, environment, and so on) are not forced to take over governments *in toto* but can concentrate on those functions they are really interested in. The 'Greens', for example, do not have to take a stand on foreign policy (for which they are dogmatically ill-equipped) but can devote their energy to FOCJ dealing with environmental issues. Similarly, an ethnic group need not disassociate itself from the state they live in as a whole but may found FOCJ which care for their particular preferences. South Tyroleans, for example, unhappy with the language domination imposed by the Italian state, need not leave Italy in order to have their demands for cultural autonomy fulfilled, but may establish corresponding FOCJ. Such partial exit (for instance, only with respect to ethnic issues) does not lead to trade barriers often associated with the establishment of newly formed all purpose jurisdictions. FOCJ thus meet the criterion of market preserving federalism (see Weingast 1993).

A federal web composed of FOCJ certainly affects the role of the nation states. They will certainly lose functions they presently do not fulfil according to the population's preferences, or which they produce at higher cost than FOCJ designed to exploit cost advantages. On the other hand, the scheme does not purport to do away with nations but allows for multi-national as well as small scale alternatives where they are desired by the citizens. Nation states subsist in so far as they provide functions efficiently according to the voters' preferences.

4.2. Overcoming Problems

Up to this point we have emphasised the beneficial effects of FOCJ. However, there are also some alleged problems with our concept which will now be discussed.

Overburdened citizens

In a federal system of FOCJ, each individual is a citizen of various jurisdictions. As a consequence, individuals may be overburdened by voting in elections and referenda taking place in each FOCUS. However, citizens in a direct-democratic FOCUS find it much easier to politically participate as they have only to assess one or a few concrete issues at a time. In contrast, in representative-democratic APJ citizens have to evaluate all political aspects simultaneously, and they have to speculate what position a political candidate will take over the next election term. Formal voting theory indeed assumes that the voters evaluate each dimension of government activity or of a candidate's policy separately (for example, Downs 1957, or for a survey Mueller 1989). This breakdown according to various aspects is to a substantial extent performed naturally by FOCJ. If the citizens find it none the less burdensome to vote on each governmental function separately, they can rely on institutions emerging to deal with the problem. For instance, in referenda they may simply follow parties' recommendations. A more innovative solution would allow citizens to voluntarily transfer the voting right on specific functions to a political agent, be it a party or an interest group, who then decides on the behalf of the citizens concerned. This kind of 'representation' is chosen by each citizen according to his or her individual preference, and can be recalled at any time.

Overburdened consumers

An individual is confronted with a multitude of suppliers of public services which is argued to make life difficult. This is the logical consequence of having more options to choose from, and is similar to supply in the private sector. If citizens find it nevertheless to be a problem, a governmental or a private advisory service can be established which offers information and support for the consumers' decisions. It should, moreover, be observed that in APJ the same problem exists. There is no all-enhancing administration managing all public services. Rather, the responsibility is divided up among specialised government departments so that the citizens/consumers are also effectively confronted with many different agencies supplying public services.

'Need' to coordinate the activities of FOCJ

While coordination is obviously often needed, coordination between governments is not a good as such. It sometimes serves to build cartels among the members of the 'classe politique' who then evade or even exploit the population's wishes (see CEPR 1993, Vaubel 1994, Frey 1994). As far as welfare increasing coordination is concerned, its need is reduced compared to APJ because the FOCJ emerge in order to minimise externalities. If major spillovers between FOCJ exist, new FOCJ will be founded taking care of these externalities. As the number of FOCJ is restricted due to the transactions cost involved, less important externalities between FOCJ will remain. However, spillovers also exist in a system of APJ between administrative units, for instance, between the department for environment and the department of transport. The crucial question therefore is in what system N-player Coase-type interfunctional bargaining is more likely to arise. The respective civil servants in APJ have a muted incentive to take these spillovers into account by bargaining. On the one hand, their sphere of influence may be curtailed if they coordinate decisions among various departments effectively. On the other hand, their income and other benefits are essentially unconnected to the possible benefits to the citizens. To overcome externalities within an APJ the respective government needs to establish interministerial commissions with appropriate incentives. In contrast, the political managers of a FOCUS have a self-interest to engage seriously in Coasian bargaining as the support received from the members of their FOCUS depends on how much they raise their members' utility. This responsiveness is achieved by the institutions of re-election and by popular initiatives and referenda on specific issues. To the extent that the citizens of some FOCJ value coordination, it behoves the FOCJ governments to provide it. Thus, coordination among FOCJ is not inherently different from coordination in economic markets, where similar problems occur all the time and are analysed in depth by much recent research in industrial organisation (see Farrell and Saloner 1988, Milgrom and Roberts 1990). Some of the solutions found there, for example, for the development of industry wide standards, might well apply to FOCJ as well.

Vote trading

In FOCJ the separation along functions prohibits vote trading and therefore restricts the expression of different preference intensities. In contrast, in a system of APJ, minorities with strong preferences in one dimension (function) can exchange votes with groups who have strong interests in other functions, leading to a Pareto-superior outcome. However, vote trading does not always induce Pareto-superior outcomes. Log-rolling is only beneficial to the groups included in the deals, but tends to damage others. According to the vote trading paradox (see Riker and Brams 1973) log-rolling may even be costly for all the groups involved, when government activity is not effectively limited to allocative functions. Furthermore, preference intensities can generally be expressed by higher vote participation and/or by a higher probability to vote for a desired alternative. Finally, a federal system based on FOCJ is flexible enough to allow minorities with intensive preferences to establish new FOCJ which care for their preferences.

Redistribution

It is claimed that all forms of federalism – including FOCJ – undermine redistribution. Moreover, FOCJ are said to emerge on the basis of income. As far as redistribution is based on the citizens' solidarity or on insurance principles, this fear is unwarranted. Only as far as redistribution is a pure public good, and thus must be enforced to prevent free-riding, may a problem arise. However, recent empirical research (Gold 1991, Kirchgässner and Pommerehne 1996) suggests that substantial redistribution is feasible in federal systems. In the US and especially in Switzerland, lower level and even local governments strongly engage in redistribution activities and are responsible for a substantive share of redistribution. In these countries, mobility is obviously not high enough to render redistribution impossible. As concerns Europe, mobility is also quite low. Less than five per cent of EU-citizens live outside their country of citizenship. This low level of mobility can be interpreted in two ways: (i) In decentralised systems mobility by persons (and to a lesser extent also firms) is countervailed by strong local attachment. (ii) Redistribution does not constitute a pure public good but provides localised benefits. However, if decentralised redistribution is considered insufficient, a FOCUS specialised in interregional redistribution may emerge but this presupposes barriers to entry (in analogy to insurance systems with cross-subsidisation). Moreover, centralisation of redistribution is still possible, of course. The European constitution may give central government the power to impose a limited amount of income redistribution.

5. WHY HAVE FOCJ NOT YET SUCCEEDED?

In view of the major advantages outlined, and the futility of much of the alleged problems of FOCJ the economist's standard question arises: if this type of federalism is so good, why is it not more successful? The organisation of states today does not follow the model of FOCJ for two major reasons. An obvious, but crucial one, is that individuals and communities are prohibited from establishing such jurisdictions, and in many countries of the European Union communities are not even allowed formally to collaborate with each other without the consent of the central government (for empirical evidence, see Sharpe 1993, esp. p. 123ff.). When spillovers exist, the normal procedure in all member countries is to shift the task to a higher level of government which leads to increasing centralisation. An example is environmental protection which to a considerable extent deals with local issues but where the existence of partial externalities have lead to a centralised administration.

Secondly a system of FOCJ is not observed because it violates the interests of politicians and public officials at the higher levels of government. The emergence of FOCJ reduces the public suppliers' power and increases citizens' influence by the newly introduced mechanisms of competition by exit and entry and by direct democratic elements. Both are regularly opposed by the classe politique (see, for example, Vaubel 1994 for the case of the EU). Politicians' discretionary room and therefore the rents appropriable are the larger, the higher the federal level.[2] Thus, they favour a shift of competencies in this direction, and oppose local decisionmaking, especially by FOCJ.

In the countries of the European Union (and elsewhere) a federal system of FOCJ will not arise if these barriers are not overcome. A necessary condition is new constitutional rules allowing the formation of FOCJ and giving the citizens and the governments the right to appeal to the Constitutional Court if they are blocked.

6. ILLUSTRATIONS

6.1. European History

Decentralised, overlapping political units have been an important feature of European history. The competition between governments in the Holy Roman Empire of German Nations, especially in today's Italy and Germany, has been intensive. Many of these governments were of small size. Not a few scholars attribute the rise of Europe to this diversity and competition of governmental units which fostered technical, economic and artistic innovation (see, for instance, Hayek 1960, Jones 1981, Weede 1993 and Baumol and Baumol 1994 who also give a lively account of how the musical genius of Wolfgang Amadeus Mozart benefited from this system of government). While the Chinese were more advanced in very many respects, their superiority ended with the establishment of a centralised Chinese Empire (Pak 1995, Rosenberg and Birdzell 1986). The unification of Italy and Germany in the nineteenth century, which has often been praised as a major advance, partially ended this stimulating competition between governments, leading to deadly struggles between nation states.[3] Some smaller states escaped unification; Liechtenstein, Luxembourg, Monaco, San Marino and Switzerland stayed politically independent, and at the same time grew rich.

The above mentioned governmental units were not FOCJ in the sense outlined in this chapter but they shared the characteristic of competing for labour and capital (including artistic capital) among each other. However, history also reveals examples of jurisdictions close to FOCJ. The problems connected with Poland's strong ethnic and religious diversity (Catholics, Protestants and Jews) were at least partly overcome by jurisdictions organised along these features, and not along geography (see Rhode 1960 and Haumann 1991). The highly successful Hanse prospered from the twelfth to the sixteenth century, and comprised *inter alia* Lübeck, Bremen, Köln (today German), Stettin and Danzig (today Polish), Kaliningrad (today Russian), Riga, Reval and Dorpat (today parts of the Baltic republics) and Groningen and Deventer (today Dutch); furthermore, London (England), Bruges and Antwerp (today Belgian) and Novgorod (today Russian) were *Handelskontore* or associated members. It clearly was a functional governmental unit providing for trade rules and facilities and was not geographically contiguous.

6.2. Contemporary Examples

The European Community started out as a FOCUS designed to establish free trade in Europe, and was from the very beginning in competition with other trade areas, in particular North America, Japan, and EFTA. Due to its economic success, it has attracted almost all European countries. But entry has not been free, rather the nations determined to enter had to pay a price. They have (with partial exceptions) to accept the 'acquis communautaire' as well as to pay their share to the Community outlays which to a large extent serve redistributive purposes. In several respects there exist FOCJ-like units within Europe such as with respect to police, education, environment, transport, culture or sports though they have been prevented from becoming autonomous jurisdictions with taxing power.

Most of these functional units are not contiguous with the area of the European Union. Some are smaller (for example, those organised along ethnic or language functions), and some are larger. Several East European countries and Switzerland which are not EU-members are certainly fully involved in, for instance, European culture, education or crime. FOCJ of the nature understood in this chapter may therefore build upon already existing structures, and are in the best of European traditions.

There are two countries in which functional, overlapping and competing jurisdictions exist (though they do not in all cases meet the full requirements of FOCJ specified above).

United States

Single-purpose governments in the form of 'special districts' play a significant role in the American federalist system (ACIR 1982, 1987). Their number has strongly increased, between 1967 and 1972 by 30.4 per cent, between 1972 and 1984 by 19.7 per cent, in both cases more quickly than other types of jurisdictions (Zax 1988). There are both autonomous and democratically organised as well as dependent special districts (for instance, for fire prevention, recreation and parks). Empirical research suggests that the former type is significantly more efficient (Mehay 1984). Our theoretical hypothesis of the opposition of existing jurisdictions against the formation of special districts is well borne out. In order not to threaten the monopoly power of existing municipalities, statutes in 18 states prohibit new municipalities within a specified distance from existing municipalities (ACIR 1982, Zax 1988: 81); in various states there is a minimum population size required and various other administrative restrictions have been introduced (see, for example, Nelson 1990). Empirical studies reveal that these barriers imposed by Local Agency Formation Commissions (LAFCO) tend to reduce the relative efficiency of the local administration (DiLorenzo

1981, Deno and Mehay 1985), and tend to push upwards the local government expenditures in those municipalities which have introduced LAFCOs (Martin and Wagner 1978).

Switzerland

Many Swiss cantons have a structure of overlapping and competing functional jurisdictions which share many features of FOCJ. In the canton Zurich (with a population of 1.2 million in 1991, a size of 1700 km² and tax revenue of SFr. 3000 million) there are 171 political communities (with a tax revenue of SFr. 3800 million) which in themselves are composed of three to six independently managed, democratically organised communities devoted to specific functions and levying their own taxes. Take a typical example for the purpose of illustration: the political income community of Niederhasli (population 5900, size 11km²) finances its expenditures of SFr. 11 million (in 1991) by raising a tax equivalent to 38 per cent of the cantonal tax rate (in addition it levies various charges and receives a limited amount of subsidies from the canton). A community that exclusively provides for elementary schools (years 1–6 of schooling) has expenditures of SFr. 5.8 million and levies a tax of 55 per cent of the cantonal tax. A corresponding community specialising in education of years 7–9 spends Sfr. 4.9 million and levies 22 per cent of the cantonal tax rate. There are two church communities having tax rates of 10 per cent and 11 per cent of the cantonal tax rate, respectively. The two school communities and the two religious communities are essentially self-financing. The sixth community (Zivilgemeinde) is devoted to providing water, electricity and a TV antenna, and finances itself solely by user charges. These communities often overlap with neighbouring political communities. In the case of Niederhasli, the advanced school community also comprises the political community of Niederglatt (pop. 3300) and parts of Oberglatt (pop. 4300) (the rest of the pupils attend school in yet another school community). In addition there are 174 functional units (*Zweckverbände* as they are aptly called in German-speaking countries) whose members are not individual citizens but communities.[4] Thirty of these Zweckverbände care for waste water and purification plants, 21 for water provision, 15 for cemeteries, 14 for hospitals, 10 for regional planning, 10 for refuse collection, and so on. The canton Zurich is no exception in Switzerland concerning the multitude of types of functional communities. A similar structure exists, for example, in the canton Glarus or Thurgau (for the latter, see Casella and Frey 1992). Various efforts have been made to suppress this diversity of functional communities, usually initiated by the cantonal bureaucracy and politicians. However, most of these attempts were thwarted because the population is mostly satisfied with the public supply provided. The example of

Switzerland – which is generally considered to be a well-organised and administered country – shows that a multiplicity of functional jurisdictions under democratic control is not a theorist's wishful thinking but has worked well in reality.

7. CONCLUSIONS

Europe owes its position as an economically rich and intellectually and artistically powerful continent in a large measure to the great variety of governmental jurisdictions in competition with each other. This basic insight was overshadowed by the unification movements, especially in Italy and Germany. The European movement follows the historic lesson by opening up trade barriers and supporting economic competition, and this with great success. However, the historic lesson has not been followed with respect to establishing competition between existing and new governments.

This chapter proposes that the future European constitution should allow, and actively promote, the evolution of functional, overlapping and competing governmental jurisdictions (FOCJ). They fulfil many of the welfare-enhancing qualities of theoretical concepts such as Tiebout's voting by foot, Olson's and Oates' fiscal equivalence, or Buchanan's clubs. It is shown that FOCJ are feasible, that there are successful historical examples, and that they partially exist in the form of US special districts and Swiss functional, democratic and overlapping communities.

NOTES

1. As always, there are precursors to FOCJ. The general idea has already been brought up by Montesquieu (we owe this information to one of the referees), but it has, to our knowledge, not been applied to the EU. In the economics literature a related concept has been pioneered by Tullock (1994), who somewhat misleadingly speaks of 'sociological federalism'. Casella and Frey (1992) discuss the concept and refer to relevant literature. A recent Centre for Economic Policy Research Publication (CEPR 1993) briefly mentions the possibility of establishing overlapping jurisdictions in Europe (pp. 54-55) but does not work out the concept nor does it refer to previous research (except for Drèze 1993 on secession). In contrast, Schmidt-Trenz and Schmidtchen (1994) focus on the role of territoriality in the framework of optimum legal areas.
2. A formal reason is that the more vote cycling is prevalent, the more alternatives (functions) there are (see, for example, Kramer 1973). Normally, lower level jurisdictions have more institutions for citizen participation, and they are used more widely, so that the politicians' discretionary room and rents are lower (see, for example, Oakerson and Parks 1988, Cronin 1989).
3. According to Sperber (1994, p. 24), in the first half of the nineteenth century average income was higher in strongly decentralised Germany than in strongly centralized France, which may at least partly be attributed to the difference in the degree of centralisation.

4. Zweckverbände also exist between cantons in which case they are called Konkordate. However, these units (clubs) are not legally independent political entities, that is, the US and Swiss single purpose communities are exceptions (see Mehay 1984).

REFERENCES

Adonis, A. and S. Jones (1991), 'Subsidiarity and the European Community's Constitutional Future', *Staatswissenschaft und Staatspraxis*, **2**, 179–196.

Advisory Commission on Intergovernmental Relations (ACIR) (1982), *State and Local Roles in the Federal System*, Report A-88, Washington, DC: US Government Printing Office.

Advisory Commission on Intergovernmental Relations (ACIR) (1987), *The Organization of Local Public Economies*, Report A-109, Washington, DC: US Government Printing Office.

Baumol, W.J. and H. Baumol (1992), 'On the Economics of Musical Composition in Mozart's Vienna', *Journal of Cultural Economics*, **18**, 171–198.

Bird, R.M. (1993), 'Threading the Fiscal Labyrinth: Some Issues in Fiscal Decentralization', *National Tax Journal*, **46**, 201–221.

Blöchliger, H. and R.L. Frey (1992), 'Der schweizerische Föderalismus: Ein Modell für den institutionellen Aufbau der Europäischen Union?', *Aussenwirtschaft*, **47**, 515–548.

Breton, A. (1996), *Competitive Governments: An Economic Theory of Politics and Public Finance*, New York: Cambridge University Press.

Buchanan, J.M. (1965), 'An Economic Theory of Clubs', *Economica*, **32**, 1–14.

Buchanan, J.M. (1991), 'An American Perspective on Europe's Constitutional Opportunity', *Cato Journal*, **10**, 619–629.

Casella, A. and B.S. Frey (1992), 'Federalism and clubs: Towards an economic theory of overlapping political jurisdictions', *European Economic Review*, **36**, 639–646.

Centre for Economic Policy Research (CEPR) (1993), *Making Sense of Subsidiarity: How Much Centralization for Europe?*, London: CEPR.

Cronin, T.E. (1989), *Direct Democracy. The Politics of Initiative, Referendum and Recall*, Cambridge, Mass.: Harvard University Press.

Deno, K.T. and S.L. Mehay (1985), 'Institutional Constraints on Local Jurisdiction Formation', *Public Finance Quarterly*, **13**, 450–463.

DiLorenzo, T.J. (1981), 'Special Districts and Local Public Services', *Public Finance Quarterly*, **9**, 353– 367.

Downs, A. (1957), *An Economic Theory of Democracy*, New York: Harper and Row.

Drèze, J. (1993), 'Regions of Europe: a feasible status, to be discussed', *Economic Policy*, **17**, 266–307,

Epple, D. and A. Zelenitz (1981), 'The Implications of Competition Among Jurisdictions: Does Tiebout Need Politics?', *Journal of Political Economy*, **89**, 1197–1217.

European Constitutional Group (1993), *A Proposal for a European Constitution*, London: European Policy Forum.

Farrell, J. and G. Saloner (1988), 'Coordination through Committees and Markets', *Rand Journal of Economics*, **19** (2), 235–252.

Frey, B.S. (1983), *Democratic Economic Policy*, Oxford: Blackwell.
Frey, B.S. (1994), 'Direct Democracy: Politico-Economic Lessons from Swiss Experience', *American Economic Review*, **84**, 338–342.
Gold, S.D. (1991), 'Interstate Competition and State Personal Income-Tax Policy in the 1980s', in D.A. Kenyon and J. Kincaid (eds), *Competition among States and Local Governments*, Washington, DC: Urban Institute Press, pp. 205–217.
Haumann, H. (1991), *Geschichte der Ostjuden*, München: Beck.
Hayek, F.A. von (1960), *The Constitution of Liberty*, Chicago: Chicago University Press.
Herman, F. (reporter) (1994), *Zweiter Bericht des Institutionellen Ausschusses über die Verfassung der Europäischen Union*, Europäisches Parlament, Sitzungsdokumente (A3–0064/94).
Hirschman, A.O. (1970), *Exit, Voice and Loyalty*, Cambridge: Harvard University Press.
Jones, E.L. (1981), *The European Miracle*, Cambridge: Cambridge University Press.
Kirchgässner, G. und W.W. Pommerehne (1996), 'Tax Harmonization and Tax Competition in the European Community: Lessons from Switzerland', *Journal of Public Economics*, **60**, 351–371.
Kramer, G.H. (1973), 'On a Class of Equilibrium Conditions for Majority Rule', *Econometrica*, **41**, 285–297.
Martin, D. and R. Wagner (1978), 'The Institutional Framework for Municipal Incorporation', *Journal of Law and Economics*, **21**, 409–425.
Mehay, S.L. (1984), 'The effect of governmental structure on special district expenditures', *Public Choice*, **44**, 339–348.
Milgrom, P. and J. Roberts (1990), 'Bargaining Costs, Influence Costs, and the Organization of Economic Activity', in James E. Alt and Kenneth A. Shepsle (eds), *Perspectives on positive political economy*, Cambridge: Cambridge University Press, pp. 57–89.
Mueller, D.C. (1989), *Public Choice II*, Cambridge: Cambridge University Press.
Mueller, D.C. (1996), *Constitutional Democracy*, New York: Oxford University Press.
Nelson, M.A. (1990), 'Decentralization of the Subnational Public Sector: An Empirical Analysis of the Determinants of Local Government Structure in Metropolitan Areas in the U.S.', *Southern Economic Journal*, **57**, 443–457.
Oakerson, R.J. and R.B. Parks (1988), 'Citizen Voice and Public Entrepreneurship: The Organizational Dynamic of a Complex Metropolitan County', *Publius: The Journal of Federalism*, **18**, 91–112.
Oates, W.E. (1972), *Fiscal Federalism*, New York: Harcourt Brace Jovanovich.
Olson, M. (1969), 'The Principle of "Fiscal Equivalence": The Division of Responsibilities among Different Levels of Government', *American Economic Review*, **59**, 479–487.
Pak, H.M. (1995), 'Effective Competition, Institutional Choice and Economic Development of Imperial China', *Kyklos*, **48**, 87–103.
Pitschas, R. (1994), 'Europäische Integration als Netzwerkkoordination komplexer Staatsaufgaben', *Staatswissenschaft und Staatspraxis*, **4**, 503–540.
Rhode, G. (1960), 'Staaten-Union und Adelsstaat: Zur Entwicklung von Staatsdenken und Staatsgestaltung in Osteuropa, vor allem in Polen/Litauen, im 16. Jahrhundert', *Zeitschrift für Ostforschung*, **9**, 185–215.
Riker, W.H. and S.J. Brams (1973), 'The Paradox of Vote Trading', *American Political Science Review*, **67**, 1235–1247

Rosenberg, N. and L.E. Birdzell (1986), *How the West Grew Rich. The Economic Transformation of the Industrial World*, London: I.B. Tauris.
Sandler, T. and J.T. Tschirhart (1980), 'The Economic Theory of Clubs: An Evaluative Survey', *Journal of Economic Literature,* **18**, 1488–1521.
Schmidt-Trenz, H.-J. and D. Schmidtchen (1994), 'A Theory of Optimum Legal Areas. Regulation of Social Interaction Through the Control of Territory', Discussion paper Nr. 9402, Universität des Saarlandes.
Schneider, F. (1992), 'The Federal and Fiscal Structures of Representative and Direct Democracies as Models for a European Federal Union: Some Ideas using the Public Choice Approach', *Journal des Economistes et des Etudes Humaines,* **3**, 403–437.
Sharpe, L.J. (ed.) 1993, *The Rise of Meso Government in Europe*, London: Sage.
Sperber, J. (1994), *The European Revolutions 1848–51*, Cambridge: Cambridge University Press.
Teutemann, M. (1992), *Rationale Kompetenzverteilung im Rahmen der europäischen Integration*, Berlin: Duncker & Humblot.
Tiebout, C.M. (1956), 'A Pure Theory of Local Expenditure', *Journal of Political Economy,* **64**, 416–24.
Tullock, G. (1994), *The New Federalist,* Vancouver: Fraser Institute.
Vaubel, R. (1994), 'The political economy of centralization and the European Community', *Public Choice,* **81**, 151–190.
Weede, E. (1993), 'The Impact of Interstate Conflict on Revolutionary Change and Individual Freedom', *Kyklos,* **46**, 473–495.
Weingast, B.R. (1993), 'Constitutions as Governance Structures: The Political Foundations of Secure Market,' *Journal of Institutional and Theoretical Economics,* **149**, 286–311.
Zarkovic Bookman, M. (1992), *The Economics of Secession,* New York: St. Martin's Press.
Zax, J.S. (1988), 'The Effects of Jurisdiction Types and Numbers on Local Public Finance', in H.S. Rosen (ed.), *Fiscal Federalism: Quantitative Studies*, Chicago: The University of Chicago Press, 79–106.

Comment

Hans-Jörg Schmidt-Trenz

FOCJ is 'fuzzy' – this seems to be a term which might come first to mind. But FOCJ is a very serious concept, that we should look at. Therefore I want to give a FOCI: a friendly opinion perhaps catching your interest.

What is FOCJ all about? I must admit that I did not get a clear-cut message about that. Who is the addressee? Is it the European Commission? Is this chapter an attempt to sell well known economic concepts such as the theory of public goods, externalities and clubs under a new brand name, hoping that politicians will buy it? This perhaps explains the widespread use of the terms 'must' and 'should'.

Or is the addressee the scientific community to which the authors primarily speak, saying: 'Hey, we have a new approach, a new theory of the state.' If we go this way, as I want to, there are several questions to be answered on which I want to focus.

1. What is the meaning of the concept of FOCJ?
2. Is it a theory?
3. What is new?

That South Tyrolians may decide to speak German without leaving the Italian State is no news; do we – as economists – really need a new theory to underline this and does FOCJ give a new insight to this old question? I do not want to follow this question further. I just want to mention it as one of the multitude of historical examples, 'illustrations' and empirical evidence, that Frey and Eichenberger indicate in order to support their approach. I would have been reluctant to do so at this stage of the theoretic elaboration of FOCJ. I think, at this stage much more effort should have been spent on developing a sound theory, including assumptions and conditions for propositions while concentrating on a few examples or just one which is precisely worked out.

So let me start with the first question: what is the meaning of the concept of FOCJ? With the term 'function' the authors seem to be very clear. This term refers to a 'public service'. But that is almost all we hear. What kind of goods are in the range of this term using the language that economists commonly do? Public Goods, Club Goods, Private Goods? What are the assumptions about the question of exclusion of non-payers and how do these assumptions influence the success of FOCJs? There is no specification of this point which leads to the impression that the concept is not very clear and lacks a theoretical basis.

The same holds for the term 'overlapping' with its two interpretations 'intersection' and 'overlapping in the narrow sense'. On the one hand, there is a lot of talking about geography: 'FOCJ emerge in response to the "geography of problems"'; 'they extend over different geographical areas'. But on the other hand the authors concede that FOCJ need not be 'physically contiguous'. This remains unclear. When the authors speak about the size of a FOCJ, what do the authors measure? Number of members or square metres?

The question to be answered is: what is the link between *members* of FOCJ and *geography* of FOCJ? We hear nothing about that link. You are in a tennis club and I am too; so – are those clubs intersecting, are they overlapping? I have tried to come to grips with the concept and I have reached the following considerations which are related to the theory of optimum legal areas, published last year (Schmidtchen and Schmidt-Trenz 1994).

The authors differentiate FOCJ (functional, overlapping and competing jurisdictions) and APJ (All-Purpose Jurisdictions). If we are precise concerning the question of territoriality, we first of all have to differentiate two kinds of FOCJs: (i) 'functional *territorial* competing jurisdictions' and (ii) 'functional *non-territorial* competing jurisdictions'.

Let me call the first one FUTCI (see, for example, the US which claims the monopoly of power within well-defined geographic boundaries), and let me call the second one FUNCTI (see, for example, the American Economic Association though it calls itself 'American'; or take my tennis club example).

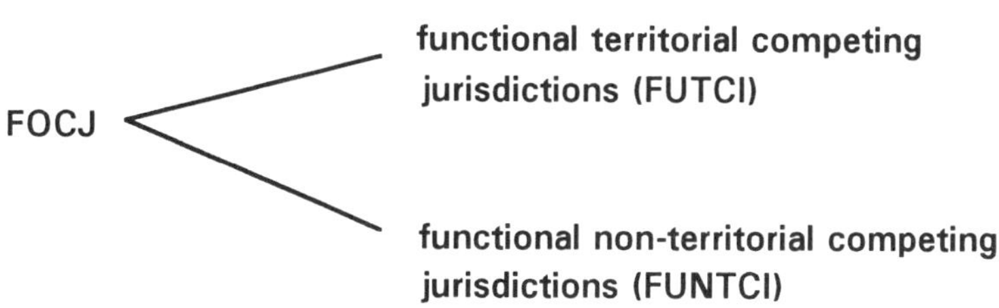

In the term APJ a second criterion is shining up: the *number* of functions to be fulfilled: a single function, multiple, or all. A complete analysis then comes to the following possibilities:

Types of FOCJs	Territorial strategy	Non-territorial strategy
Single-function	Single-FUTCI	Single-FUNCTI
Multiple-function	Multi-FUTCI	Multi-FUNCTI
All-function	All-FUTCI	All-FUNCTI

Let me give an example of what may be the case according to Figure 7.1 below. Let us regard six individuals: Bruno, Rainer, Hans, Joerg, Daniel and Torsten. These individuals are symbolised by a square. First of all, they have joined a single-FUTCI producing the service A. Think, for example, of A as the fundamental protective state in the sense of Buchanan providing a property and a contract law with police forces, courts and prisons. Here, this club A works on a territorial basis which is indicated by the rectangle. This club provides law and enforcement by controlling territory. Let us skip for a while the question of whether this is good or not. On the basis of A, the six individuals can play the market and other games and form other clubs, for example tennis clubs, which correspond to the function B. In this case, the individuals may choose to apply a non-territorial strategy. To be members of the same tennis club does not necessarily mean that you have to be neighbours. So, Bruno, Rainer and Joerg join tennis club 1, and Hans, Torsten and Daniel tennis club 2. Those tennis clubs are FUNCTIs.

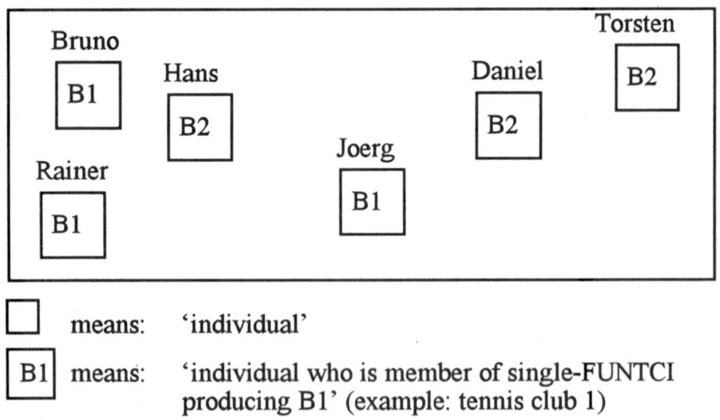

Figure 7.1 Single-FUTCI producing A (example: the protective state)

In the language of Frey and Eichenberger, the tennis clubs 'intersect' (as there are two FOCJ fulfilling the same task in the same area) and they 'overlap' with the protective state A. The term 'overlapping' seems to be quite meaningful in this context but what do we learn by saying that both tennis clubs 'intersect'? If exit and entry are possible, then it says nothing more than that they compete, which is another part of the FOCJ-definition. If exit and entry are not possible, the term says nothing to the economist.

But things could also be like that in Figure 7.2: nothing has changed concerning the nature and membership of both our tennis clubs. But the protective function A is organised in another way. Its governance structure is no longer a FUTCI but a FUNTCI, meaning that the protective function is executed in a non-territorial way. It applies the personality, not the territoriality principle and in my example there are two intersecting, that is, competing protective states A1 and A2. You can easily see that the example is chosen such that there is *no* perfect overlapping of tennis clubs and protective states. Torsten, Daniel and Hans belong to the same tennis club but not to the same protective state. That might create problems. What happens if Hans does not pay his tennis club membership fee? Do Torsten and Daniel have to apply to the courts and police forces of A1 or A2, their own protective state? How will A1 behave, when the police of A2 try to enforce the payment? One solution to this problem are collision norms and enforcement treaties. But there is another solution – the rearrangement of memberships because a perfect overlapping between protective states and tennis clubs might prove cheaper, that is, the transaction cost minimises governance structure.

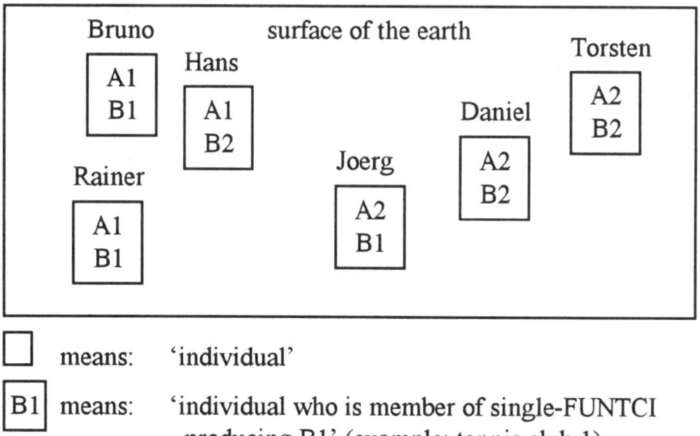

Figure 7.2 Single-FUNCTI producing A

To this end we would, for example, have to convince Hans to join protective club 2 and Joerg to join protective club 1. But this membership switch might be costly for them. Perhaps they have to learn new rules of the game. These costs might be so high as to impede a change.

Let us have a look at a last figure. People do not sit in space, they move. So the protective states 1 and 2 have to engage on the whole surface of our landscape which implies identification costs: individuals have to find out to which protective state the people they meet belong. Again, that might be very costly compared with a territorial strategy. Figure 7.3 shows a situation where A1 and A2 decide to become FUTCIs, introducing a border between them and claiming a territorial monopoly of power within these boundaries.

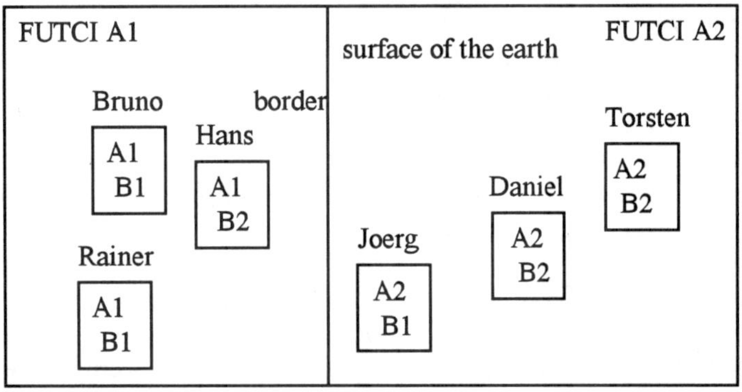

☐ means: 'individual'

B1 means: 'individual who is member of single-FUNTCI producing B1' (example: tennis club 1)

Figure 7.3 Multi-FUTCI producing A

It can easily be shown (as in the theory of optimum legal areas) that such a strategy has huge advantages but at some cost. There arises a problem of border trespassing which has to be regulated. If Joerg and Hans do not change tennis clubs, they are now 'foreigners' in their tennis club. This raises some new questions.

I could easily proceed with further examples but I have to stop here. As I said, the chapter very often uses the words 'must' and 'should'. So let me ask the authors:

- How many FOCJs of type A should exist?
- What is their optimal size?

- How many functions should it fulfil? Perhaps not all, but only a single function?
- Does competition lead to an optimum?
- Should FOCJs follow a territorial strategy or not?
- How should exit and entry be regulated?
- How should collisions be regulated?
- How many FOCJs of type B should exist?
- Should they follow a non-territorial strategy?
- How should they regulate exit and entry?
- Is there an interdependency between the FOCJ A and the FOCJ B and if so, as I guess, what is it?
- Do they have to overlap?
- How do FOCJs have to be organised internally?
- How do all these questions depend on the nature of the good considered?
- How about the working of competition and the possibility of free-riding?
- Then, might FOCJs depend on coercion?
- Then, what are the incentives of the FOCJ-managers?

All these questions would have to be answered by a theory, indicating assumptions and conditions under which certain propositions hold. But I found almost none of these questions; I saw almost no assumptions and conditions; rather what I read was a description about what a FOCJ is and that the authors believe in FOCJs. I am quite sure that the term FOCJ may be useful, but this has to be shown in a clear-cut theory which can then be finally tested, concentrating on a concrete problem.

This theory has to be built on the existing literature of constitutional economics, public goods, clubs, federalism and the new institutional economics of international (say for this purpose, inter-group) transactions from which I have heavily borrowed. We also have to be aware of the fact that this literature is able to answer many of the questions I have asked above. A new theory would have to fill the gaps and analyse whether the existing answers are right or not. An even bigger challenge would be the attempt to integrate all the different strands of literature in a single theory. From the standpoint of FOCJ, this remains the task to be fulfilled. I like the idea of a fifth freedom along the lines of FOCJ. But its efficiency gains have to be shown in a more precise way. This seems to me a necessary, though not sufficient, condition in order to convince the European Commission to become a FOCJ.

REFERENCES

Schmidt-Trenz, H.-J.(1990), *Außenhandel und Territorialität des Rechts. Grundlegung einer Neuen Institutionenökonomik des Außenhandels*, Baden Baden: Nomos.

Schmidt-Trenz, H.-J. and D. Schmidtchen (1991), 'Private International Trade in the Shadow of the Territoriality of Law: Why does it work?', *Southern Economic Journal*, **58**, 329–338.

Schmidtchen, D. (1993), 'Neue Institutionenökonomik internationaler Transaktionen', in U. Schlieper and D. Schmidtchen (eds), *Makro, Geld und Institutionen*, Tübingen: Mohr, pp. 57–84.

Schmidtchen, D. and H.-J. Schmidt-Trenz (1990), 'The Division of Labor is Limited by the Extent of the Law. A Constitutional Approach to International Private Law', *Constitutional Political Economy*, **1**, 49–71.

Schmidtchen, D. and H.-J. Schmidt-Trenz (1994), 'Theorie optimaler Rechtsräume. Die Regulierung sozialer Beziehungen durch die Kontrolle von Territorium', *Jahrbuch für Neue Politische Ökonomie*, **13**, 7–29.

8. Toward Ever Closer Union – Or Ever Larger? Or Both? Entry to the European Union from the Perspective of Constitutional Economics

Manfred E. Streit and Stefan Voigt

Resolved by thus pooling their resources to preserve and strengthen peace and liberty, and calling upon the other peoples of Europe who share their ideal to join in their efforts.
(from the preamble of the treaty establishing the European Community)

1. INTRODUCTION

The collapse of the centrally planned economies in 1989 has fundamentally changed Europe's political and economic landscape. Not only do the societies of Central and Eastern Europe have to rewrite their constitutions, international and supranational entities such as the OSCE, NATO, and the European Union (EU) have to redefine scope and depth of their tasks. This constitutes formidable test cases for the applicability of constitutional economics. Here, an attempt is being made to apply the framework of constitutional economics to the question of entry into the European Union. The question of entry is not limited to the countries of Central and Eastern Europe as the applications of Turkey, Malta and Cyprus show. Entry changes the size of the Union which can also be changed by its opposite, namely exit. Further, entry is not only possible on the collective level but also on the individual one which leads to a 2x2-matrix:

Considered entity	Action	entry	exit
Individual		1	2
Collective		3	4

Case 1 reminds us of the necessity of a (common) migration policy. Case 2 should not constitute a serious problem for a liberal entity (unrestricted right to exit). Case 4 has been a blind spot not only of economics but also of social philosophy and discussion has only emerged recently (for the point of view of a philosopher, see A. Buchanan (1990/1991, 1991); for treatments within the framework of constitutional economics, see Sunstein 1991, Chen and Ordeshook 1994). Mention of this case also has to be made because the *spiritus rector* of constitutional economics, James M. Buchanan, assumes a collective right to exit as a device constraining Leviathan from systematically exploiting certain groups (J. Buchanan 1990). The main thrust of this chapter will, however, lie with case 3.

The choice of a constitution can be thought of as a choice of rules as opposed to a choice within rules. We will thus have to look for rules that could be chosen by rational actors to admit entry of additional states. Before doing that, the current *status quo* is described and possible costs and benefits of enlarging the Union are sketched. This includes possible effects on the EU budget as well as on trade with potential member states (section 2). In the following section 3, we first try to make use of the theory of clubs in order to conceptualise the European Union for our analytical problem. Section 4 is an attempt to further substantiate the analysis by applying constitutional economics to the question of entry. The word attempt is to be stressed here because we take a rather critical stance concerning the advice that can be deduced from contractarian constitutional economics à la Buchanan. Constitutional economics in that vein is entirely normative and primarily interested in the legitimacy of rules. Good normative theory must, however, be grounded on positive theory. This is why an attempt at incorporating knowledge available through political economy is being made in section 4.2. Since we are sceptical regarding the present effectiveness of constitutional economics but trust in its potential relevance, it will be no surprise that two groups of conclusions are presented in the last section of the chapter: the first concerning ways to improve upon the effectiveness of constitutional economics as an analytical instrument; and the second concerning the material question of more countries entering the Union. With regard to the second group, our central hypothesis advanced is that the deepen or enlarge alternative frequently discussed today is probably only half the story. If a decision to enlarge the Union by a considerable number in its South and its East is taken, people might be better off if the scope of tasks delegated onto the European level was diminished.

2. THE STATUS QUO AND SCENARIOS OF POSSIBLE DEVELOPMENT

2.1. Basic Possibilities

In 1957, the European Economic Community was founded with six member states; currently it has 15 members. Although the goals of this European supranational entity have been broadened several times[1] and its name has been changed to European Union, the basic decision rules have not been fundamentally changed. Nine states have already been admitted to the Union after its founding, a whole series is seeking entry now: Turkey, Malta and Cyprus have been knocking at the door for years, the Višegrad countries (the Czech Republic, Hungary, Poland, and Slovakia) have also formally applied. Applications from Bulgaria, Romania, Slovenia as well as the Baltic states Estonia, Latvia, and Lithuania are expected. In Switzerland, the pros and cons of a possible accession are heatedly discussed. Because the population has turned membership in the European Economic Region down, Switzerland's formal application for full EU-membership is unlikely within the next couple of years.

The Treaty on the European Union (TEU, 'Maastricht') contains one article dealing with the accession of new members. Article O states that the Council has to act unanimously after having received the consent of the European Parliament which has to approve of new members by an absolute majority of its members. The agreement on the conditions of admission not only has to be ratified by the applicant state but also by the contracting states. Article O thus specifies the formal procedure. It has been argued that Article F (TEU) and Article 3a of the Treaty on the European Community (TEC) serve as substantial requirements that have to be fulfilled before accession is considered (Article F states that the governments are founded on the principles of democracy; Article 3a that all the policies pursued have to be based on 'the principle of an open market economy with free competition'). Besides the fulfilment of these 'essentials', the Council conducting the negotiations with applicants has substantial discretionary leeway.

In discussions concerning the development of the EU, the enlargement and the deepening options are often presented in a dichotomous way as if one could only have one or the other. On logical grounds, however, two additional possibilities are conceivable, leading to a 2x2-matrix again:

Enlarge	Deepen	no	yes
No		1	2
Yes		3	4

Case 1 simply constitutes the preservation of the present situation while case 2 would mean a deepening of the Union (that is, assigning still more tasks to the European level and supposedly somehow modifying the decision procedures). Since this chapter is mainly concerned with entry, these cases are not of primary interest. Case 3 – which will be mainly discussed here – means that a given set of goals and instruments is to be applied to a significantly larger number of member states. 'No deepening' does not necessarily have to mean 'standstill' though, it could also mean 'rollback'. This might be the price for enlargement. Case 4 would mean moving in two directions at the same time which is difficult to conceive of.

We have just argued that deepening and simultaneously enlarging the Union makes little sense. Hence, if politicians decide in favour of the deepening option, alternatives to entry become relevant. Since our topic is entry, their consequences are merely presented here in a summarised fashion.

Table 8.1 Trade policy consequences of alternatives to entry

Trade policy instruments / Option	Exception clauses	Safeguard clause	Anti-dumping	Local content
Europe-Agreements	textiles, coal and steel, agrar	applicable to all product groups	applicable	> 60% for Common Market rules to apply
EFTA-membership	would be omitted	not applicable	applicable	> 60% for Common Market rules to apply
EER-membership	access to Common Agrarian Market barred	not applicable	applicable	not applicable
EU-membership	not applicable	not applicable (see, however, Art. 115 TEC)	not applicable	not applicable

2.2. Effects of Enlarging the Union

a. Budgetary effects

Based on the EC Budget of 1989, the Centre for Economic Policy Research (1992) has estimated the national contributions to the budget as well as eligibility to the structural funds and the price support scheme under the Common Agricultural Policy (CAP). It turns out that national GNP is a very good predictor of the respective national contributions. Neglecting that the structural funds heavily favour Ireland, CAP's allocations can be explained by the country's share of agriculture and its *per capita* income. After having introduced a dummy variable for The Netherlands and Germany, the allocation of the CAP price support scheme can be fairly well explained with agricultural output.[2]

Using the CEPR equations and assuming a doubling of *per capita* income combined with a 25 per cent decrease in the structural relevance of the agricultural sector, Stehn (1994) estimates that the accession of the Višegrad-countries plus Bulgaria and Romania would cost some 11 billion ECUs annually which amounts to an almost 20 per cent increase of the total budget.

Leipold (1995, p.131) chooses another way of calculating possible budgetary consequences. The *per capita* amount that the poorest EU-members received from the structural fund in 1992 varied between 89.6 ECU (Spain) and 289.1 ECU (Ireland). Since *per capita* income in the would-be member countries still is substantially lower, he assumes 300 ECU to be a realistic amount. For the Višegrad-four with their almost 65 million inhabitants, this would mean an extra 19.5 billion ECU (if one adds Bulgaria and Romania, the sum increases to 30 billion ECU).

In the meantime, the EU has been supplemented by still one further instrument of redistribution, namely the cohesion fund which is to help member countries whose *per capita* income remains below 90 per cent of the Union average. Obviously, all of the Central and Eastern European countries would be eligible. The costs of integrating only the Visegrad-states could run up to 30 to 40 billion ECU which adds up to almost 70 billion ECU annually, a sum that is compatible with the estimates of the European Commission (*Frankfurter Allgemeine Zeitung*, No. 161, July 14, 1994; p.2). Based on his lower figures, Stehn concludes that from a fiscal point of view, enlargement would be possible especially if the 'peace dividend' consisting of reduced military expenditure, export growth, and benefits derived from increased environmental quality were properly taken into account. He remains sceptical concerning the integration of the Central and Eastern European economies into the agricultural and structural funds, pointing to possible drawbacks concerning the incentives for wide-ranging reforms, especially in agriculture (*ibid.*, esp. p. 214).[3]

Considering the budgetary effects, it would be inappropriate to neglect an argument of reform: the additional cost of accession would be caused to a considerable extent by ill-conceived common policies, like the Common Agricultural Policy. Hence they could be avoided by a corresponding revision of the *acquis communautaire*.

b. Trade effects

Puffing up the EU budget by another 20 per cent has to be paid by somebody. Regarding costs, however, many people would probably argue that total costs of accession will most likely exceed the additional burden imposed upon the EU budget because of trade effects: the cheaper imports from the Central and Eastern European economies would cause substantial adjustment costs, sectorally most likely in the sensitive branches of steel, textiles and clothing, chemicals and food products, and geographically supposedly in the countries with similar cost structures in production, that is, Spain, Portugal, and especially Greece. A number of recent papers show that most of these fears are unfounded. For the textiles and clothing sector, Corado (1995) finds that increasing trade with the Central and Eastern European countries may have benefited EU producers in two ways: first, by increased exports to those economies primarily in high value-added products; and secondly by transferring the labour-intensive parts of the value chain to those countries, thus making Western European producers more competitive in comparison with producers from developing countries.

The effects on the steel sector have been analysed by Winters (1995) who finds that consumers in the Union and producers in Central and Eastern Europe could gain substantially. He also finds that the costs to EU and EFTA producers would be fairly small, namely long-run output reductions of 1.6 per cent and 3.0 per cent respectively. Presupposing further market liberalisation, Winters predicts overall (EU and Central and Eastern Europe) net welfare gains of over 100 million ECUs.

Concerning the regional effects of an enlargement of the Union, the predictions are similarly positive: based on estimates by Baldwin (1994), Dimelis and Gatsios (1995) find that Greek exports should increase by 191 per cent whereas Greece's imports from the Central and Eastern European economies would only increase by 91 per cent. Spanish trade with the Central and Eastern European economies is quite small. According to Gual and Martín (1995), this will remain so even after the completion of the transition period. Adjustment costs appear thus to be negligible.

Turning to the overall benefits, reduced military expenditure is welfare enhancing at least for Western European taxpayers as long as one supposes the CIS not to be a military threat. But savings on military expenditure are not by themselves an argument to inflate the EU budget by another 20 per cent, because this would reduce net gains. However, the argument could be modified. If one supposes accession to the Union to increase political and economic stability in Central and Eastern Europe, 11 billion ECU *per annum* might be a price worth paying. But this argument has a strong *ad hoc* flavour. Similar difficulties appear when scrutinising the other components of the 'peace dividend' cited by Stehn: there is no direct nexus between improved environmental quality and inflating of the funds. There remains the argument of additional exports. This is, of course, a good argument but it does not directly depend on a stark increase of the EU budget.

c. Effects on EU decision procedures

Besides budgetary and trade consequences, it is interesting to inquire into the decision procedures supposing that the Union's organs were simply enlarged, too. Currently, there are 87 votes in the Council; the qualified majority being 62 votes, the blocking minority is thus 26 votes. If the Višegrad-four plus Bulgaria and Romania were admitted, the number of Council votes would increase to 118, the qualified majority being subject to renewed negotiation. The number of votes that additional members could hope to be assigned can be found in column 1 of Table 8.2. In the Commission, the six new members would consist of one large country (Poland) and five small ones. In the past, large member states have dispatched two commissioners, small ones one, thus the number of commissioners would increase from the current 20 to 27. The same procedure can be applied to the composition of the European Parliament, and, of course, to an even larger number of new member countries. The decision procedure within the Union could therefore become even more complicated. This is not only costly in terms of decision costs but also in terms of employees solely occupied in translating all the documents into the then 17 official languages (see Table 8.2 for the effects of an even larger number of entrants)!

It has often been argued that a balance of power between large and small members has to be found, assuming that size was a major factor of a country's interests. In the future, one dividing line that appears to be more likely is that between rich and poor. Up to now, Ireland, Greece, Spain and Portugal have been the main beneficiaries. With an enlargement toward Central and Eastern Europe, the group of poor countries would consist of ten countries, almost half of the club. Adding the three potential entrants south of the Union (Cyprus, Malta, Turkey) would change the balance completely. Since an increase in the European Union budget with a constant scheme of receipts would reduce the net amount received by the poor current members (they would also have to contribute to the extra 20 per cent of the EU budget), they would most likely oppose this development.

Table 8.2 Possible consequences of an EU enlargement on decisionmaking structures under the assumption that decisionmaking rules remain unchanged

	Number of votes in the Council	Number of seats in the Commission	Number of seats in the Parliament	Official language
EU (15)	87	20	626	11
Czech Republic	5	1	25	Czech
Hungary	5	1	25	Hungarian
Poland	8	2	64	Polish
Slovakia	3	1	16	Slovak
Bulgaria	4	1	22	Bulgarian
Romania	6	1	48	Romanian
Slovenia	2	1	9	Slovene
Estonia	2	1	7	Estonian
Latvia	2	1	11	Latvian
Lithuania	3	1	15	Lithuanian
Turkey	10	2	87	Turkish
Malta	2	1	6	Maltese
Cyprus	2	1	6	Greek, Turkish
EU (28)	141	35	967	23

A modified scenario, namely that of widening the Union and freezing the current budget, would reduce the net receipts of the poor current members even further.[4] The alternative, an ever increasing EU budget, might eventually provoke adverse reactions by voters and might therefore reduce the political chances of politicians who consented to an inflation of the budget. This seems to be a real possibility in the two largest contributor countries, namely the UK and Germany. A rational answer of politicians facing this threat would be to use the subsidiarity-principle as a 'protective shield': they could claim that some of the perceived objectives could very well be 'sufficiently achieved by the member states' as Article 3b of TEC demands. Furthermore, some of the activities of the EU enumerated in Article 3 could simply be suspended. Measures in the sphere of tourism, as named in Article 3t might be a case in point. An explicit modification of the treaty seems unlikely. It is more likely that some policy areas will simply be 'forgotten'. The ultimate consequence would then be, as already indicated in section 2.1, a widening combined with a 'rollback' or 'flattening'.

3. THE EUROPEAN UNION AS A CLUB

3.1. Heuristic Quality of the Notion

The idea that the EU could be conceptualised as a club almost suggests itself. To interpret the founding of a club as a contract corresponds, of course, to one of the central notions of constitutional economics. Originally, the pure theory of clubs was Buchanan's tool for transforming Samuelson's dichotomy between public and private goods into a continuum with club goods ranging somewhere in the middle. The possibility to produce club goods is based on three assumptions: (1) there is a quantity-range in which the *per capita* production costs decrease when an additional individual is admitted, (2) exclusion is possible and (3) rivalry in consumption sets in at some membership level below the entire population. The purpose of inquiry into the theory of clubs is to identify the optimal level of the good to be produced given a certain membership size or to identify the optimal number of members given the supply of the club good respectively. In a second step, one can solve for optimal size and amount simultaneously. The problem with this approach is that it is based on (1) identical individuals (identical preferences, identical resource endowment) and that (2) (re-)distribution is excluded by assumption.

Although the notion of the European Union as a club is appealing at first sight, a number of questions have to be dealt with before one can talk of a useful conceptualisation: (1) who are the members of the supposed club? (2) what are the club goods produced, what sorts of costs are incurred producing them, and what sorts of benefits arise consuming them?, and (3) does the conventional category of club goods suffice so that employing the notion is appropriate in all cases?

The European Union is a club of states, not of individuals. Considered like this, it currently consists of 15 and not of 360 million members. One could, however, argue that states only exist because their existence is instrumental for individuals in improving their individual lot. In this case, governments are simply agents of their population, the principal. If the principal–agent contract – the constitution – on the national level is devised and effectively used in such a way that it largely excludes self-servicing behaviour of the agent, the club here analysed could also be considered as a club consisting of 360 million members who are represented by 15 agents (governments). This question will have to be taken up again in the section on constitutional economics proper (section 4.2).

Even more difficult is the identification of the club goods produced by the European Union. The common market, the single most important instrument of the European Union in reaching the tasks enumerated in

Article 2 of the treaty, seems a prime candidate for analysis. An (internal) common market can be characterised by the absence of barriers to trade and by the realisation of the so-called 'four liberties', that is, by the absence of obstacles to the free movement of goods, persons, services, and capital. Suppose some basic regulatory framework necessary for such a common market which is independent from the number of member countries making up the common market club. It would then hold that an additional member to such a club would always cause a reduction in *per capita* costs. Consequently, the optimal club size would include all economies of this globe and the good 'common market' would not qualify as a club good. This argument can be modified on the grounds that the basic regulatory framework of the present club, that is the so-called *acquis communautaire*, might not correspond to the preferences of the members of a would-be member state. The common market would then turn into a club good because of the specificity of the regulatory framework. It could then be argued that potential entrants are not prepared to pay the price of accepting the club as it is.

3.2. Deviations and Modifications

Not all elements which constitute the *acquis communautaire* pass the test of being club goods. This holds particularly true for those common policies which are based on funds to be used as instruments. The Common Agricultural Policy, structural and regional policy, as well as the promotion of cohesion imply that the corresponding funds are used in a redistributive way. This means that they cannot qualify as club goods because of rivalry in consumption. Some authors have raised the idea that the benefits of redistribution via funds could be considered as income insurance. To be convincing, this would require one to assume that the decision to establish those funds has been a constitutional one made under a 'veil of ignorance' by agents who are risk-averse. But to uphold the assumption of such a veil would require one to ignore the history of European integration.

The pure theory of clubs provides neither for the possibility of discrimination nor (re-)distribution. If one can observe that some member states are systematically net payers and others net recipients, then this phenomenon cannot be made plausible within club theory. Applying the rationality principle, it is hard to see why one or two member states should persistently be net payers with all the rest being net recipients. To declare that the part of the accruing cooperative surplus generated by the European Union and realised by the member states in question would far outweigh their budget shares is a tempting way out. However, this comes close to ad hockery. Nevertheless, it cannot be excluded that package deals between member states exist, for example, an initial deal between France and Germany which balances Germany's net contribution to the agricultural fund with its access to French markets for industrial products.

It could also be argued that some of the policies of the EU have become genuine club goods only because they have been in existence over a number of years and are thus able to generate stable expectations not only on the level of national governments but also on the level of individual actors. For some national government, entry into the EU might even be an opportunity to commit itself to a specific policy – such as the policy to establish a system of undistorted competition leading, for example, to a reduction of subsidies and to deregulation – that it could not credibly commit to otherwise. If this were the case, that is, if some EU policies would produce pay-offs mainly because they have been in existence over a number of years, these policies would have acquired the status of capital goods (see also Buchanan 1977, chapter 7). Since the pay-offs are limited to the respective members, one could talk of 'club capital goods'.

Regarding the problem of deepening the EU and relying on the economic theory of clubs, one (normative) conclusion might be drawn: as long as one is discussing a number of separable club goods and different members of the club have different preferences concerning their provision, it might be welfare enhancing to realise a *géométrie variable* as proposed by the former President of the European Commission, Jacques Delors. Its organisation would, however, have to take place outside the established decision procedures of the European Union. To see this, simply suppose France and Germany wanted to establish common military forces, which all other member states evaluated as being either premature or even superfluous. If these forces were to be established within the structure of the Union, all other member states would have a say concerning their tasks via their representatives in the Council, the Commission, and the Parliament.[5] However, a deepening outside the present structure of the Union may produce unwarranted spillover effects for the Union.

4. OPTIONS FOR CONSTITUTIONAL CHANGE

4.1. The Normative and Analytical Bases of Constitutional Economics

Constitutional economics breaks with the analysis of welfare economics in some major respects: it is not known end-states that are analysed but rules that coordinate behaviour in a world of uncertainty. The welfare economic procedure of comparing a given state with an idealised, hypothetical one and demanding policy measures in case these two differ is judged as futile from the point of view of constitutional economics. As early as 1954, Buchanan advanced the argument that the fiction of a social welfare function was useless. Although Demsetz (1969) is not exactly a constitutional economist, his dictum that welfare economists often commit the 'Nirvana' fallacy could probably be subscribed to by most constitutional economists. Constitutional economists are interested in the analysis of rules that coordinate interaction. Wicksell (1896) showed that Pareto superiority for collective choice could only be secured using the unanimity rule. Consequently, a proposed rule is only deemed to be an improvement of the *status quo* if unanimous consent can be generated. Using the concept of efficiency therefore only makes sense on the rule level: by definition, a rule is efficient if it can secure unanimous consent among the population.[6]

There is one central value judgement underlying the whole approach: only individuals count. And since, *a priori*, no single individual is to be weighted more heavily than any other, everybody has to consent. Although J.Buchanan slips in a number of additional value judgements without explicitly referring to them (for some examples and critique, see Voigt 1994a), the described value judgement is the central norm on which the entire theory is built.

4.2. Trying to Apply the Analytical Framework to the Question of Entry

a. The contractarian veil of ignorance

Only very few papers on the development of a European constitution within the framework of constitutional economics exist. In 1990, J. Buchanan published a paper entitled 'Europe's Constitutional Opportunity' (on which one of us wrote a rather critical note concluding that this topic was not an appropriate example for applying constitutional economics to real-life problems).[7] In the meantime, Kirchgässner (1994) has published a paper in which he claims it to be relevant positively as well as normatively (see also the volume edited by Leschke 1994).

The veil of uncertainty (Buchanan and Tullock 1962, p. 78) or of ignorance (Rawls 1971) is a central trait of constitutional economics. Rational individuals are supposed to choose the most basic rules according to which they want to live from behind a veil that makes them ignorant with regard to their individual resource endowment, their individual production function, and their preferences in consumption, or in short: their real-life identity. Rules unanimously chosen from behind such a veil, it is claimed, will most likely be 'fair' or 'just' norms. In the meantime, even Buchanan has become somewhat sceptical regarding the possibility of making the veil thick enough in order to exclude any distributional considerations (Brennan and Buchanan 1985, p. 140). Attempts to systematically thicken the veil would amount to establishing a meta-constitutional rule, specifying the procedure under which a society chooses to choose its rules. It would have to be agreed upon unanimously. It seems doubtful, however, that unanimous consent could be generated for such a procedural rule.

With regard to the EU, the representatives of the member states know very well who they are and what their specific interests are. New members are admitted after having taken a close look at their factual identity. Hence decisions from behind a veil are difficult to conceive of. Kirchgässner (1994) does use the concept of a veil, albeit in a modified way: today's politicians decide upon tomorrow's constitution. If the time span between a decision and its coming into effect is long enough, politicians expect not to be in power at the time the rules come into force. They will therefore have few or no personal interests at all. 'In such a situation, they might have an incentive to act "morally" and, therefore, to vote for fair rules' (1994, p. 325). But even if a politician expects to be out of office ten years from now, she will still recall whether she is representing a poor or a rich country, whether it is large or small, has a high share in agriculture, what its situation concerning the sensitive sectors is and so forth. Furthermore, she will have to sell the contract to domestic interest groups and to the current electorate. The argument is thus not based on genuine ignorance but rather on the hope that politicians will be ignorant concerning the interests of citizens in the country they represent. Hence, trying to use the concept of the veil is hardly promising.

However, let us assume for a moment that there is a veil and that it makes politicians decide more 'morally'. If 'morally' is then interpreted in the sense of Rawls who founded his considerations largely on Kant, one could be tempted to ask whether the law of our own actions could be the general – in this case: global – law. Is the CAP applicable on a world-wide scale? The answer is no unless one decides that one wants to induce the farmers of the world to produce output to be largely destroyed later on. But is this argument likely to impress any politician in such a way that she will be ready to change the respective policies? Again, the answer is no, it being based on public choice theory. This is, of course, not an argument against moral discourse. It is just a reminder that moral agreement as contained in the normative strand of constitutional economics will most likely be of rather limited relevance in real-world politics.

b. Further problems of using the contractarian approach

We would also like to draw attention to two other problems that make the contractarian model difficult to apply to the European Union: first, Buchanan's standard question concerning the justifiability of the current *status quo* ('could the rule system presently in force have been the result of unanimous consent at some former time?') is of no help. Given that the national Leviathans are not sufficiently constrained by the national constitutions, and there is a broad consensus on this, one could argue that the insufficiently binding constitutions could not have been brought about by unanimous consent at some former time and are thus not justified. If the competences on the national level are insufficiently constrained, it seems most likely that this defect will be perpetuated onto the European level.[8] It could be argued that the subsidiarity principle is already a case in point since it is not enforceable by individuals at court. But what follows from this apparent legitimacy gap of national constitutions, as well as the European one? Basically nothing if the 'we start from here' approach (Buchanan 1977, p. 80) is taken seriously. 'Starting from here' means taking the institutions currently in force as a starting point. Changing this set of rules is only justified if unanimous agreement for reform can be secured today. Buchanan's standard question is thus completely superfluous.

Secondly, the clear-cut concept of unanimous consent is often tempered by introducing a companion concept, namely hypothetical consent. According to this concept, Pareto-superiority of rule changes is already secured if an observing scientist – or a politician – believes that unanimous agreement *could* be secured. This opens considerable leeway which eventually empties the concept of any meaning.

4.3. Trying a Different Path

a. Choice of decision-rules – the pure case

From the perspective of constitutional economics, the central question with regard to entry is: what procedure would a group of rational individuals agree upon? One answer seems to be very straightforward: they would only let additional members in as long as unanimity concerning their entry is secured. In the case of the EU the constitutional situation is different. The decision units are not the individual citizens of the member states. Instead, they are represented by their governments. If the member governments are considered as parties to the contract on entry, observance of the basic procedural norm applying to individuals is secured via article F of the TEU already quoted above, that is, the requirement of democratic government. But let us first take a closer look at the decisions a rational individual and not a rational government has to make.

In founding a club, a rational individual would have to decide upon the following: (1) which goods should be provided by collective action and which ones by private action (either purely individualistic or by private contractual arrangements), (2) on which level should the goods provided by collective action be supplied, and (3) what should be the respective majorities used in order to decide upon the provision of public goods? In 'the calculus of consent', Buchanan and Tullock (1962) gave basic theoretical answers which could be read as interpretations of the subsidiarity principle: (1) goods should be provided by collective action only if private action is more expensive (p. 57f.), (2) where possible, collective action should be organised in small rather than in large units (p. 114f.), and (3) the decision rule should lead to the minimisation of interdependence costs which are defined as the sum total of external costs ('costs that the individual expects to endure as a result of the actions of others over which he has no direct control') and decisionmaking costs ('costs which the individual expects to incur as a result of his own participation in an organised activity', p. 45f.). Discussing the second question, Buchanan and Tullock advance an abstract solution for the optimum size of government: 'The group should be extended as long as the expected costs of the spillover effects from excluded jurisdictions exceed the expected incremental costs of decisionmaking resulting from adding the excluded jurisdictions' (p. 113). With regard to the third question, they point out that the decisionmaking costs will be lower, at any given collective choice rule, in communities with a homogeneous population than in those with a heterogeneous one. From this observation, they draw the normative conclusion that 'the more homogeneous community should adopt more inclusive rules for the making of collective decisions. However, the homogeneity characteristic affects external costs as well as decisionmaking costs. Thus, the community of homogeneous persons is more likely to accept less restrictive rules even though it can 'afford' more restrictive ones' (p. 115).

Applying these considerations to the question of entry and still considering the rational individual, yields the following conclusions: first, given that every entrant makes the club more heterogeneous, every entrant causes a change in decisionmaking as well as in external costs. Both costs will increase with every additional member. Following the optimisation calculus, entry should then be accompanied by a change in the decision rule: the larger and more heterogeneous the club, the smaller the influence of any member chosen at random, that is, the higher the external costs that can be imposed on the randomly chosen individual. If the randomly chosen individual is prepared to accept some maximum level of external costs, increasing the heterogeneity should be accompanied by *more* inclusive decision rules (see Figure 8.1).

However, external costs are not the only relevant cost category: since decisionmaking costs also increase with larger membership, it is at least theoretically possible that the optimising rule will require *less* inclusive majorities (see Figure 8.2).[9]

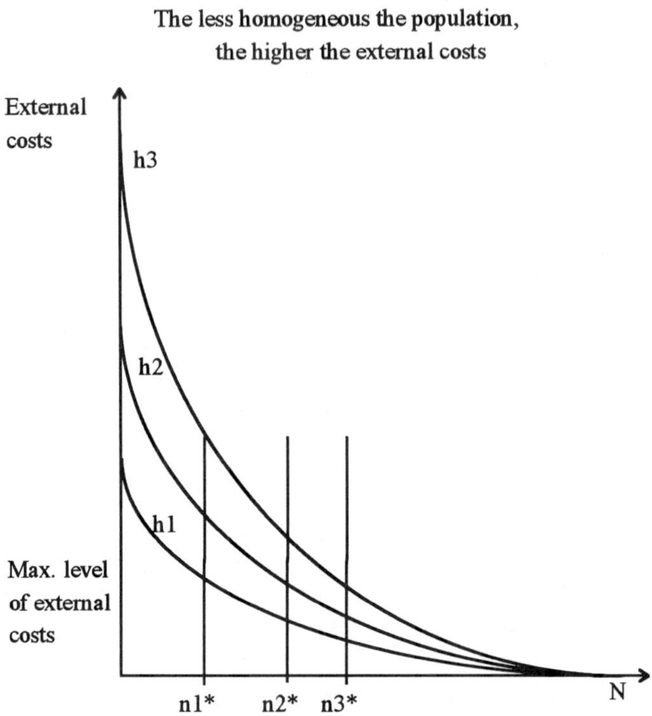

Figure 8.1 Individually optimal decision rules under a given maximum of external costs and different degrees of homogenity

The second effect of making a society more heterogeneous is that interdependence costs will increase systematically. The interdependence costs indicated in Figure 8.2 are for different degrees of homogeneity but for only one level of decisionmaking and collective action, that is, the supranational level. Every increase in interdependence costs on this level makes it more likely that the provision of the good in question becomes (relatively) less costly on a level beneath the supranational one, that is on the national one or possibly on an intermediate one *à la géometrie variable*. In other words, the larger the club, the fewer become the areas of collective action reasonably assigned onto this level. Enlarge *or* deepen is thus indeed the alternative. Assuming that the amount of collective action currently assigned to the EU is optimal, enlarging the Union would then even mean stripping it of some of its current tasks, that is enlarge *and* flatten.

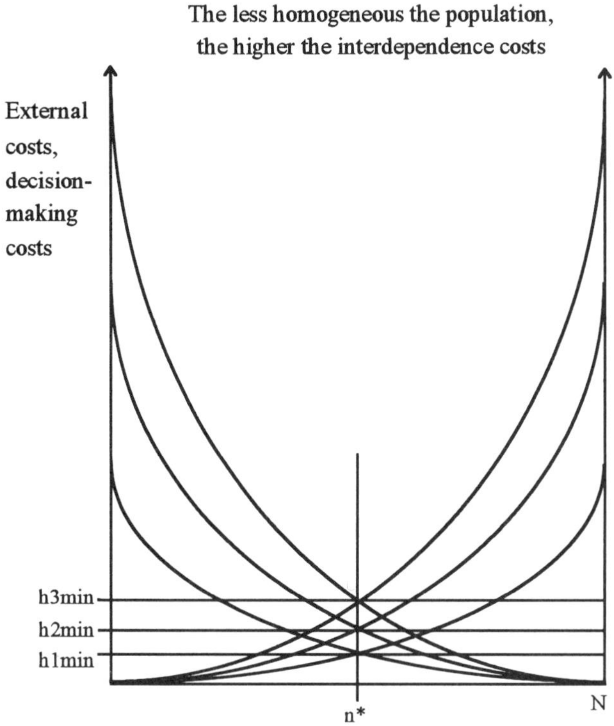

Figure 8.2 Increasing heterogenity always means increasing interdependence (external plus decisionmaking) costs

b. The choice of rules taking political economy into account

Normative constitutional economics is interested in the legitimacy of the procedure for choosing rules. Although it has emerged from public choice theory, it is basically void of any aspects that play a role in real-world politics: organised interest groups, for example, do not have a systematic place in that theory. Similarly, some of the more down to earth normative theories such as the principal–agent theory have not been systematically integrated into this theory. Instead of offering some hints of how to get to a more applicable economic theory of constitutions, we will just sketch some possibilities to deal with the question of entry.

1. Since heterogeneity raises the relevant cost categories in various ways, a uniform constitutional rule regarding the substantial requirements for admission of new members does not appear to be sufficient. Given

the economic and social individuality of every potential entrant, strictly universal conditions of entry are hardly sufficient.

2. Given heterogeneity, there might be a provision in the principal–agent contract between citizens and governments that gives the politicians acting on behalf of their populations discretionary powers for negotiating with applicants for entry. As principals, rational individuals will, however, anticipate that their agents will use the mandate for maximising their own utility (if we assume monolithic blocs to exist for a second). As a consequence, the principals will try to devise an instrument that allows them fairly direct sanctioning.
3. The executive body of the club (that is, the Commission) will also be constrained by a principal–agent contract, the principals in this case being the governments of the member states. It is in the interest of this executive body to maximise tasks and its budget. This is especially relevant when one remembers that the larger the club, the fewer the goods rationally supplied by collective action on the top level.
4. From 2. and 3. it follows that the rational citizen-voter is confronted with a two-tiered principal–agent relationship. Most likely, this arrangement contains many loopholes. Anticipating this – plus having knowledge of Popitz's law – the rational citizen-voter has every incentive to devise a fairly direct sanctioning mechanism.
5. Given 4., one mechanism immediately comes to mind: the principals commission the (two-tiered) agents to negotiate the terms of entry on a case-by-case basis. The agents then turn to their principals – that is, ultimately to the voters – to get their placet. In other words, entry has to be confirmed by referenda in the member states.[10] The admission of new members can be interpreted as requiring an amendment and hence a change in the club constitution. At this fundamental level, it is therefore rational for the citizen-voters to decide for themselves and not be represented by some (imperfectly controlled and controllable) politician. Even if politicians decide unanimously and one would therefore expect a Pareto-superior solution to emerge, the Pareto-superiority of the politicians might not be identical to that of the citizens (Faina Medin and Puy Fraga 1988, p.143).[11]
6. What would be a good decision rule for referenda on constitutional change? Currently, the admission of a new member has to be ratified by every member state. It would therefore only be straightforward to demand that all referenda in the current member states be favourable with regard to the potential entrant(s). This means assigning the borders defined by the member states special significance. Economically, this can be justified by supposing higher homogeneity of citizen-voters within the member states than between them. This

consideration also points the way to the 'optimal quora' of the referenda within member states: since their populations differ with regard to their homogeneity, the optimum will vary between member states. It will therefore make little sense to prescribe a certain quorum that has to be uniformly reached.

7. Drawing on the minimisation-of-interdependence-costs calculus, the rational citizen will be in favour of modifying the decision rules to be applied by the governing body of the club with every change in membership size. If the decision rules to be applied are also part of the referendum, the citizen-voter can expect that its agents will be constrained by the threat of being voted down.
8. An alternative way of constraining the agents could be based on the insight that it makes little sense to put the fox in charge of the chickens, in this case to delegate three fundamental powers to one organ which decides 1. upon the identity and number of the members, 2. upon the bundle of collective goods to be produced and which 3. does indeed produce them. It can, of course, be argued that there exists some separation of powers between the Council, the Commission and the European Parliament. It might, however, be rational to redesign the dividing line between these three and possibly even to devise another decisionmaking body (for the logic of power within Europe's constitution, see Cooter and Drexl, 1994).
9. Up till now, the proposed admission procedures have been based on the implicit assumption that there are genuine club or collective goods to be produced. Concerning the provision of (re-)distributive measures, they have to be somewhat modified. It seems strange to endow the beneficiary of (re-)distributive measures with a vote on the sum and structure of these transfers. This should be restricted to the net-payers. On the individual level (and within nation-states), (re-)distribution could be interpreted in some cases as flowing from an insurance contract. Because, from behind the veil, nobody can be sure that she will not be tomorrow's worst-off, it can be rational to opt in favour of (re-) distribution. However, as we have argued before, the governments know very well who they are and there are no convincing reasons to artificially thicken the (non-existing) veil.
10. If our proposals should be relevant at all, somebody has to make them publicly known and to demand their implementation. Here, the rational citizen-voters face a problem of collective action: everybody would be better off with a set of modified constitutional rules even if she has to invest time and effort in bringing them about. But everybody would be even better off if only the others did the work. In other words, there are strong incentives to take the free-rider position.

Since this is generally valid, the public good 'modified set of constitutional rules' will not be produced unless the prerequisites identified by Olson (1965; [1] small numbers, [2] private good coming along with the public one, and [3] unequal distribution of benefits) hold. It is even conceivable that the publication of a potentially Pareto-superior set of constitutional rules already depicts a public good. Its non-publication could then be termed 'articulation failure' (as argued in Voigt 1994a). The possibility of its existence makes Buchanan's evaluation that 'change in this "contract", if it is desirable at all, can always find unanimous support, given the appropriate time for compromise' (1977, p. 233f.) appear overly optimistic.[12] Taking public choice theory seriously thus leads us to predict that the constitutional rules including those concerning entry will most likely remain unchanged.

5. CONCLUSIONS AND OUTLOOK

Our main conclusions can be divided into instrumental and material ones. Regarding the analytical instruments used, we hope to have demonstrated:

- that the (pure) theory of clubs shows, like constitutional economics, contractual features and has analytical appeal when approaching the question of entry to the European Union. However, closer inspection reveals its limitations as a heuristic tool due to strong assumptions.
- that the contractarian approach to the choice of rules, again, appears quite suitable in discussing entry. However, the basic assumption of a 'veil of ignorance' turns out to reduce the validity of this instrument as significantly as it did already when discussing the compatibility of redistribution with the theory of clubs.
- that political economy can be quite useful in three directions: (1) it can help to identify weaknesses of the two above-mentioned instruments, (2) it can be used to improve the analytical quality of these instruments, and (3) it can give access to some vital problems related to entry.

Turning to the material results and concentrating on widening by giving access to possibly 13 countries to the east and south of the present EU, it appears worth emphasising:

- that particularly after 'Maastricht', redistribution among member states looms large and may well not be tenable at the present scale after a widening by countries which all qualify as net-recipients. As a consequence, a 'roll-back' or 'flattening' may be a realistic scenario instead of the *status quo* or even a deepening. Thereby the subsidiarity principle could become a 'protective shield' for net contributors.

- that the widening will probably significantly increase the heterogeneity of the Union in many respects which will have two effects: (1) decisionmaking costs and external costs will increase, with – under normal conditions – more inclusive decision rules being optimal. (2) Interdependence costs will systematically increase, making it likely that a growing number of tasks so far delegated to the Union may be better handed down to lower levels of government; thus strengthening the case of 'flattening'.
- that the constitutional rules for accession should reflect two factors: (1) the heterogeneity within and between member states and (2) the two-tiered principal–agent relationship consisting of the relation between member-state citizens and their government, on the one hand, and member-state governments and the executive agent of the Union (the Commission) on the other. A closer inspection leads to two constitutional propositions: (1) To handle the principal–agent problem in favour of the citizens as the prime principals, entry should be subjected to referenda and to the requirement of unanimity among member states. (2) To take into account heterogeneity within member states, no uniform quorum should be prescribed for the referenda on accession.

Considering the likely effects of the envisaged entry of up to 13 countries into the EU, the chances that the *acquis communautaire* – including the present constitutional arrangements – will be sustainable are pretty slim. Much more can be said in favour of a 'flattening'. However, the question of entry can be a cause for optimism in European affairs: many European politicians have tied their credibility and reputation to the European Monetary Union (EMU) and to further moves toward a Political Union. Already the fall of the toy version of EMU – the European Monetary System – should have been read as a clear sign that the degree of economic unity hitherto reached in the Union is far from being sufficient to uphold such a system. Further, the discussion of the Political Union after 'Maastricht' shows verbal and practical signs of retreat by politicians from an idea which was left open to speculation anyhow. The reason for our optimism is straightforward: the entry of countries from the east and south of the Union should provide an excellent opportunity to return to sober solutions, including overdue reforms (like the reshaping of the CAP), and to provide

Europe as a whole with a structure which is economically and politically viable.

NOTES

1. For an analysis of these changes and an assessment of their consequences for the economic constitution of the European Community see Streit and Mussler 1994.
2. The equations used by the CEPR (1992) are:
(1) National contribution in mn ECU=2.9+0.91 National GNP in mn ECU (R^2=0.99)
(2) Structural funds by country (ECU per person) = 84.31 – 4.87 *per capita* income (thousand ECU) + 3.66 share of agriculture (percentage of GDP) + 122.90 dummy (Ireland) (R^2=0.98)
(3) CAP funds received (mn ECU) = 0.153 agricultural output (mn ECU) + 1666.4 dummy (for The Netherlands and Germany).
3. One might add that the integration of Central and Eastern Europe into the CAP could cause further repercussions in the 'rest of the world', that is those who suffer from the trade diversion caused by the enlargement of the agricultural 'market order'.
4. A budget freeze relative to the development of the gross national products has been in place ever since the 1992 'Delors-II-package': According to it, the budget will not surpass 1.27 per cent of GNP until 1999.
5. The Protocol on social policy is constructed as an exception to this general logic: it states that 11 Member States (that is, all the current members except the UK) wish to continue with the policy of the 1989 Social Charter and it authorises them (but not the UK!) to 'have recourse to the institutions, procedures and mechanisms of the Treaty'. The protocol shows how complicated a ***géométrie variable*** within the structure of the Union would be, since it states another qualified majority than stated in Article 148 TEC. A ***géométrie variable*** would thus mean different qualified majorities for all the policies only subscribed to by a (variable) subset of the member states.
But a qualified majority for *x* countries is not always the same qualified majority since it would depend on the size of the countries participating in the respective policy. Additionally, suppose a specific policy is only aimed at by two member states. They would clearly use the rule of unanimity to establish and administer such a policy. As one increases the number of participating countries marginally, one would have to ascertain some threshold level which constitutes a switch from quantitative to qualitative change, that is, the threshold where unanimity becomes too costly and qualified majority is expedient. This level could, again, also depend on the size of the participating countries.
The problems a ***géométrie variable*** would bring about can be illustrated by pointing to the introduction of some Non Tariff Agreements as a consequence of the Tokyo Round which can be interpreted as the introduction of such a geometry into the GATT. It has decreased the stability of expectations concerning the rule system because it has made the GATT rule system less transparent (Bael 1988, p. 73).
In his Monnet lecture, former member of the European Commission Peter Sutherland commented upon the prospects of a ***géométrie variable***: 'It is a dangerous terrain because the corollary of progress by the core is the ability to opt-out by "the unable" or "the unwilling" and the temptation to try out a Europe à la carte with all of the legal uncertainties and centrifugal tendencies to which losses of the Community method would give rise' (1995, p. 9).
6. Constitutional economics in its contractarian formulation is neither the only nor the first research programme within economics to focus on the choice of rules instead of the choice within rules. The Freiburg School of Law and Economics already concentrated on this in the 1930s and 1940s. Its most obvious connection to constitutional economics is the elaboration of the concept of the 'economic constitution' (see Streit, 1992). Hayek can, of course, also be

considered a constitutional economist. Whereas J. Buchanan's programme is clearly dominated by normative interests, Hayek is also interested in more positive questions (for a critical evaluation of Hayek's constitutional economics, see Voigt, 1992).

7. See Voigt 1994b. For the question whether constitutional economics constitutes a genuine challenge for the established disciplines of political economy, see Voigt (1996).
8. This appears to be clearly the case. The changes of the economic constitution of the Community after 1957 have paved the way for a system which allows rent-seeking activities and a corresponding growth of the public sector comparable to the member states (see Streit and Mussler, 1994).
9. This counterintuitive result depends on the actual functions describing external costs and decision costs. It is at least theoretically possible that their aggregation, leading to interdependence costs as the decisive criterion, will suggest a less inclusive decision rule. In any case, one has to be aware of the rather stringent assumptions underlying the calculus.
10. Blankart (1993) arrives at the same conclusion by way of a different argument: starting with the two extreme forms of the delegation of powers – pure direct democracy on the one hand and pure representative democracy on the other – and supposing that any mixture between the two can be realised, he asks whether utility-maximising individuals would ever rationally choose pure representative democracy, that is, a form of government in which the Kompetenz-kompetenz (the power to grant power or the power to change the constitution) lies with the government. He concludes that this will never be the case because the control costs would go towards infinity when the power to grant power is delegated.
11. Recently, Frey (1994) has argued that referenda on fundamental questions lead to a societal discourse at large, and are thus to be valued of and by themselves. Additionally, passing a referendum on a specific decision increases the acceptance of the resulting measures among the population and is thus stability enhancing.
12. See Tullock (1987) for a rather pessimistic evaluation of the consequences the 'calculus of consent' had on research as well as its applications for proposing constitutional reforms. Witt (1992) is concerned with the fact that recommendations on how to improve institutional arrangements must take precisely that set of institutions deemed to be defective as their starting point.

REFERENCES

Bael, I.v. (1988), 'The GATT Dispute Settlement Procedure', *Journal of World Trade Law*, **22** (4), 67–77.

Baldwin, R. (1994), *Towards an Integrated Europe*, London: CEPR.

Blankart, C. (1993), *The State as a Club*, Discussion paper, Economic Series 4, Humboldt-University Berlin.

Brennan, G. and J. Buchanan (1985), *The Reason of Rules*, Cambridge: Cambridge University Press.

Buchanan, A. (1990/91), 'Toward a Theory of Secession', *Ethics*, **101**, 322–342.

Buchanan, A. (1991), *Secession – The Morality of Political Divorce from Fort Sumter to Lithuania and Quebec*, San Francisco: Westview.

Buchanan, J. (1954), 'Social Choice, Democracy, and Free Markets', *Journal of Political Economy*, **62**, 334–343.

Buchanan, J. (1965), 'An Economic Theory of Clubs', *Economica*, **32**, 1–14.

Buchanan, J. (1977), *Freedom in Constitutional Contract – Perspectives of a Political Economist*, College Station/London, Texas: A&M University Press.

Buchanan, J. (1990), Europe's Constitutional Opportunity, in *Europe's Constitutional Future*, IEA Readings, London.

Buchanan, J. and G. Tullock (1962), *The Calculus of Consent – Logical Foundations of Constitutional Democracy*, Ann Arbor: University of Michigan Press.
Centre for Economic Policy Research (1992), *Is Bigger Better? The Economics of EC Enlargement*. Monitoring European Integration 3, London.
Chen, Y. and P. Ordeshook (1994), 'Constitutional Secession Clauses', *Constitutional Political Economy* **5** (1), 45–60.
Cooter, R. and J. Drexl (1994), 'The Logic of Power in the Emerging European Constitution, Game Theory and the Division of Powers', *International Review of Law and Economics*, **14**, 307–326.
Corado, C. (1995), 'The Textiles and Clothing Trade with Central and Eastern Europe: Impact on Members of the EC', in R. Faini and R. Portes (eds), *European Union Trade with Eastern Europe*, London: CEPR, pp. 236–268.
Demsetz, H. (1969), 'Information and Efficiency – Another Viewpoint', *Journal of Law and Economics*, **12**, 1–22.
Dimelis, S. and K. Gatsios (1995), 'Trade with Central and Eastern Europe: The Case of Greece', in R. Faini and R. Portes (eds), *European Union Trade with Eastern Europe*, London: CEPR, pp. 123–166.
Faina Medin, J.A. and P. Puy Fraga (1988), 'A Framework for a Public Choice Analysis of the European Community', *Economia delle Scelte Pubbliche*, **2**, 141–158.
Frey, B. (1994), 'Direct Democracy, Politico-Economic Lessons from Swiss Experience', *American Economic Review*, **84** (2), 338–342.
Gual, J. and C. Martín (1995), 'Trade and Foreign Direct Investment with Central and Eastern Europe: Its Impact on Spain', in R. Faini and R. Portes (eds), *European Union Trade with Eastern Europe*, London: CEPR, pp. 167–200.
Kirchgässner, G. (1994), 'Constitutional Economics and Its Relevance for the Evolution of Rules', *Kyklos*, **47** (3), 321–339.
Leipold, H. (1995), 'Zur Osterweiterung der Europäischen Union, Chancen und Hindernisse', *Außenpolitik*, **46** (2), 126–135.
Leschke, M. (ed.) (1994), *Probleme der deutschen und der europäischen Integration – Institutionenökonomische Analysen*, Münster.
Olson, M. (1965), *The Theory of Collective Action*, Cambridge: Harvard University Press.
Rawls, J. (1971), *A Theory of Justice*, Cambridge: Harvard University Press.
Stehn, J. (1994), 'Stufen einer Osterweiterrung der Europäischen Union', *Die Weltwirtschaft*, 194–218.
Streit, M.E. (1992), 'The Freiburg School of Law and Economics', *Journal of Institutional and Theoretical Economics*, **148**, 675–704.
Streit, M.E. and W. Mussler (1994), 'The Economic Constitution of the European Community – From "Rome" to "Maastricht"', *Constitutional Political Economy*, **5** (3), 319–353.
Sunstein, C. (1991), 'Constitutionalism and Secession', *University of Chicago Law Review*, **58** (2), 633–670.
Sutherland, P. (1995), 'The European Union – A Stage of Transition', 17th Jean Monnet Lecture at the European University Institute, in *EIPA Scope*, European Institute of Public Administration, 1995/2, 2–9.
Tullock, G. (1987), 'The Calculus after 25 Years', *Cato Journal* **7** (2), 313–321.

Voigt, S. (1992), 'On the Internal Consistency of Hayek's Evolutionary Oriented Constitutional Economics – Some General Remarks', *Journal des Economistes et des Etudes Humaines*, **3**, 461–476.

Voigt, S. (1994a), 'Die kontraktorientierte Theorie der Verfassung, Bemerkungen zum Ansatz Buchanans', *Homo Oeconomicus*, **XI** (2), 173–209.

Voigt, S. (1994b), 'European Political Union – An Appropriate Example for Applying Constitutional Economics to Real-Life Problems?', *ORDO*, **45**, 273–286.

Voigt, S. (1996), 'Die konstitutionelle Ökonomik als Herausforderung für die Theorie der Wirtschaftspolitik – zugleich eine Skizze zur Weiterentwicklung einer ökonomischen Theorie der Verfassung', in J. Pies and M. Leschke (eds), *James Buchanans konstitutionelle Ökonomik*, Tübingen: Mohr (Siebeck), pp. 157–183.

Wicksell, K. (1896), *Finanztheoretische Untersuchungen*, Jena: Fischer.

Winters, L. (1995), 'Liberalization of the European Steel Trade', in R. Faini and R. Portes (eds), *European Union Trade with Eastern Europe*, London: CEPR, pp. 201–235.

Witt, Ulrich (1992), 'The Endogenous Public Choice Theorist', *Public Choice*, **73**, 117–129.

Comment

Michael G. Faure

INTRODUCTION

What are the contents of this chapter? The authors attempt to analyse the problem of entry to the EU from an economic perspective, using several economic models, but especially looking at it from the angle of constitutional economics.

Their goal is to contribute to the literature by providing a critical analysis of the constitutional economics approach *à la* Buchanan. In addition the authors attempt to provide hints for the procedural rules that should be applied when decisions concerning entry are made.

First the authors discuss the *status quo* and the basic possibilities to come out of this *status quo* (section 2). The basic message of that section is that a choice will have to be made between the so-called enlarging or the deepening of the EU. Achieving both at the same time, meaning both more member states and more competences for the union, does not seem to be possible.

Next, the authors analyse the effects of enlarging the union and present several analytical frameworks to analyse the question of entry. Their conclusion is that enlarging the Union with new member states will increase its heterogeneity. A second major conclusion of the chapter is that a decision on entry should be based on a referendum because of the principal–agent problems between politicians and citizens in the member states (see section 5).

SOME GENERAL OBSERVATIONS

1. A first general problem is that the authors merely analyse the problem of entry from a procedural perspective. Their conclusion that a strong case can be made in favour of a referendum to control the principal–

agent problem in member states, is obviously not only appropriate for entry decisions. Many authors in the fields of constitutional law and economics and public choice have advocated referenda,[1] so this conclusion hardly comes as a surprise.

2. A more fundamental question is whether it is possible to discuss the desirability of either enlarging or deepening of the EU without providing a theoretical framework regarding the principal question of whether centralisation within a European framework is needed at all for specific topics. The authors use the theory of Clubs to discuss entry. It seems, however, only possible to discuss the optimal size of the Club if one first establishes why the members want the Club in the first place. Only if the common goals and advantages of cooperation via a Club are known, useful comments can be made concerning the optimal size of the Club. If one does not address this fundamental question first, one will unavoidably be left with a rather superficial analysis of the possible budgetary effects of enlarging the Union that says very little about the qualitative benefits or disadvantages of the Union as such.

   Therefore the authors should have first looked into the economics of federalism that addresses the question under what circumstances centralisation may be desirable.[2] Only if such a theoretical framework is used, may it be possible to design the scope of an optimal legal area for a specific subject matter that has to be regulated.[3] Moreover, van den Bergh has recently provided an interesting analysis of the subsidiarity principle from a law and economics perspective indicating that centralisation, for example, via the European Union could be desirable in order to control transboundary externalities and to remedy prisoners' dilemmas.[4] Only if first the fundamental question is answered why a European Union is needed in the first place and for what kind of topics, can a useful analysis be provided concerning the optimal size and necessity of enlargement.

3. The authors point to both an enlargement of the market and the creation of military stability (section 2.2.b). However, these goals can easily be reached without the need for a total market integration, which the European Union achieves at this stage. Once more this shows that inevitably first the question will have to be answered what topics will be dealt with before the question of enlargement can be decided.

4. The authors assume that the larger the Union will be, the greater the heterogeneity will be. Although this statement seems intuitively correct, the question, however, arises whether this is necessarily the case. First, one should point at the fact that already within the existing

European Union a large amount of heterogeneity, generally speaking, exists. For instance, environmental problems in Greece or Ireland are totally different. Nevertheless European directives impose similar emission standards for all member states.[5] If heterogeneity is an argument in favour of referenda, as the authors seem to suggest, they should consequently argue that already now member states should have the right to vote via referendum on every new directive coming from Brussels. Second, one can not decide on the question of heterogeneity either before or after enlargement without focusing on the topics that the EU should regulate. Indeed, if the number of topics to be regulated is small and if with respect to these topics a similar approach would be followed in all member states there thus should not be a large degree of heterogeneity.

This leads to the conclusion that the authors' finding that one can not combine an enlargement with a deepening must not necessarily be true. Again, this seems at first blush intuitively correct. The larger the Union the more preferences might differ. However, it might well be the case that in a number of specific areas new entrants may have a legal regime that complies very much with existing legislation within the Union so that an enlargement does not necessarily lead to more heterogeneity. In sum, whether there will be more heterogeneity as a result of an enlargement can only be answered if the topics to be regulated by the European Union are designated first.

A FEW SPECIFIC POINTS

Following these general comments a few additional specific points can be made.

1. In section 2.2.a Streit and Voigt discuss budgetary effects of a possible enlargement, arguing that, for instance, France, Germany and the Benelux might have to contribute a lot more if East Europeans joined the EU. However, one can not simply look at the costs of enlargement without also looking at the benefits. If one were to use a theoretical framework of centralisation indicating that one of the reasons to have a European Union in the first place would be the control of transboundary externalities, the fact that some Eastern European countries were to join the Union may well have substantial compensating benefits, for example, because they would be forced to comply with European environmental directives. This could lead to a substantial reduction of environmental damage precisely in the

Benelux, France and Germany. If curing externalities is indeed seen as one of the goals for centralisation, one way to look at the territorial scope of the Union would be to examine what the scope of the externality to be regulated is.

2. A related point is advanced in section 4.3.a, arguing that from the perspective of the constitutional economics, the central question with regard to entry is: what procedure would a group of rational individuals agree upon? One could wonder whether this procedural question is indeed the fundamental one. The more fundamental question that individuals should first ask is what kind of tasks or topics they want to regulate at the central level, at the local level or in FOCJ.[6] An institutional framework should then be worked out to determine what is to be regulated at the various levels. The question of scale would be then automatically answered depending upon the topics to be regulated. Thus it would automatically be clear whether it would be efficient to have more entries into the Union.
3. For the reason discussed above, I have difficulty with the authors' assumption that every entrant makes the Club more heterogeneous (4.3.a). This seems to be based largely on the non-motivated feeling that a Hungarian may be different than a Belgian. From a legal point of view the question of heterogeneity obviously depends on the topic that has to be regulated within the Club. If the entrants' law is quite similar to the average of the already included legal systems, the entry will not lead to more heterogeneity. The remainder of the authors' analysis rests on the non-motivated assumption that every entry provides more heterogeneity, which I believe to be doubtful.
4. Finally the authors, still in the same section, seem to be quite enthusiastic about the current competences attributed to the EU, since they assume that the amount of collective action currently assigned to it is optimal. This statement can certainly be attacked from a law and economics perspective. Given the influence of pressure groups, there is a serious risk, and some empirical evidence, that too many competences are attributed to the European Union. Pressure groups will obviously choose the level of government where their influence is largest.[7] Given the low degree of transparency, lobbying by the industry might be a lot easier in Brussels than at the local level where a countervailing power by, for instance, non-governmental organizations exists.[8] The basic problem with the chapter is therefore that the authors apparently incorrectly assume that the current working of the EC is efficient. Literature has, on the contrary, demonstrated not only that more competences than would be efficient are attributed to the

European level,[9] but also that the competences are used in a way which lead to overregulation.[10]

CONCLUDING REMARKS

The authors provide a lot of interesting material and information on the question of entry. The chapter also contains an interesting overview of the literature in that respect. My only doubt concerns the fact that I do not believe that one can analyse the question of entry without looking at the fundamental questions related to the economics of federalism which indicates what an optimal legal area to regulate a specific problem is. The chapter does not address the probably more interesting and inevitable question, being: if you want to say anything about entry, should you not first focus on the question of how large in general a unity or organization that sets rules for different topics should be?

In sum, I do not believe one can usefully discuss entry or enlargement of the European Union if one does not analyse what competences should be attributed to it in the first place.

NOTES

1. See, for example, B.S. Frey (1983), and J. Rourke, R. Hiskes and C. Zizakzadeh (1992).
2. See, for example, with respect to fiscal federalism R. Inman. and D. Rubinfeld (1994).
3. See H.-J. Schmidt-Trenz and D. Schmidtchen (1993).
4. See the inauguration address of R. van den Bergh (1994a), and R. van den Bergh (1994b). See also van den Bergh's contribution on the meaning of the subsidiarity principle for competition law (Chapter 6 of this volume).
5. This is criticised in M. Faure and J.G.J. Lefevere (1995a), and in M. Faure and J.G.J. Lefevere (1996).
6. See B.S.Frey and R. Eichenberger, Chapter 7 of this volume.
7. See E. Noam (1982).
8. See M. Faure, R. van den Bergh and J. Lefevere (1996).
9. See generally R. van den Bergh (1994b), and for environmental policy, M. Faure and J.G.J. Lefevere (1995b).
10. For nice examples see A. Ogus (1995).

REFERENCES

Bergh, R. van den (1994a), *Subsidiariteit rechteconomisch bekeken. Adieux Bruxelles?*, Arnhem: Gouda Quint.

Bergh, R. van den (1994b), 'The Subsidiarity Principle in European Community Law: Some Insights from Law and Economics', *Maastricht Journal of European and Comparative Law*, 337–366.

Faure, M. and J.G.J. Lefevere (1995a), 'Protecting Drinking Water Quality Against Contamination by Pesticides: An Alternative Regulatory Framework', *Review of European Community and International Environmental Law (RECIEL)*, 321–326.

Faure, M. and J.G.J. Lefevere (1995b), 'Some Public Interest and Private Interest Aspects of Environmental Standard Setting in the European Community', in D. Mayes (ed.), *The Evolution of Rules for a Single European Market, II, Rules, Democracy, and the Environment*, Brussel: EC, pp. 320–351.

Faure, M. and J.G.J. Lefevere (1996), 'The Draft Directive on Integrated Pollution Prevention and Control: an Economic Perspective', *European Environmental Law Review*, 112–122.

Faure, M., R. van den Bergh and J. Lefevere (1996), 'The Subsidiarity Principle in European Environmental Law: an Economic Analysis', in E. Eide and R. van den Bergh (eds), *The Law and Economics of the Environment*, Oslo: Juridisk Forlag, pp.121–166.

Frey, B.S. (1983), *Democratic Economic Policy*, Oxford: Blackwell.

Frey, B.S. (1994), 'Direct Democracy: Political-Economic Lessons from Swiss Experience', *American Economic Review*, 338–342.

Inman, R. and D. Rubinfeld (1994), 'The EMU and Fiscal Policy in the New European Community: An Issue for Economic Federalism', *International Review of Law and Economics*, 147–161.

Noam, E. (1982), 'The Choice of Governmental Level in Regulation', *Kyklos*, 278–291.

Ogus, A. (1995), 'Quality Control for European Regulation', *Maastricht Journal of European and Comparative Law*, 325–338.

Rourke, J., R. Hiskes and C. Zizakzadeh (1992), *Direct Democracy and International Politics: Deciding International Issues through Referendums*, London: Boulder.

Schmidt-Trenz, H.-J. and D. Schmidtchen (1994), 'Die Theorie optimaler Rechtsräume', *Jahrbuch für Neue Politisch Ökonomie*, **13**, 7–29.

Comment

Roland Vaubel

In current discussions about the Intergovernmental Conference, it is frequently taken for granted that the Eastern enlargement requires a transition to widespread majority voting in the Council of the European Union. Streit and Voigt demonstrate that this conclusion is premature because, for any given quorum, enlargement will not only raise the cost of decisionmaking but also the cost of being outvoted (the external cost). Even though it is not necessarily true that 'every entrant makes the club more heterogeneous' – entry can, for example, reduce the standard deviation of *per capita* income – there can be no doubt that, in the special case of the Eastern enlargement, heterogeneity in the Union would increase. The external cost would have to be borne by the most deviant member countries – for example, by the richest and the poorest member states.

The richest member states would be outvoted on European budgetary issues so as to redistribute at their expense. The poorest member states would be outvoted in 'harmonising' national regulations and tax rates. This is because those member states which are highly taxed and regulated are interested in imposing their own level of regulation and taxation on the more liberal member states in order to reduce the latter's competitiveness. This is 'the strategy of raising rivals' costs' which is well known from industrial economics (for example, Salop and Scheffman, 1983) and the positive theory of regulation (Goldberg, 1982). Stigler (1970, p. 2), Heller (1986, p. 271f., 277) and Bartel and Thomas (1987), for example, have suggested that this strategy has played an important role in centralising regulatory policy in the United States. Majority voting in the European Union would enable the decisive voter in the Council to force his own level of regulation and taxation upon the less restrictive member states – most notably on the Eastern entrants – just as West Germany has imposed its regulations and tax rates on East Germany. The consequences are well known.

Moreover, as the increase of regulation and taxation in the less restrictive member states reduces the competitive pressure on the more highly regulated and taxed member states, the latter will raise their own regulations and taxes even further; and the decisive member state will impose this increase on the less restrictive member states as well. Thus, majority voting triggers an iterative process of regulation and taxation and leads to a new equilibrium in which all member states have a higher level of regulation and taxation than they used to have in isolation or would have had under the unanimity rule.

Streit and Voigt argue that 'a uniform constitutional rule regarding the substantial requirements for admission of new members does not appear sufficient'. This statement has to be qualified. It probably does not hold for a Union confined to a common or internal market, a customs union or a free-trade area. In these cases, a general rule – as exists under GATT or WTO – seems to be preferable. Without such a rule, existing trade blocs which use external protection to exploit their market power will exact tribute from entrants who are too small to affect their terms of trade. The negotiations over the European Economic Area were a case in point. Norway and Iceland were asked to pay tribute in terms of fishing rights, while Austria and Switzerland were pressed to accept more environmental damage from Alpine transit traffic.

For analogous reasons, a general entry rule would work well if all public or club goods of the Union were produced in optimal quantities and priced according to the equivalence principle (at least at the margin). Thus, what Streit and Voigt are suggesting is a second-best solution. They presuppose that fiscal equivalence cannot be attained.

As a matter of fact, the European Union produces very few public or club goods and is mostly engaged in redistribution (for the benefit of interest groups). Streit and Voigt note that redistribution 'could be interpreted in some cases as flowing from an insurance contract'. But they argue that this interpretation does not apply to the EU because the decision to redistribute has not been 'a constitutional one under a veil of ignorance'. I agree with their conclusion but I am not convinced by their line of reasoning. Constitutional decisions do not necessarily presuppose a veil of ignorance (even though they are facilitated by it). As Buchanan (1975) has explained in some detail, a constitutional contract may also be concluded in an anarchistic equilibrium, that is, in the absence of a Rawlsian veil of ignorance. Even in an imaginary world of perfect foresight, there would be scope for Pareto-improving unanimous decisions at the constitutional level. The problem about EU redistribution is not that 'the governments know very well who they are' but that the decision to insure is not one that has to be taken by the governments of the member states. Since individuals differ with regard to risk aversion, the decision whether, how much, and with whom to insure must ultimately be left to the individual. If some or even most citizens wished to insure with their government or the EU, they could, of course, do so but they should not have the right to impose their will on the others.

The Eastern enlargement of the European Union has further implications for constitutional reform which have not been mentioned so far. Enlargement will aggravate the principal–agent problem because it weakens each principal's incentive to control the agent. The share of the benefits which can be internalised by the individual member state declines, and the external benefit for the others increases as the number of members grows (Olson 1965). Econometric evidence suggests that the growth of membership does in fact explain bureaucratic waste in other international organisations like the International Monetary Fund and the World Bank (Vaubel 1996). As the incentive to control weakens, it becomes all the more important to introduce more effective instruments of control. EU legislation and policies ought to be directly controlled by the parliaments of the member states and by the citizens in referenda (European Constitutional Group 1993; Vaubel 1995: 59–63).

Finally, by raising heterogeneity, the Eastern enlargement will increase the power of the European Commission and the European Court of Justice at the expense of the Council and the member states. This is because the Commission and the Court decide by simple majority while the Council and the member states usually cannot reverse such decisions except by unanimity. Thus, enlargement strengthens the case for the following two reforms which the European Constitutional Group (1993) has suggested. First, the Commission – as a civil service – must cease to be a legislator. This follows also from the principle of the separation of powers, the democratic principle and the principle of subsidiarity. Second, again for the sake of subsidiarity, the judges of the European Court of Justice ought to be empanelled from, and selected by, the highest courts of the member states.

Will the Intergovernmental Conference really clear the way for Eastern enlargement?

REFERENCES

Bartel, A.P. and L.G. Thomas (1987), 'Predation Through Regulation: The Wage and Profit Effects of the Occupational Safety and Health Administration and the Environmental Protection Agency', *Journal of Law and Economics*, **30**, 239–264.

Buchanan, J.M. (1975), *The Limits of Liberty – Between Anarchy and Leviathan*, Chicago/London: Chicago University Press.

European Constitutional Group (1993), *A Proposal For a European Constitution*, London: European Policy Forum.

Goldberg, V.P. (1982), 'Peltzman on Regulation and Politics', *Public Choice*, **39**, 291–297.

Heller, T. (1986), 'Legal Theory and the Political Economy of American Federalism', in M. Capelletti, M. Seccombe and J. Weiler (eds), *Integration*

Through Law – Europe and the American Federal Experience, Berlin, New York: de Gruyter, pp. 254–317.
Olson, M. (1965), *The Logic of Collective Action*, Cambridge, Mass.: Harvard University Press.
Salop, S.C. and T.D. Scheffman (1983), 'Raising Rivals' Costs', *American Economic Review, Papers and Proceedings*, **73**, 267–271.
Stigler, G.J. (1970), 'Director's Law of Public Income Redistribution', *Journal of Law and Economics*, **13**, 1–10.
Vaubel, R. (1995), *The Centralisation of Western Europe – The Common Market, Political Integration and Democracy*, London: Institute of Economic Affairs.
Vaubel, R. (1996), 'Bureaucracy at the IMF and the World Bank – A Comparison of the Evidence', *The World Economy*, **19** (2), 195–210.

9. Non-coercion, Decision Rules and Europe's Constitutional Debate

Frank Vibert

INTRODUCTION

The member states of the European Union (EU) have now started an Intergovernmental Conference to review the Maastricht agreement (the Treaty on European Union) and to prepare the ground for the next stage of enlargement of the Union. The member states are torn in two different directions – in one direction by a desire for stability and consolidation (in part because it is not clear that public opinion is ready for large changes) and, in the other direction, by a desire to maintain the momentum towards closer European political integration as well as by knowledge that significant changes will in fact have to be made if enlargement is to take place.

A number of commentators have suggested that the way through the dilemma is for Europe to formalise the rules of political association in Europe. This would mean putting the existing Treaties into the form of a constitution or possibly prefacing the existing Treaties with a set of constitutional principles. In the absence of a more fundamental constitutional discussion, the existing Treaties perform the role of a 'surrogate' constitution. In my view the present position is an entirely unsatisfactory situation because the Treaties have not been drawn up as constitutional documents and would look very different if they were. There has always been a political agenda behind the Community but the Treaties have not been drawn up as articles of political association. As a result, the key principles of political association are fudged rather than addressed. The treaties obfuscate when they need to be clear. The desired outcomes of association are stressed rather than the processes and rules of association.

One of the most important topics for discussion concerns decision rules in the Council of Ministers – what voting rules should apply to which subjects. This is a highly sensitive area from a political perspective since it concerns the balance between the small and large member states. The way in which it is resolved will also have far reaching institutional and constitutional repercussions:

- The outcome will have crucial consequences for the effectiveness of the Council itself and thus help determine what kind of role the Council will play in European structures.

- A further part of this discussion will concern to what extent 'opt-outs' or 'opt-ins' are possible and desirable in different areas of policy and will thus be critical to the evolution of 'variable geometry' in the Union.

- Yet another dimension concerns the procedures for rule changing and rule keeping. The Maastricht agreement came close to defeat during the ratification process – triggered by difficulties in one of the smaller member states. The question thus raised is whether, in future, rule changes should continue to require unanimous consent or whether a lower threshold should be considered. This same question is presented in somewhat different form when the suggestion is made that if all member states cannot agree on the next stages of political integration, then some should be able to press ahead.

- If high thresholds for rule changes are retained, then the further consequence must be faced – Treaty amendment will become increasingly difficult. This sparks another crucial question – what are the likely consequences for the rules and rule keeping when the amendment process becomes increasingly difficult?

In order to get some guidance on these questions about decision rules it is useful to explore what constitutional economics has to offer.[1] This will bring the reader fairly quickly to the non-coercion principle (attributed by Buchanan to Wicksell, although it has an earlier incarnation with Rousseau's theory of the general will). The non-coercion principle has provided the point of departure for a discussion of decision rules in constitutional economics. In the way it has been formulated in constitutional economics, the non-coercion approach states that, in principle, the best rule for collective decision taking is that decisions should be taken by unanimity. This is because unanimity provides the only decision rule which allows each participant to decide for themselves whether a choice improves their position or not. At the same time, it is recognised as a practical matter that unanimity is a counsel of perfection – a largely impractical and costly standard. One of the major reasons for agreeing on constitutional arrangements is to reduce the cost of collective decisionmaking in the post-constitutional setting. Unanimity is retained as the criterion for constitutional choice. But the approach to decision rules for collective choice applicable to the 'operational' setting is one of cost.

This chapter explores the role played by this way of formulating the non-coercion principle. In particular it discusses whether it offers a clear way of distinguishing between normative and positive elements in decision rules and can thus provide a persuasive approach to formulating constitutional rules in the EU including decision rules in the Council. The discussion is based on the original statement of the principle in the Calculus of Consent ('The Calculus'). While a discussion of the way decision rules are now analysed in constitutional economics would have to take into account later developments (in particular, for the reasons mentioned in the text, the developments in game theory) the non-coercion principle remains a key principle in constitutional economics and the discussion in 'The Calculus' remains a basic text for distinctions between the normative and positive elements in it.[2]

The conclusions of the discussion relate both to the thrust of the research programme of constitutional economics as it applies to questions relating to a developing European constitutional order and to the normative elements of Europe's constitutional debate.

1. THE ROLE OF THE NON-COERCION PRINCIPLE

The non-coercion principle serves four quite distinct roles in constitutional economics. Each of these roles raises different questions:

(i) *As a demarcation device between constitutional choice and political choice:* The rules governing political choice in the operational setting are distinguished from the rules governing constitutional choice itself. The question is whether an approach to decision rules in politics through the notion of 'cost' provides an adequate guide to their formulation.

(ii) *As the criterion for constitutional choice:* The formulation of constitutional economics suggests that while the rules for deciding on collective choices in the political setting can be analysed as cost driven, the rules for deciding on constitutional choices should be centred on the unanimity principle. The question is whether 'unanimity' works for this purpose. Is there a 'bright line' between the rules governing political choice and those governing constitutional choice?

(iii) *As an underpinning for methodological individualism:* The unanimity model poses questions of choice about rules from the stand-point of the individual chooser. Two questions arise. The first stems from the fact that Europe (aside from Switzerland) does not practise direct democracy but various forms of representative democracy. In the context of the European Union, the Council represents the constituent member states. What is involved in this transition from the individual to the individual constituent state? More fundamentally, does the unanimity principle succeed in keeping separate the methodological individualism of economics and individualism as a normative political doctrine?

(iv) *As a justificatory principle for a constitutional arrangement:* The final role played by the non-coercion principle is as a criterion for the legitimacy of the constitutional arrangements. The claim is that if the constitutional rules are unanimously agreed then they are legitimate – no further questioning is allowed. The issue is whether unanimity can serve as a validation principle that excludes further question.

These questions are distinct. It would be possible to reject the cost based account of the formation of decision rules for political choice but retain unanimity for constitutional choice. It would be possible to accept the approach to decision rules about constitutional choice and to collective choice in the post-constitutional setting but at the same time distinguish more clearly between the positive and the normative aspects of the theory. It would also be possible to retain the entire approach but reject unanimity as a justificatory principle for constitutional arrangements. In the discussion below each of the four questions is examined separately.

2. UNANIMITY AS A DEMARCATION DEVICE

The proposition underlying the cost based approach to decision rules in collective choice is that participants in a political association will agree on decision rules that involve less than unanimity first as a means to reduce decisionmaking costs in society. The second determinant of the voting rules will be the fears of the participants of costs imposed on them if overruled in an area of collective choice. There are two implications. One implication is the trade-off between agreement on rules that reduce decision costs and the fear of imposed costs that may result. Another implication is that decision rules will be differentiated according to the area of choice.[3] Starting from the point that ideally decisions should be taken by unanimity, in practice, voting rules will be more relaxed the less the area of collective policy is seen as likely to involve the participants in costs if they find themselves outside the decisive majority.

One initial question concerns the sense in which the term 'cost' is being employed. The term can be seen entirely in a financial sense. Some decisions are more likely to involve the imposition of higher financial costs than others. For example, environmental decisions are likely to be seen as potentially more costly than certain other decisions about the market and this might justify more stringent rules for environmental decisions within the Single Market voting procedures. Similarly, defence decisions are likely to be viewed as routinely carrying high financial costs and might therefore generally justify more stringent decision rules. The practical complication is that the degree of costliness cannot easily be ascribed to general areas of policy. Within each broad area of policy – defence, the environment, the social chapter, there are some decisions with very high potential costs and others that may be low cost. Nevertheless, the general approach is quite straightforward – being outside the decisive majority in different policy areas will have different financial costs attached and so decision rules can be graduated accordingly. The complication of the unpredictability of the costliness of measures within broad areas of policy is one that can, in part, (in relation to economic policy) be met by voting rules which distinguish between regulatory and deregulatory action.

There is an immediate objection to this rather restrictive sense of cost in that it appears to ignore the importance of purely normative elements in collective choice. From a normative perspective, some areas of collective choice may be seen as 'intrinsically' more important than others. One response is to try to deny the relevance of normative orderings on the ground that they are subjective and arbitrary. Another response is to suggest that the notion of 'cost' is being used in a broader sense than financial cost to stand as a proxy for any reasons (including normative reasons) why participants may fear to be excluded from a decisive majority. It is this broader notion of 'cost' that is being used in constitutional economics – even if the illustrations used are often those of financial cost.[4]

In this broader sense 'cost' can stand as an analytic proxy for normative differences. For example, wealthier member states of the EU may place a higher valuation on environmental standards than poorer member states. But precisely because of these normative differences, the poorer member states may fear the costs of having expensive regulations imposed upon them.

'Cost' can also stand as a proxy for the more sensitive areas of collective decision taking. Currently the more sensitive areas of collective policy in Europe are recognised in the so called 'pillars structure' of the Maastricht Treaty. Through the separations brought about by the pillars, decisions relating to the law and order issues of the Home Affairs pillar are distinguished from the decisions under the Economic Community – for example on the engine sizes of motor bikes. These sensitive areas in decision taking can also be said to reflect normative orderings of importance – a decision on law and order is more important than a decision on engine sizes. However, even in this case 'cost' can also be said to capture the sense in which a wrong decision on law and order will be more costly for the ties of political association than wrong decisions on most issues of economic regulation.

One weakness in this account so far is that the perception that different choices have different costs attached to them would not by itself justify differentiated voting rules in societies. Where the appreciation of different areas of choice is similar, participants would have no fear of imposed costs – in addition all participants will be approaching costly areas of choice with a similar degree of caution and would have similar preferences about incurring decision costs. Homogenous societies do not need complex decision rules. It is different preferences which give rise to fears of imposed costs. 'Cost' therefore must also be used in the different sense of referring to 'preferences' and different intensities of preferences. The conclusion drawn in the Calculus is either that differing preference intensities will give rise to such constitutional features as bicameral legislatures or that decision rules themselves will be more stringent in areas where participants fear that their strongest preferences will be overridden.[5]

Moving the argument into the area of preference theory opens up other considerations familiar in that context. It puts the focus on the bargaining context of collective decisionmaking and in particular it emphasises the importance of the setting in bargaining situations – whether a setting is zero or positive sum for example.

In the Calculus, bargaining and the setting in which bargaining takes place are treated in two different ways. First, the setting is treated as a positive sum game in the overall constitutional agreement. Unless there is an overall perception of mutual gain there will be no constitutional agreement on the rules. Because there is this perception of net overall gain, participants may allow for decision rules in particular areas to be framed in ways that lead to their interests in that area being overruled. Second, within the operational rules, participants will use other devices to try to stop their interests being overruled – notably by log rolling (vote trading) and side payments.

While vote trading and side payments are an important feature of decision taking in the Council it seems difficult to confine the bargaining setting to the positive sum perceptions of the constitutional bargain. The bargaining setting also seems highly relevant in considering decision rules in particular areas of operational choice. For example, decisions related to creating the

Single Market could be seen to be part of a positive sum game – since all participants benefit from the removal of trade barriers. By contrast, decisions on say a common foreign policy might be seen as more likely to involve issues where participants anticipate zero sum situations – for example, a decision by some participants to recognise Macedonia might be seen by others as against their interest or, to give a different example, France may see itself as being impacted by events in Algeria in a way not shared by other members of the Union. The implication is that decision rules can be less stringent in areas where a positive sum setting is identified (where preferences are more likely to be aligned) than in settings where participants fear a zero sum outcome and preferences are seen as likely to hold the possibility of conflict. This seems to characterise the actual distinctions being made at least as much if not more than the attempt to nuance decision rules through log rolling and side payments.

Trying to be clear about the different bargaining settings in which different decisions will need to be made seems important, but, it too seems an incomplete guide to the rules of collective choice. One qualification already mentioned is that it may be difficult to characterise different areas of decision taking in any pure way. A positive sum setting (such as the mutual reduction of trade barriers) may be seen to have some negative aspects (when declining industries have to shut in response to open markets) and the foreign policy setting would also likely offer some choices which are positive sum as well as those that may be seen as zero sum.

What is being introduced by this sort of qualification is not that the setting is indeterminate but the concept of risk. Different choice settings offer different perceptions of risk to the participants (the risk of finding interests in conflict). There is a further reason why risk and uncertainty seem to have a direct relevance to the choice of decision rules. This is because the choice about decision rules involve other key uncertainties – in particular, the uncertainties attached to the behaviour of other participants. Can a country like Finland always count on the support of other Scandinavian members in situations of collective choice? If it can, then it is less exposed to being overruled in majority decisions and can therefore live more easily with lower majority thresholds. To give a different example, can Germany always count on the support of France and the Benelux countries? Different categories of choice also pose different degrees of risk about voting behaviour. On an issue like regional aid the voting line up of member states is fairly predictable, but on an issue of foreign policy it may not be. Moreover behaviour may change over time – France may see a greater risk of being at odds with Germany now than it did say 10 years ago. Similarly, the voting line up on financial issues has changed as the balance between the net contributors to the budget and the net recipients has changed.

Uncertainty is recognised as a fundamental factor in choice in the Calculus but there is nevertheless an attempt to exclude it from the analysis of decision rules. The suggestion is that an individual player will assume that over a series of decisions preferences will be randomly distributed. It is also suggested that a player cannot anticipate which specific rules might benefit him in a particular area. Thus the conclusion is drawn that the individual player will devise rules for the average player.[6]

These are very strong assumptions. The alternative assumption is that member states will have ideas where they could be most at risk and where the behaviour of other participants may be most unpredictable or most likely to be in conflict. As a result they will attempt to frame decision rules to try to deal with situations of risk – risk in the setting, in the behaviour of other participants and in the (in)stability of preferences of others. In such circumstances participants will approach decision rules with a view to minimise the risk of being overruled in the areas of maximum significance to themselves.

In short, approaching the choice of decision rules as a matter of cost has the great advantage of providing a unifying analytic framework. But it does seem that other factors need to be given additional prominence – in particular the bargaining setting and the risk perceptions. The bargaining setting cannot just be thrown into the constitutional bargain and detached from the consideration of the rules of choice in the operational setting.[7] The risk setting also cannot be put to one side. The attitude of member states in the EU is more accurately described by a minimax rule addressed to the risks and uncertainties of the bargaining setting and of the behaviour of others rather than to cost alone.

While constitutional economics is defined broadly to include bargaining theory which sheds light on rules for treating risk, it remains less than fully satisfactory to treat normative differences under the rubric of 'cost'. It is possible to say that risk reduction is motivated by 'cost' and directed towards minimising potential costs. But it will be necessary and important to explain in what sense the term 'cost' is being used. As mentioned above, they may be costs in the conventional sense of economic or financial costs but the most sensitive areas of decision taking appear rather to reflect costs in a normative sense – the fear of immigration on established social habits, or different approaches to law and order, different environmental preferences, concerns about military involvements. The reason why it is important to distinguish in what sense 'cost' is being used is that when it comes to giving reasons that justify differences between the decision rules in different areas it would be seen as odd to give a proxy reason of 'cost' if it is normative reasons rather than financial reasons that are involved.

3. UNANIMITY AS A CRITERION FOR CONSTITUTIONAL CHOICE

Constitutional choices set the rules of the game for all aspects of political association and are thus the most important choices to be made. For this reason Rousseau suggested that constitutional choices should be made by unanimity. Similarly, constitutional economics suggests that in matters of constitutional choice it is essential that participants can choose for themselves through the unanimity rule whether the rules are in their own interest.[8] A sharp distinction is thus made between the rules of constitutional choice and the rules for political choice within an agreed constitution.

Again there is a problem of practicalities. Unanimity is going to be difficult to achieve and in practice a high threshold and special procedures are likely to be adopted – as for example in the United States or Switzerland. Unanimity might be retained for agreement on the original constitution but rule changes through amendment procedures are likely to involve high majorities. Once unanimity is removed, minorities can still block but, nevertheless, it becomes possible for an individual member state (or a few member states) of a Union to be overruled on an issue of the most fundamental importance. It leads to the possibility of changes being made to the rules originally agreed without the consent of all participants. For this reason constitutional economics stresses the importance of the right of secession. The threat of secession may lead other participants to modify their behaviour. But, in any event, the right to withdraw from the Union provides an ultimate safeguard for participants against being persistently overruled in areas of importance to them or on any area concerning changes to the original constitutional contract.

There are, I suggest, two shortcomings in this account. First, it places over reliance on the right of secession. The insights of constitutional economics have to be extended to opt outs in areas of collective choice within a constitution. Second, it overemphasises the amendment procedure as the source of rule changes. The insights of constitutional economics have to be extended to look at rule keeping and rule changing through the interpretation process.

3.1. Secession

The right of secession provides an ultimate safeguard for a participant in a political association. It is therefore of crucial importance in any political association resting on voluntary consent to the rules. But it should also be recognised that secession is very much a weapon of last resort – to be used only in the extreme situation when the balance of advantage of membership has swung against continuing in the Union in the view of the member state concerned. In practice, the more pertinent question for Europe is whether in a Union where there exists considerable diversity of preferences it is permissible for members to 'opt in' or 'opt out' of participating in areas of collective choice within a political union or whether all policies should be decided and conducted as common policies.

In the European debate, the right of secession may become an issue and indeed it is a right that should be made explicit in the Treaties. Insofar as Europe's embryonic constitution (the Treaties) can be viewed as a contract between member states, the right to secede should be vested with the contracting parties (the individual member state). But more central to current concerns is the debate about 'variable geometry' and the opt ins or opt outs that accompany it. Analysis of opting in or out puts the argument back to the rules of collective choice within the constitution and the benefits of voluntary consent to rules governing policy choice as well as constitutional choice. It extends the nature of the analysis into such areas as the nature and costs of 'free riders'. The ability to opt in or out also seems to offer one of the key ways in which a competitive supply of public policies can be maintained in a system of distributed powers and thus must be supported by analysis of the advantages of competing jurisdictions and how those are best maintained.

There is also an important sense in which the right of secession is a normative rule about the values associated with the constitution itself. The right of secession has the consequence that a participant can be allowed to go their own way even if the preference differences which lead to the parting of the ways are fundamentally objectionable to other members of the Union. It could mean, for example in the context of Europe, that a member state which flagrantly disregarded the Council of Europe's Convention on Human Rights and refused to acknowledge the procedures for adherence would be allowed to leave the Union rather than have common standards of behaviour imposed by Union procedures. The rule is saying that the differences in even the most important values in a political association are less important than the principle that a constitutional contract should always have the voluntary consent of each participant. The value of voluntary consent to political association is being put above other values. I find this a defensible position. Otherwise there are no limits to what might be imposed in the name of a Union. The balance of powers within a system of distributed powers is otherwise also tilted decisively in favour of the central jurisdiction. At the same time the normative aspect of the unanimity rule in constitutional choice does need to be made explicit.[9]

3.2. Amendment

As far as amendment is concerned there is a dilemma. If amendment is made easy, then rules lose their stability. However, if amendment involves high thresholds of consent, then it may become an impractical procedure and fall out of use. In this case rule change will take place not through amendments but through interpretation. If constitutional economics is to have something relevant to say about rule changes then it must focus on rule keeping and rule-change through interpretation and not focus too exclusively on amendment. If one looks at the United States it seems fairly clear that rule interpretation has often been the route to rule change rather than the amendment process. If one looks at the Economic Community it is also clear that the interpretation process has introduced the equivalent of rule changes. Common to both is the role of a central court in Treaty or constitutional interpretation.

In the United States the role of the Supreme Court is taken as a given – subject only to important questions about the way in which it carries out its duties. In the case of Europe the role of the Court of Justice is not settled. There are questions about the way it has handled Treaty interpretation under the Economic Community pillar, it is excluded at present from the other two pillars, and more fundamentally, since the Treaties have not been devised as constitutional documents the question of how best to keep the rules of a rule-based political association is only just beginning to be debated.

Lawyers tend to assume automatically that if rule change is to come through interpretation that judges are best equipped to do it. It would follow that many see the European Court of Justice developing a role analogous to that of the US Supreme Court with the Court of First Instance handling lesser issues. However constitutional economics does have a number of pertinent questions to ask about interpretation. The questions are those that form the traditional focus of constitutional economics – the effect on a rule-based system of government of incentives, of different majorities, and of the division of jurisdictional responsibilities.

a. Incentives

Questions about incentives concern the consistency between institutional responsibilities and the stability of the rules. In the context of interpretation, the questions include whether the rule keeper can possibly be neutral keeper of the rules when it itself belongs to the central jurisdiction in a Union. What would be the effect on incentive signals for a central court if another central body (the European Parliament) had a hand in the appointment process? Would there be a case for a special court of competence conflict to settle certain types of constitutional questions for example when there is a dispute over Union versus member states jurisdiction?

b. Necessary majorities

The Calculus quite rightly emphasises the importance of the power to block in decision rules relating to operational choice.[10] However it is also a crucial concern in relation to constitutional choice. If rule change in a constitution comes through an interpretation procedure the right to block is lost unless the rules specifically address change through interpretation. The basic reality of a judicial process of interpretation is that the contracting parties (the constituent states) will have been frozen out of the rule change process and minorities will have lost their blocking powers. If there is a high level of dissatisfaction with a court judgement it would be possible for the member states to nullify or modify the judgement by subsequent Treaty amendment (the Barber case). But this will require a high majority to reverse a judgement. The power of a blocking minority will have disappeared even on issues of far reaching importance to the contracting parties. To make a regular habit of nullification would in any case tend to undermine judicial interpretation.

c. Jurisdictional responsibilities and rules

Constitutional economics also asks further questions about the relationship between institutions and the rules which seem highly relevant in this context. Is it desirable to allow for a monopoly supplier of interpretation – such as a single court? If competing sources of interpretation are to be kept alive (for example, a role for the constitutional courts of the contracting states) how is that to be achieved without having disorder in the rules? Does it make sense to retain the Court of Human Rights as a specialised court for matters concerning fundamental rights? Would it make sense to have national parliaments involved in rule keeping?

Some of these questions were present in the original American debate about the 'least dangerous' branch. Others were present in the early debate about 'interpositioning'. Europe needs to go through an analogous debate in considering rule-keeping structures. What adds to the difficulty in the case of Europe is a much more prevalent tradition of law as the instrument of government, as well as the acceptance by some of a legal theory of courts being able to act according to 'authorising norms'. The theory of a constitution or Treaty providing authorising norms adds substantial scope for judge-made law, is intimately connected with a hierarchical view of political organisation and is difficult to reconcile with the safeguards offered by the separation of powers.

4. UNDERPINNING FOR METHODOLOGICAL INDIVIDUALISM

The stress on the unanimity principle as the rule for constitutional choice helps underpin the methodological individualism of constitutional economics – the view that the rules of political association can be explained by the rational behaviour of individuals. It helps underpin this view because it offers a model whereby individual actors (the constituent states) each decide for themselves whether it is in their rational self-interest to be a party to the constitutional contract.

In this context it has been pointed out that it is important to distinguish between the methodological individualism of economics and political individualism – the view that concern for the individual ought, as a normative proposition, to underlie the structuring of the rules of political association. The Calculus recognises the importance of distinguishing in its analysis between these two types of individualism and between the normative and the positive.[11] The question is whether it achieves this aim.

One important aspect is whether analysis of decision rules for collective choice should start from unanimity or from simple majority rules. A related question concerns the transition from rules viewed as the outcome of the rational choices of individuals and rules viewed as the outcome of choice between the constituent states of a union. Are normative assumptions involved in this passage from the individual to the individual constituent state of a union?

The Calculus treats simple majority voting as one rule among others with no special status. The reason given is that equal intensity of preferences between individuals cannot be assumed and interpersonal comparisons of utility cannot be made.[12] However, politics does involve summations which is one reason why rules are needed to guard against the imperfections of politics as a process. Moreover, as a starting point for a discussion of decision rules, simple majority voting has two important characteristics: it gives equal weight to doing something as compared with not doing something and it is also the only voting rule in which a minority cannot prevail over the majority. The implication is that the asymmetry inherent in the unanimity principle, in terms of making it more difficult to do something than not to do something, as well as the special position into which it places the minority in giving it the power to block, is in fact not placing the individual in a neutral choice setting but instead is making a political assumption – that the individual should be protected, that minorities need special treatment in the rules and that government inaction is better than government action.

One defence of a bias against collective action in the voting rules is indeed that the spontaneous order provides more efficient solutions than public choice to coordination problems and therefore there should be a bias against the collective decisions of politics and a defence against the problems of government failure. However, in my view the systemic problems of government failure are best recognised in other parts of a constitution (for example, in the fiscal and other rules that are intended to set limits on politics) and through asymmetries within the voting system (for example, making it easier to deregulate than to regulate). The spontaneous order is itself an abstraction while constitutional rules have to do with the real order which already includes substantial or excessive degrees of government. In respect of the real world, I am inclined to agree that the point of departure for voting rules should be the simple majority because of the equal weighting it gives to the choice of doing (including rolling back the frontiers of government) as compared to not doing (and leaving government interventions in place).

One implication of taking the simple majority as the point of departure for a discussion of voting rules is that the other non-voting rules that constrain collective choice must be seen as carrying a greater burden in a rule-based system of governance. Constitutional economists have been in the forefront of recognising the need for fiscal rules in a constitution and these are important in the European context. But also important in the European debate, is the use and abuse of various declarations of 'rights'. While this is an area of long standing interest for political theorists it has not in recent times received the attention it deserves from constitutional economists.

The principal reason that asymmetries in voting are justified is because of inequalities in situations of collective choice. It is not simply, or mainly, a question of different intensities of preference. The more important inequality is that choices are not equal – as earlier discussed, there are different perceptions of risk attached to different areas of choice. The other inequality is that the choosers are not equal. This is really the crux of the matter when political association is seen to be between states rather than between individuals. Clearly the states in Europe are not equal – and the proliferation of small states in contrast to a few very large ones and the predominant weight of Germany lies at the heart of the difficulty of decision rules in Europe.

It can also be pointed out that viewing states as the relevant unit for decision rules is not the same as viewing individuals and must rest on other grounds. The Calculus makes a number of simplifying assumptions so that the transition from the individual to the representative unit at the union level can be handled as an issue of bicameralism. Different interests in society can be aggregated by function or by geography and represented in a two-chamber system. In turn a bicameral system can be orchestrated to produce any set of decision rules. However a right of secession or the right to block constitutional change has to do with the rights (both operational and rule-keeping) of the constituent states in a union and their peoples and not necessarily with bicameralism at the union level. There are some in Europe who would wish to see the Council of Ministers become a second chamber – but this depends on viewing the Council not as a policy making body but in the role of a representative assembly.

The grounds for explicit treatment of constituent states in a union exist – in terms of giving weight to existing political associations and the ties of sentiment and civil association that they embody, as well as in terms that they provide a ready made basis for a system of multiple jurisdictions. But here one is bringing in other considerations of both positive analysis (the benefits of competing sources of public policy) as well as normative considerations – the advantage of building on the existing habits of civil association. It leads in the direction of looking at systems of concurrent majorities – albeit for different reasons than some of those advanced by Calhoun (1851).

The point about distinguishing more clearly in any discussion of decision rules between the normative and the positive elements of the analysis has been made a number of times in the discussion above. However, when it comes to deploying the non-coercion principle as a justificatory principle for constitutional arrangements the normative becomes all important.

5. UNANIMITY AS A JUSTIFICATORY PRINCIPLE

As a justificatory principle the non-coercion principle has been interpreted in constitutional economics to mean that the rules of a constitution are justified if all participants agree on them. Agreement is the only test of mutual gain. In other words voluntary agreement legitimises the rules of political association.

There are in my view two problems with this formulation. One is the view (associated with Ackerman) that one cannot maintain that something is good just because it is agreed – reasons have to be able to be given. Here the methodology of economics has a problem. Preferences have been expressed and bargains concluded but concepts such as cost or utility do not characterise the content of the preferences and choices. Buchanan seems to take the position that it is improper to question whatever has gone into the agreement – one is playing 'God' if one attempts to raise questions about perceptions of mutual gain. But there is no reason to be intimidated in this way. In what sense is it improper to ask for reasons behind choices? It is perfectly possible for what is generally agreed to be wrong by objective standards. It is also possible for what is generally agreed to be challenged on normative grounds. The assertion that constitutional bargains cannot be challenged places Buchanan far too close for comfort with the view of an otherwise quite dissimilar theorist – Kelsen (1986) – that there are authorising norms to be found in a constitution which are valid by virtue of the fact that there is a basic norm to be found in an original constitution, while failing to answer questions either about the basic norm or the original constitution.

The second problem with the view that the normative is in the agreement is that made by Gauthier (1986) – that in an important sense the rules of political association are the rules of constraint (constraint on individual behaviour and on collective behaviour and on those with political power). The concept of constraint is difficult to reconcile with the maximising assumptions of economics. If constraint or precautionary motives are involved in the agreements on the rules then they need to be made explicit. Rules of restraint are easier to explain in terms of the bargaining situations of game theory but still the setting and the character of the scale of measurement have to be taken into account in considering the nature of any equilibrium reached.

In my view it is a mistake to try to avoid the normative in justifying the rules of political association and one must face up to a discussion of the values that underlie constitutional agreement. This does not lead me to wish to back away from the importance of coercion. On the contrary, the coercive powers of any system of government represent the central problem of political association. There is much to be said by characterising political association in terms of cooperation, and in terms of exchange and bargaining. However, in the end there is no getting away from coercion and it cannot be confined to a box not open to question called the constitutional agreement. For liberals the question is how the view that coercion should be minimised can be justified on normative grounds. I would suggest that there are two paths: one is to assert the value of the individual. The other is to view the rules of political association as based on prudential values – rules of restraint, rules which help to manage choice, particularly longer term choices, and as rules which safeguard other values such as participation. Prudential values have been somewhat out of favour, or even neglected. But I suggest it is time for their reinstatement.

6. CONCLUSION

The conclusions I would like to draw from this discussion about the non-coercion rule and decision rules relate first to the research programme of constitutional economists and secondly to the normative debate which is taking place in Europe about what the rules of political association in Europe should be.

6.1. The Research Programme

Until recently constitutional economists have made a relatively small contribution to the debate about Europe's developing political structures. This partly reflects a split among those interested in rule-based political association as to whether or not contributing to the debate would lead to errors of 'constructivism' or 'rationalism'. Once this hurdle has been jumped, there is the difficulty that a number of problems that seem of the greatest importance in the European context have not received sufficient research attention. Certain of these areas emerged in the course of the discussion above of the non-coercion principle. First, on voting itself there is the question as to whether insights can be offered on questions of concurrent voting which seem to offer one promising way of dealing with inequalities between member states of the Union and inequalities between the subject matter of policy choice. Secondly, insofar as voting rules offer only one means by which political choice can be constrained, there is a need to look further at other non-voting constraints – in particular the role of declarations of rights. Historically declarations of rights were seen as a way of setting limits on political power but their recent evolution has been in the direction of trying to preset the outcome of law and politics. The legitimate and illegitimate use of devices to try to pre-order preferences in settings of collective choice needs much greater attention. A third important area relates to rule-keeping. Is the European Union to follow the American example and look to a central court (the European Court of Justice) as the rule keeper and to judicial interpretation as the source of rule change, or is there a place for representative methods of rule keeping (for example, by national parliaments or by referenda)? Insofar as judicial rule keeping is to have a prominent place, are there better ways of maintaining a decentralised system of competing jurisdictions than through entrusting rule keeping to a central court? Fourth, there are questions relating to the norms for judge made law. Kelsenesque theories of authorising norms in a constitution can run counter to the doctrine of the separation of powers and of course in the context of individual European countries the parliamentary systems of government are usually regarded as representing systems of fused or shared power rather than the separation of powers. What research can constitutional economists draw on in talking about judge-made law and the separation of powers in the context of the European Union and a European constitution?

6.2. The Normative

Differences about how to shape the rules of political association in Europe can ultimately be traced to a debate about legitimating principles. Some simply see a European political construction as 'good in itself' and thus requiring no further justification. At a more sophisticated level, and one which is the most appealing to politicians, is the view that Europe's constitutional structure can be legitimated as long as it embraces a basket of values including both traditional liberal values as well as strong rules to achieve social justice. These and several other principles put forward as legitimating principles are expressed in a manner that open the way for the justification of an expansive and centralised system of European government quite at odds with the constitutional economist's view of the advantages of rule-based, decentralised and limited government. When the non-coercion principle of constitutional economics is expressed in the form that whatever is unanimously agreed (for whatever reason) represents a valid constitutional contract it not only fails as a justificatory principle in itself but also equally fails to provide counter arguments about what legitimises a decentralist view of government. The liberal tradition is that the problem of the coercive power of government is the central issue that has to be treated if a system of government is to be legitimated. The non-coercion principle has to be expressed in a normative form and has to be justified with reasons if it is to be influential in upholding the liberal tradition in Europe's constitutional debate.

NOTES

1. In the discussion which follows, the account of decision rules in the Calculus of Consent is taken as the basic source. References in the text are to 'The Calculus' and page references in endnotes are to the 1962 edition.
2. See, for example, the discussion in Stefan Voigt, 'Positive Constitutional Economics – A Survey', in *Constitutional Political Economy* September 1996 (forthcoming). In his subsequent writings, Buchanan has in my view tried to keep within the normative and positive distinctions of 'The Calculus' (see also Voigt).
3. 'All potential governmental or collective activity should not be organized through the operation of the same decision rule', p. 73.

4. 'Economic theory does not depend for its validity or its applicability on the presence of the purely economic man ... . The man who enters the market relationship ... may do so for any number of reasons', p. 17.
5. These two approaches are distinguished on page 130.
6. 'Since no player can anticipate which specific rule might benefit him during a particular play of the game he can, along with all the other players, attempt to devise a set of rules that will constitute the most interesting game for the average or representative player. It is to the self interest of each player to do this', pp.79–80.
7. 'The categorical opposition of interests that many theorists assume to arise to prevent unanimity is much more likely to characterize the operational as opposed to the constitutional level of decision, and it is essential that these two levels of decision be sharply distinguished ... Conceptually, men can reach agreement on rules, even when each party recognizes in advance that he will be "coerced" by the operation of agreed-on rules in certain circumstances', p. 251.
8. 'Only if a specific constitutional change can be shown to be in the interest of all parties shall we judge such a change to be an "improvement"', p. 14.
9. It is difficult to defend the claim that the unanimity principle is 'a very weak ethical postulate', p. 172.
10. 'This relevant distinction between the power of determining action and the power of blocking action has not been sufficiently emphasized in the literature of political science', p. 258.
11. 'Methodological individualism should not be confused with "individualism" as a norm for organizing social activity. ... This work is 'individualist' only in the first, or methodological, sense', p. vii (Preface). 'Our theory of constitutional choice has normative implications only insofar as the underlying basis of individual consent is accepted', p. 7.
12. 'Unless equal intensity of preferences is postulated, there are no particular characteristics attributable to the 51 per cent rule for choice', p. 256.

BIBLIOGRAPHY

Ackerman, B.A. (1980), *Social Justice in the Liberal State*, New Haven: Yale University Press.

Blaug, M. (1980), *The Methodology of Economics*, Cambridge: Cambridge University Press.

Buchanan, J.M. (1991), *The Economics and Ethics of Constitutional Order*, Ann Arbour: University of Michigan Press.

Buchanan, J.M. and G. Tullock (1962), *The Calculus of Consent*, Ann Arbour: University of Michigan Press.

Calhoun, J.C. (1851), *A Disquisition on Government and a Discourse on the Constitution.*

Dietze, G. (1973), *Two Concepts of the Rule of Law*, Indianapolis: Liberty Fund Inc.

European Constitutional Group (1993), *Proposal for a European Constitution*, London: European Policy Forum.

Gauthier, D. (1986), *Morals by Agreement*, Oxford: Clarendon Press.

Hirschman, A.O. (1970), *Exit, Voice and Loyalty*, Cambridge: Harvard University Press.

Kelsen, H. (1986), 'The Function of a Constitution', in R. Tur and W. Twining (eds), *Essays on Kelsen*, Oxford: Clarendon Press.

Rae, D.W. (1969), 'Decision Rules and Individual Values in Constitutional Choice', *American Political Science Review*, **63**.

Schwartz, T. (1981), *The Logic of Collective Choice*, New York: Colombia University Press.

Vibert, F. (1995), *Europe: A Constitution for the Millennium*, Dartmouth: Dartmouth Publishing.

Voigt, S. (1996), 'Positive Constitutional Economics – A Survey', *Constitutional Political Economy*, (forthcoming).

Comment

Boudewijn Bouckaert

> *'A good constitution is infinitely better than the best despot'.* T.B. Macaulay: Milton, 1825, *Edinburgh Review*, August

As a lawyer, dealing with property rights and their economic analysis, I am somewhat puzzled by Vibert's condensed treatment of the non-coercion principle and its place within Europe's constitutional debate. His article cuts through many disciplinary fields: political economy, political philosophy, ethics and law. As such it provides us with many interesting reflections on the rationality and morality of voting procedures and institutions. I do not discover, however, straight lines of thought leading to one or another policy advice regarding the European Constitution. Lacking strong positions to attack, I limit myself to some reflections on theoretical notions and viewpoints developed in the paper, in the hope that they may be helpful for someone somewhere in the discussion about our future European institutions.

1. THE 'COST' OF INSTITUTIONS

Vibert raises several questions about the use of the notions of costs concerning the choice of voting rules. He rightly points to the fact that (1) the notion of cost should be wider than mere financial costs, (2) that costs can differ substantially with regard to where rules are applied in areas of policy voting and (3) that the evolution of costs can be unpredictable. To cope with these difficulties Vibert introduces several new notions, such as costs in the sense of 'normative reasons' and 'intrinsically' important areas of collective choice. These notions are quite unclear to me and seem even to complicate, rather than to clarify the debate on the optimal voting procedures.

Once economics leaves the world of the computing entrepreneur, who is comparing his factor costs with the measuring rod of market prices, the notion of costs gets a meaning which must be wider than the mere financial.

One does not need to refer to morally loaded areas of action for this. Giving up a consumer good with a certain uniqueness already implies a cost for the concerned individual, which cannot be expressed exactly in financial terms. Therefore economists moved to the very formal, but widely applicable, notion of 'opportunity costs',[1] that is, the value of the second best alternative one has to give up for his choice. This notion is also applicable to the area of choice of voting rules: what is the cost of my choice for a unanimity rule? If we suppose that a 90 per cent majority is the available second best, then the foregone benefits of this latter rule constitute the cost of unanimity.[2]

Although this answer is impeccable, its content is very thin. It only indicates to where one has to direct further research. For instance, the benefits of the 90 per cent-majority rule, compared to the unanimity rule, lie in the fact that decisions will be reached quicker and with less negotiation effort, because a minority of 10 per cent is unable to veto. But even this preciseness leaves us with numerous questions. For instance, how to measure the value of time, gained by something less than unanimity rule?

It must be clear that institutional economics is unable to provide 'hard' answers in this field and unable to arrive at conclusions about 'optimality' in its strictest sense, that is, the best solution there is. It is nevertheless possible, and this is witnessed by much literature and research in this field, to structure historical and empirical data into cost categories, which serve as tools for generating more or less plausible comparisons. The lack of a common measuring rod, such as market prices, has to be compensated by qualitative criteria. Irreversibility, for instance, is a quality which points to high cost. This might explain why the choice about life is not put into a voting basket, but put under a regime of constitutionally shielded individual rights. The irreversible and common value of virgin forests may explain why we prefer a protection of them based on a regulation. The eventual private owner of them has to convince a majority of voters to make irreversible changes in these natural resources.

A distinction between political action and political reaction might be another qualitative criterion. With political action, initiated by the political actor, time decision costs caused by delay due to unanimity or qualified majority rules, consist of the foregoing of the projected benefits of this action. With political reaction, in which the political actor has to cope with a situation not planned nor controlled by him (for instance, a military invasion, a temporary offer for a treaty), time decision costs can be substantially higher due to urgency. This might explain why we rely in the case of foreign affairs which imply a lot of reactions, more on executive power, with an *ex post* control by parliament, than on *ex ante* majorities. Both examples illustrate that institutional economics can work with a monistic cost notion, that is, opportunity costs, but has to rely for its precision on qualitative criteria. These criteria lead us, at best, to conclusions of optimality in the weak sense, that is, the best rules given the inherent uncertainties concerning costs. This also explains why many conclusions in this area of economics imply rather prudential rules than optimal rules – rules with which we will avoid the worst instead of obtaining the best.

2. AMENDMENT AND INTERPRETATION

Vibert makes several interesting remarks on the role of courts in the interpretation of the European treaties and other secondary European rules. He rightly points out that interpretation by judges may change rules, without the consent of the member states, who had agreed upon the rules. A shorter procedure for amendments may alleviate this problem, but cannot eliminate it. Relying entirely on amendments is even conceptually impossible, for each reading and application of a text implies an act of interpretation. Making use only of amendments with no judicial interpretation would then mean that a litigating party could always claim before court that it has a different interpretation of the applicable text and that the text has to be amended.

Vibert raises the question whether one really needs a monopoly supplier of interpretation. In fact, no modern liberal legal system relies on a monopolistic interpretation of the law. Legal interpretation is made by a multitude of courts, advisers and legal scholars. The basic question, however, is whether we need an 'interpretor of the last resort', that is, a court which has the competence to solve the legal question definitively and which decision is enforceable upon the parties. Such an 'interpretor of the last resort' is nearly always assumed as a necessity. This assumption stems probably from the needs of a legal system designed to solve legal conflicts between citizens. A final authority for these conflicts is necessary in order to restore peace and certainty at micro-levels of society. The 'price' of such a final authority, that is, the risk of an ill-founded decision, does not threaten the cohesion of society, because the decision only affects a small segment of the members of society. In a context of a limited number of players, such as a Treaty-community (for example, the Union, with fifteen players, fourteen members plus the union-authority itself), the inherent quality of the decision becomes more important than the urgency of the decision. A swift, but divisive, decision of an interpreter of the last resort could trigger a process of disintegration within the Union.

For this reason it is recommendable to abandon the path of a final interpreter and to discuss models of arbitration and of competing jurisdictions. The crucial function of such systems is their capacity to produce 'good reasons' in the legal contest, about which all *bona fide* partners can reach a consensus.[3] Arbitrators are nearly driven by an invisible hand to produce good reasons, which can convince both litigating parties, even the convicted one. By doing so, they increase their reputation for future cases. If parties do not reach an agreement on an arbitrator, they can go to a court or a separate arbitrator of their choice, which will also produce reasons, which may be either convincing or less convincing. If the decisions of different courts concerning the same legal conflicts between members of the treaty-community remain incompatible, it is clear that the conflicts have a rather political character and that they should be solved by the highest political authorities of the treaty-community.

3. MORALITY, CONSTITUTION AND POLITICAL DECISION

In the last section, Vibert questions Buchanan's view that agreement on institutions and choices also justifies these institutions and choices. Vibert argues for a more normative justification of the rules of political association. Indeed, the moral message of the viewpoint of Buchanan, as presented here, is very thin and will probably gain little support from people looking for a moral underpinning of politics. On the other side, Buchanan's viewpoint reflects the sound liberal suspicion of essentialist values, such as 'social justice', 'sense of community', 'solidarity', and 'patriotism', in the name of which some groups legitimise their domination and their pillaging of morally less vocal groups.

It is, in this regard, useful to distinguish between the constitutional rules on one hand, and the political decisions made following these rules. The former regard the scope of individual rights versus the scope of collective action and the procedures for collective action. The latter regard measures, in which ways the possibilities for collective action, provided by the constitution, are effectively used.

If we could succeed in establishing constitutional rules, which are based on genuine unanimous consent of all members of a political community, these rules would reflect the highest political morality which could ever be attained. This is because unanimous consent means at the same time full respect for the individual rights of all members in society. A genuine consent on a constitution means that all citizens freely agree that some of their rights can be ceded to a common body, which will make decisions on their behalf. It is difficult to see which constitution could be more moral than such one.

The same reasoning, however, does not apply to the political decisions, taken within the framework of the constitution. Here we have to apply the same distinction as with regard to individual action, taken within the framework of individual rights. Such action can be lawful, that is, it does not violate other peoples' rights, but can be, morally seen, of a poor quality.

Rights can be understood as metanorms, which limit the domain of our norm-guided individual action.[4] A rights-based political view, such as for instance classical liberalism, does not necessarily imply a moral relativistic view, according to which all possible lawful decisions deserve the same moral regard.

Under a unanimously agreed constitution, collective decisions are to be considered as an extension of individual action, through aggregation and delegation procedures. As such, the same distinction between lawfulness and morality apply. Political decisions are lawful as long as they respect the (unanimously agreed upon) constitution and the rights of outsiders to the concerned political community. Their lawfulness is, however, only a necessary condition and not a sufficient condition for their 'goodness'. Suppose that within a political community, with a correctly established constitution, a constitutionally correct political decision is made to cut down all trees in the country in order to enhance immediate monetary returns, thereby completely denying the interests of future generations. Such a political decision might be lawful, but reflects a very poor moral concern.

The distinction between lawfulness and morality of political decisions does not prevent the establishment of causal relationships between both. It is very reasonable to suppose that political communities, whose institutions reflect a high respect for the freedom of their citizens, are rather inclined to moral perfectionism. Political communities, whose institutions allow oppression and collective theft, will tend also to degrade morally. Historical examples of this latter relationship are not very hard to find.

NOTES

1. For a wide notion of costs see for instance G.P. O'Driscoll Jr. and M.J. Rizzo (1985), *The Economics of Time and Ignorance*, Oxford: Basil Blackwell.
2. About the costs of the different voting rules, see D.C. Mueller (1989), *Public Choice II*, Cambridge: Cambridge University Press.
3. A good historical comparison for such a competition process in producing 'good reasons' is provided by the middle ages, more precisely the period between 1200 and 1400. See for instance H. Berman (1983), *Law and Revolution. The Formation of the Western Legal Tradition*, Cambridge: Harvard University Press.
4. For further readings on this viewpoint see D.B. Rasmussen and D.J. Den Uyl (1991), *Liberty and Nature. An Aristotelian Defense of Liberal Order*, La Salle, Illinois: Open Court; see also by the same authors 'Rights as meta-normative principles', in T.R. Machan and D.B. Rasmussen (eds) (1995), *Liberty for the 21st Century. Contemporary Libertarian Thought*, London: Rowman & Littlefield Publishers, pp. 41–59.

Comment

Friedrich Schneider

This chapter is an interesting one and raises some important topics, such as the decision rules in the Council of Ministers in the EU, the problem whether 'opt-outs' or 'opt-ins' are possible and desirable, and whether the role of the 'Non-Coercion Principle' should be adopted. The author tries to make some valuable points with respect to these issues and provides an economic analysis of some elements of a possible constitution of the European Union.

However, as the chapter stands now, I have some difficulties in understanding it and realising what it's goal really is. I will group my criticism in the following five remarks.

1. AIM/GOAL OF THE PAPER

As one reads the paper, it is not clear what the message of the paper is. Does the author want to raise some normative questions about constitutional economics when applying it to the EU? Or does the author want to provide a positive analysis of possible constitutional elements in the EU? Or, if the paper is a mixture of both, then why the switch from normative to positive issues and how do we benefit from such switches?

2. THE BACKGROUND OF THE PAPER WITH RESPECT TO CONSTITUTIONAL ECONOMICS

The author basically refers to the book 'The Calculus of Consent' written by Buchanan and Tullock in the year 1962. However, since then a quite extensive literature has been published on the topics of constitutional issues and in constitutional economics. Let me only mention, for example, the special issues of *Kyklos* (Vol. 47/3, 1994) entitled 'Democratic and Federal

Rules for a Future Europe'.[1] I find it somewhat unjustified just to refer to some famous books and articles in this field as there has been some progress made in constitutional economics and a lot of detailed discussion has taken place especially in regard to the problems raised by the author in his paper. Thus one might learn more if one were to consider the latest development in the literature.

3. IS 'UNANIMITY AS A DEMARCATION DEVICE' GOOD ADVICE FOR CONSTITUTIONAL ISSUES?

In section 2 the author treats the problem of 'unanimity as a demarcation device'. When reading this it is again not clear what the message is. I think the author should have much more clearly worked out the very strong trade-off between the decision costs in agreeing on a certain decision rule, which can be infinitely high if unanimity is applied, and the costs which arise from a decision (when unanimity is not applied) which, for example, overrules a country or state. We all know, and there is an enormous amount of literature about this, that this is a trade-off quite often 'solved' by coming up with a decision rule of simple, two-third, or even three-quarter majority. But very rarely does one come out with unanimity as a decision rule. The unanimity rule gives every state (or even every voter or every politician) the absolute veto-power over all other members. This might block every decision, even when the *status quo* is the worst outcome for most states, with the exception of one.

Also, it is not clear why the author can make statements like that relatively more relaxed decision rules will be possible in the environmental area than in the areas of security and defence. Environmental decisions, such as the introduction of 'green' taxes or other instruments might effect the economy as severely as additional measures in the area of security and defence. If environmental catastrophes create massive negative external effects, the consequences and damages might be even greater.

4. THE PROBLEM WITH UNANIMITY FOR CONSTITUTIONAL CHOICE AND THE PROBLEM OF SECESSION

In section 3 'Unanimity as a criterion for constitutional choice' the author should clearly define what he means by unanimity. In principle, as one reads this, it is not clear whether according to the author 'unanimity' means direct democratic decisionmaking institutions like the referendum process or a high approval of a two-third or three-quarter majority in representative democracies. It is not clearly pointed out in this chapter how one should approach representative democracies with a qualified majority and which direct democratic elements should be adopted. Also in this chapter the secession or opt-out argument should be much more clearly worked out. For example, is a secession also possible for provinces/cantons/member states of a state in the Union? Can, for example, a rich state in Germany, like Baden-Württemberg or Bavaria, become an independent member in the EU? Or can a rich town (like Milano or Turin in Italy) also secede and become a member of the EU? If we then have a lot of small members in the EU, would the European Union be more easily manageable? Would there not be a temptation to have trade barriers and other restrictions so that, for example, poor people could not immigrate into theses rich provinces/towns? I think it is simply not enough to state the argument of secession and not clearly spell out, in a much more precise way, what is meant by it.

5. SOME REMARKS ON METHODOLOGICAL INDIVIDUALISM

In section 4 'Underpinning for methodological individualism', it is not clear why the voting procedure is so important for methodological individualism. Are there not other much more important procedures? As long as the costs and benefits of the different voting rules in the different situations are not discussed and evaluated in contrast to each other, that is, first in the formation of a constitution and later in working within this constitution, I cannot see that the voting procedure is one of the most essential points for methodological individualism.

NOTE

1. Compare for example G. Kirchgässner (1994), 'Constitutional Economics and Its Relevance for the Evolution of Rules', *Kyklos*, **47** (3), 321–340; I. Bohnet and B.S. Frey (1994), 'Direct-Democratic Rules: The Role of Discussion', *Kyklos*, **47** (3), 341–354; F. Schneider (1993), 'The Federal and Fiscal Structures of Representative and Direct Democracies as Models for a European Federal Union: Some Ideas Using the Public Choice Approach', *Journal of Economistes et des Etudes Humaines*, **3–4**, 403–438; D.C. Mueller (1989), *Public Choice II*, Cambridge: Cambridge University Press; V. Vanberg and J. Buchanan (1989), 'Interest and Theories in Constitutional Choice', *Journal of Theoretical Politics*, **1**, 49–62.

10. Constitutional Problems of the European Union – A Lawyer's View

Ulrich Everling

1. PRELIMINARY REMARKS

Constitutional Problems of the EU and Community were broadly discussed in most of the member states in connection with the ratification procedures of the Maastricht Treaty. The most important example of these disputes was the judgement of the German Federal Constitutional Court (*Bundesverfassungsgericht*) which confirmed the conformity of the Treaty on European Union to the German Constitution but expressed important conditions and limitations (BVerfGE 89, 155). The debate is now being enforced under the auspices of the Intergovernmental Conference 1996, which is determined, *inter alia*, to strengthen the Union on the eve of its envisaged enlargement by a number of Eastern Countries.

The actual debates are not free of emotions, preconceptions and even ideological tendencies. It is, therefore, particularly useful to examine the main problems by means of the Economic Analysis of Law and, by this way, to contribute to a more objective and rational discussion. This has been done in the preceding articles but cannot be foreshadowed by this chapter prepared by a lawyer who is accustomed to the application of traditional legal methods.

This chapter is based on the understanding that law is not only to be interpreted as being formed by economic and social factors and by the requirements of efficiency. Law is also the expression of traditions, of social structures and demands, of political attitudes and interests and in particular of values and sense of justice. These aspects may be less important in the field of technical rules where practical requirements are predominant. But they have a higher degree of influence on the regulations concerning the social and economic order, and, on the constitutional level, fundamental values are to be respected and are not at the disposal of the legislator. One of the crucial problems of European integration consists in the fact that the mentioned traditions, structures and understandings of values are quite different in the member states. They must gradually be assimilated to such a degree that they may form the basis of a common consciousness of the citizens.

Every method determined to analyse Community law must take into account these imponderables in order not to risk failing the test of reality. In the following, such aspects will be stressed. They will be discussed in four issues: first, remarks on the origin and structure of the Union and Community; second, questions of the decisionmaking process and its democratic basis; third, problems of federal organisation such as distributions of competences and subsidiarity; and fourth, in a short look at perspectives of enlargement. This chapter will be mostly concerned with the Community because it is, in difference to the Union, a legal entity equipped with sovereign powers.

2. ORIGIN AND LEGAL STRUCTURE OF THE EUROPEAN UNION AND COMMUNITY

2.1. Basis of European Integration

The Community was from the beginning, and is at present, not a simple club determined to further economic wealth and welfare, even if this is one of its important aims. For the war generation, European integration was an answer to the experiences of dictatorship, war and genocide. Whilst after the First World War the allied States tried to keep down Germany through humiliation, suppression and reparation (which must inevitably fail), after the Second World War the western part of Germany was included under the auspices of cold war and rearmament, in the alliance of western democracies, and in particular in the European Community, on the basis of equal conditions, rights and duties for all member states.

Membership in the Community has contributed and currently still contributes to Germany's external and internal security and to peace and freedom in Europe. The Community is, therefore, according to its origin and objectives a genuine political entity even if its subject matters essentially concern economic policy (Hallstein 1979). For this reason German governments often accepted common regulations which were economically disadvantageous, unreasonable or at least risky. The Monetary Union is, in the view of many economists, the most important example of this kind.

This impetus of the founders seems to be mostly forgotten by the post-war generation. Today the dominant understanding of integration is that the problems of the modern industrialised world cannot be solved by each of the states alone (Hrbek and Wessels 1984). But it is not sure whether this utilitarian perception will have a sufficient integrating force to incite a common consciousness between the peoples as a basis for a supranational political entity. Most of the governments believe, therefore, that it is necessary to strengthen the political elements of the Community which are already in place through the founding of the EU. This perspective will be the most important issue of the Intergovernmental Conference 1996.

Such a result of the Conference would continue the gradual development of the Community of the last decades. At the beginning politicians and scholars discussed the appropriate method of integration (Schneider 1992). Some scholars and in particular economists, proposed a functionalist approach primarily with the aim of the opening of the markets and of free competition whilst politicians and lawyers mostly believed that only powerful institutions could create an international or even supranational entity. The result of this dispute was, as always, a compromise which combined the opening of the markets with an institutional system and its own legal order. Both were in a manifold way linked. This demands a closer explanation.

2.2. Common Market and Common Politics

The starting point of the Community's development was the opening of the national markets accompanied by a system of undistorted competition. The fundamental liberties of goods, services, persons and also to a certain degree capital within the Common Market are up to today the hard core of the Community. At the beginning, these liberties were only understood as interdicting the member states from discriminating against goods imported from other member states as well as the activities of their nationals or enterprises. But step by step the European Court of Justice also established the principle that regulations which are applied equally to national goods and persons, as well as to imported goods and to nationals of other member states, must not prevent free trade except when that is justified by requirements of public order, security or health or by reasons of general interests (P.C. Müller-Graff, in Groeben, Thiesing and Ehlermann 1991, notes to Articles 30 *et seq.*).

This jurisprudence started with the free movements of goods and was applied to services. For individuals this principle was finally established only in 1995. The limitations on the free market caused by national reservations based on public order, security and health or on interests of common wealth could only be overruled by harmonisation of law (Curral 1985). This harmonisation was executed extensively up to now, in particular to establish the internal market proclaimed by the Single European Act.

The Common Market is ensured by rules of competition which are effectively applied to practices of enterprises as well as to state based aid. Exemptions exist particularly in the field of agricultural policy where a dirigistic set of provisions regulates the market. But apart from this special field, the coordination of the economic policy based on the competition rules had the encouraging result that all of the member states, as well as the Community itself, consequently seem more or less to orientate their policies on the principles of a market economy. Thus they ensure price stability and liberty of economic activities enforced by competition.

On the background of these efforts, the measures taken to achieve the Monetary Union, must be considered. The introduction of a common currency is intended to accomplish and to consolidate the Common Market. Consequently the rules established for this purpose must be, in the first place, judged according to economic and technical criteria. But if the Community succeeded in carrying out the plan under really stable economic conditions it would have the impact of a great leap towards increased political integration. Common economic and financial policy would then be inevitable, and the member states would be bound in such a way so that they would not any more be able to go their own way without serious consequences (Tietmeyer 1995).

2.3. Legal Order of the Community

The results reached hitherto in the economic field could only be achieved because the Community was equipped with an institutional and legal order which ensured the functioning of the open market. As has already been mentioned, the Court interpreted the rules on the free movement of goods, services and persons in such a manner that they could correspond to their *effet utile* in order to eliminate the obstacles of trade and business between the member states (Oppermann 1991, p.215). By deciding that most of the provisions of the Treaty are directly applicable, the Court entitled the citizens to claim for themselves the fundamental liberties of the Common Market. It also confirmed the supremacy of Community law over national law, and thus secured the unity and uniform execution of the common rules and by this way the commonly adopted economic measures (Oppermann 1991, p.194).

The Community institutions decided on numerous rules to harmonise the national laws, thus eliminating obstacles preserved by member states within the Common Market and determining the framework for the economic activities in the open market. It also decided on common policies like agricultural, transport and social policies. Particularly important are the rules concerning commercial policy, which determine, under economic aspects, the degree of free trade with third countries. They also influence, under political aspects, essential elements of the relationships to third countries and, through this, the foreign policy of the member states (Stein 1992).

The main instruments of the Community's legal actions are, on the one hand, regulations which are binding on all institutions, member states and citizens with priority over national law and, on the other hand, directives which the member states are obliged to transpose into national law but can nevertheless also be directly applicable within all member states as far as they are exactly and unconditionally formulated and necessitate no further execution (Prechal 1995).

In addition, the numerous atypical decisions without legal force should be mentioned. Leaving aside the common foreign and security policies and the fields of justice and home affairs, one should refer to the overwhelming mass of resolutions, declarations and protocols emanating from informal sessions of the Council or the representatives of the member states. They demonstrate that the legally binding actions of the institutions are complemented by a broad field of cooperation outside the Treaties (Wellens and Borchardt 1989).

Thus the Community has established its own legal order which is originally based on the Treaties but in its application is not dependent on the consent of the member states and instead follows its own genuine rules. All the member states have accepted the supremacy of Community law over their national laws but most of them – openly or silently – claim reservations concerning the hard core of their constitutional orders, for instance the rule of law or the essentials of fundamental rights (Lorenz 1990).

As to the last point, it is emphasised that the Court has established numerous fundamental rights or rights similar to those which are protected by Community law and limit the power of the Community institutions. These rights are important for the legal positions of the citizens. But they are also important for the integrating power of the Community because they are the expression of unchangeable values which attribute to the Community a destination higher than that of mere utilitarianism (Frowein, Schulhofer and Shapiro 1986). The Community institutions have to respect them even if they would prefer to disregard them in the interest of economic effectiveness.

2.4. Legal Nature and Constitution of the Community

The member states founded or appointed the Community by international treaties. Through these treaties they transferred sovereign powers in specific fields to the Community to fulfil formerly national functions through its own institutions and based on its own legal order. This 'transfer' must be understood as equipping of the Community with sovereign powers whilst the member states, to the same extent, reduce their claim of exclusive dominance in their legal orders of their territories (Lorenz 1990, 83). The position of the member states is, therefore, essentially diminished even if they claim in the final analysis to be responsible for the welfare of their peoples. In most fields of economic policy they can only act with the consent or participation of the Community. The execution of sovereign powers is divided between Community and member states (Obradovic 1993, Frowein 1995).

But in spite of its widespread functions and competences, the Community cannot be qualified as being a state and therefore not as a federal state. Up to now it has only limited competences; it does not dispose of territory, people and public power by itself and is not based on the common awareness of the citizens. Its qualification as a state is made even more difficult since the European Union claims to head the Community without being, according to most of the interpreters, a legal personality itself having legal competences (Blanke 1993). But the Community is more than a mere *Staatenverbund* (of allied States) as the German Federal Court stated. It is also, at least beginning to be, a *Bürgerverbund* (compound of citizens) since it addresses its rules directly or indirectly to the citizens, lets them participate in the decisionmaking process by their elected representatives in the European Parliament, and opens the national frontiers to develop interstate connections on all levels of society (Everling 1995).

The rules determining the functioning of such a political body like the Community reflect all the characteristics of a constitution. There is no reason to reserve this notion to states but, on the other hand, its use alone does not justify analogies to states. This notion only underlines that the Community has reached an autonomy and independence which detaches it, at least to a certain degree, from the treaties by which it was founded.

Nevertheless it is difficult to connect formally a notion of Constitution to the existing Treaties on Union and Community. Both are in such a lamentable formal condition that they are not apt to fulfil the essential function of a written constitution; that is, to radiate integrative power to all member states, regions and citizens concerned (Everling 1992, 1056).

One of the most important tasks of the Intergovernmental Conference is, therefore, to establish a text worthy to be declared a Constitution of the Community. Here is not the place to deal with this problem. But it must be emphasised that this is also a necessity in terms of economics because the free European market will only be attractive if its legal framework is presented in an understandable form.

3. DECISIONMAKING PROCESS OF THE COMMUNITY

3.1. Procedures of the Community's Law-making

Secondary Community law is decided by the common institutions according to a complex variety of rules. The starting point was a simple system consisting of three phases: namely, the proposition by the Commission, consultation by the European Parliament and a decision of the Council. From the beginning there were exceptions, in particular, concerning the commercial policy where the Parliament need not be consulted. The balance of power existed primarily between the independent Commission which had, and still has today, the right and monopoly to present propositions, and the Council, composed of ministers from the member states, which decided on nearly all legal acts of general importance. The European Parliament on the other hand had only a limited role.

This situation has been step by step essentially changed. Today the Parliament has effective influence on the decisionmaking process by means of the procedures of cooperation and codecision. The latter attributes a right of veto, in particular the consent of parliament is necessary in regard to associations with third countries or their access to the Community (Boest 1992). But it is difficult to understand according to which criteria the different procedures were attributed to the respective competences for Community activities. It seems that the particular interests of the member states to reserve their influences on certain fields led to compromises so that no overarching pattern is apparent. The necessity to act quickly and effectively may also have been decisive, for instance, in the field of agriculture where the original procedure persists (Winter 1993).

These somewhat disordered rules should be revised by the Intergovernmental Conference. Certainly the simplification of the procedures will be one of its important issues in order to further the effectiveness of the decisionmaking process. But nevertheless preference must be given to the political necessity of enforcing the participation of the Parliament which represents the citizens in order to make the procedures more transparent for the citizens.

In this context, the European Council composed of the heads of states and governments must be mentioned. According to Article D of the Union Treaty it 'shall provide the Union with the necessary impetus for its development and shall define the general political guidelines thereof' but it is not entitled to make law. This Council is a re-animation of the old Fouchet-plans of the Sixties which intended to head the Community by the national governments in order to control and direct the activities of the Community. Apart from the provisions concerning the Monetary Union, the

Maastricht Treaty was, therefore, not a progression to more supranationality but, at least partly, a rollback to more influence of the member states which claim to remain masters of the Union's development. But it is not certain whether they will succeed in this regard because they have to respect the Treaties, the Community law, and in particular the independence of the institutions. The power of the European Council is built primarily on the factual authority of their members (Everling 1992, p. 1062).

3.2. Legitimacy of the Community's Legislative Power

The diffuse construction of decisionmaking provokes the often discussed question of legitimacy of the legislative power of the Community institutions which is the crucial point of the above mentioned Maastricht Judgement of the *Bundesverfassungsgericht*. Law is accepted by the citizens concerned not because some persons equipped with power make a decision, but because the authority of the relevant institutions is recognised as being legitimate. Legitimacy of law is based on democratic procedures applied by those authorities and on criteria concerning its content with particular regard to human rights and justice as well as to the rule of law. The principle of democracy as expressed by the German Basic Law that 'all the State power emanates from the People' is – *mutatis mutandis* – also applicable for the Community.

The *Bundesverfassungsgericht* stated that being a compound of states the Community could derive its legitimacy only from the member states whilst the European Parliament may have a 'supporting' function as long as there does not yet exist one European People but different peoples. Legitimacy of the Community is, in the view of the Constitutional Court, at the present state procured by the legal acts of the national parliaments by which they agree to the European Treaties and, through this, to the transfer of limited competences to the Community. Thus, the *Bundesverfassungsgericht* tends to restrict the Community's capacities to act and to develop and to claim a certain supervision by the national Constitutional Courts which may turn in the last instance to renationalisation (Tomuschat 1993, Meessen 1994, Herdegen 1994).

This cannot be right. The legitimacy of Community law cannot be ensured in the same way as in states; the special structure of the Community must be taken into account. Its law is legitimated in a double way. On one side, the Community is certainly a compound of states and must derive its legitimacy primarily from the member states acting in the Council by ministers responsible to their parliaments. But the Community is also, at least to a certain degree, a compound of citizens. The position of the individuals and in particular their participation in the decisionmaking process by elected members of the European Parliament has already reached such a degree that they contribute to the legitimacy of common legislature (Everling 1995).

But this second pillar must be furthermore enforced. The rights of the Parliament must be step by step promoted in such a manner that Community legislation will finally need the consent of the Council as well as the Parliament with reconciliation procedures securing effectivity.

3.3. Decision Procedure in the Council

A main problem to deal with is the decision procedure of the Council. The Council had from the beginning a double function. On the one hand, it is the place where the member states search for consensus and compromise. On the other hand, it is the central decision maker which has to promote the functioning of the Community. This double character explains the special kind of working in a style mixed of elements of decisionmaking and international negotiations. It also explains the long-time practice of unanimity vote following the so-called Luxembourg protocol of 1966. But since the south enlargement in the 1980s the Council decides more and more by qualified majority even if it always tries first to find a common agreement. Effective decisionmaking of a body of twelve or now fifteen members is not possible if each position of the member states must be respected. Also, the participation of the European Parliament led to a broader application of the majority rule (Götz 1995).

The dilemma existing in this regard may be demonstrated by the procedure of approximation of laws. The related directives deeply intervene in traditions, interests, social structures and vested rights existing in the member states. Newspapers mocked the Council which negotiated more than fifteen years on subjects like insurance, pharmacists or architects under the unanimity rule. But when the directives were finally adopted they were accepted by the professionals concerned because their different points of view had been sufficiently discussed. Everybody welcomed the proclamation of the free internal market in 1986 which was in substance mainly a broad programme of approximation of law under the majority rule. But when in the following years a flood of half-discussed and hastily formulated directives surprised the professionals the reaction was negative. The roll-back of European engagements which appeared during the ratification procedures of the Union Treaty has been at least partly caused by the rigorous application of majority rule (Jickeli 1995).

As a consequence of this experience it should not be proposed to restrict the majority rule because it is necessary to guard the capability to act. But before its application the institutions should, as in national parliaments, patiently try to come as much as possible to a consensus, and they should allow sufficient time and the occasion to profoundly discuss the related problems with the professionals concerned. At present it is doubtful whether the majority practice should be widened to fields where it is not yet applied like, for instance, tax rules.

In this context the so-called comitology must be mentioned. The first administrative committees were introduced by the agricultural market orders in the sixties. To secure effective administration, the member states could not but delegate power of executive legislation to the Commission. They intended, however, to preserve their influence since in practice the technical details are often the most important rules for the professionals concerned. The Commission has, therefore, been obliged to hear Committees composed of experts of the national administrations whose reactions have different procedural consequences from case to case, even, under certain conditions, a reversion of the competence to the Council. This system has also been foreseen in directives on approximation of law and generalised by the famous decision on comitology offering different models of procedure. Some of these procedures may be questioned and may be simplified (Bradley 1992). But in principle this system seems to be reasonable. It gives the member states the security that their arguments are heard and that regulations are taken neither without deepened debate nor against the interest of most of them and their relevant professionals. Thus it may be regarded as a method to further the peoples' acceptance of law which is rendered by – judged from a democratic point of view – an incomplete institutional order.

3.4. European Judiciary

Special attention must be given to the role of the European Court of Justice, a concept which in the following also includes the Court of First Instance (Kirschner 1995). The Court possesses a central position in the institutional system of the Community. According to Article 164 EC-Treaty it has the mission 'to ensure that in the interpretation and application of the Treaty the law is observed'. The Court interprets the Treaty according to the teleological method, understanding the 'telos' of the Community as it has been defined by the Treaties and later on developed by the political instances and public opinion. On this basis, it tends to decide in such a way that the institutions are able to effectively fulfil the tasks confided to them (Dauses 1994).

But nevertheless the Court has to decide in applying the law even if it is not clear and incomplete. Judges are not entitled, like political institutions, to actively pursue political aims. On the other hand, legal texts are never clear and complete. Courts are more than the *bouche de la loi*, gaps must be closed and new economic or social developments must be taken into consideration. Such a jurisprudence must not be understood as 'judicial activism' but as *Richterrecht* or *richterliche Rechtsfortbildung* which means judge-made law (Ukrow 1995).

Great parts of the national law are judge-made law, it is indispensable and, therefore, recognised in all member states. But it has always been disputed because in modern democracies law-making is reserved for the legislature. Legitimacy, formation and limits of judge-made law have steadily been discussed. Legal texts of the Community are even more incomplete than those of the member states, and judge-made law of the Court of Justice is, therefore, even more indispensable. But it is also more questioned because it is not, as in member states, built upon the basis of common traditions, values and conceptions of law which in the Community are only beginning to exist (T. Stein 1986).

The Court derives the legitimacy of its jurisprudence from the mandate formulated in the cited Article 164 EC-Treaty. It takes the material guidelines from the principles and aims underlying the Treaties founding the Communities and from the common conceptions of the national constitutions and legal orders as well as international conventions. It controls the conformity to Community law of the measures and legislation taken by the Community's institutions as well as by the member states. Under the first aspect it decides relatively cautiously, sometimes too cautiously. The crucial aspect is the second one, however.

The problem concerns primarily the distribution of competences which will be treated in the next section. Here it is only to underline that there is no reason to place the Court under the supervision of another Community court or national court, because no human institution is immune of errors. The only controller of high courts is public opinion and professional criticism. It can be effective as has been shown in the last few years when the Court, influenced by the debate concerning the ratification of the Maastricht Treaty, has changed or moderated its jurisprudence in several fields.

4. RELATIONSHIP BETWEEN MEMBER STATES AND COMMUNITY

4.1. Distribution of Competences between Community and Member States

A central point of the Community constitution is the distribution of powers between the Community and the member states. From the beginning member states resisted the steady extension of Community activities and, in particular, against the extensive use of the competences. As already explained, the Community obtains its sovereign powers by the transfer of tasks and competences by the member states in the Treaties. According to the dominant legal theory, as confirmed by Article 3b paragraph 1 EC-Treaty, this transfer followed the principle of limited special authorisation, '*begrenzte Einzelermächtigung*' as it is called in German (Kraußer 1991). But in practice some authorisations are open to broad interpretation.

To give some examples: a small subparagraph of Article 43 EC-Treaty is the basis for the excessive building of rules governing the agricultural policy. It includes about 20 market organisations comprising a variety of intervention instruments like production quotas, aids or levies, and even special monetary systems and rules for product quality. The competences for approximation of laws in Articles 100, 100a and others of the EC-Treaty put nearly the whole national economic law at the disposal of the Community. This competence is particularly important since harmonised law prevents the member states from legislating this respective field with the consequence that every harmonisation leads to a widening of the competence of the Community (Everling 1987, 217).

Meriting special consideration is Article 235 EC-Treaty which authorises the Council to decide by unanimity if actions by the Community are necessary to achieve one of its objectives and no other competence exists. This article is sometimes regarded as making possible the self-authorisation of the Community, but such a sort of 'competence-competence' which means the ability of the Community to determine its competences on its own does not correspond to the present state of integration. Member states, therefore, mostly demand a narrow application of this article (Everling 1987, 218).

Consequently, competences of the Community including the cooperation fields of the Union are more than a patchwork quilt. Nearly every public function in the member states is concerned or at least touched by Community law or action. It is obvious that this furthers the trend to centralisation. As long as the Council decided by unanimity, member states were believed to dominate the development. But because of the already mentioned experiences following the Single European Act, resistance in the member states is growing.

In Germany, particularly the *Länder* revolted against the – in their view, excessive – legislative activities of the Community by which they believed to be threatened in their already eroded competences. In the context of the ratification of the Maastricht Treaty they succeeded in fighting for effective participation in the preparation of German voting in the Council. But the problem concerning the limitation of the Community's competences remained open.

4.2. Discussions on Limitations of the Community's Competences

The adequate distribution of legislative power on the different levels of decisionmakers like Community, member states, Länder or regions and local government bodies has been discussed for a long time. For the Community, this question is only relevant as far as their relation to the member states is concerned. Distribution of powers inside the member states remains their free discretion. On the other hand, it is irrelevant whether a competence claimed by the Community belongs, according to the constitutional order of a member state, to the genuine tasks of its *Länder* or regions. Only if the Community's competences went so far that their constitutionally secured existence was endangered, the question of constitutionality might be raised. But the Community is far away from this limit (Schwarze 1995).

It has been discussed whether a list of competences of the Community could be useful. Such a list would perhaps better the transparency but solve nothing in substance because the borderline between the different domains remains to be determined. Most of the Community's competences are not defined by the attribution to a determined subject matter but by their functional role in establishing the Common Market. They are, therefore, open to dynamic interpretation.

Most of the existing federal states have conferred to constitutional courts the responsibility to decide about the borderline between different competences. In the EC-Treaty this task is given to the Court of Justice which is competent to interpret the Treaty, including its provisions attributing competences to Community institutions. Consequently the constitutional or supreme courts of the member states are not entitled to decide in this field. This result cannot be avoided, as the *Bundesverfassungsgericht* believes, under the pretext of interpreting the national legal act by which the Parliament had given its agreement to the ratification of the Treaties, since the competences of national constitutional courts are limited by the competence attributed to the Court of Justice (Everling 1995, 12).

It is obvious that the existence of the Community would be questioned if each of the constitutional or supreme courts of the member states would follow the German claim and decide according to its own traditions, interests and understandings whether Community law is applicable in its territory. This question must be decided by one institution for all member states, and this is, according to the Treaty, the Court of Justice (Everling 1995, 15).

4.3. The Principle of Subsidiarity

To counter the tendencies of centralisation the Maastricht Treaty established in Article 3b paragraph 2 EC-Treaty the principle of subsidiarity. It was introduced in the debate by the German *Länder* and is regarded by some of them, in connection with the dubious idea of a 'Europe of Regions', as a sort of magic formula to protect their particularities. Certain observers seem to hope that it may be used for the reduction of the Community's activities or even for renationalisation (Goppel 1993) whilst other observers, exactly for this reason, regard it as danger for the integration (Pescatore 1995).

In view of these controversies it is necessary to emphasise that the principle of subsidiarity does not concern the competences of the Community but their exercise. The competences of the institutions are determined in the Treaty; they must be interpreted according to their sense and *effet utile* and are not touched by the principle of subsidiarity. But this principle must be taken in consideration if the competences shall be used.

The estimation whether 'the objectives of the proposed action cannot be sufficiently achieved by the member states' and can be 'better achieved by the Community' is primarily the task of the political institutions of the Community. For this purpose they have to evaluate the relevant facts and conditions and to consider the situation in all member states. It may well be that certain actions can be taken by some of the member states alone because of their intellectual or financial resources, but not by the smaller and poorer among them. Only the capacity of all member states is decisive.

The decisions of the Community institutions to legislate are in every aspect subject to the control of the Court of Justice. There is no doubt as to the justifiability of the principle of subsidiarity, only the extent of judicial control is questionable. The Court always accorded the institutions a broad discretion to evaluate economic and technical situations. Also, with regard to the application of the principle of subsidiarity, it is supposed that it will only supervise the limits of the discretion, in particular concerning errors of facts or law or apparently unfounded decisions (Pipkorn 1992).

But the Court has always compensated for the attribution of discretion to the institutions by a certain strictness with regard to the respect of the rules of procedures. The most important effect of the principle of subsidiarity consists, therefore, in the duty of the institution to estimate, in every state of procedure, whether the conditions of taking a Community action are fulfilled, and to motivate it in the preamble of the decision concerned. This obligation is stated by the heads of government and confirmed by an inter-institutional agreement in 1993. It should be transposed in a protocol to the Treaty.

Such rules of procedure may not only constitute a basis for the judicial control but influence the practice of the institutions. If they are forced to explicate the motives of their activities, they have to reflect on their motives in the first instance. Understood in this sense, the principle of subsidiarity may contribute to the balance between Community and member states.

A negative effect of the principle, however, must be mentioned. Since its application and effect must be judged case by case, the security of law, which is indispensable as a basis for economic activities may be jeopardised. The control of subsidiarity also has the consequence that decisions having political effect were more and more transferred to the Court of Justice.

4.4. Administrative Execution of Community Law

The picture shall be completed by remarks concerning the administration in the Community (Schwarze 1988). As a rule, Community law is administratively executed by the national authorities. The only exceptions are the competition rules for enterprises and the control of national state aids. In all other fields the application of Community law to enterprises and citizens is decentralised. National authorities levy, for instance, customs duties on the basis of the Common Tariff and common regulations. They also apply the intervention instruments of the agricultural market organisations; and all the directives on approximation of laws must be transformed into national law which is applied by national authorities.

Thus the Community follows, according to the European tradition, a concept of federalism different from the United States where federal authorities and courts execute federal law. Even in the genuine field of the Commission's administration, namely the competition rules for enterprises, national administrations are entitled to act under certain conditions as long as the Commission is not engaged. Since the Commission is not able to prosecute all infringements on the competition rules, it recently invited the national authorities to act in its place. In this instance, the Community system seems to be secured against centralisation.

But it must be added that in practice the Commission has instruments to influence the measures taken by the national authorities. Particularly, in the field of agricultural policy, the execution regulations of the Commission often concern concrete situations. Remarkably effective is the indirect influence by the agricultural guidance and guarantee fund. The Commission only repays expenditures of the national authorities caused by the application of market organisations if the payments are, in its opinion, in conformity to the relevant dispositions. To avoid difficulties during the future settlement of the fund, the national authorities therefore often ask the competent services of the Commission for their opinion concerning concrete cases. The answers are not binding for the authorities, but they mostly follow the advice. This is because they otherwise risk that their refunds will be rejected and that they will be consequently criticised by their courts of auditors. This example shows tendencies of interlacings between Community's and national administrations.

5. OUTLOOK: ENLARGEMENT OF THE UNION

The preceding considerations are based on the present state of the Union and Community and need to be completed and further developed in light of the prospective and envisaged fourth enlargement of the Community. This subject demands a special examination which cannot be delivered here; only some concluding remarks may be presented on the related problems.

It seems to be the common opinion that the admission of at least four and perhaps up to nine Eastern European States to the Union will be indispensable. All politicians regard it as necessary to stabilise the region after the collapse of the Soviet Union, and the states concerned are not satisfied by cooperation agreements as experience shows. Demands of Mediterranean countries must also be answered. At the end of this process, the Union and Community may have more than 24 and perhaps 30 member states. Will this still be the European integration we have discussed here? Politicians pretend that there will be no contradiction between deepening and enlargement of the Community. But nobody knows how the institutions will be able to work effectively if they must represent such a number of member states. In addition, nobody knows how, for instance, the free movement of workers is possible in light of the nearly unlimited number of people intending to go to the West or how agricultural policy could function if the enormous production reserves existing in these countries were mobilised.

Proposals for a *géométrie variable* are under discussion, but this may lead to a *Europe à la carte* and put the unity of the Union and its consistence in question. Transitional periods and even exemption rules for certain sectors may be accepted. A particular example of the latter may be the Monetary Union for which the participation of all member states may not be demanded. But exemptions without time limit are barely possible with regard to the hard core: that is, the internal market for goods, persons and services governed by undistorted competition. Otherwise Union and Community would change their nature (Maillet 1995).

The main problem of the envisaged enlargement by the accession of a great number of differently structured states consists in the repercussion on the long-time objectives of Union and Community which has been explained in the introductory remarks. The envisaged developments will force both the politicians and the scholars to constantly reconsider the problems of European integration.

REFERENCES

Blanke, H.J. (1993), 'Der Unionsvertrag von Maastricht – Ein Schritt auf dem Weg zu einem europäischen Bundesstaat?', *Die öffentliche Verwaltung*, **46**, 412.

Boest, R. (1992), 'Ein langer Weg zur Demokratie in Europa. Die Beteiligungsrechte des Europäischen Parlaments an der Rechtsetzung nach dem Vertrag über die Europäische Union', *Europarecht*, **27**, 182.

Bradley, K. (1992), 'Comitology and the Law: Through a Glass, darkly', *Common Market Law Review*, **29**, 693.

Currall, J. (1985), 'Some Aspects of the Relation between Articles 30–36 and Article 100 of the EEC Treaty, with a Closer Look at Optional Harmonisation', *Yearbook of European Law 1984*, **4**, Oxford, 169.

Dauses, M. (1994), 'Die Rolle des Europäischen Gerichtshofes als Verfassungsgericht der Europäischen Union', *Integration*, **17**, 215.

Everling, U. (1987), 'Gestaltungsbedarf des Europäischen Rechts', *Europarecht*, **22**, 214.

Everling, U. (1992), 'Reflexions on the Structure of the European Union', *Common Market Law Review*, **29**, 1053.

Everling, U. (1995), 'The Maastricht Judgment of the German Federal Constitutional Court and its Significance for the Development of the European Union', *Yearbook of European Law 1994*, **14**, 3.

Frowein, J.A., S. Schulhofer and M. Shapiro (1986), 'The Protection of Fundamental Human Rights as a Vehicle of Integration', in M. Capeletti, M. Seccombe and J. Weiler (eds), *Integration Through Law*, Book 3, p. 231.

Frowein, J.A. (1995), 'Die Verfassung der Europäischen Union aus der Sicht der Mitgliedstaaten', *Europarecht*, **30**, 315.

Goppel, T. (1993), 'Die Bedeutung des Subsidiaritätsprinzips', *Europäische Zeitschrift für Wirtschaftsrecht*, **4**, 367.

Götz, V. (1995), 'Mehrheitsbeschlüsse des Rates der Europäischen Union', in O. Due, M. Lutter and J. Schwarze (eds), *Festschrift für Ulrich Everling*, Baden-Baden: Nomos, p. 339.

Groeben, H. v.d., J. Thiesing and C.-D. Ehlermann (eds) (1991), *Kommentar zum EWG-Vertrag, 4th ed.*, Baden-Baden: Nomos.

Hallstein, W. (1979), *Die Europäische Gemeinschaft*, 5th ed., Düsseldorf: Econ.

Herdegen, M. (1994), 'Maastricht and the German Constitutional Court: Constitutional Restraints for an "Ever Closer Union"', *Common Market Law Review*, **31**, 236.

Hrbek, R. and W. Wessels (eds) (1984), *EG-Mitgliedschaft: ein vitales Interesse der Bundesrepublik Deutschland?*, Bonn: Europa-Union-Verlag.

Jickeli, J. (1995), 'Der Binnenmarkt im Schatten des Subsidiaritätsprinzips', *Juristenzeitung*, **50**, 57.

Kirschner, H. (1995), *Das Gericht erster Instanz der Europäischen Gemeinschaften*, Köln: Heymann.

Kraußer, H.-P. (1991), *Das Prinzip begrenzter Ermächtigung im Gemeinschaftsrecht als Strukturprinzip des EWG-Vertrages*, Berlin.

Lorenz, N. (1990), *Die Übertragung von Hoheitsrechten auf die Europäischen Gemeinschaften*, Frankfurt.

Maillet, P. (1995), 'Convergence et géométrie variable', *Revue du marché Commun et de l'Union européenne*, 145.

Meessen, K.M. (1994), 'Hedging European Integration: The Maastricht Judgment of the Federal Constitutional Court of Germany', *Fordham International Law Journal*, **18**, 511.

Obradovic, D. (1993), 'Community Law and the Doctrine of Divisible Sovereignty', *Legal Issues of European Integration*, **1**, 1.

Oppermann, T. (1991), *Europarecht*, München: Beck.

Pescatore, P. (1995), 'Mit der Subsidiarität leben', in O. Due, M. Lutter and J. Schwarze (eds), *Festschrift für Ulrich Everling*, Baden-Baden: Nomos, p. 1161.

Pipkorn, J. (1992), 'Das Subsidiaritätsprinzip im Vertrag über die Europäische Union – rechtliche Bedeutung und gerichtliche Überprüfbarkeit', *Europäische Zeitschrift für Wirtschaftsrecht*, **3**, 697.

Prechal, S. (1995), *Directives in Community Law*, Oxford: Oxford University Press.

Schneider, H. (1992), 'Europäische Integration: die Leitbilder und die Politik', *Politische Vierteljahresschrift, Sonderheft 23*, 3.

Schwarze, J. (1988), *Europäisches Verwaltungsrecht*, Baden-Baden: Nomos.

Schwarze, J. (1995), 'Kompetenzverteilung in der Europäischen Union und föderales Gleichgewicht', *Deutsches Verwaltungsblatt*, **110**, 1265.

Stein, E. (1992), 'Foreign Policy at Maastricht: "Non in commotione Dominus"', *Common Market Law Review*, **39**, 663.

Stein, T. (1986), 'Richterrecht wie anderswo auch? Der Gerichtshof der Europäischen Gemeinschaften als "Integrationsmotor"', in *Richterliche Rechtsfortbildung*, Festschrift der Juristischen Fakultät der Universität Heidelberg zu deren 600-Jahr Feier, Heidelberg: Müller, p. 619.

Tietmeyer, H. (1995), 'Zur politischen Fundierung der monetären Integration', in O. Due, M. Lutter and J. Schwarze (eds), *Festschrift für Ulrich Everling*, Baden-Baden: Nomos, p. 1575.

Tomuschat, C. (1993), 'Die Europäische Union unter der Aufsicht des Bundesverfassungsgerichts', *Europäische Grundrechte Zeitschrift*, **20**, 489.

Ukrow, J. (1995), *Richterliche Rechtsfortbildung durch den EuGH*, Baden-Baden: Nomos.

Wellens, K.C. and G.M. Borchardt (1989), 'Soft Law in European Community Law', *European Law Review*, **14**, 267.

Winter, G. (1993), 'Institutionelle Strukturen der Europäischen Union', *Die öffentliche Verwaltung*, **46**, 173.

Index